Joining the Dialogue

Joining the Dialogue

PRACTICES FOR ETHICAL RESEARCH WRITING

BETTINA STUMM

broadview press

BROADVIEW PRESS – www.broadviewpress.com
Peterborough, Ontario, Canada

Founded in 1985, Broadview Press remains a wholly independent publishing house. Broadview's focus is on academic publishing; our titles are accessible to university and college students as well as scholars and general readers. With 800 titles in print, Broadview has become a leading international publisher in the humanities, with world-wide distribution. Broadview is committed to environmentally responsible publishing and fair business practices.

Library and Archives Canada Cataloguing in Publication

Title: Joining the dialogue : practices for ethical research writing / Bettina Stumm.
Names: Stumm, Bettina, author.
Description: Includes bibliographical references and index.
Identifiers: Canadiana (print) 2021020317X | Canadiana (ebook) 20210205458 | ISBN 9781554813957 (softcover) | ISBN 9781770487598 (PDF) | ISBN 9781460407134 (EPUB)
Subjects: LCSH: Academic writing. | LCSH: Academic writing—Moral and ethical aspects. | LCSH: Research. | LCSH: Research—Moral and ethical aspects.
Classification: LCC P301.5.A27 S78 2021 | DDC 808.02—dc23

Broadview Press handles its own distribution in North America:
PO Box 1243, Peterborough, Ontario K9J 7H5, Canada
555 Riverwalk Parkway, Tonawanda, NY 14150, USA
Tel: (705) 743-8990; Fax: (705) 743-8353
email: customerservice@broadviewpress.com

For all territories outside of North America, distribution is handled by Eurospan Group.

Broadview Press acknowledges the financial support of the Government of Canada for our publishing activities.

Copy-edited by Emma Skagen

Illustrations by Bettina Stumm

Book design by Chris Rowat Design

PRINTED IN CANADA

CONTENTS

PREFACE

People like to be connected. Whether we're talking, emailing, instant messaging, posting on social media, or catching up on current events, we want to interact with other people and with the world around us. We like to be "in the know" and to communicate what we know to others. While the way we communicate has changed dramatically in the last century, the desire to connect is nothing new. Over two millennia ago, the Greek philosopher Aristotle asserted that "man is a social creature" (*Ethics*, Book 9:9, p. 304). He suggested that we are naturally constituted to live in relationships with other people and that community life is key to our human flourishing. The role of language in our societies proves that we are part of a relational network that is rooted in communication. We communicate to connect with each other.

As social beings, our desire to connect through language is natural to us. But that doesn't make it easy. In fact, we could argue that communication is always a risk. We can put our words out there and be ignored or misunderstood. We can listen to others who don't listen to us. We can feel threatened by opposing viewpoints or flooded with too much information and find ourselves attacking others or shutting down. We can "open up" or "close down" connections with others by means of our words, and others can do the same to us. So how do we connect ethically with each other in and through our communication?

This question of how to connect ethically is one that has long interested scholars in philosophy and in communication studies. Ethics, broadly understood, is concerned with "how we should live our lives" (Jaksa & Pritchard, 1994, p. 3), and communication ethics, in particular, focuses on how we should engage and communicate with others so that our interactions are mutually beneficial and build the common good.

Fifteen years ago, I became interested in this question of how to connect with others ethically, particularly in our writing. As a scholar in autobiography studies, I had been working with stories of Holocaust survivors and was trying to figure out how to share their traumatic accounts with readers in honourable and meaningful ways. How should their stories of suffering be told and how might readers be encouraged to respond ethically to their accounts?

My research led me to the concept and practice of ***dialogue*** as the most ethical way to engage with others, not just in the context of trauma and suffering but across all forms of communication. Why? Because dialogue is a reciprocal and responsible way of interacting with others. In a dialogue, each person is free to speak and each person takes responsibility for truly listening and responding. To be in dialogue means to be genuinely open to others, to be receptive and responsive in our interactions, and to be willing to learn and change through those interactions.

In this textbook I bring my background in ethical dialogue to bear on academic communication. While we normally think of dialogue as a *verbal interaction* between two or more people, this textbook focuses on academic dialogue in its *written form*, in the research writing that occurs among scholars. Experienced writing instructors have long agreed that writing is a "social, conversational act" (Graff & Birkenstein, 2014, p. xvi), and that writing well in an academic context means expressing our research and ideas in relation and response to the work of other scholars.

In our college and university studies, our goal is to participate in these dialogues with our own research writing, both practically and ethically. Practically, we aim to understand what scholars are saying in their research writing and to learn the techniques necessary for engaging and responding to their work. Ethically, we strive to be open and responsive to the scholars whose work we're studying, acknowledging how their research and ideas have come to shape our own.

This textbook is geared to help us learn to interact practically and ethically with academic research as we explore subjects that interest us and step into research dialogues with other scholars. It is unique in this twofold approach. While most writing manuals teach us the practical skills necessary to develop our research writing or participate in current research dialogues through our writing, this textbook considers both the practical skills *and* the ethical orientation needed for genuine dialogue to occur and for research interactions to flourish. While we want to be able to join research dialogues effectively with our writing, we also want to be researchers who interact ethically with the research and ideas of other members in the academic community through our writing.

In this textbook, then, the term *dialogue* is used in two ways: First, it refers to *a practice of reciprocal communication* between people in a particular community. Second, it refers to *an ethical way of relating to one another* within that practice of communication. Taking these two meanings together, we can define dialogue as a reciprocal, interactive approach to communication in which we relate meaningfully to one another in and through language.

Communication scholars Cissna and Anderson (1994) describe this relating as a "process and quality of communication in which participants 'meet,' which allows for changing and being changed" (p. 10). When we truly relate to another person, we become mutually open to each other's views and ideas. "What a good conversation that was!" we might exclaim after the fact, but we struggle to explain what made it so good. Something mysterious about our encounter made us feel truly engaged and inspired. We may think of it as a meeting of the minds, in which we suddenly came to understand something or someone in a new way. Between us, through our dialogue, something changed and new meaning emerged (Arnett et al., 2009, p. 55).

This kind of "meeting" isn't limited to face-to-face interactions. We are also capable of genuine encounters with written words (Bakhtin, 1986, p. 75), in which we open ourselves to other views and ideas and discover new meanings as we read. In fact, many of us can point to an "Aha!" moment we've experienced while reading, when we've understood something in a new way or felt that the words *really spoke* to us as we read them, compelling us to respond.

As we truly encounter and relate to others, we find that dialogue has the power to astonish, invigorate, and transform us. It is not surprising, then, that dialogue is often promoted in academic contexts as a catalyst for learning. At college and university we have the unique opportunity to engage with many different people and, in the process, be exposed to new ideas, be challenged in our thinking, become invested in certain issues and concerns, and join the scholarly discussions happening around us. In other words, academic communities provide an excellent forum for dialogue because in them we regularly encounter new viewpoints that encourage our engagement and response.

With this in mind, this textbook takes a dialogic approach to academic research and writing practices. Taking a "dialogic approach" means two things: First, it means learning how to participate in research dialogues with other scholars and how to structure our research writing to reflect those dialogues. Second, it means learning how to dialogue ethically in our writing so that our research interactions are meaningful and respectful. We will pursue these two objectives as follows:

1. LEARNING HOW RESEARCH WRITING WORKS AS A DIALOGUE

Academic research writing is used among scholars to share their research findings and ideas. When scholars write in an academic context, they engage and interact with other scholars who are invested in the same subject. Together, they are committed to developing knowledge about that subject collectively as they build on each other's work. While research writing may seem to be made up of stuffy prose and rules, scholars see it as a lively, socially responsible way to communicate in order to build knowledge and share it with others for the benefit of the community. Our goal, as students, is to become familiar with the genres of research writing so that, when we become interested in a particular research area, we can contribute our ideas to the ongoing dialogue about it in ways that other scholars can recognize and appreciate.

This textbook illustrates how academic dialogue is formed and practised in research writing across disciplines and fields of study. It will help us to recognize how dialogue is used in knowledge development and how to apply the interactive structures that scholars use to share their research findings and ideas. To learn how to recognize research writing as a dialogue:

- We will be introduced to genres of research writing, the academic communities who use them, their purpose in these communities, and the expectations of communication that have developed around them.
- We will see how scholars explore their interests with like-minded thinkers and engage in dialogue with them by means of their research writing.

- We will discover how scholars represent the work of other researchers as a dialogue in their prose.
- We will learn how scholars present their own stance in relation and response to the research material and scholarly views of others.
- We will see how scholars support their ideas with research evidence and reasoning so that readers can understand their views and recognize their value.

Once we have a solid understanding of how research writing functions as a dialogue, we will put our learning into practice:

- We will analyse a range of research examples across the disciplines to help us see how to interact dialogically with the research and ideas of other scholars.
- We will learn the dialogic skills necessary for research writing—attentive reading, notating, summarizing, orchestrating, citing, critical thinking, responding to others, arguing, reasoning, crafting, editing, and revising—by means of relevant exercises and reflection questions.
- We will be introduced to various templates that help us represent the research and ideas of others and situate ourselves in dialogue with them as we write.

To develop our dialogic skills, then, this textbook uses three key strategies. First, it relies heavily on examples from academic research writing to illustrate concepts and dialogic practices. While these examples are initially difficult to read and understand, they are consistent with the context and genres of communication that we are aiming to learn, emulate, and participate in as we write our research papers. To write like researchers, we need examples of how researchers write.

While we benefit from academic models, we also need opportunities to develop our own composition practices. This book uses a template approach to help us step into the structures of dialogue modelled by researchers as we communicate our findings and ideas. Templates offer a practical, hands-on way to craft our prose, especially when we're not sure what to say or how to say it. While we may have written essays in the past, academic research papers rely on different patterns and conventions that we may not be familiar with. Templates give us an easy way into the writing process so that we feel comfortable and confident as we join the research dialogue.

Finally, this book uses a developmental approach in which each composition skill builds on the one before. In the early chapters, we begin with how to read and represent what research scholars are saying about a topic before we move to the more difficult practices of assessing their research and ideas and responding with our own stance. These skills are brought together in the latter part of the book, where we take a step-by-step approach to writing an academic research paper: from choosing a topic to writing the paper to editing and revising it. At each stage, examples, exercises, and templates will help us understand and practise our academic reading and writing.

2. LEARNING THE ETHICS OF DIALOGUE FOR RESEARCH WRITING

In addition to fostering strong composition practices, this book upholds an ethics of dialogue as the basis for effective research communication. It sees ethics at the heart of academic dialogue, shaping how we relate to other researchers, how we develop our knowledge, and how we structure our research writing. Specifically, an ethics of dialogue describes the *orientation* of open responsiveness we have towards others behind our communication practices, the basis by which we come to respect the ideas of others, acknowledge their research, collaborate with them, and contribute beneficially to the academic community and beyond.

As we work through this textbook, we will discover how to think ethically about academic communication and how to practise ethical dialogue in our research writing. In particular:

- We will become familiar with the ethical philosophies of dialogue that help us interact receptively and responsibly with other research scholars.
- We will discover the ethical dimensions of dialogue that underpin each of our composition practices—summarizing the work of others, orchestrating their ideas, citing their work, thinking critically, developing our own stance, supporting our ideas, structuring our prose, and communicating clearly.
- We will develop an ethical orientation of open responsiveness towards other research scholars by learning to exercise attentiveness, reciprocity, acknowledgement, accountability, responsible agency, and respectful interaction in our research writing.

In order to highlight both the practical and ethical dimensions of academic dialogue, this textbook is organized as follows:

Part 1 sets up a two-part framework for approaching academic dialogue. Combining an ethical and a rhetorical approach, it focuses on how we relate to one another in and through dialogue in an academic context. Chapter 1 considers our "ethical orientation" towards others, the way we situate ourselves receptively and responsively in our academic communication. Chapter 2 considers our "communication situation," the way our words and ideas are shaped by our location (where we are and who we're with) and by the genres of communication that have come to be used in various situations, including an academic one.

Part 2 focuses on the foundational skills needed to set up a dialogue in our research writing. Setting up a dialogue begins with identifying what other scholars have said about a research topic. We need to be aware of the research conversations happening on that topic and be able to convey the various views accurately to our readers. This takes an ethical orientation of open *receptivity*—the ability to listen attentively with the intent to understand and represent the ideas of others. It also takes practical reading and writing skills—the ability to read closely and critically, take notes, and summarize research texts (which we focus on in Chapters 3 and 4); orchestrate different research viewpoints on a topic (Chapter 5); and acknowledge the research of scholars in a conversation through citation (Chapter 6). These chapters are indebted to the work of Janet Giltrow et al. (2009) and are set up incrementally, stressing the steps involved in reading and representing scholarly research ethically. Chapters include academic examples drawn from different disciplines, writing templates and exercises to practise each skill, and clear directions for composing a research summary and a literature review, two common genres we encounter across research fields and disciplines.

Part 3 focuses on developing the analysis and argumentation skills we need to respond meaningfully to the research and ideas of other scholars in our writing. Chapter 7 highlights the main components of a research stance—a claim, reasons (evidence), and reasoning—and how to recognize them in the research writing of others. Chapter 8 turns to critical thinking—how we analyse and assess the claims, reasons, and reasoning of others in order to respond meaningfully to them. In this chapter, special attention is given to writing a critical analysis paper, the sort found in disciplines like literature, film, art history, and gender and cultural studies, where analyses of texts and images are central to our research dialogues. Chapter 9 helps us to develop our own research stance with particular focus on composing a response-able research claim and using common styles of argumentation to convey our reasons and reasoning. These three chapters combine traditional rhetorical strategies with current composition practices in order to equip us to join research conversations effectively and responsively. They also provide ethical frameworks for thinking critically and developing response-able claims.

Part 4 applies the dialogic skills of reception and response to the specific genre of the academic research essay, highlighting the steps involved in writing this kind of paper—from choosing a topic and writing a proposal and bibliography (Chapter 10) to crafting the essay itself (Chapters 11 to 13) to editing and revising it (Chapter 14). In the process, special attention is given to distinctions between analytical and argumentative research essays as well as the structural differences between essays in the humanities, social sciences, and sciences. These final chapters focus on the forms and functions of dialogue that make up our academic composition. In particular, they help us to assert ourselves as responsible agents of research who interact with other research scholars and communicate our findings and ideas effectively to readers. They highlight the importance of organizing our work and writing it clearly and logically for our communication to be successful and for the research dialogue to flourish.

Over the course of 14 chapters, *Joining the Dialogue* provides the dialogic skills necessary to be effective and ethical communicators in academic contexts and in the world beyond. Dialogue is the method of communication we use to develop knowledge together and share that knowledge with others in our research community. Ethical openness is the means by which we truly encounter each other's viewpoints so that new discoveries can be made and new ways of thinking can emerge between us. We have the opportunity to develop our dialogic skills in an academic environment as we learn to share our research, test each other's ideas, and respect each other's viewpoints. These skills are valuable, not only in academia but also in our social relationships, work environments, and political activities. They help us to broaden our frames of reference, learn to collaborate, mitigate conflict, reach consensus, and proceed democratically in all our interactions.

ACKNOWLEDGEMENTS

This textbook would not have taken shape without the lively dialogues with colleagues and students at UBC and Corpus Christi College whose questions, interests, and needs shaped the focus, direction, exercises, and templates in this textbook. A special thanks goes to those at Corpus who encouraged this project in its preliminary stages, including Paul Burns, Mazen Guirguis, Jamie Paris, Shawn Flynn, and Shawna Buhler. I would also like to thank Ryan Uyeno and Fatema Al-Shaeel for allowing their work to appear as student exemplars in Chapter 11.

In addition to the support of colleagues and students close at hand, I am grateful for the many discussions, conferences, and forums in autobiography studies, writing, and phenomenology that helped me hone the ethical and dialogic focus of this book. I want to thank IABA, CASDW, CLSG, ACCUTE, the Verge Arts Series, and the many other academic communities that have created spaces for engaging in intellectual and ethical inquiry. These are the dialogues that stimulated my research and ideas.

I am particularly indebted to the dialogic and template approach to academic writing modelled by Gerald Graff and Cathy Birkenstein in their textbook *They Say, I Say: The Moves That Matter in Academic Writing.* I have also been deeply influenced by Janet Giltrow's genre approach and organizational strategy in *Academic Writing: An Introduction*. This textbook emerged largely in response to their remarkable work.

This textbook would not have made it into print without my editor at Broadview Press, Marjorie Mather, who showed keen interest in the book while it was still in its conception stages, offered helpful feedback at various points during the writing process, and gave me the space (and extensions!) to work on it at my own pace—believing that it would, in fact, get done. I am also grateful to Tara Lowes for catching the niggling errors and inconsistencies in the final stages of the editorial process.

Alongside Marjorie, Tara, and the other editors at Broadview, I had a number of tireless readers who each contributed invaluable editorial comments during the writing process. Particular thanks goes to Andrea Heidebrecht for her helpful suggestions as the chapters were first taking shape; to Keith Hyde for his rigorous engagement, useful questions, and honest feedback on early chapter content; to Jackie Rae for prompting inclusive language and variations of dialogue across fields of study; to Jeff Severs and Stephen Ney for reviewing the

Preface and offering ongoing encouragement to finish the project; to Kasey Kimball for her clear recommendations for refining the prose and clarifying the ideas; and to Irmgard Stumm for her close attention to detail and her painstaking review of the whole book, twice over.

Finally, I am very grateful for the regular prods and nudges from supportive friends and family members that helped me bring this textbook to completion. Thank you all!

PART I
APPROACHING ACADEMIC DIALOGUE

CHAPTER ONE

GENUINE DIALOGUE AND THE ETHICS OF COMMUNICATION

Academic research and writing are acts of communication. Scholars communicate their research findings and ideas about a wide range of topics in order to build knowledge within their research communities and share new discoveries or new ways of thinking with others. In college and university settings, we want to develop our ability to communicate with other scholars in ways that fit this community. In order to do that well, we first need to understand what communication is and what it involves. In this chapter we will explore the nature and ethics of communication, and see how the practice of genuine dialogue is involved in our academic interactions.

A. THE NATURE OF COMMUNICATION

When we think about the nature of communication, three critical features stand out:

1. Communication Is Relational

Communication presupposes a community. We don't exist in a void, but in relationships and in a world shared with other people. We use language—verbal sounds and written signs and symbols—to communicate with and relate to others. In fact, in English there is a direct link between the words *communication* and *community*, as they both share the same root word: *commune*.

Commune: To share

Communal: Sharing a common life; relating to a community

Community: A body of people associated by common status, pursuits, practices, etc.

Communicate: To share of/to share in; to participate; to exchange information through a common system of symbols, signs, or behaviours

Notice the repeated ideas of sharing, commonality, connection, participation, and belonging that are embedded in our language. To ***commune*** means to connect, to hold things in common, to belong together. We communicate in order to connect, relate, and share our lives with each other. Our communication, then, is ultimately social and meant for the common good.

Communication is also the main way we come know ourselves and define who we are in relation to other people. Linguistic theorist Mikhail Bakhtin (1984) describes this relationship as follows: "*To be* means *to communicate*.... I am conscious of myself and become myself only while revealing myself for another, through another, and with the help of another" (p. 287). We can understand what Bakhtin means when we think about how we have been shaped by the words and views of other people and how we have come to know ourselves by interacting with them. Through our interactions, we determine who we are and find our meaning and place in the world.

In fact, we are in communication with others from the moment of our birth. We interact through coos, smiles, squeals, and cries. Then we learn specific signs, sounds, and behaviours by mimicking our parents, caregivers, or siblings, mirroring back to them what we have seen and heard. In doing so, we essentially become what is modelled for us. As children, if we hear something often enough—you're a good kid, you're a princess, you're an artist, you're a nerd, you're athletic, you're so funny, you're sweet—we can internalize it and define ourselves by it. We become what we're told we are, or we work hard to fight against it: I am *not* a princess! I am *not* a nerd!

These personality markers as well as other markers of identity—family, nationality, race, class, gender, religion, etc.—are the main ways we define ourselves and share who we are with other people in language (Taylor, 1994, p. 32): I'm from Syria. I am Chinese Canadian. I have three siblings. I'm 20. I'm transgender. I'm Catholic. I'm from a working-class family. Notice how each of these identity markers locates the speaker in a certain community and is used to identify the speaker to others. This model of identity by and with others is called ***relational identity***. It suggests that connection and communication with others make us who we are.

2. Communication Is Active

Communication is meant to do things in the world, and it does different things depending on the context. It can share information, make plans, sell houses, spark rebellions, create identities, develop knowledge, etc. For example, consider what these road signs communicate:

When we see these signs, we are meant to do something, to act in response: stop, yield, verify our route, check our speed, decide whether we need a rest, or laugh.

The ability to act in the world through language is empowering. Words have power to make or break, give or take, create or destroy. For example, saying "I do" in a marriage ceremony is considered an act of fidelity to another person in many cultures. Saying "thank you" is an act of gratitude and acceptance. Saying "turn right at the next intersection" directs someone's movement. Saying "you're fired!" changes someone's work status. Actions performed by or as a result of an utterance are called "speech acts" and they occur regularly in our conversations (Austin, 1962).

Written communication is also active and able to do things in the world. It can bind people to certain laws, inform, persuade, entertain, motivate, and challenge. Often writing does not feel active or social. In fact, we normally write alone. Nonetheless, we are always talking to someone (whether actual or imagined) when we write—someone we want to engage with and whom we hope will respond to us. Consider the following excerpt by Iranian writer Marjane Satrapi from the introduction to her graphic narrative, *Persepolis: The Story of a Childhood* (2003). What does she expect her story to do in the world through her readers?

EXERCISE 1
DOING THINGS WITH WORDS

As you read Satrapi's introduction to *Persepolis*, consider the following questions:

1. Whom is Satrapi writing for?
2. What is Satrapi trying to do in the world by writing about her childhood experiences of the Iranian Revolution in 1979?
3. What are readers meant to do in response to reading her account?

In the second millennium B.C., while the Elam nation was developing a civilization alongside Babylon, Indo-European invaders gave their name to the immense Iranian plateau where they settled. The word "Iran" was derived from "Ayryana Vaejo," which means "the origin of the Aryans." These people were semi-nomads whose descendants were the Medes and the Persians. The Medes founded the first Iranian nation in the seventh century B.C.; it was later destroyed by Cyrus the Great. He established what became one of the largest empires of the ancient world, the Persian Empire, in the sixth century B.C. Iran was referred to as Persia—its Greek name—until 1935 when Reza Shah, the father of the last Shah of Iran, asked everyone to call the country Iran.

Iran was rich. Because of its wealth and its geographical location, it invited attacks: from Alexander the Great, from its Arab neighbors to the west, from Turkish and Mongolian conquerors, Iran was often subject to foreign domination. Yet the Persian language and culture withstood these invasions. The invaders assimilated into this strong culture, and in some ways they became Iranians themselves.

In the twentieth century, Iran entered a new phase. Reza Shah decided to modernize and westernize the country, but meanwhile a fresh source of wealth was discovered: oil. And with the oil came another invasion. The West, particularly Great Britain, wielded a strong influence on the Iranian economy. During the Second World War, the British, Soviets, and Americans asked Reza Shah to ally himself with them against Germany. But Reza Shah, who sympathized with the Germans, declared Iran a neutral zone. So the Allies invaded and occupied Iran. Reza Shah was sent into exile and was succeed by his son, Mohammad Reza Pahlavi, who was known simply as the Shah.

In 1951, Mohammed Mossadeq, then prime minister of Iran, nationalized the oil industry. In retaliation, Great Britain organized an embargo on all exports of oil from Iran. In 1953, the CIA, with the help of British intelligence, organized a coup against him. Mossadeq was overthrown and the Shah, who had earlier escaped from the country, returned to power. The Shah stayed on the throne until 1979, when he fled Iran to escape the Islamic revolution.

Since then, this old and great civilization has been discussed mostly in connection with fundamentalism, fanaticism, and terrorism. As an Iranian who has lived more than half my life in Iran, I know that this image is far from the truth. This is why writing *Persepolis* was so important to me. I believe that an entire nation should not be judged by the wrongdoings of a few extremists. I also don't want those Iranians who lost their lives in prisons defending freedom, who died in the war against Iraq, who suffered under various repressive regimes, or who were forced to leave their families and flee their homeland to be forgotten. One can forgive but one should never forget.

Satrapi, M. (2003). Introduction. In *Persepolis: The story of a childhood.* Pantheon Books.

3. Communication Is Interactive

Combining the relational and active dimensions of communication, we can say that communication is ultimately interactive, a "two-sided act" (Voloshinov, 1986, p. 86) that involves a relationship of exchange. This exchange is typically called a ***dialogue***. A dialogue is often described as a social, verbal interaction between two speakers or interlocutors. A standard diagram of this process looks something like this:

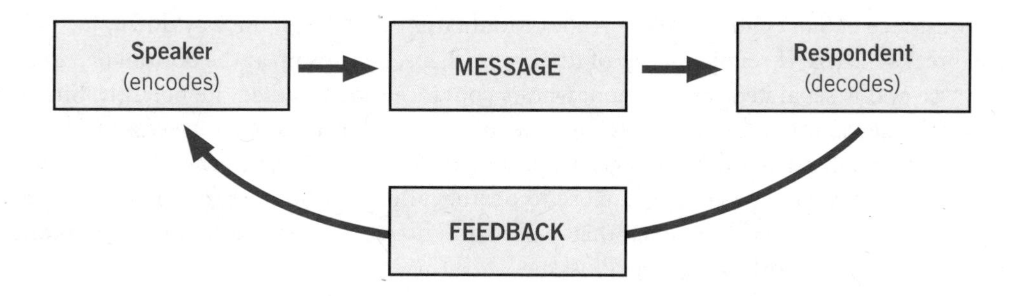

However, this diagram is somewhat simplistic and misleading. Dialogue involves much more than communicating a message to someone else who has to decode it and respond with feedback. This illustration seems to suggest that communication is primarily one-sided. It's about the first speaker and his or her message. The respondent's only purpose is to be a sounding board, giving feedback. In reality, speakers and respondents change places as they interact, speaking and listening to one another. This interaction creates a relationship that shapes what is said, how it is said, and what effect the words have. In the next section, we'll see how this relationship works.

B. GENUINE DIALOGUE: THE ETHICS OF COMMUNICATION

If communication is relational and interactive, then it has ethical implications for how we share our lives and ideas with each other. Ethics is concerned with how we can engage with others so that our interactions are mutually beneficial and build the common good. To engage in that way, we first need to see each other as valuable human beings, worthy of respect and attention. In particular, being ethical means being able to accept people who are "other" than we are with ideas that are different from our own. It also means being able to interact with them from that place of acceptance (Buber, 1965, p. 69).

In communication, this kind of mutual, attentive, and respectful interaction takes the form of a genuine dialogue. In every genuine dialogue, we engage in mutual address and response: speaking and listening, giving and receiving. As philosopher Kelly Oliver points out in her book *Witnessing: Beyond Recognition* (2001), to fully function as human beings we need to be able to address ourselves to others and respond to and be responsible for others. From her perspective, our personhood (or sense of self) depends on address-ability and response-ability. To address others we need to assert our agency—our ability to speak and take action in the world. To respond to others we need to be receptive and open to them, allowing them to assert their agency too. When we are silenced or unheard, when we are unable to express ourselves or respond to others, we lose something of ourselves.

This kind of loss is directly illustrated in the mountaineering docudrama *Touching the Void* (2003), which tells the story of two climbers—Joe and Simon—who attempted to climb the west face of Siula Grande in the Andes Mountains in 1985. On the way down, Joe falls and breaks his leg. Through a series of further mishaps, he ends up at the bottom of a deep crevasse and is separated from Simon, who is convinced Joe has died. Reluctantly, Simon descends the mountain alone. Hours later, Joe manages to crawl out of the crevasse and take his own perilous journey down the glacier and rocky terrain. When he nears the base camp a couple of days later, he collapses, close to death, calling out Simon's name, hoping that by some chance he is still there. Of that experience, he recalls, "At that point when no one answered the call, I lost something. I lost me."

In this extreme example, we can see that losing all human connection and response undoes us. This is because we exist by means of our relationships with other people. Most of the time we are not in dire situations where a response from someone else will literally save our lives. However, we do find that if our ability to address others or respond to others is taken away from us we lose something of ourselves. We can all think of situations where mutual interactions break down and we experience a sense of loss as a result. For instance, think of the friend who gives us the silent treatment, the date who ghosts us after a night we thought went well, or the colleague who chatters endlessly, never asking questions or giving us space to talk. In each of these experiences, we can feel disregarded, disrespected, or devalued.

However, if we're honest, we must admit we sometimes find ourselves doing exactly the same things to others. We can easily tune others out, engage half-heartedly in discussions, nod agreeably despite what we really think, criticize without actually listening, talk over people, or interrupt them when they're talking. We all have the capacity to take over our conversations, dominating others with our agency until they feel they cannot speak out in response. We all have the capacity to ignore or avoid responding to others, damaging their dignity or sense of identity.

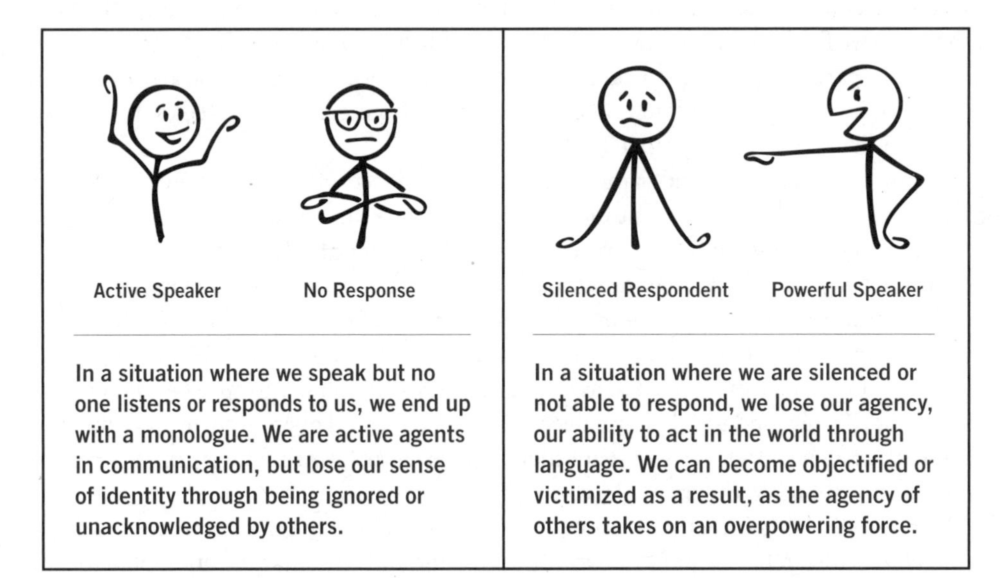

In a situation where we speak but no one listens or responds to us, we end up with a monologue. We are active agents in communication, but lose our sense of identity through being ignored or unacknowledged by others.

In a situation where we are silenced or not able to respond, we lose our agency, our ability to act in the world through language. We can become objectified or victimized as a result, as the agency of others takes on an overpowering force.

Bakhtin (1984) suggests that genuine dialogue, unlike these negative extremes of communication, "presuppose[s] a communality" that endows each of us with equal rights and equal responsibilities (p. 292). When we engage in dialogue we take turns actively listening and actively responding to each other. We are fully present and fully engaged with one another in the process. Here is what Bakhtin says about it:

> The single adequate form for *verbally expressing* authentic human life is the *open-ended dialogue*. Life by its very nature is dialogic. To live means to participate in dialogue: to ask questions, to heed, to respond, to agree, and so forth. In this dialogue a person participates wholly and throughout [his/her] whole life: with [his/her] eyes, lips, hands, soul, spirit, with [his/her] whole body and deeds. [He/she] invests [his/her] entire self in discourse, and this discourse enters into the dialogic fabric of human life. (p. 293)

What Bakhtin describes here is far from easy. It takes a radical shift in our orientation towards others to truly engage in dialogue.

Martin Buber (1958) describes this shift in orientation as moving from an "I-It" attitude towards others to an "I-Thou" encounter with others. When we have an ***"I-It" attitude***, we see ourselves and our experiences of the world as the centre of reality and treat others as objects or things revolving around ourselves (i.e., we treat a person as an "it"). This attitude is often described as *egoism*. With an "I-It" attitude, we treat our own experiences and viewpoints as absolutes. As a result, we do not take the views or experiences of others as equal to our own. With an "I-It" attitude we may also avoid real encounters with others and focus on gathering knowledge or information about them instead. This sometimes happens in academic research. We can feel intelligent and objective when we gather knowledge about certain people, communities, or populations, but in the process the people themselves become objects for us to view, define, analyse, and categorize as we think best.

In politics an "I-It" orientation can lead to the oppression of others. In social communities it can lead to stereotypes and stigmas. In personal relationships it can lead to domination or disengagement. In short, an "I-It" attitude undermines our ability to engage in genuine dialogue with others because it keeps us from seeing them as equals and encountering them as they truly are. They are limited by our image of them and reduced to our ideas about them.

In contrast, an ***"I-Thou" encounter*** approaches others as truly "other"—not entirely knowable and not easily pinned down or boxed in by categories. Instead of capturing the characteristics of others with stereotypes or even with objective analysis, an "I-Thou" encounter meets others openly and sincerely as they are; as equals with different ways of being in the world. As Buber (1958) describes it, "The *Thou* meets me. But I step into direct relation with it.... I become through my relation to the *Thou*; as I become *I*, I say *Thou*. All real living is meeting" (p. 11). What Buber is suggesting here is that genuine dialogue occurs when we truly meet someone else on equal terms, and when our orientation towards each other is open to difference and reciprocal interaction.

In genuine dialogue, we affect each other. We inform each other. We prove each other's prejudices wrong and grow in our openness and ability to understand. When we talk about genuine dialogue, then, we are talking about an ethical orientation towards others that works itself out in mutual and reciprocal interactions. This orientation towards others is open and receptive, respectful of difference, and fully engaged. The interactions that result have the potential to be life giving and affirming to all members of a conversation.

C. ETHICAL POSTURES FOR GENUINE DIALOGUE

As we can see, genuine dialogue depends on ethical "postures" or ways of orienting ourselves towards others in our interactions, treating them as a "Thou" rather than an "It" as we communicate. These ethical postures include our ability to be receptive, response-able, and reciprocal. Let's look more closely at these terms, as they will be used throughout this textbook to describe how to engage ethically in academic dialogue.

1. Receptivity

Genuine dialogue begins with a posture of receptivity towards others. When we are ***receptive*** to others, we take a position of openness and attentiveness to them in our encounters. We are "open" to others when we are willing to listen to what they have to say and willing to learn from them, even if their viewpoints are new to us or different from our own. Hence, being "open-minded" refers to our ability to welcome unfamiliar ideas with interest and curiosity rather than feel threatened by them. In genuine dialogue, we choose to be open to others, acknowledging that what they know is worth listening to. Through our openness, we develop our knowledge and understanding of the world around us so that we can engage well with others in it.

If openness refers to our willingness to listen to others, attentiveness describes the way we listen. Attentiveness means offering our full attention to others as we listen to what they have to say. When we "attend to" others and their ideas, we are fully present to them, with the intention of understanding their views and experiences. In fact, the act of attentive listening is deemed essential to ethical dialogue, because only when we are fully present in our listening can another person genuinely speak and feel heard (Scarafile, 2014, p. 3).

2. Response-ability

Genuine dialogue also depends on our ability to actively respond to one another, what we might call ***response-able agency***. Agency refers to our ability to speak and act in the world in relation to one another. In a dialogue, we listen to what others have to say and respond to their ideas with our own. We each have a voice that we are responsible for using in order to contribute to our relationships with others and to the world around us. As Bakhtin (1993) describes it, my voice is my *unique* action in the world (p. 34). No one else sees things exactly as I do and no one else can take my place: "That which can be done by me can never be done by anyone else" (p. 40). When we speak, we take action with our voice and assert our own particular viewpoints in ways that no one else can do for us.

Voicing our views may take the form of speaking out about something important to us, whether personal or political. It may involve standing up for ourselves when others put us down, or it may involve joining forces with others in a political movement like Black Lives Matter or Idle No More. We may want to contribute our views to an intellectual discussion on a particular idea or theory, or speak up about a personal matter with friends or family members. In all these ways, we engage with and respond to other people and situations, taking action with our voices and impacting our relationships and communities.

It feels good to discover our own unique voices and share our ideas with others. However, response-able agency also involves taking responsibility for our voices and using them for the good. As Bakhtin (1993) argues, because only I can act, relate, and respond to others from the specific place and situation in which I am located, I am answerable for all that I say or do from that position (p. 42). To be answerable means that I am accountable to others and take responsibility for my own words and actions. As I prove myself responsible, others can count on me as a reliable person and trust what I say. I am committed to what I say and take responsibility for how I say it (Ricoeur, 1992, p. 165). As we learn to take responsibility for our own voices, we use them to benefit and build up the community. We also ensure that they do not dominate or drown out anyone else's voice. Being a response-able agent in genuine dialogue means that we are each accountable to keep the agency of others intact—their ability to speak and act in the world in their own unique way—as we voice our views.

3. Reciprocity

Lastly, genuine dialogue depends on mutual interaction. Receptivity and response-ability must go both ways for genuine dialogue to happen. We call this mutual interaction ***reciprocity***—the mutual exchange of words and ideas between two or more people established on the golden rule: to treat others as we want to be treated (Ricoeur, 1992, p. 266). Each member of the dialogue takes turns speaking and listening, sharing ideas and responding to the other. In this mutual exchange, members commit to engaging with and responding to each other in the ways they want others to engage with and respond to them.

Karl-Otto Apel (1996), a philosopher of language and ethics, highlights a further dimension of reciprocity in genuine dialogue. He suggests that a genuine dialogue occurs when all the members have equal rights in the conversation and share equal responsibility (p. 321). He argues that one of the main purposes of dialogue is to present rational arguments to one another in order to raise and solve problems together. This kind of equality and rational reciprocity requires an attitude of mutual respect among all members involved in the conversation. We respect that other people have their own ideas and ways of being in the world, and we respect their ability to speak and act in the world as they think best (Nevo, 2013, pp. 270, 282). When we respect one another, it means we value what each person can contribute to the dialogue and we treat one another with dignity in the process.

D. GENUINE DIALOGUE IN ACADEMIC COMMUNICATION

An ethics of genuine dialogue sounds virtuous and even inspiring, we may think, but what exactly does it have to do with academic research and writing? How do we engage in genuine dialogue with other scholars in the academic community when we are not actually face to face with them, but rather "communing" over a written text?

In order to think about how genuine dialogue functions in academic communication, we need to recognize that dialogue can take the form not only of an oral or verbal conversation, but also a written exchange. The academic texts we read—scholarly books, research articles, reports, reviews, etc.—function as "written discourse" among scholars. ***Discourse*** refers to concrete discussions that can occur either in oral or written form. Academic writers use written discourse to share their research on a particular topic with readers. Academic readers who are interested in that topic will actively study the material and respond to it with their own research writing, and so on. Each writer is a reader and researcher. Each reader and researcher is also a writer. Through their writing, academics share their work with each other, engaging in reciprocal interactions and building their mutual understanding about the subject. The process may be slower than oral dialogue, but the interaction is no less dialogic.

In order for research writing to function as a genuine dialogue, though, it requires an ethical orientation—a posture of receptivity, response-ability, and reciprocity—towards others in our academic interactions, particularly as we approach research texts and connect with research subjects and other scholars as we write. Engaging in genuine dialogue means that we don't treat a research text we read as an "It," an object to be used, exploited, or appropriated. While research writing may appear dense, detached, and objective, we recognize that behind each text is a person, an academic writer who wants to communicate information and ideas to us for a particular purpose. We can think of a research text, then, as a "Thou" to be carefully read, respected, and acknowledged as the words and ideas of someone else. Consequently, we take a posture of open receptivity towards the research texts we read.

Similarly, when we engage with a particular group of people for research purposes, we must adopt an ethical orientation to establish a mutual and reciprocal dialogue with them. A human subject is never an "It," an object to be analysed for the sake of developing our own projects or academic goals. Each research subject is a "Thou" who has full agency to engage with our research, challenge it, and benefit from it. Ultimately, our goal is to interact reciprocally and develop knowledge together, not to turn people into projects.

Finally, our ethical orientation impacts how we write. We are always respondents first as we write, open and receptive to new ideas and checking our own perspectives against those of experts who have long been involved in scholarly study. We make every effort to get to the heart of their research and their ideas in order to understand and respond to them. This means we don't think of ourselves as the centre of knowledge, treating our own research and viewpoints as absolutes. Nor do we steal other people's ideas, pretending they're our own, or manipulate research material to suit our own purposes. In fact, academic research writing is ultimately not about us as individual researchers at all, but about extending our understanding as a community through meaningful and reciprocal interaction.

Genuine academic dialogue, then, is an invitation to actively engage with and respond to the ideas of other researchers. We are each a "Thou" to one another. We each have a voice and can use it to be an agent of action, using our words for the good of the research community. While each one of us is responsible for ensuring our voice is informed and well supported by the research and ideas of others, we also want to bring our own unique stance to the research dialogue in order to help the community rethink its current ideas and consider new ones. Together, as we move the conversation forward in mutual interaction, our collective understanding grows.

E. PRACTISING GENUINE DIALOGUE IN READING AND WRITING

Positioning ourselves in an "I-Thou" relationship and participating in a genuine dialogue with the research and ideas of others has practical dimensions in our academic reading and writing. When we read, we situate ourselves in a posture of open and attentive listening. When we write, we situate ourselves as active respondents to what we have read. Let's consider some of the ways that an ethical posture works itself out in our actual reading and writing practices.

1. Reading Orientation: A Posture of Receptivity

Imagine that you are engaging with a person and a community every time you pick up a research text to read it. As you read, try to take a position of open reception to the research and ideas of others. Our primary goal is to listen closely to the text and do our utmost to understand the content in all its facets. In doing so, we orient ourselves responsibly towards the text and its writer(s). Here are some practical ways to inhabit a posture of open reception in our academic reading:

- **Read Openly**
  When we read openly we take a receptive attitude towards a text, as someone who has something to learn from the writer. A research text is written by a scholar for a particular reason or purpose. He or she has something meaningful to share with the research community. With this in mind, we want to consider what the scholar has to share and be willing to listen. This means putting aside our preconceived ideas about the subject in order to learn something new or to see things in a different way.

- **Read Attentively**
  Reading attentively means reading slowly and carefully with the goal of understanding a text. It is the opposite of reading quickly and superficially with the goal of taking from the text only what proves useful to us. When we read to suit our own purposes, we of-

ten wrench the text out of its context and take only the bits and pieces that support our points. Instead, we should seek to understand the scholar's purposes and perspective as a whole. We want to notice the nuances of the scholar's stance and avoid simplifying content where he or she offers complexity and shades of grey.

- **Read Generously**
  When we read generously, we do so with a positive mindset and the best assumptions about a scholar's ideas and research. In other words, we should always begin by looking for the good in what others communicate. We focus on the aspects that build our knowledge, develop our understanding, and prove beneficial to the community.

- **Read Critically**
  When we read critically, we notice the limitations of a scholar's perspective, findings, or analysis in the text. We can only truly see these if we have already engaged in the other three reading practices. Without them, we risk pointing to limitations that don't actually exist or expose a need to "be right" or "sound smart" rather than engage in genuine dialogue. As we will come to discover later in this textbook, reading critically is not a practice of criticizing a research text but a practice of analysing and assessing it.

- **Recognize Reading Lenses**
  When we read, we always do so through a particular lens with a particular perspective. Our lens is our way of seeing the world based on our background, current knowledge, history, interests, and life experiences. Often our lenses are so much a part of us that we are unaware of their existence, but they determine how we read and interpret a text nonetheless. Do we automatically look at research with an eye towards gender issues, politics, class struggle, historical context, or religion? In our reading, we want to become aware of our particular lens and realize that others might read the same research material equally well through a different lens. In other words, there is always more than one way of looking at an issue or a text. The more we are aware of our own lenses and the more we are willing to accommodate the views of others, the richer and deeper our knowledge will be.

2. Writing Orientation: A Posture of Response-Able Agency

Imagine that you are engaging a reader and a community every time you write. Assume that you are writing for an audience who is invested in your topic, and that you are responding to other scholars as you address the topic with your readers. Here are some practical ways to address others responsively when you write:

- **Know the Conversation**
  When we write academically, we are always entering a conversation between scholars in a research community who have been considering and discussing the subject long before we join in. We need to know that conversation—what they have been saying about the subject—in order to genuinely interact with them. If we don't, we will be unable to engage in the dialogue.

- **Acknowledge Others in the Conversation**
  In a regular conversation, we acknowledge the people we are talking to. The same goes for written dialogue. When we write academically, we recognize and acknowledge the ideas of other researchers in a practice called "citation." In effect, when we cite someone, we are saying, "I got this idea from someone else who was already talking about it before I entered this conversation." Plagiarism is the act of ignoring that someone else has given us an idea. It is disregarding someone else in the scholarly conversation and treating his or her words as if they are our own. Nothing could be more detrimental to genuine dialogue than disregarding others, stealing their words, and lying to our community. It is contrary to an "I-Thou" relationship.

- **Represent Others Accurately**
  When we are trying to make a case or prove a point, we sometimes fail to listen to the whole story or recognize the viewpoint of the people we are interacting with. We take bits and pieces of what they have said in order to challenge them or to add fuel to our own views. Similarly, in academic writing we can be so intent on proving a point that we distort the words of other scholars in the community to make our case. This is an example of an "I-It" attitude. While we might accidentally misunderstand another scholar's work, we should never deliberately misappropriate someone else's words or ideas to suit our own purposes. We want to represent the whole dialogue between us, not just the parts that prove our point.

- **Acknowledge Limitations**
  When we engage in dialogue, we acknowledge what we know and what we don't know about a subject. We acknowledge that our views are limited and that there are more perspectives on the subject than our own. When we write academically, we want to be up front about the fact that we are focusing on one particular issue or question from one specific viewpoint. We don't need to know everything about everything to address that issue or question. But we do need to be clear that we are coming at it from a particular perspective by stating our lens or stance directly.

- **Anticipate Readers and Expect a Response**
  When we write, we always take our readers into account. We write as though we are talking to someone and we know who that someone is. As students, we mostly imagine

our professor as the key reader of our research writing, but if we stick around academia long enough, we will also start imagining other readers too—like interested researchers in our field of study and perhaps even a broader community who may benefit from our knowledge and insights. As we keep our readers in mind, we are better able to write for their knowledge level and degree of interest, as well as to anticipate their questions and concerns. In fact, our goal is to write in such a way that stimulates a response from our audience and invites further dialogue on the subject.

CONCLUSIONS

The nature and ethics of communication are key issues to bear in mind as we approach research and writing in the academic community. All communication is relational, active, and interactive, engaged with others and meant to do something in the world. Like other forms of communication, research communication comes with ethical imperatives—ways to treat others and engage responsibly with them in order to grow our understanding and build up our knowledge together. We can practise communicating ethically through genuine dialogue, approaching research receptively, response-ably, and with respect for all the members in the conversation so that our interactions are mutual and reciprocal. In our research communication, genuine dialogue involves orienting ourselves towards texts and their authors in an "I-Thou" rather than "I-It" manner. This orientation means that we read and write with others—specifically our research community and readers—always in mind. We will return to this idea of genuine dialogue throughout this textbook as the fundamental and ethical foundation from which to communicate in an academic context.

QUESTIONS FOR REFLECTION

1. Think about the ways you communicate with others. What things do you do in the world through your communication? How is your communication active and relational?

2. When you interact with other people, do you regularly engage in ethical dialogue? What are some ways to develop your interactions so that they are receptive, response-able, and reciprocal?

3. What do you see as the main differences between "I-It" and "I-Thou" interactions?

4. Why is an "I-Thou" relationship necessary for academic research and writing? How can you treat a text and an author as a "Thou" in your reading and writing practices?

5. As you develop your academic research skills, which ethical reading posture do you most want to cultivate?

6. As you develop your academic communication skills, which ethical writing posture do you most want to develop?

CHAPTER TWO

THE COMMUNICATION SITUATION

Respecting Genre

In Chapter 1, we looked at the nature and ethics of communication. We saw that ethical communication is rooted in dialogue and that genuine dialogue depends on our ability to be receptive, response-able, and reciprocal with others, treating each of them as a "Thou" rather than an "It." We also saw how ethical communication works in an academic context through our reading and writing practices. In this chapter, we will look at a second dimension of dialogue: our communication situation. We cannot communicate in a vacuum. Our words and ideas are always shaped by where we are and who we're with. Thinkers in communication studies call this our ***situation***. With this in mind, we will look closely at how our situation shapes the way we engage with other people in general and the way we dialogue in academic research contexts specifically. We will also look at the forms of communication or "genres" that develop over time and become the norm for interacting in particular situations.

A. INTRODUCING GENRE

When we examine how communication works in practice, we realize that different situations require different kinds of communication. We communicate differently at home with our parents than we do at university with our professors. We communicate differently when we're texting a friend about a show we both watched last night than when we're writing a book review for our literary blog. We communicate differently when we're instructing our neighbour about how to look after our dog while we're on vacation than we do with a sales representative when shopping for a new cell phone. Who we are communicating with and what context we are communicating in shape what we say and how we say it.

If we don't speak or write for the context we are in, our audience will be confused and struggle to respond to us. There won't be enough common ground between us to make dialogue possible (Bakhtin, 1984, p. 183). In communication studies, ***common ground*** refers to the principles and practices we share in common or agree upon in a community in order to be able to communicate with one another. We can think of common ground as the language norms we adopt and share that make it possible for us to understand and be understood by others in a specific context (Holquist, 1990, pp. 60–61). When we have basic practices in common, we can depend on that shared foundation to help us communicate with one another and build our understanding of the world.

Some forms of communication have been long established in particular contexts, like the medical terminology used among doctors in a hospital or the legal language used by lawyers in a courtroom. These forms of communication take practice to learn and are not usually used elsewhere. Other forms of communication may be easy for us—such as texting with abbreviations and emojis—but only because we have long shared a common ground with others who text and have come to learn what certain things mean in this context. We communicate easily when we share common ground, but we experience disconnection when we don't. Whether consciously or unconsciously, we are constantly assessing our level of common ground with others, navigating how to communicate effectively with them in the situations we find ourselves.

The forms and styles of communication that we use to fit our audience and shared situation are called genres. A ***genre*** is a commonly held practice of communication that has become standard in a certain situation within a given community. Genres are the *types*, *forms*, or *styles* we use to categorize, construct, and understand written, oral, and visual communication. They are "the habitual forms of expression available for saying such and such a thing in such and such a situation" (Holquist, 1990, p. 64).

We learn forms and styles of communication very early on as young children: we imitate what we hear and we are drilled on what to say and what not to say in certain contexts. For instance, we may have been taught how to ask politely for something; how to "use our words" instead of throwing a tantrum; how to speak in a normal tone of voice instead of whining; when to whisper and when to use our "outside voice"; etc. As we develop and grow into adults, we continue to learn new forms of communication that fit certain situations and are used in certain communities. We may be acquainted with genres like detective fiction, weather reports, docudramas, business letters, tweets, birthday cards, and rental agreements. The norms that have developed around these forms of communication will be familiar to us if we belong to a community that uses them.

In order to communicate effectively with others, then, we need to be aware of our situation and the genres of communication already used in that situation. This may, at first, sound obvious. In fact, it is more complicated than most of us realize. When we are not aware of the genre of communication in which we are engaging or the social cues and expectations around that genre, the results can be awkward, hilarious, or dire. Consider the possibility of substituting a text message for a professional email. If we interact with a prospective boss who expects a professional interaction, a text message will lack the tone and structure that suits the situation. The problem here is not the texting genre, but the disconnect between the texting genre and the professional situation; texting is an inappropriate style of communication for this context. It may result in a laugh, or it may cost us the job.

These errors in genre are made on a regular basis in communication, and often they spring from simple misunderstandings of a social situation or of the kind of interaction expected.

Someone wants a question answered with a quick fact, but gets a long-winded story instead. Someone wants a brief overview of a film to decide whether to see it and gets a full plot summary (along with spoilers!) instead. Someone wants an in-depth discussion on a political issue and gets some superficial comments instead. Someone wants a persuasive literary essay and gets a book review instead. We experience these cross-genre miscommunications any time one person does not understand the social situation or the kind of interaction expected by the other person or by the larger community.

With this in mind, we need to think about genres not simply as forms or styles of communication that can be memorized and produced, but as practices of communication that occur in specific contexts with specific people for specific purposes. As Janet Giltrow et al. (2009) describe it, the practice of genre depends on our *situation* and our *form* of communication working together in tandem (p. 5). If we were to picture this symbiotic relation as an equation, it would look like this:

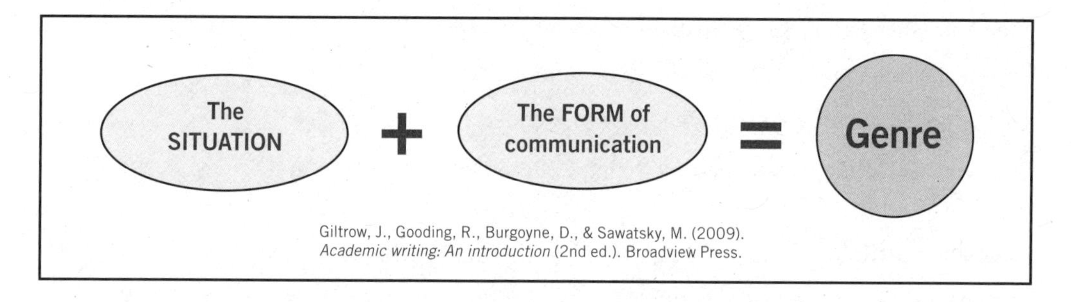

Giltrow, J., Gooding, R., Burgoyne, D., & Sawatsky, M. (2009). *Academic writing: An introduction* (2nd ed.). Broadview Press.

This formulation can be used to describe any genre, whether oral, visual, or written. However, since writing is our focus in this textbook, let's turn our attention to genres of *written communication* and consider these two dimensions—situation and form—more closely.

1. The Writing Situation

Before we begin any form of written communication, we need to be aware of the situation in which we are writing: our context, audience, and purpose. In fact, we usually need to assess our situation before we can meaningfully write within it. There are at least four questions to consider when assessing our writing situation:

- **What is the context of our communication?**
  Is the context educational, commercial, familial, professional, personal, impersonal, creative, recreational, occupational...?

- **Who is our intended audience and what is their level of knowledge or interest?**
  Is it a general audience, an expert audience, a peer audience, an interested audience, a diverse audience, an intimate audience, an unknowledgeable audience...?

- **What is the relationship between us and our audience?**
  Is the person our peer, a community member, a family member, a student, an instructor, an employer, an employee, an authority figure, a consumer...?

- **What is the purpose of our communication?**
  Is our purpose to instruct, to inform, to reflect, to question, to analyse, to persuade, to compare, to narrate, to describe, to entertain, to motivate, to assist, to confide...?

For example, consider the multiple ways the documentary film *The Salt of the Earth* (2014) showcasing the photography of Sebastião Salgado can be communicated in written form, depending on the situation.

Theatre Overview

The Salt of the Earth (Biography Documentary) 110 min.

Directors: Juliano Ribeiro Salgado; Wim Wenders

Screenplay: Juliano Ribeiro Salgado, Wim Wenders, David Rosier

Rated: PG; Not Recommended for Young Children, Disturbing Content.

Academic Article

Steven J. Gold (*Sociological Forum*)

As sociologists celebrating Salgado's contributions to the understanding of society, we are moved to reflect on our discipline's relationship with visual studies. According to Howard Becker (1974), sociology and photography trace their origins to the same time and place—France in the 1840s. Further, both disciplines are devoted to exploring humanity's relationship to technology. Given their common origins and concerns, the two disciplines have much to offer one another.

Text Message

Hey Jon, meet you at the theatre at 7 tmrw for S of the E. Should be good ☺

Film Review

Joe Morgenstern (*Wall Street Journal*)

Moving pictures are supposed to move, but the most moving ones in "The Salt of the Earth" are stills. This exemplary documentary celebrates the work of the Brazilian photojournalist Sebastião Salgado; it was directed by Wim Wenders and the subject's son, Juliano Ribeiro Salgado.... Mr. Salgado has chronicled anguish, suffering and the vicissitudes of human labor over the course of four decades, always in black-and-white and often with a tension between hellish circumstances and heavenly lighting. The film is suffused with his anguish over the state of our species, and our planet. Yet it ends with a change of heart and a turn of events that make a plausible case for hope.

We can see that the contexts range from personal to informational to academic. The audience for each genre is different too, ranging from avid filmgoer to scholar to friend. The purpose for each genre of communication also varies. The theatre overview is written to inform, while the text message is written to make a plan. The academic article is written to discuss and analyse the film, while the film review is written to describe, reflect on, and comment intelligently about it. Given what you now know about genre, try the following exercise to see how well you can pinpoint the communication situation in different writing contexts.

EXERCISE 1
THE WRITING SITUATION

Read the four excerpts below. Determine the communication situation of each by answering the following questions:

- What is the context of the written communication?
- Who is the intended audience?
- What is the relationship between the writer and the audience?
- What is the writer's purpose?
- What is the genre of each excerpt?

Excerpt 1

Any change or addition to this... agreement must be agreed to in writing and initialed by both the landlord and the tenant. If a change is not agreed to in writing, is not initialed by both the landlord and the tenant or is unconscionable, it is not enforceable. The requirement for agreement under subsection (2) does not apply to: a) a rent increase given in accordance with the Residential Tenancy Act; b) a withdrawal of, or a restriction on, a service or facility in accordance with the Residential Tenancy Act; or c) a term in respect of which a landlord or tenant has obtained an arbitrator's order that the agreement of the other is not required.

BC Residential Tenancy Branch. (2016). *Residential tenancy agreement.* Office of Housing and Construction Standards.

Excerpt 2

- 3 cups of spinach leaves
- 1 pear, cored and thinly sliced
- ½ cup pomegranate seeds
- ½ cup roughly chopped pecans
- 2 oz. crumbled blue cheese
- ¼ cup vinaigrette dressing

1. Layer spinach with pear slices.
2. Add the pomegranate seeds and the chopped pecans.
3. Finish with crumbled blue cheese.
4. Add vinaigrette dressing and serve.

Adapted from Mirabella, J. (2014). Pomegranate and pear salad. In *Mason jar salads and more* (p. 65). Ulysses Press.

Excerpt 3

"This must be a simply enormous wardrobe!" thought Lucy, going still further in and pushing the soft folds of the coats aside to make room for her. Then she noticed that there was something crunching under her feet. "I wonder is that more moth-balls?" she thought, stooping down to feel it with her hand. But instead of feeling the hard, smooth wood of the floor of the wardrobe, she felt something soft and powdery and extremely cold. "This is very queer," she said, and went on a step or two further. Next moment she found that what was rubbing against her face and hands was no longer soft fur but something hard and rough and even prickly. "Why, it is just like the branches of trees!" exclaimed Lucy. And then she saw that there was a light ahead of her; not a few inches away where the back of the wardrobe ought to have been, but a long way off. (p. 8)

Lewis, C.S. (1978). *The lion, the witch and the wardrobe.* Scholastic.

Excerpt 4

According to the classical definition by Olweus (1978), bullying is an intentional aggressive act that is repeatedly carried out on a victim in a situation in which there is an imbalance of power. Victims of bullying have been found to suffer from anxiety, post-traumatic stress, depression, and suicide ideation (Klomek et al., 2009; Matthiesen & Einarsen, 2004; Nielsen et al., 2015) as well as somatic conditions such as headaches and stomach aches (APA, 2000; Gini et al., 2014;

> Løhre et al., 2011). Bullies also suffer from anxiety, depression and suicidal ideation, and those who are involved both as aggressors and victims appear to suffer most severely (Hymel & Swearer, 2015; Kowalski & Limber, 2013; Smokowski et al., 2014; Turner et al., 2013). (p. 87)
>
> Donoghue, C., & Meltzer, L. (2018). Sleep it off: Bullying and sleep disturbances in adolescents. *Journal of Adolescence, 68*, 87–93. https://doi.org/10.1016/j.adolescence.2018.07.012

2. The Writing Form

The form of our written communication is inseparable from the situation in which it occurs—its context, audience, and purpose (Giltrow et al., 2009, pp. 6–7). When we communicate, we always need to decide what form of writing makes the most sense for our situation. Or, as is more often the case, we come to learn what form of writing is already commonly used to communicate in that situation. The ***form*** of our writing is the structure, format, and organization we use to arrange our words and ideas. For example, we might structure our writing in a linear way—in a *sequence* or *chronology*—using lists, numbers, or bullet points. We might organize our writing with categories, putting ideas together in groups according to their similarities and/or differences. We might structure our writing *narratively*, as a story unfolding in space and time. We also might use patterns like *cause and effect* or *problem and solution* to organize our ideas.

As we determine what form of writing makes the most sense in a particular situation, we also consider what style of writing is most effective for our communication. Our ***style*** of writing is the way we express ourselves and the language we use to convey our ideas—our word choice, sentence structure, point of view, and tone. For example, our style could be described as chatty, informal, emotional, passionate, matter-of-fact, detached, objective, descriptive, prescriptive, minimalistic, effusive, forceful, formal, etc. depending on the kinds of words and punctuation we use, how we structure our sentences, the point of view we choose, and the tone we take.

When we focus purely on form and style in our written communication, we can easily get caught up in language rules and writing directives. For example, when it comes to writing essays, we have all probably heard rules like these: Never use "I." Keep an objective tone. Write formal sentences. Avoid bullet points. Use three body paragraphs. This way of writing feels rigid and formulaic to most of us. We are so busy following rules that we might find it hard to be invested in what we're saying. We need to start with what we want to say, and then decide what form and style will be most effective and appropriate for communicating it to our particular audience in our particular situation. Form and style, in other words, are our tools for communicating what we care about so that our readers will sit up and listen, so that they want to interact and respond to us.

EXERCISE 2
THE WRITING FORM AND STYLE

Return to the four writing excerpts in Exercise 1 and answer the following questions:

- What is each excerpt's form (structure, organization, arrangement of ideas)?
- What style of language is used (word choice, sentence structure, punctuation, tone, point of view) in each?
- How are the form and style reflective of and effective for each excerpt's communication situation?

In sum, genres of communication and the various forms and styles they take depend on the communities that produce them and those communities' interests, needs, and priorities. Each writing example that we looked at represents a distinct situation of communication. They reveal our conventional ways of communicating information, ideas, directions, stories, research, or legal agreements. Each genre of writing serves a particular purpose and its form and style are appropriate for its situation and audience. With this in mind, we begin to realize that many of the "mistakes" we make in our writing are not errors per se, but simply acts of mistaking one situation for another. They occur when we are unclear about our audience and their expectations, or when we are unaware of the forms and styles of writing that are customarily used in a particular situation. As we become more aware of our communication situations and the conventions of writing typical to them, we become more effective communicators.

B. THE GENRE OF ACADEMIC RESEARCH WRITING

Our goal in this textbook is to learn the genres of research writing in an academic situation. What kind of research writing takes place in a university context? How do different communities of scholars typically communicate their research with one another? Academic research writing represents a distinct situation: academics communicating with other academics. Academic research writing also serves a particular purpose: to build on current knowledge about a subject in order to develop new knowledge and deeper understanding. Each community of scholars will do this differently, but some basic characteristics of writing remain the same.

- **Goal**
  The aim of research writing is to engage deeply with other scholars' research and ideas, as well as to produce new ideas and insights through that engagement.

- **Form**
  Research writing is structured as a dialogue: scholars share their knowledge and understanding in research texts in order that other scholars will read this research and respond with their positions, interpretations, and ideas.

- **Research**
  All research is built on other research. No ideas exist in a vacuum; rather, they exist in dialogue with other ideas. Academic writing is rooted in research—that is, the established ideas and findings of other scholars who are experts in their field of study.

- **Stance**
  All research writing presents a stance—where a scholar *stands* in relation to other research experts, thinkers, and writers. This stance is typically formulated as a *claim* (often called an *argument* or *hypothesis*). No one stands alone. Each stance is located in a larger dialogue about the topic at hand.

Consider how the following examples from different disciplines use these four basic characteristics regardless of the topic or field of study. The dialogic form is highlighted alongside each example, using terminology from Graff and Birkenstein's *They Say, I Say* (2014), while the research is represented in bold and the writer's stance is underlined.

The Dialogic Form
Example 1: Social Sciences (Field of Study: Higher Education)

Recent higher education guidelines in both the United States and the European Union (**e.g., Berlin Communique 2003; European Consortium for Accreditation in Higher Education 2004; National Commission on the Future of Higher Education 2006**) have underlined the fact that employability is the priority for higher education and that the role of the university is to promote competent and ethical professional practice. Nonetheless, **researchers in Europe** have recently pointed out that "there is still much to be done to translate this priority into institutional practice" (**Crosier et al., 2007, p. 7**). In particular, <u>we consider it important to seek to understand what the most effective educational practices are at the undergraduate level for the promotion of a professional approach to work</u>. **There is acknowledgement** that inquiry-based forms of teaching and learning...can improve the quality of learning in higher education (**Association of**

Researchers say

In response we consider

Researchers say

American Colleges and Universities 2007).... In this article we explore whether and how an inquiry-based form of teaching and learning can develop a professional approach among students. (pp. 245–46)

In response we explore

Gilardi, S., & Lozza, E. (2009). Inquiry-based learning and undergraduates' professional identity development. *Innovative High Education, 34*(4), 245–256. https://doi.org/10.1007/s10755-009-9109-0

The Dialogic Form
Example 2: Natural Sciences (Field of Study: Climate Change)

Data for global surface temperature indicate little warming between 1998 and 2008 (**Jones et al., 2009**). Furthermore, global surface temperature declines 0.2 °C between 2005 and 2008. Although temperature increases in 2009 and 2010, the lack of a clear increase in global surface temperature between 1998 and 2008 (**Jones et al., 2009**), combined with rising concentrations of atmospheric CO_2 and other greenhouse gases, prompts some **popular commentators (Carter, 2007; Easterbrooke, 2008**) to doubt the existing understanding of the relationship among radiative forcing, internal variability, and global surface temperature. This seeming disconnect may be one reason why the public is increasingly sceptical about anthropogenic climate change (**Gronewald, 2009**).

Recent analyses address this source of scepticism by focusing on internal variability or expanding the list of forcings. Model simulations are used to suggest that internal variability can generate extended periods of stable temperature similar to 1999–2008 (**Easterling & Wehner, 2009**). Alternatively, expanding the list of forcings to include recent changes in stratospheric water vapor (**Solomon, 2010**) may account for the recent lack of warming. But neither approach evaluates whether **the current understanding** of the relationship among radiative forcing, internal variability, and global surface temperature can account for the timing and magnitude of the 1999–2008 hiatus in warming.

Researchers say

Here we use a previously published statistical model (Kaufmann et al. 2006) to evaluate whether anthropogenic emissions of radiatively active gases, along with natural variables, can account for the 1999–2008 hiatus in warming. To do so, we compile information on anthropogenic and natural drivers of global surface temperature, use these data to estimate the statistical model through 1998, and use the model to simulate global surface temperature between 1999 and 2008. (p. 11790)

In response we say

Kaufmann, R.K., Kauppi, H., Mann, M.L., & Scott, J.H. (2011). Reconciling anthropogenic climate change with observed temperature 1998–2008. *Proceedings of the National Academy of Sciences of the United States of America, 108*(29), 11790–11793. https://doi.org/10.1073/pnas.1102467108

The Dialogic Form
Example 3: Humanities (Field of Study: Ethics of Autobiography)

Much recent attention to the topic of ethics and life writing has centred on a series of issues such as privacy and misrepresentation. The focus has been on the ethics of authorial performance. **This has been important work**, articulating the tacit moral assumptions we bring to the reading of lives and thereby outlining a new possibility in the way we think about the writing of them—the possibility that, in the memorable formulation of **John Eakin, "ethics is the deep subject of autobiographical discourse" (p. 123)**. [Researchers say]

The fundamental question in this new work is: *What is it right for the life writer to do?* On any philosophical account of ethics, *What is it right to do?* has to be a central question. On some accounts, however, such as the one I draw on here, this question occupies only part of the space of the broader ethical domain, which is defined by **the question as it was posed by the Greeks**: [In response I say] *How should a human being live?* My claim is that this broader formulation contains another question which can be found at work at the heart of most, if not all, written lives: *What is it good to be*? (p. 53) [In response I say]

Parker, D. (2004). Life writing as narrative of the good: *Father and son* and the ethics of authenticity. In P.J. Eakin (Ed.), *The ethics of life writing* (pp. 53–72). Cornell University Press.

As we study these examples and become more familiar with academic research writing, we will begin to notice some common ways that scholars signal a dialogue between the research of others and their own research stance. They usually begin with the research of others to inform readers of the topic at hand and what other scholars in the community have been saying about it. Then they respond by asserting their own research stance in one of the following ways:

- by **agreeing** with the current research and building on it with their own research
- by **complicating ideas** or **filling gaps** in current research in light of their own research
- by **questioning** an aspect of current research in light of a particular problem or set of reasons discovered in their own research
- by **solving a problem** (or answering a question) in current research by means of their own research
- by **disagreeing** with an aspect of current research and showing why by means of their own research

These five dialogic activities (and variations on them) are so common in academic research writing that we can easily draw from their structures and use them in our own work. In fact, we will learn how to do so in the second half of this textbook. For the time being, consider the following five templates below that reveal positions of agreement, complication, inquiry, problem/solution, and disagreement as meaningful ways to respond to current research:

Position 1: Agreeing with and Adding to Current Research

- Recent studies show __X__. I build on these observations to suggest __Y__.

Position 2: Complicating or Filling a Gap in Current Research

- While recent research has focused on __X__, I suggest we also consider __Y__.

Position 3: Questioning an Aspect of Current Research

- I question the recent findings that indicate __X__ to argue that __Y__.

Position 4: Solving a Problem Raised in Current Research

- Current scholarship has discerned the problem of __X__. There are a number of solutions to this problem, but I propose __Y__.

Position 5: Disagreeing with an Aspect of Current Research and Showing Why

- Contrary to the current views on __X__, I contend __Y__ because of __Z__.

These five positions represent a starting point on which to build our awareness of the dialogic form that academic writers use in the genre of research writing. As we work through this textbook, we will have the opportunity to use these and other templates to structure our research stances as we join the academic dialogue.

C. ACADEMIC RESEARCH WRITING VS. HIGH SCHOOL ESSAYS

When we look closely at the dialogic form, the level of research, and the researcher's stance in academic writing, we can see that the genre of research writing looks quite different from that of the high-school essay. This is because academic research writing *is* different from the high-school essay. High-school institutions are meant to help students develop foundational skills in a wide variety of subjects. The high-school essay, then, is geared towards teaching basic communication skills to students and assessing whether they can make observations, formulate thoughts, and support ideas with evidence in a logical and coherent way (Giltrow et al., 2009, p. 10). The five-paragraph essay, with its structured form and sentence style, fits this purpose.

In contrast, academic institutions are primarily communities of research that are working to develop new knowledge and hone understanding. Students are invited to participate in those communities and may eventually become experts in their fields of study through ongoing research, focused experimentation, and practice over time. In an academic classroom or online course, students do their learning under the direction of professors who are trained as researchers and who read and write research publications.

The knowledge gained at university or college is focused and specific, shaped by the issues that are important to each research community or discipline. The issues that concern one research community might not concern another research community. For example, a literary community might be interested in asking, "How do poetic conventions help us understand a Shakespearean sonnet?" A community of historians might ask, "What kinds of political and social ideologies in Europe led to World War II?" A religious studies community may focus on questions about the role of the gods or spirituality in human experience, while a community of biologists may be interested in questions about musculature and tissue connection in human anatomy. While research communities sometimes overlap in their broader concerns—such as species interaction, the natural environment, ethical practices, and human cultures—their studies are still specific and focused (rather than general and vague), meant to move knowledge forward through innovative research.

It makes sense, then, that the high-school essay doesn't fit the academic context and its research situation very well. In fact, using it in an academic context is rather like writing a book report for an application to work at the public library. A book report has some connections to that working environment (a library is full of books), but it will not land the applicant a job. Similarly, knowing how to make observations, find evidence, and write paragraphs are all aspects of academic research writing, but a high-school essay can't "land the job" of an academic research paper. Given the kind of research interests and inquiries that academic scholars have, research writing has a different approach. As you begin to learn more about the genres of research writing you will discover how to implement the following skills:

- discern and represent the research ideas and findings of experts in a field of study or research community
- take a research stance on a problem, concern, idea, theory, concept, or text that is important to that research community
- frame a research stance in response to the ideas of others in the research community, with the purpose of contributing something meaningful to the dialogue
- support a research claim with the kind of evidence and reasoning that is clear, convincing, and credible to an academic audience—that is, the researchers and experts in your field of study
- write and structure your research and ideas in ways that are fitting for your academic context, as a participant in a scholarly conversation with critical thinkers and research experts

Making the shift from high-school essays to academic research writing is actually quite a leap. The context is different. The purposes for writing are different. The audience is different. The expectations are different. The form and style are different. It is important to realize these differences up front. In effect, in college and university we are asked to learn a whole new way of writing that may draw upon some of the writing genres familiar to us from the past, but remain distinct from them.

CONCLUSIONS

There are many genres of communication in our culture. Some we know very well and use often. We know the situations from which they arise as well as the forms and styles they take to reach an audience. Other genres we do not know as well because we haven't been in situations that use them. We may not be clear about their context or community, the expectations of that community, or their particular forms and styles of communication. Trying to write in these little-known genres feels as awkward as walking into a party where we don't know anyone in an outfit that clearly doesn't fit the occasion. It is helpful to have a guide in such situations: someone to tell us what to wear, when to arrive, what to bring, and, ultimately, to show up *with us* so we do not have to go alone. Think of this textbook as a guide to the party of academic research writing!

QUESTIONS FOR REFLECTION

1. Which everyday genres of writing do you use most often? To what purpose?

2. How are these everyday genres of writing different from university research writing? Why are they different?

3. Why do academics use a dialogic form to structure their research writing?

4. Imagine you are studying the housing market crisis in Toronto. You have just finished reading a number of research articles that (a) examine how the crisis has affected Toronto's poorest neighbourhoods and (b) observe that solutions like social housing are not working to meet the needs of financially reduced or impoverished Torontonians. What position might you take in response to this research? Choose one of the five templates outlined in Section B and create a stance that you could potentially hypothesize or argue in a research paper.

5. What are some of the key distinctions between the genre of the high-school essay and the genre of academic research writing?

PART 2
DEVELOPING SKILLS OF RECEPTION

CHAPTER THREE

THE ART OF SUMMARY

Representing Others

In Chapters 1 and 2 we learned that effective dialogue in an academic context depends on two things: our ability to engage ethically with other scholars and our ability to understand the academic situation we're in and the genres of communication we're being asked to use. We come now to our first genre of academic research writing: the summary. We begin with the summary because it is the foundation of most academic writing. Summaries are used and incorporated in almost every research genre—book reviews, literature reviews, lab reports, research proposals, academic essays, scholarly articles, and books.

We write summaries to report what other research scholars have said about a topic in order to show readers how we are engaging with their research and responding to their ideas. In other words, we use summaries to set up an academic dialogue between other scholars and ourselves in our research writing. In this chapter we will explore the genre of summary in detail. We will look at what summary is and how we use it to represent what others have said in a research dialogue. We will examine the underlying ethics of summary and learn how to compose one ourselves.

A. WHAT IS SUMMARY?

In everyday conversations we constantly report what other people have said. We hear all sorts of things that we want to pass along. In fact, most of our conversations are made up of summarizing and sharing these things with others. Another way of putting it is that we constantly represent others by sharing their words and ideas—sometimes to pass along information, sometimes to make sense of something, sometimes to entertain others, sometimes to persuade them. Consider the following examples we might say or hear in everyday conversation. Notice how each example points to what someone else has said as part of the conversation (highlighted in bold):

"I really want to go to your party, but **my mom said** I have to go to this family gathering she's been planning for weeks. It's on the same night. I'm so sorry."

"I was reading a blog the other day, that one by Jeff Peters, and **he wrote** that the chocolate industry is notorious for child labour, slavery, and deforestation. So how do we find chocolate that is ethically produced and made with sustainably grown cocoa beans?"

"You wouldn't believe the massive fight that broke out on the bus on my way home yesterday. This guy, who was obviously drunk, freaked out on the bus driver and then tried to punch him! And **the bus driver's like**, 'Get off this bus, buddy, or I'm calling the police.' The man stood there and kept yelling, and **the bus driver's like**, 'Get off the bus!' Finally, he and two other passengers literally carried the guy off the bus. I can't believe people actually freak out like that. I think it'd be kinda scary to be a bus driver."

"**My doctor told me** I'm going to have to go on antibiotics for this cough; it looks like it is turning into pneumonia. I'm really worried to hear that it's getting worse. I hope the antibiotics help."

Please note that any connections between invented examples and actual circumstances, people, or resources are coincidental.

Just for fun, try spending one day being objectively aware of what you and others talk about. You may be surprised to find how many conversations are made up of short summaries reporting what other people have said that we pass on for reasons of our own. You will probably also notice that we often conclude our summaries with our own commentary—what we think about what we have just reported.

What exactly is a summary, then? A ***summary*** is a brief report of what we have seen, heard, or done, or what someone else has seen, heard, or done. The content of our summaries is endless. We summarize situations, events, information, experiences, and ideas. We summarize stories, films, conversations, and podcasts. We also learn, with time and experience, that the people we are addressing (our audience) tend to have short attention spans. This means that whatever we want to report has to be done clearly and succinctly while we have their attention if we want to engage in a dialogue with them. If our summaries are too long, our discussion quickly turns into a monologue. Consider the following situations:

1. Your two cousins, ages seven and nine, have recently seen (for the twentieth time) their favourite Disney film, *Frozen*. Out of politeness and to make conversation with them, you ask, "So what's the film about?" They proceed to tell you in comprehensive detail every single thing that happens in the film, chiming in together with voices raised in excitement. This goes on for fifteen minutes until, mercifully, your aunt interrupts them to direct their attention elsewhere.

As adults, we know that if someone asks us, "What's the film about?" we have about three minutes to sum up the plot without giving away any crucial information so that the movie isn't ruined for an interested person or before a polite person's eyes glaze over. In short, when faced with this question we give a brief summary of the film unless the person has specifically asked for details. Children, not realizing the social codes and expectations surrounding the question, take it literally and report everything.

2. You have just returned from a weeklong holiday in Costa Rica. A friend asks you the typical question, "So how was your trip?" the first time you get together. What does your friend expect to hear in response?

A polite friend is probably expecting something brief, like, "Yeah, it was really good. We stayed at this nice hotel on the beach and went swimming basically every day. We took a couple day trips into the rainforest too—I finally got to go zip lining!—but mostly we just relaxed on the beach and danced at the club near our hotel." That is, the response should be a short summary highlighting the best or worst or most remarkable parts of the trip. A more interested friend might ask further questions, but generally speaking, we realize that the response to such a question is meant to be brief. We probably all know someone who has pulled out a scrapbook or hauled out a laptop to show every picture and highlight every detail of the trip, including backstories of each image. For most recipients, this kind of description is overwhelming.

In both situations, the speaker is meant to summarize or report in brief the material or experience requested in the question. Brevity is one of the main characteristics of summarizing. Knowing our audience, culture, and situation will help us to assess how brief our summary should be. Generally speaking, summaries do not report material extensively or in minute detail, but highlight the most significant points.

B. THE ETHICS OF SUMMARY

Reporting what others have said takes *receptivity*—the ability to listen to and understand others. Receptivity takes effort to develop. When we don't put in the effort, we can easily misrepresent the words of others as we pass them along. As young children, we may have played a game called "Telephone" that illustrates this point. In this game, children sit in a circle and one child starts off the telephone conversation by making up a message. The message is whispered from child to child, making its way around the circle. In the process, the message becomes distorted, especially if it is long or complicated to begin with. The last child who hears the message repeats it back to the group. The children all laugh hysterically at how bizarre the message has become, and then they play the game again!

As adults, we easily slide into a "Telephone" situation. We don't intend to misrepresent the words of others as we pass them along, but the message can be distorted nonetheless. It is important to realize that summarizing the ideas of others involves a number of ethical practices in order to avoid distortion or misrepresentation. These practices are not only relevant in ordinary conversations; they are also critical in our academic writing, as they involve our ability to listen, interpret, synthesize, represent, and acknowledge the research and ideas of other scholars to our readers. Let's consider each practice in turn.

1. Attentive Listening

Before we can summarize someone else's ideas, we need to be able to understand the content of those ideas and recognize where the other person is coming from in speaking them. This means cultivating attentive listening skills. As we saw in Chapter 1, attentive listening means offering our full attention to others as we listen to what they have to say, especially if what they have to say is new to us or different from what we expect to hear. Truly attending to others and their ideas means we are fully present to them with the intention of understanding their views and experiences.

Clinical counsellors, therapists, and psychologists practise this kind of careful listening in sessions with clients. For example, after a client has shared his or her situation, a therapist will often summarize what the client has said and report it back to ensure that he or she has understood the message. The therapist may introduce this summary with a phrase like, "So what I hear you saying is...." The client can then agree, clarify misunderstood material, or add more information. It is crucial that therapists grasp all the nuances of their clients' experiences because the type of counsel they give depends on the accuracy of their understanding. Medical doctors, too, take careful notes about patients' ailments, listening to their bodies and their description of symptoms in order to discern what the problem is. If they do not listen carefully or if they neglect to record something, someone's health or even life may be at stake.

We take similar care in an academic context when we read the research of other scholars. We cultivate attentive reading and note-taking practices that honour the scholars' words and seek to understand all aspects of their communication. This careful listening practice becomes the basis by which we summarize. It is as if we're saying to the scholars whose work we're reading, "What I hear you saying is...," and reporting to others the content of their message in our own words.

2. Interpretation

The listening process does not simply involve our ability to parrot back what someone else has said, but to interpret the crux of what the person *means* in what he or she is saying. Someone might say, "The film was interesting," and could mean that the film was truly fascinating or that the film was peculiar or bizarre. Because language is *multivalent* (words hold multiple meanings), we recognize that there could be a number of ways to understand the meaning of someone else's words.

In a face-to-face dialogue, we can ask a person directly to clarify their meaning: "By 'interesting,' do you mean fascinating or bizarre?" In most academic contexts, however, research scholars are not available for us to consult about the meaning of their words. Hence, we need to draw out the meaning of a research text by examining its context, its intended audience, and any purposes of the text that its research writers have directly stated. In doing so, we respect their ideas and intentions for their work. However, we are also free to point out the fact that multiple interpretations are possible, noting how a text could mean different things to different audiences in different contexts beyond what the scholars may have intended.

3. Synthesis

If summarizing involves reporting the ideas of others *in brief*, then it requires another cognitive process alongside understanding and interpretation: that of synthesis. *Synthesis* is the practice of sifting through ideas, selecting the key ones, and adding them up so that their "sum total" can be communicated. It is this "sum total" that we pull together when we summarize things like the plot of a book, the highlights of our vacation, the quality of a date, or our uncle's political views. We choose which key elements to pass along to others and which material to leave out.

Similarly, when we summarize academic research we carefully choose what material to include and how to organize that material in such a way that the essence of the original meaning is retained in our retelling of it. This practice takes concentration, insight, and care. It requires us to get to the heart of what a scholar is saying and understand it from the inside in order to make effective decisions about what to include in, and how to organize, our summary.

4. Representation

When we summarize, we are effectively taking the words and ideas presented to us and *re-presenting* them in brief to someone else. In representing someone's words and ideas to others, we function as a *representative*, standing in for that person or communicating on behalf of that person. Just like an elected representative stands in for a political party or social community and speaks on their behalf, we stand in for other people when we represent what they have said. We probably do not usually think of reporting what others say as representing their words on their behalf. That is, we do not consider the ethical implications of re-presenting someone's words to someone else. Perhaps if we did, we would try harder to be accurate or be less inclined to put a spin on others' words.

- *You'll never believe what she told me. She said....*
- *He couldn't stop talking about you. He said....*
- *What was she thinking when she said...?*
- *I am so mad that he said....*
- *I'm just telling you what I heard her say....*

We often represent the words of others according to what *we think* about them rather than their intended meaning, and most of the time others are not present to check whether we are representing them accurately or not. We can probably all point to times when we have not represented others accurately or when we have felt the sting of being misrepresented ourselves.

Representation is a trusted task. In an academic context, we summarize the words and ideas of other scholars, representing them in our research writing. We give these scholars voice as we represent their research and ideas to our readers. In academic writing it is critical that we do not misrepresent other scholars, their work or their words, despite the fact that we are summarizing them in the context of our own work for our own purposes. We need to be careful to convey to our readers what scholars have actually said about their research and ideas, and represent their work as accurately, neutrally, and respectfully as we can.

5. Acknowledgement

Finally, when we report the words and ideas of others, we clarify who said what and distinguish their ideas from our own. We indicate, for instance, that it is our uncle who has these particular political views (not us), it is our date who said those awkward things (yikes), it is our friend who had that awesome idea (that we agree with), or it is the blogger who offered that helpful perspective on chocolate production (that we want to get behind). In short, we acknowledge the people whose ideas we're summarizing and engaging with in our conversations.

In the context of academic research writing, we also acknowledge the scholars whose research and ideas we're summarizing so that readers are able to distinguish them from our own. This acknowledgement is called "citation," a process we will learn more about in Chapter 6. Put briefly, *citation* is the practice of acknowledging that our knowledge stems from the research and ideas of other scholars. When we cite their work in our research writing, we give them credit for their ideas and demonstrate our respect for their research by documenting their studies.

C. THE PURPOSE OF ACADEMIC SUMMARIES

Research writers rely on summaries to communicate the research and ideas of other scholars to their readers. Whatever the research genre or field of study, writers tend to use summaries in two main ways: to outline the current research knowledge that expert scholars have established on a topic, and to convey particular scholars' research material in order to engage with, build on, and respond to it with their own stance. Let's consider these two purposes in more detail.

1. Summaries that Outline Current Research Knowledge

We outline current research knowledge to introduce readers to a topic and to show them which aspects of the subject scholars have been studying and discussing. By establishing what other scholars have said on a subject, we set the stage for our own contribution to the discussion. Consider the example summary below. Note how the academic writer outlines the topic of EMIs and the current research on them by drawing on a wide range of scholarship. Within a few sentences, readers have a basic sense of the topic, its key areas of study, and the scholars invested in its research.

> Several examples of EMIs [Ecological Momentary Interventions] to reduce depression have been created and evaluated.... EMIs intended to reduce depression do so through interventions aimed at various proximal outcomes such as engagement in pleasurable activities (Ly et al., 2014), increasing positive emotions (Tugade & du Pont, 2014), or other pathways. EMIs for depression have also made use of diverse conceptual treatment strategies including acceptance and commitment therapy (Ahtinen et al., 2013; Lappalainen et al., 2013; Ly et al., 2012) and interpersonal therapy (Dagoo et al., 2014), but the majority have been cognitive-behavioral in focus including cognitive-behavioral therapy (CBT), behavioral activation (Burns et al., 2011), relaxation (Grassi et al., 2007), and self-monitoring (Agyapong et al., 2012). (pp. 541–42)
>
> Schueller, S.M., Aguilera, A., & Mohr, D.C. (2017). Ecological momentary interventions for depression and anxiety. *Depression and Anxiety, 34*(6), 540–545. https://doi.org/10.1002/da.22649

2. Summaries that Convey Specific Research as the Basis for Making a Point

We also outline the research of other scholars in order or to build on it or respond to it with our own work. In this context, our summaries focus on a specific research finding or idea that we want to respond to or rely on as evidence to develop a point. Consider the summary below. Note how the research writer outlines the work of two key scholars—James Dodd and Ernst Bloch—in order to build on their research and develop her own ideas about the subject of hope and futurity.

> Hope is not a first-order emotion, like pleasure or pain, but rather it is an affective configuration of other emotions such as optimism and joy. My aim here is to understand hope in relation to the question of the future.... James Dodd, describing the phenomenon of hope, writes that hoping is often posed between two extremes: "on the one hand, it is an effort to bring oneself out of a today into a tomorrow, which is sustained by a temporal brush with the goodness of what is anticipated; or it is the attempt to avoid at all costs the consciousness of what today has become, by fervently believing in a fiction that has been set up as an alternative mode of being" (pp. 119–120). Also posing hope in relation to futurity and an anticipatory consciousness, Ernst Bloch, in his extensive work *The Principle of Hope*, takes hope as integral to external reality: "Expectation, hope, intention towards possibility that has still not become: this is not only a basic feature of human consciousness but, concretely, corrected and grasped, a basic determination within objective reality as a whole" (p. 7). Bloch's project centres on a utopian reality principle that combines wish and knowledge, affect and cognition in such a way that anticipates that which has not yet been realised. In effect, for Bloch, there is no uncertainty about the future, or the not-yet, as the future is already there and we must discover how to approach it. Hope then is both an emotion...and a "directing act of a cognitive kind" (p. 12). (p. 140)

Smaill, B. (2010). *The documentary: Politics, emotion, culture.* Palgrave Macmillan.

As we can see from these two examples, we write summaries to display our research capabilities and our level of knowledge about a topic to our readers. In doing so, we establish ourselves as informed and reliable representatives of the research dialogue, well equipped to contribute our own stance to the discussion.

These two examples also show us that our summaries will look different depending on whether we are drawing on a wide range of research to establish the current knowledge on a topic or focusing on a key text by a particular scholar as a means to develop a point. In this chapter and in the following one, we will learn how to summarize one text at a time. We will focus on representing a particular scholar's research findings or ideas in brief. Later, in Chapter 5, we will learn how to bring the work of various scholars together in order to highlight their different views and outline how their ideas intersect.

D. READING TO SUMMARIZE

Writing a summary of a research text begins with attentive reading; that is, reading with an aim to understand the scholar's research and ideas and to represent them accurately to others. The best way to understand a piece of research writing is to read through it slowly and take notes. When we take notes, we ask ourselves, "What is this text about? What key ideas and research findings does the researcher communicate? Do I get what the researcher is saying? Could I explain it to someone else?" As we carefully read and take notes on a research text, we make sense of it, interpret its findings, and synthesize its ideas. The clearer our notes are, the more easily we will be able to represent that research material to others.

When we take notes with an intent to summarize, we look for and highlight particular things in a research text:

- the *title*, the *name(s)* of the scholar(s) who wrote it, and the *date* it was published
- the *key points*, *concepts*, or *ideas* in each paragraph
- the *concrete details* (examples, evidence) that best illustrate the scholar's key points
- the *transition* and *direction words* that help us understand the structure and organization of the scholar's key points, including *connecting words* (and, also, in addition to, similarly), *contrasting words* (in contrast, but, yet, however), *conclusive words* (therefore, thus, hence), and *sequential words* (first, second, next, then)

In our note-taking process, we also benefit from writing the central idea of each paragraph in the margins as we go along. This central idea is called the ***gist*** of the paragraph (Giltrow et al., 2009, p. 59). When we finish reading, we consider the gist of each paragraph to help us get a sense of the article or excerpt as a whole. We could call this the *overarching gist* of the text. The following example shows how we can use the suggestions above to annotate a research text. It has been annotated for its key points/ideas (bold), its concrete details (underlined), and its transition or direction words (shaded). It also includes the gist of each paragraph in the boxes on the right hand side of the text.

> ***GIST: A teacher-centred approach vs. reflective-practitioner approach to college & university education for developing an effective professional practice***

> There are **different approaches** to **the relationship between academic knowledge and professional practice**. In a **traditional teaching-centred approach**, the overall mission of colleges and universities was to provide a scientific knowledge base by transferring disciplinary content knowledge from faculty members to students. An **effective professional practice** was considered to be the result of the **application of...theoretical principles to a specific situation**: <u>students have to learn the theory and, when engaged in the workplace, transfer that knowledge from the educational context to the job context</u>. Since the 1980s, however, the emphasis on the **reflective practitioner has called this approach into question**. Professional practice cannot be reduced to the application of theory to practice through a linear and automatic process. <u>The issues that workers must face</u> are often ambiguous and complex, with multiple solutions. Therefore, being an **effective practitioner means being able to construct situated and local**

knowledge. The ability to learn from experience through reflection on one's own action becomes crucial in this situation.

The **concept of reflective practice** has **several components** which have been expressed in different ways by scholars. First, it is an **inquiry attitude**: new practitioners cannot work out problems without **a "reflective conversation with the situation"** (Schön, 1983, p. 242), which means working through provisional hypotheses verified with constant monitoring of the effects of their actions. [Second], reflective practitioners must also **question the beliefs, values, feelings, and implicit assumptions** that influence their way of defining and solving a problem.

> ***GIST:** Two components of reflective practice: analyzing the situation & self-questioning*

Korthagen and Vasalos (2005) have suggested that there are **different areas** in which **reflection** can take place: environment, behaviour, competencies, beliefs, identity, and mission. The attention paid to these aspects has led some scholars to recommend a shift from being a **reflective practitioner** to being a **reflexive practitioner**, where **reflexivity** is defined as "**awareness of self-in-practice**" (Warin et al., 2006, p. 234). Moreover, in the work context, **reflexivity is a social activity** occurring within a "socially situated, relational, political, and collective process" (Reynolds & Vince, 2004, p. 6); therefore, a **reflexive practitioner** needs to be able to listen to and negotiate with others and to reflect on tacit assumptions shared within the community.

> ***GIST:** Recommended shift from reflective practitioner to reflexive practitioner = social and self-awareness*

These **theoretical perspectives** suggest that **reflexivity** may be **a learning outcome** connected with **professional identity development**. By the term "**professional identity**" we mean **the understanding of one's self as a professional**. Paraphrasing Korthagen and Vasalos (p. 52), the **concept** refers to the **question**: "what kind of practitioner do I want to be?" We think that this question includes some **underlying issues**. What is the subject of my work? What do I deal with as a practitioner? Which services do I provide? Upon which values, beliefs, paradigms, and theories do I depend when I build knowledge and solve problems? What are my strengths and my weaknesses? In other words, **professional identity** includes **internalized models of professionalism** and of **the concept of a "good professional,"** which arise from **experiences** and **are socially situated**. These **internalized models** influence knowledge-building and problem-solving processes. Therefore, a professional approach to work cannot be reduced to a list of disciplinary knowledge and technical skills: it is also driven by what individuals understand as "being a professional" and how they acknowledge their active roles in building meaning. (pp. 246–47)

> ***GIST:** Professional identity development = reflecting on what kind of professional to be*
>
> ***How we understand professionalism and see ourselves as "good professionals" is social and experiential; it influences how we build knowledge and solve problems***

Gilardi, S., & Lozza, E. (2009). Inquiry-based learning and undergraduates' professional identity development. *Innovative High Education, 34*(4), 245–256. https://doi.org/10.1007/s10755-009-9109-0

As we can see, note-taking is an involved practice that takes into account all the key points (concepts and ideas), details (examples), and verbal directions in a text. The key points in the excerpt above focus on various approaches to college and university education in relation to professional practices, particularly *reflective* and *reflexive* practices. Details and examples help to explain these approaches and define the terms, while verbal directions show readers how ideas connect and contrast.

As we take notes, we are engaged in the cognitive practices of understanding, interpreting, and synthesizing the various points in a text so that we can discern the meaning of the text as a whole. The more attention we can give a research text at this stage, the easier it will be to write a summary of it. Many summaries falter because we do not put in the cognitive work of making sense of a document. When we take the time to engage thoughtfully with a text in order to understand it, the process of summarizing goes much faster.

E. WRITING AN ACADEMIC SUMMARY

Once we have carefully read and annotated a text we plan to summarize, we are ready to write the summary itself. An academic summary is composed of three things:

- *reported speech*: what a scholar (or group of scholars) has said about a topic
- *the scholar(s) speaking*: the scholar(s) whose speech we are reporting
- *signal verbs*: the verbs we use to introduce the speech we are reporting

Let's begin with the reported speech and consider the scholar(s) speaking and signal verbs in connection with that speech. We can report "the speech" of scholars—by which we mean their research and ideas—in two ways: by quoting what they have written word for word or by paraphrasing what they have written in our own words. We ***quote*** research scholars word for word when we want to convey to our readers the exact language used in their original document. We ***paraphrase*** research scholars in our own words when we want to convey the gist of what they've said—the heart of their ideas, findings, or conclusions.

When we write academic summaries, we usually rely on paraphrase rather than quotation to represent the research and ideas of scholars. We do so because summaries are meant to be brief overviews of a scholar's work, not detailed reports of their exact words. Think of the root word of summary: *sum*. The "sum" of something is its "total amount resulting from the addition of two or more items, facts, ideas, etc." (*Canadian Oxford Dictionary*). Hence, a summary focuses on the "total" or "whole" of an idea, its overarching gist rather than its details. This doesn't mean that summarizers do not need to know the details of the research ideas they are summarizing. In fact, they need to know them inside and out in order to determine what they add up to. However, the readers of a summary do not benefit from a list of word-for-word details to understand the whole. Hence, we synthesize and represent the research and ideas of others in our own words, relying on paraphrase and using quotations sparingly.

Consider the following example of an academic summary within the context of a larger research paper. The authors are summarizing one aspect of the work of Brazilian educator and philosopher, Paulo Freire, from his text *Pedagogy of the Oppressed.* They rely on a publication of this text from the year 2000 (represented in parentheses below).

> In an era defined dialogically by bias and difference, learning becomes the pragmatic home of a minimal hope for communicative justice. Freire, the Brazilian educator for justice, plays out the focus on bias even more strongly. Historicity and bias situated within a given historical moment obscures our sight; Freire (2000) gave us insight into the limits of our vision through a "critical consciousness"—one that permits us to see with clarity that literacy opens the door to learning and a dialogic questioning of formerly taken-for-granted limits. Freire (2000) stated that dialogue cannot take place between those who hold significantly different positions of power, arguing that a common set of power interests makes dialogue possible. He works at face saving for the disadvantaged, not just for those in power who are inattentive to the needs of those who have no, or attenuated, power.... Someone who assumes the position of telling and has enough power to be heard without listening to the Other is not a candidate for Freireian dialogue. For Freire, awareness of the bias of inequities opens the door to beginning conversation, new learning, and change. (p. 121)
>
> Arnett, R.C., Fritz, J.M.H., & Bell, L.M. (2010). Dialogic learning as first principle in communication ethics. *Atlantic Journal of Communication, 18*(3), 111–126. https://doi.org/10.1080/15456871003742021

As we can see, most of this summary is written in paraphrase, focusing on key concepts in Freire's text. The authors do use quotation, but only sparingly, to highlight the exact wording of a key concept: "critical consciousness." Beyond that, the content of Freire's concept of critical consciousness and his views on dialogue are interpreted, synthesized, and represented in the authors' own words.

As we paraphrase the research material of other scholars, we need to acknowledge that the findings and ideas we are representing are not our own, even if the words are ours. We signal that we are representing someone else's words by referring to the scholar who wrote them. Notice how the academic writers in the example above directly state the name of the scholar whose work they are summarizing: "Freire, the Brazilian educator for justice." In fact, they repeat Freire's name at least three times to keep signalling to readers that the research and ideas they are summarizing belong to Freire.

As we write our summaries, we not only signal that we are representing someone else's words by referring to the scholar who wrote them, we also use a ***signal verb*** to introduce the content of his or her ideas. If we return to the example above, we can see how the authors provide signal verbs to indicate Freire's research activity as they represent his ideas:

Freire ... plays out....
Freire gave....
Freire stated..., arguing....
He works at....

One of our challenges as research summarizers is to choose signal verbs appropriate to the actions that the scholar carried out in his or her research. Did the scholar *observe* something? *Analyse* something? *Explain* something? *Describe* something? *Argue* something? We need our verbs to reflect that action.

Unintentionally, we often draw on the same three boring verbs—*says*, *states*, or *writes*—to convey a scholar's research: "Smith *says* _____. Then Smith *states* _____. Next she *writes* _____." While using these verbs does signal to our readers that it is Smith doing the research and that the ideas belong to her, these verbs are dull and imprecise. They do not get to the heart of Smith's research activity. When we choose signal verbs to describe Smith's work, we want to show what Smith is *doing* in her research, not just that she is *saying* something about her research. With this distinction in mind, here is a list of signal verbs to help us extend our verbal vocabulary:

account for
analyse
argue
assert
assess
assume
claim
clarify
compare
complicate
conclude
criticize
defend
define
demonstrate
depict
describe
determine
distinguish
emphasize
evaluate
examine
exemplify
exhibit
explain
explore
identify
illustrate
imply
indicate
investigate
judge
justify
observe
persuade
propose
question
recognize
refer to
reflect
refute
reveal
review
state
suggest
support
urge
verify

It is also worth noting that in most academic contexts, signal verbs are written in the present tense. Even though we are reporting the research and ideas that scholars have published in the past, we usually summarize it in our own work *in the present*. Because we are writing *right now*, our signal verbs are written in the present tense:

Smith *argues*....
Smith *claims*....
Smith *demonstrates*....
Smith *indicates*....
Smith *proposes*....
Smith *examines*....

While we report on what scholars have said in the present tense, we still sum up historical facts in the scholars' research material by using the past tense. We may even use past and present verb tenses in the same sentence, where one verb is a signal verb and the other verb refers to a historical fact.

Smith ***observes*** that in premodern societies, wealth and rank largely ***coincided***.

Using more than one verb tense in our writing can feel confusing. And some academic communities prefer to use only the past tense for both signal verbs and historical facts. However, most summarizers are encouraged to distinguish between present and past tense, depending on whether they are referring to a scholar's work (present tense) or to a past event or historical data in their research (past tense).

To review, then, we rely on paraphrase to summarize the content of what scholars have said in their research, only using direct quotations if we want to highlight a particular word, term, concept, or phrase that helps readers understand a key aspect of that content. We also attribute scholars' words to them by identifying scholars by name and using signal verbs, indicating that the original research and ideas come from them, not from us.

EXERCISE 1
STUDYING SUMMARY

1. Read the following academic summary and note whose research is being summarized.

2. Highlight where the authors use paraphrase and where they use quotation to represent the scholar's research. Determine their purpose in using each.

3. Circle the signal verbs that the authors use to report the verbal actions of the scholar.

Prosecutors face particular legal and procedural difficulties in establishing businesses' responsibility. Among the most relevant ones, Zerk (2014) highlights the following: the difficulty of identifying the appropriate entity or entities against which to lodge a private law claim in cases involving large transnational groups of companies; objections to lawsuits based on doctrines of sovereign immunity, "act of State," and "political question" frequently encountered by claimants in ATS cases; the nonapplicability of criminal law provisions to corporate entities in some jurisdictions; and the existence of rules that place restrictions on the ability of individual victims, their representatives, and other organizations (e.g., nongovernmental organizations) to initiate and participate in legal proceedings. She also includes practical obstacles blocking accountability in domestic courts, including but not limited to scarce availability (or nonavailability) of legal aid, "loser pays" rules, and lack of resources and specialized expertise within prosecution bodies. (p. 72)

Payne, L., & Pereira, G. (2016). Corporate complicity in international human rights violations. *Annual Review of Law and Social Science, 12*(1), 63–84. https://doi.org/10.1146/annurev-lawsocsci-110615-085100

F. ORGANIZING AN ACADEMIC SUMMARY

We now know that an academic summary is a brief representation of what other scholars have said in their research, which is attributed to them with signal verbs and paraphrased in our own words. But how do we begin our summary? And how do we organize the key ideas and details in such a way that they are accurate to the original, clear to our readers (who probably haven't read the original), and brief? Holding these three goals together as we write can be tricky.

As new research writers, we often find ourselves unsure of how to begin writing a summary or what exactly to include in it. As a result, we try to include every key idea and organize it as a list, laid out in the order in which we read it. This results in a *chronological* or *linear* representation of the material, in which we are forced to repeat the phrase "and then" to connect the key ideas together. For example, if we return to the excerpt by Gilardi and Lozza that we annotated in Section D, we may be tempted to summarize it as follows:

Silvia Gilardi and Edoardo Lozza talk about approaches to university education and then they compare the approaches. They focus on a reflective-practitioner approach and then describe its elements. Then they talk about reflexive practitioners and how they're different from reflective practitioners. Then they....

Not only does this approach make for a boring list of information that is sure to lull readers to sleep, it also condenses the excerpt by repeating its key points without synthesizing or making sense of them by means of an *overarching gist*. In other words, it avoids adding the information together (in sum) to present readers with a coherent whole.

Rather than compiling a chronological list of information, we use a spatial organization instead. *Spatial organization* presents information by moving from the overarching gist to specific points, from the whole to its parts. We begin by focusing on the big picture: What is this research text or excerpt about *as a whole*? What is its sum total? Then we delve into the key ideas that we've added up to come to that big picture.

To illustrate, think of spatial organization in a summary as a tree rather than a line (Giltrow et al., 2009, pp. 63–64). Like a tree starting at its trunk, a summary starts with the overarching gist of the whole text. This "trunk" is the base out of which all the key points and details stem. Once we've established the overarching gist, then we highlight the most applicable key points that branch out from it. Points that are really abstract or that we think will be confusing for our readers can be illustrated with concrete details or examples (often located in parentheses), like leaves on the tree.

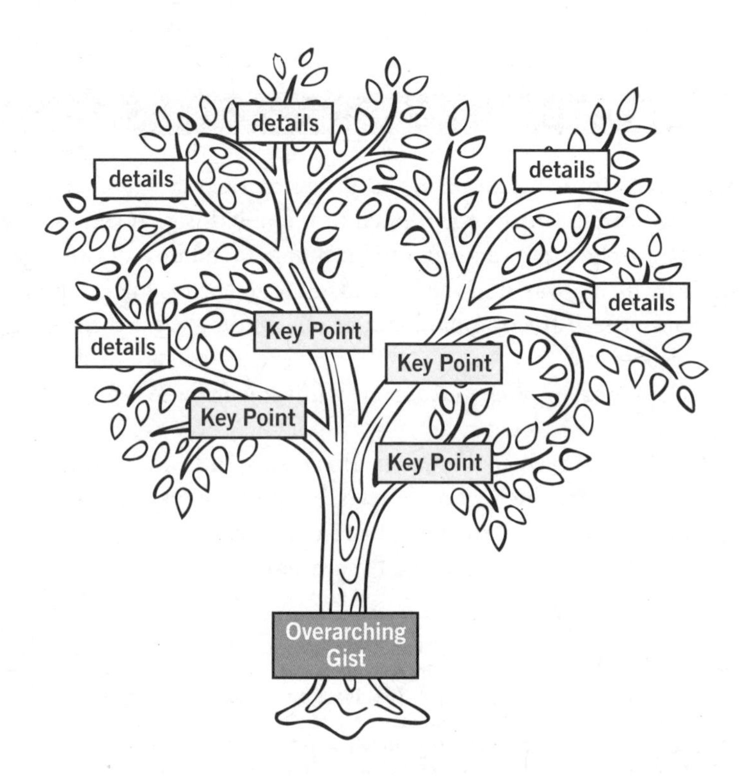

Using this spatial approach, writing summaries can be broken down into five steps:

Trunk

1. Begin by introducing the scholar(s), the text being summarized, and the date it was published.
2. Write the overarching gist of the whole article or excerpt in a sentence or two.

Branches and leaves

3. Highlight the key points that develop the overarching gist.
4. Incorporate some concrete details (examples/evidence) to clarify these points.
5. Acknowledge the scholars throughout with signal verbs and use transitions to help readers understand how the points link together and relate to each other.

Let's return to the excerpt by Gilardi and Lozza we annotated and summarize it using spatial organization. Notice how it incorporates the five elements above—the "trunk" in the first two sentences and the "branches" throughout the rest of the summary.

> In this excerpt of "Inquiry-Based Learning and Undergraduates' Professional Identity Development" (2009), Silvia Gilardi and Edoardo Lozza introduce two approaches for teaching professional practices to post-secondary students: a "teaching-centred approach" (where students gain knowledge of best practices from professors) and a "reflective practitioner approach" (where students learn professionalism by experience and self-reflection). Gilardi and Lozza focus on the latter approach as a means to prepare students to become "good professionals" in the workforce. Through self-reflection and experience, students can learn *to think* critically about complex work situations and question their own assumptions and views in order to address workplace problems. As they develop awareness of themselves (individually) in relation to others (socially), they can become reflexive practitioners, able *to practise* listening and negotiating with others in their work environments. These skills, Gilardi and Lozza argue, are not simply technical know-how, but are experientially derived and rooted in internalized models of what it means to be a "good professional."

As we can see, the summary begins by introducing the article, its date, and its authors so that readers know exactly what is being summarized. The summary also outlines the overarching gist in the first two sentences. Then it covers the key points about reflective and reflexive practices, adding details throughout to help readers make sense of these concepts. Notably, the points do not occur in exactly the same order in the summary as they do in the original text. Because the organization is spatial rather than chronological, key points are incorporated in the order that makes the best sense to the summarizer (in light of his or her purposes) rather than the order originally used by the researchers. Finally, the summary relies largely on paraphrase—the summarizer's own words representing Gilardi and Lozza's ideas—and uses signal verbs to attribute the ideas to them.

G. BECOMING EFFECTIVE SUMMARIZERS

Functionally speaking, our summaries report the research and ideas of other scholars. However, to be truly effective, our summaries also depend on how we situate ourselves in relation to the material we are representing. To be effective summarizers, we need to put ourselves in the shoes of the scholar we are summarizing. This means putting aside our own views to inhabit those of the scholar. From this position, we are able to see their research and ideas from their perspective and represent them as neutrally and fairly as possible. In fact, we should be so neutral in our summary that readers cannot tell whether we agree or disagree with the scholar whose work we're representing (Graff & Birkenstein, 2014, p. 31). We aim to be strictly informative without sliding into glowing reports or negative criticisms.

For example, the summary of Gilardi and Lozza's excerpt above reads respectfully and neutrally. But imagine if the summary read this way instead:

In "Inquiry-Based Learning and Undergraduates' Professional Identity Development," Silvia Gilardi and Edoardo Lozza dismiss a "teaching-centred approach" as a ridiculous way to prepare college and university students to be "good professionals" in the workplace. No one learns by being spoon-fed technical knowledge. The only way to teach professionalism is through a "reflective practitioner approach," which is a far superior method of learning.

Rather than a neutral and informative representation of the material, this example reveals a negative bias with words like "ridiculous" and "dismiss," and extremes like "no one" and "only." The summarizer does not try to inhabit the shoes of these scholars or present their ideas in a neutral way, but reduces the complexity of the original excerpt and reinforces his or her own preconceived ideas. Such a summary sounds inaccurate and unreliable as a result. To write effective summaries, then, we need to be able to inhabit other viewpoints and represent them in a considerate and impartial manner.

How effective our summaries are also depends on how we situate them in the larger context of our writing. In research writing, summaries are usually not stand-alone pieces. They are part of a larger document (a report, a review, a research essay, etc.). With this in mind, we need to ask ourselves, "What is the purpose of my summary within the larger piece of prose I am writing? Why am I reporting the research of this scholar or group of scholars to my readers?" As we saw in Section C, summaries are used to introduce readers to the current knowledge about a topic or to address and discuss a particular theory, concept, or area of research that we are studying. With this in mind, we balance our summary of other scholars' work with our own ideas, integrating what they have said in relation to what we are saying.

Consider how the following example balances a neutral summary of "minority stress theory" in the research of Meyer (2003) with the research writers' response to that theory, setting up a written dialogue between them. This summary is shaded and the research writers' response is underlined for clarity:

Minority stress theory argues that individuals with marginalized identities experience unique stress from their minority status in society, including both distal and proximal stressors that impact the individual. Distal stressors are objective stressors that are independent of the individual perceptions such as prejudice events (Meyer, 2003) that act concurrently with proximal stressors, which are subjective and operate internally, such as internalized transphobia or racism (Meyer, 2003). Minority stress theory assumes that stress is cumulative and is compounded to create more stress on those with both a minority status and a minority identity. For individuals of multiple marginalized identities, stressful environmental conditions are compounded. These stressful situations may lead to poor outcomes for individuals because there is no buffer or mediating factor of stress in the social environment. Using this theory, it is reasonable to suggest that, due to the impacts of both racism and transphobia that transgender/GNC people of color experience, they are at greater risk for adverse health outcomes due to the stressors of their marginalized gender identity and racial identity status in our society. (pp. 220–21)

Kattari, S., Walls, N.E., Whitfield, D.L., & Langenderfer-Magruder, L. (2017). Racial and ethnic differences in experiences of discrimination in accessing social services among transgender/gender-nonconforming people. *Journal of Ethnic & Cultural Diversity in Social Work, 26*(3), 217–235. https://doi.org/10.1080/15313204.2016.1242102

In this example, the research writers (Kattari et al.) summarize Meyer's theory of minority stress in order to show how it applies to the topic of their article—discrimination and adverse health outcomes among transgender individuals and gender-nonconforming people of colour. In effect, they have set up a dialogue with Meyer, in which they uphold the theory and apply it to their own work.

Ultimately, our summaries of scholarly research are balanced with our own ideas in the context of a larger research document. We can imagine this balance of ideas as an interactive dialogue between what other scholars have said about a topic and what we are saying in response to their views. We will learn more about how to structure this kind of dialogue when we get to Chapter 5. At this stage we want to make sure we can represent in brief what other scholars are saying in a respectful and reliable way, so let's practise summarizing with the following exercise.

EXERCISE 2
SUMMARY PRACTICE

1. Read the following excerpt. Annotate the key points, details, transition/direction words, and gist in each paragraph. Then determine the overarching gist of the passage: What do the paragraphs add up to say?

2. Write a short summary of the excerpt in four to five sentences (150–200 words).

- Try your hand at spatial organization by introducing the scholars' names and the title and date of the text you are summarizing (found at the end of the excerpt), as well as stating the overarching gist of the whole passage, in your first sentence or two.

- Next, cover the main points of the excerpt and incorporate useful details. Use your own words to paraphrase this material rather than quoting sections of the text.

- Use signal verbs and transitions throughout to help readers follow you.

- If in doubt, use the examples throughout this chapter to help you.

Concern about climate change has grown over the past 25 years. Today, thousands of climatological scientists and researchers across related fields are conducting research on topics ranging from the specifics of obscure climate processes to the likely impacts of climate change on everything from alpine ecosystems to financial markets. The pace of discovery and the growth in understanding have been sufficiently rapid, the breadth of impacts sufficiently wide, and the implications of social concern sufficiently broad that a major international organization was created to synthesize scientific evidence on climate change. The Intergovernmental Panel on Climate Change, or IPCC, operates under the auspices of the United Nations Environment Programme and the World Meteorological Organization. Every six years or so, the panel publishes assessment reports that summarize the state of the research on climate change science, impacts, and policy (*Climate Change*, 2014). Many other organizations, too, have assessed aspects of the problems inherent in climate change, resulting in projects ranging from the 2007 *Stern Review*—a UK government study emphasizing the economic benefits of early action against climate change—to the 2014 philanthropically funded American Climate Prospectus, which summarizes the expected economic risks of climate change in the United States (Sterne, 2007; Houser et al., 2015).

Perhaps the most important point about the science of climate change is that our knowledge arises from four very different sources: direct observations of the climate system and changes within it, including everything from almanac records to satellite-based imaging; paleoclimate evidence of Earth's climate in the distant past—for example, what we can deduce by examining air bubbles trapped in the Antarctic ice sheet by snow that fell hundreds of thousands of years ago, or by analyzing the chemical composition of fossilized marine animal shells trapped in sedimentary layers at the sea bottom for tens of millions of years; laboratory studies of the chemical and physical processes that take place in the atmosphere; and—perhaps most important for forecasting—numerical, computer-based models of climate circulation and other climate properties, which in many respects are similar to the meteorological models used for generating weather forecasts. Our understanding of climate change is based on all four of these sources, which together paint a consistent picture of carbon's current and future warming effects on the planet.

Scientists are nearly certain that climate change is occurring and has the potential to be extremely harmful. Climate change nonetheless has several unique characteristics that combine to present a very challenging mix for policy makers. Climate changes—both those already observed and those anticipated—will affect different countries and different regions very differently. But, eventually, the changes will affect humans in every nation on the planet; in no place will climate remain unchanged. Moreover, every country's carbon dioxide emissions affect the climate in every other country because carbon dioxide's long lifetime means that it achieves a nearly uniform distribution in the atmosphere. Thus climate change is a global commons problem at the largest conceivable scale; the atmosphere is an easily damaged, open-access resource whose preservation will demand increasingly active coordination across the full complexity of human social interactions. Climate change's global nature thus distinguishes it from almost every other major environmental policy problem—except, perhaps, the effects of ozone depletion or large-scale nuclear warfare.

Another implication of carbon dioxide's very long lifetime is that a significant fraction (about 25 percent) of today's emissions will remain airborne even a millennium from now unless we invent a technology to affordably capture and bury the carbon dioxide, meaning that many expected changes are effectively irreversible. Furthermore, the huge mass of the oceans is absorbing a large portion of the climate's thermal energy as Earth warms, and the resulting thermal inertia means that the effects of today's emissions will take several decades to appear. Even if we could eliminate emissions entirely today, enough greenhouse gases have already been released to gradually warm the planet for the rest of the current century and beyond.

Climate change science is also rife with uncertainty. Even though scientists are increasingly certain about the general characteristics of global climate changes under certain emissions scenarios, extensive uncertainties remain when it comes to details of how the climate will respond at time and spatial scales relevant to humans. The answers to such questions as how fast the sea level will rise are so uncertain that scientists can offer policy makers only a very limited basis for making decisions, much less tell them with confidence how high to build a seawall. When combined with the fact that, in the coming years, humans will change their emissions behaviors in response to changes in energy supply and economic development, uncertainty about what will happen becomes daunting.

The combination of universality; effective irreversibility; lags between emissions, policy actions, and system responses; and general uncertainty means that policy makers will need an unusual degree of foresight, extraordinary powers of judgment, and a willingness to act without getting credit (or suffering opprobrium) for the outcomes. It's no wonder that many leaders have resisted grappling with climate change—all the more so because of the potential costs of reducing greenhouse gas emissions. (pp. 13–15)

Oppenheimer, M., & Anttila-Hughes, J.K. (2016). The science of climate change. *The Future of Children, 26*(1), 11–30. https://www.jstor.org/stable/43755228

CONCLUSIONS

Summaries can be seen as the foundation of academic research writing. We use summaries to represent what other scholars have said about a topic, issue, theory, text, or set of findings. As we begin to develop our summary-writing skills, it can be helpful to examine how other scholars write summaries in the field of research in which we are studying. Different research communities produce different kinds of summaries, so we will notice, for instance, differences between summaries in the field of environmental science and those in literature, psychology, or business. However, they share in common the impulse to represent in brief what scholars are saying on the topic in order to develop a dialogue with them. It can be a challenge to understand and represent the work of other scholars briefly in our own words while at the same time being accurate and objective in our representation. But as we practise attentive reading and note-taking, signalling and paraphrasing, synthesizing and spatial organization, we will develop the skills we need to write effective academic summaries.

QUESTIONS FOR REFLECTION

1. Which ethical aspects of summary do you find most difficult: attentive listening, interpretation, synthesis, representation, or acknowledgement? What are some practical ways to advance your skills in these areas?

2. Why are academic summaries seen as the foundation of all research writing?

3. Why are attentive reading and annotating skills so important for summarizing the research and ideas of scholars?

4. Why do summarizers find spatial organization more conducive to writing academic summaries than a linear or chronological organization?

5. Two of the hardest aspects of summary writing are synthesizing material and paraphrasing it in our own words. To practise these aspects, try paraphrasing the two excerpts below in your own words, synthesizing the material in a single sentence. In your paraphrase, directly acknowledge the name of the writer(s) and use signal verbs to indicate their activity. Consider the example paraphrase of the following excerpt and use it as a guide to help you.

Example Excerpt

From *Interventions: A Life in War and Peace* by Kofi Annan (2012)

While the past quarter century has witnessed an extraordinary escape from poverty on the part of hundreds of millions in Asia, Africa, and Latin America, the scourges of war, terror, and weapons of mass destruction still remain as present as ever. What has changed is the power of individuals—men and women in every part of the world emboldened by education and rising expectations of a better life in larger freedom—to demand a say in how they are governed and by whom. (pp. ix–x)

Example Paraphrase

Kofi Annan (2012) observes that in the last twenty-five years, poverty has declined in many developing countries and individuals have become increasingly vocal and powerful in shaping political power, despite the fact that acts of human destruction continue (pp. ix–x).

Excerpt 1

From *Communication Ethics Literacy: Dialogue and Difference* by R.C. Arnett, J.M.H. Fritz, and L.M. Bell (2009)

The fundamental requirement for classroom learning, whether in face-to-face or mediated environments, is showing up. Absence from classroom discussion or from the public conversation about ideas takes away our opportunity to texture and nuance understanding. Something happens when we show up—the ideas become embodied, understood more richly and deeply. Absence hurts learning; it impoverishes engagement with ideas and masks our responsibility.... Each time we do not show up for a given responsibility, we lose a chance to practice a simple act that makes communication ethics possible—showing up. (p. 7)

Excerpt 2

From *The Challenge for Africa* by Wangari Maathai (2010)

Often the soil in tropical forests is not well suited to agriculture and can be farmed for only a few years. Unless the subsistence farmers practice good land management, the soil degrades quickly, and they are forced to encroach further into the forests and grasslands. When rains fall, the earth is washed into the rivers, leaving barren land behind. As the trees are cut, the landscape is transformed, and the risks of soil erosion and desertification increase. In this way, a cycle is set in motion that not only threatens the survival of the people who rely on the ecosystem's resources—its watersheds and rainfall patterns, its flora and fauna—but also has the potential to endanger the climatic systems on which the entire planet depends. (p. 14)

CHAPTER FOUR

ETHICAL INTERPRETATION

Summarizing Difficult Material

As we develop our ability to summarize what others say in academic writing, we discover pretty quickly that some documents are easier to summarize than others. Some academic texts use abstract concepts that we don't understand and we struggle to read and summarize them. Other texts offer case studies or narratives that could be understood in more than one way, so we're not sure how best to summarize them. In this chapter, we will take a closer look at how to read and interpret difficult passages in order to summarize them. Relying on the summary frameworks developed by Giltrow et al. (2009), we will look specifically at the following:

- how to summarize abstract concepts and ideas
- how to summarize case studies and interviews
- how to summarize stories or narratives

We summarize difficult material through the act of *interpretation*—making sense of what we read by examining the words and ideas closely and contextually, and bringing our own viewpoint to bear on the material. As we saw in Chapter 3, an ethical interpretation begins with a posture of open reception to a text, as we take time to read carefully and listen attentively to what has been written. A receptive orientation is critical to our reading and interpretation practices because the way we read and interpret a text will determine how we summarize it and how we position our response to its ideas.

A. A FEW WORDS ABOUT INTERPRETATION

Every time we pick up something to read, our brains seek to make sense of the words, images, and ideas presented to us. This process is called ***interpretation***. We often interpret or make sense of things without even being aware that we're doing so. Certain ways of understanding become well-worn pathways in our brains as we make repeated connections between certain kinds of information and interpret new information in light of what we already know or believe about a subject. Take the well-known examples below:

Do you interpret this image as a duck or a rabbit?

Do you interpret this image as a vase or two faces?

Images, words, ideas, situations, and people can be interpreted in more than one way. How we interpret something shows us how we see and understand the world around us.

In academic studies, we recognize that there may be a number of ways to interpret or make sense of a research study, a lab report, a piece of literature, or a historical event, depending on how we see things from where we stand. For example, consider a hypothetical study examining why 20 per cent of college students are late to or absent from their classes. Some instructors might interpret this behaviour as problematic and in need of solution while other instructors might interpret this behaviour as immaterial and leave student attendance and level of class engagement in the students' hands. The instructors who interpret the behaviour as a problem would need to analyse what the behaviour means in order to determine its best solution. For instance, instructors who interpret lateness and absence as a sign of disrespect for the learning environment may pose the solution of grade penalties as a way to address the problem. In contrast, instructors who interpret lateness and absence as a sign of disinterest in course material may pose the solution of an interactive class environment as a way to address the problem. The solution to lateness and absence, then, depends on how one interprets the problem.

Multiple interpretations lead to interesting dialogue and discussions. However, it is important to realize that there is no such thing as limitless interpretation. A study, behaviour, narrative, or event can be interpreted in more than one way, but it cannot be interpreted in any old way. There are a limited number of interpretations or ways to make sense of a subject, and some interpretations are better than others.

For example, consider the first two lines of "The Ship of Death," a poem by D.H. Lawrence: "Now it is autumn and the falling fruit / And the long journey towards oblivion." We might interpret these lines literally, as describing the season of autumn and the natural death and decay that occur at this time of the year. Alternatively, we might interpret these lines metaphorically, as likening the autumn season to human decay and death. Both these interpretations make reasonable sense of the words and the tone of the lines. The second one especially so, if we read these lines in the context of the rest of the poem. However, if someone were to interpret the lines as a spaceship falling from the sky, or a restorative hike through the wilderness, or the festive celebration of Thanksgiving, we would question the interpretation because it doesn't adequately make sense of the content. Our interpretations need to be logical, relevant, and convincing ways of understanding a subject in order for them to make a contribution to the academic dialogue we are joining.

In our academic studies we become increasingly aware of our interpretations: how we come to make sense of words and ideas and why we understand a subject in the way that we do. We also learn to hone our interpretations to make the best possible sense of the documents we read and to engage respectfully with the researchers who have written them. We are, after all, reading research texts in order to participate in a thoughtful and analytical dialogue with other researchers. Consequently, we do our best not to jump to conclusions or make quick assumptions about what we have read. Instead, we genuinely seek to understand research texts through attentive listening and careful analysis. This practice of attention is called ***close reading***.

Close reading requires patience and effort as we, the readers, mentally labour through words and ideas to discern their possible meanings and respond accordingly. After a close reading, it may turn out that we do not agree with or support the ideas in a text. In fact, we may see an underlying bias in the author, find the analysis weak, or notice the research evidence is thin. However, before we can make judgement calls like these, we first need to go through the trouble of understanding a researcher's ideas from the inside. A quick or superficial glance at an academic text will not result in a genuine understanding of it. Moreover, any stance or position we take on academic material that we do not understand will be shallow and unconvincing, closing down conversation rather than opening it up.

Okay, fair enough, we may think. Close reading it is. But how do we understand an academic text that is really difficult? We may read it closely and respectfully a number of times and still not understand it. What then? How do we make sense of complex material or develop a valid interpretation of a case study or narrative in order to respond to it meaningfully? This chapter will show us how.

B. SUMMARIZING HIGH LEVELS OF ABSTRACTION

Material containing abstract concepts, ideas, and theories is perhaps the most difficult to interpret and summarize (Giltrow et al., 2009, p. 89). Before we can summarize an abstraction and put it into our own words, we first have to make sense of it ourselves. These ideas are hard to understand precisely because they are intangible and nonconcrete, and often discussed using theoretical language or jargon.

Abstractions are precisely those ideas that leave most of us confused and tired because they take so much effort to understand.

However, understanding them is a big part of our academic practice and we feel capable and confident when we do finally "get it."

How, then, do we work through abstract concepts to make sense of them and summarize them accurately in our own words? The answer requires us to be able to cultivate our reading, thinking, and writing skills and use them to get to the bottom of a complex text.

- **Reading (Comprehension)**
  We determine the gist of an abstract concept or idea in an article by searching through each paragraph for the words we already know and understand, underlining or highlighting them as we go. Often we can figure out complex ideas by putting the understandable details together piece by piece until the whole picture becomes clear, like putting together a jigsaw puzzle. This involves reading each paragraph a few times closely and looking up words we don't know in a dictionary. As we saw in Chapter 3, it also helps to be aware of verbal transitions or directions—like *connecting words*, *contrasting words*, *conclusive words*, *sequential words*, and *repeated words*—in order to makes sense of the structure and organization of the researcher's ideas.

- **Thinking (Interpretation)**
  Next we ask ourselves questions: What is this paragraph about as a whole? If our readers were new to this concept and needed it to be explained briefly, how would we do it? What are the key words that we should include in our summary so that they would be able understand these ideas?

- **Writing (Summation)**
  Lastly, we summarize the abstract ideas in our own words. We add details or examples to our summary to help our readers understand the original article so they do not have to muddle through it like we did. Summarizing abstract texts is hard work because we have to make abstract and complex ideas clear and concrete so that readers can understand them. As a result, our summaries may be almost as long as the original text due to the details that need to be added. A good rule of thumb for summarizing abstraction is that the summary should always be clearer and more concrete than the original text.

Consider the following example of abstract academic writing:

> [H]istorical discourse might be considered as an enunciative modality of events that truly happened. Barthes (1967) highlights how the "facts," which are supposed to be the subject matter of history, reveal an evident dependence on the process of attribution of meaning, and so take on a discursive nature. Historical data gain relevance thanks to sense-making procedures: the comprehension of events and their organization into a textual format demands a complex cognitive elaboration that, through the "dialogue" between different types of documents, allows the formulation of an evaluation and/or a judgment that specifies the meaning of the reconstructed events. Historical facts are a genre of reality that cannot reveal themselves: rather, they are discursively constructed, as long as the analysis of different sources shapes a series of events into a "form of life." Besides having a "side," history is also necessarily "partial;" that is both "under-determined" as well as "over-determined." It invests with novel, emergent facts and elaborations as a consequence of the interpretative process. Moreover, it comes to be understood according to the emotional and affective resonance that individuals retain of past events, thus keeping them alive within collective memory (Halbwachs, 1950). (p. 34)
>
> Mininni G., Manuti, A., & Curigliano, G. (2013). Commemorative acts as discursive resources of historical identity. *Culture & Psychology, 19*(1), 33–59. https://doi.org/10.1177/1354067X12464982

Upon first encounter, most readers (including academics in fields outside history and cultural studies) will be puzzled by this excerpt. Abstract passages like this take work to figure out. Notice how the three strategies of reading, thinking, and writing suggested above can help us take this passage apart in order to interpret and summarize it.

1. Reading (Comprehension)

As we read the passage closely, we start by highlighting the words and details we already know (in bold below). We also highlight key verbal directions (shaded below). Then we look up key words in the document that we probably don't know, like *discourse* and *discursive*. When we look these words up in the *Canadian Oxford Dictionary*, we find that the most applicable definition of *discourse* is "a formal discussion of a subject in speech or writing," and that *discursive* means "proceeding by argument or reasoning." Other words may also need looking up, like *enunciative*, *modality*, *cognitive*, *elaboration*, *reconstructed*, *emergent*, *affective*, etc.

> [H]istorical discourse might be considered as an enunciative modality of **events that truly happened**. Barthes (1967) highlights how the "**facts**," which are supposed to be the subject matter of **history**, reveal an evident dependence on the process of attribution of meaning, and so take on a discursive nature. **Historical data** gain relevance thanks to **sense-making procedures**: the comprehension of **events** and their **organization** into a textual format demands a complex cognitive elaboration that, through the "**dialogue**" between **different types of documents**, allows the formulation of an evaluation and/or a judgment that specifies the meaning of the reconstructed **events**. **Historical facts** are a

genre of **reality** that cannot reveal themselves: rather, they are discursively constructed, as long as the analysis of different sources shapes a **series of events** into a "**form of life**." Besides having a "side," **history** is also necessarily "partial;" that is both "under-determined" as well as "over-determined." It invests with novel, emergent **facts** and elaborations as a consequence of the interpretative process. Moreover, it comes to be understood according to the **emotional** and affective resonance that **individuals** retain of **past events**, thus **keeping them alive** within collective **memory** (Halbwachs, 1950).

2. Thinking (Interpretation)

As we read this passage carefully, we can see that it is about the relationship between historical facts or events that truly happened and the way they are recorded in writing and understood. The words *facts* and *events* are repeated numerous times, and when we look up words like *discourse* and *comprehension*, we realize that the article is addressing the way we make sense of facts and events and reconstruct them through memory, analysis, and language.

It is also evident that various ideas are being added together here, by means of connecting words like *and*, *besides*, *also*, and *moreover*. The ideas presented are: (a) historical facts are discursively constructed into a series or form that makes sense to us; (b) history has a "side" and is thus partial; (c) history depends on interpretation; and (d) history has an emotional dimension that keeps its events alive in our collective memory. These four ideas will need to be included in our summary.

After rereading the paragraph a few times, we realize the scholar is saying that formal historical texts about past events are assumed to be objective facts; but, in fact, they are crafted and constructed in ways that make sense to a collective community and emotionally move that community to keep its memories alive.

3. Writing (Summation)

In the following summary of the original passage, notice how the major term *discourse* is defined and how the four ideas about historical discourse that are imbedded in the original are emphasized. Details to clarify the abstract concepts have also been added (in bold) and words that are more straightforward and clear are used. The summary is almost as long as the original due to these added details, but it is kept as brief as possible by eliminating excess words and repetitions. The sentences have also been carefully organized to make sure the ideas are clear and will make sense to a reader who is unfamiliar with the original text. Finally, the title of the article and its research writers are cited, so readers know what document is being summarized, and careful signal verbs are used to highlight the actions of the authors.

In this excerpt from "Commemorative Acts as Discursive Resources of Historical Identity" (2013), Mininni et al. analyse the way historical discourse (**oral and written material about the past**) reconstructs events through "sense-making" practices that historians use to shape and organize past events into texts that we can understand. Mininni et al. imply that historical events are not objective facts that speak for themselves. Rather, historians interpret historical documents and piece them together in a logical sequence to make sense of them and to create a meaningful story of the past for a particular community. This is why the same historical event can be understood differently by different communities involved in it. **For example, historians in France interpret the event of World War II differently from those in Germany, and differently again from those in the United States**. Mininni et al. thus see historical discourse as a partial, emotionally salient interpretation of past events for the collective communities who are living in the present.

EXERCISE 1
SUMMARIZING HIGH LEVELS OF ABSTRACTION

Given the suggestions and example above, read closely, interpret, and attempt to write a short summary on the following abstract excerpt. While your summary will probably be almost as long as the original excerpt on account of the added details, aim to keep it as brief as possible. You can do this by cutting out as many adjectives, adverbs, and repetitions as you can, and by reviewing your sentence construction and organization to ensure that your summary flows and makes sense to a reader unfamiliar with the original text.

> Torture is such an extreme event that it seems inappropriate to generalize from it to anything else or from anything else to it. Its immorality is so absolute and the pain it brings about so real that there is a reluctance to place it in conversation by the side of other subjects. But this reluctance, and the deep sense of tact in which it originates, increase our vulnerability to power by ensuring that our moral intuitions and impulses, which come forward so readily on behalf of human sentience, do not come forward far enough to be of any help: we are most backward on behalf of the things we believe in most in part because, like ancients hesitant to permit analogies to God, our instincts salute the incommensurability of pain by preventing its entry into worldly discourse. The result of this is that the very moral intuitions that might act on behalf of the claims of sentience remain almost as interior and inarticulate as sentience itself. (p. 60)

Scarry, E. (1985). *The body in pain: The making and unmaking of the world.* Oxford University Press.

C. SUMMARIZING CASE STUDIES AND INTERVIEWS

Case studies and interviews are also difficult to interpret and summarize, but for different reasons. They are made up of details and concrete examples that need interpreting so that we can construct their meaning and significance in our summaries (Giltrow et al., 2009, p. 92). Constructing the meaning of someone else's details can be complicated because we don't know if we are interpreting those details in the way they were intended by the author or researcher. We must try to discern what the details point to and what the passage means as a whole.

Details and examples are easy to follow and understand, but their larger meaning and significance can be unclear.		The summarizer's job is to interpret the details and present the reader with one meaning that makes sense.	

Because the higher levels of meaning are determined by our interpretations, they reveal our take on the details, our perspective of the material. For example, how do you interpret the following details?

> Two girls went into a clothing store.
> The store was offering a 25 per cent discount on all merchandise.
> The girls left the store two hours later with five bags of clothes each.

One interpretation might be that the girls benefitted from the discount and made large purchases. Another interpretation might be that the girls were drawn in to buying too many clothes at a relatively small discount, only benefitting the store. Same details, different interpretation.

How, then, do we work through case studies and interviews to interpret their meaning and summarize them in our own words? The answer requires us to continue developing our reading, thinking, and writing skills, but our focus takes a different direction than it does when we summarize abstract documents.

- **Reading (Comprehension)**
  We determine the meaning of details by searching for concepts in each paragraph that help us pull the details together into a meaningful whole. Concepts are the *categories* or *headings* in which all the details could be sorted. They are often abstract or Latinate

terms that end in "-tion," "-logy," or "-ism." For example, the overarching category for *cutting down trees* is "deforestation." Adding together *2+2* falls under the heading of "addition." Studying *what people understand about God* is called "theology." We begin by looking for categorical or conceptual terms in our reading of the details. If there are no categories or concepts mentioned, we must figure out higher levels of meaning by adding up the details and deciding what they equal, show, or prove. In other words, we must create the headings under which they can be gathered. In order to interpret details meaningfully, it may help to diagram them visually under relevant headings.

- **Thinking (Interpretation)**
  Next we ask ourselves questions: What is each paragraph about as a whole? If someone asked us to organize this list of details, how would we make sense of them in a way that is logical and meaningful? What key concepts are these details pointing to?

- **Writing (Summation)**
  Lastly, we summarize the details using our meaningful categories, incorporating a few of the original details into the summary to illustrate the whole. The main focus of summarizing case studies and interviews is to highlight the overarching meaning or significance of the details.

Consider the following case study. Upon first encounter, most readers will understand the content without difficulty. However, in order to summarize, we will need to interpret what the details mean, because their meaning is not made clear in the passage.

> Nanna plays basketball and attends a fitness centre in her leisure time. In the interview she makes it clear that she likes sport and thinks she is a good athlete/player but also that she wishes to retain her position as 'one of the girls'. Her statements clearly show that she has given much thought to her role as a girl in PE [Physical Education] lessons. She calls attention to a number of manoeuvres that make her recognisable as a good athlete and an attractive female.... Although she likes to 'hang out' with the girls, she often prefers to do sporting activities with the boys. She is aware of the fact that she has to act seriously and show endeavour in order to be accepted and respected as a good PE student. (p. 652)
>
> With-Nielsen, N., & Pfister, G. (2011). Gender constructions and negotiations in physical education: Case studies. *Sport, Education and Society*, *16*(5), 645–664. https://doi.org/10.1080/13573322.2011.601145

Notice how the three strategies in reading, thinking, and writing suggested above can help us pull the details of this passage together in order to summarize them.

1. Reading (Comprehension)

As we read the passage, we take it apart and highlight the higher-level concepts among the details (in bold below). We can categorize the passage in terms of concepts directly in our own words (in bold after each section). We may also want to circle the key verbal directions to help us see the relationship between details (shaded below).

> Nanna plays basketball and attends a fitness centre in her leisure time. In the interview she makes it clear that she likes **sport** and thinks she is a **good athlete/player** but also that she wishes to **retain her position** as 'one of the girls'. Her statements clearly show that she has given much thought to her **role** as a girl in PE [Physical Education] lessons. ***[Concept: gender position in regard to sport]***
>
> She calls attention to a number of **manoeuvres** that make her **recognisable** as a **good athlete** and an **attractive female**.... Although she likes to 'hang out' with the girls, she often prefers to do **sporting activities** with the boys. ***[Concept: navigating gender roles]***
>
> She is aware of the fact that she has to **act seriously** and **show endeavour** in order to be **accepted** and **respected** as a good PE student. ***[Concept: ways to be accepted and recognized for athletic capabilities as a female]***

2. Thinking (Interpretation)

Figuring out what this paragraph means as a whole requires that we make sense of the relationship between the gender roles of boys and girls in regard to sport, and the way girls must navigate between athletic capability (determined as masculine) and connection with their female peers (determined as feminine). We may interpret these ideas in a number of ways. For example:

(a) Athletic girls reinforce conventional gender roles in sport by minimizing their femininity to be respected in this "masculine" context.

(b) Athletic girls challenge gender stereotypes in sport with their ability to enact masculinity and become "one of the guys" when they engage in sport.

(c) Athletic girls seek social acceptance among male and female peers as they try to balance their femininity with expectations of masculinity in playing sport.

If we sketched out these categories, they might look like this:

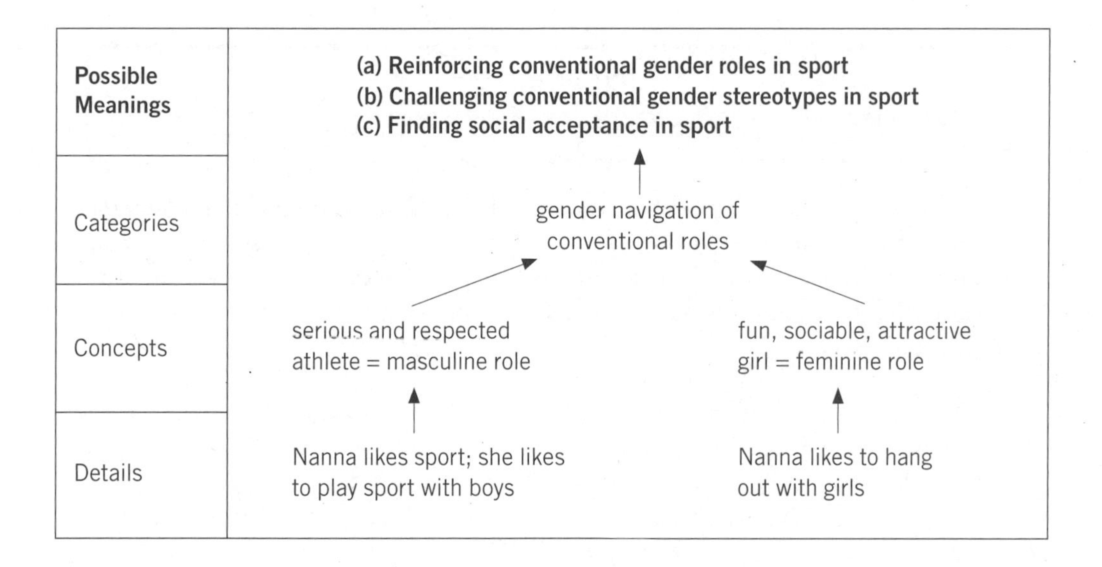

As we can see, more than one interpretation of the details could be correct. However, we need to choose one interpretation, the one that makes the most sense to us as we interpret the details in the context of the text as a whole. Let's imagine we have chosen the first interpretation: reinforcing conventional gender roles in sport. Our intention now will be to summarize this case very briefly so that it reflects the original article while also representing our interpretation of it.

3. Writing (Summation)

In the following summary of this case study, notice how the details have been categorized as "gender navigation," and that this gender navigation has been interpreted as the first meaning: "reinforcing conventional gender roles." These concepts appear in bold. Also note how short the summary is once the details have been interpreted into concepts and once it has been carefully edited to remove repetitions and verbal clutter.

> The case of Nanna reported in With-Nielsen and Pfister's "Gender Constructions and Negotiations in Physical Education: Case Studies" (2011) illustrates how athletic girls must **navigate gender roles** as they engage in sport during PE classes. To be accepted and taken seriously as competent athletes, teenage girls feel they must **minimize their femininity** and **take on a masculine role**, **reinforcing conventional gender stereotypes** that surround sport.

EXERCISE 2
SUMMARIZING CASE STUDIES AND INTERVIEW MATERIAL

Given the suggestions and example above, read closely, think through, and attempt a short summary on the following case study excerpt. To keep your summary brief, remove as many adjectives, adverbs, and repetitions as you can, and review your sentence construction and organization so that your summary flows and will make sense to your readers.

> Tamara, age 21, was told that because her birth parents were unmarried, they decided to place her for adoption as her birth mother's older sister had placed her child for adoption years earlier. Her birth mother was still in school and did not have enough money to support a child and her birth father "wanted nothing to do with a baby." Tamara's birth mother chose open adoption because she "knew what her sister had gone through after choosing a closed adoption of her daughter." Tamara recalls seeing and talking to her birth mother on the phone when attending a family vacation and meeting up with her when she was in her preteens. There has been no contact with her birth father.
>
> Tamara's contact with her birth mother "dwindled off" and she has not spoken to her or heard from her in the last four years. Tamara described how her adoptive parents have tried to reach her the last few times, but Tamara has "given up even attempting." When asked about how she feels that her contacts are no longer acknowledged, she reports experiencing varying emotions: "now I just don't care, however I do resent her for being there when I was young and completely dropping out of my life now that I'm older—I blame it on negative impacts in her life, difficult situations, and she is possibly nervous about contacting me after so long perhaps anticipating my feelings towards her, or perhaps it has become painful and has regrets about giving me up." As her words describe, Tamara has fluctuated between resentment and ambivalence about the current level of contact between her and her birth mother. She goes on to describe hesitancy in initiating any change in the current contact saying, "I really don't care at this point. There is such a large divide between us now that I wouldn't even know where to begin and I fear that if I did happen to put myself out there and give her the time of day and get to know her again, the same thing would happen, she would disappear again, and the whole process would start all over again, I have no doubt." (pp. 56–57)

Farr, R.H., Grant-Marsney, H.A., Musante, D.S., Grotevant, H.D., & Wrobel, G.M. (2014). Adoptees' contact with birth relatives in emerging adulthood. *Journal of Adolescent Research, 29*(1), 45–66. https://doi.org/10.1177/0743558413487588

D. SUMMARIZING NARRATIVE: INTERPRETING STORIES

In some ways, summarizing narratives is similar to summarizing case studies and interview material. Like case studies and interviews, narratives are about particular people and things, actions and events. They are made up of concrete details that need to be interpreted and categorized as concepts or themes in order to be summarized.

Unlike many case studies and interviews, however, narratives are often organized chronologically; things, people, and places are mentioned according to the order in which events occurred (Giltrow et al., 2009, p. 95). At first glance, this chronological ordering seems like a godsend. Beginner summarizers simply take the chronological order from the narrative and reproduce it as a "plot summary." While plot summaries are sometimes used in book reviews, they are not recommended in most academic contexts because they lack synthesis and interpretation (see Chapter 3). In fact, in literature and history courses students are often warned not to include plot summaries in their essays for this very reason.

Rather than write plot summaries, research scholars interpret the plot of a narrative and related details as meaning or illustrating something significant about the story as a whole. Plot and details may be retold sparingly, but only to point to the major issues, concepts, themes, or ideas that they illustrate.

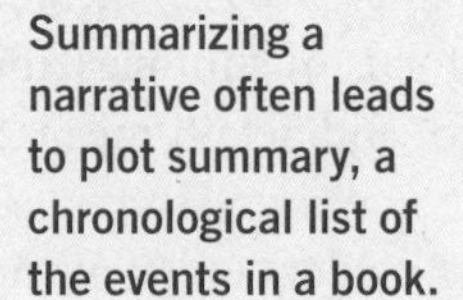

Summarizing a narrative often leads to plot summary, a chronological list of the events in a book.

"And then this happened. And then that happened. And then this other thing happened...."

The summarizer's job is to interpret the plot and details to illustrate something significant about an event or issue in the story or about the story as a whole.

Notably, a narrative always has multiple meanings and can be interpreted in various ways. Because the higher levels of meaning are determined by our interpretations, they reveal our position on the story—our perspective on the plot, the characters, and the other narrative material. For example, Shakespeare's *Othello* lends itself to multiple interpretations. Thematically, it could be read as illustrating the futility of love and self-sacrifice, the lust for power, the betrayal of friendship, or the insanity of envy. Historically, it could be read as representing the oppression of women or the problems of race and politics in the Elizabethan period. The various meanings that narratives stimulate make them very interesting to literary scholars. But in summarizing narratives, they will usually focus on the one meaning they think is most critical for understanding the story.

How, then, do we work through narratives to interpret their meaning and summarize that meaning into our own words? The answer requires us to hone what we have already learned about summarizing case studies and interviews. Again, our focus is on interpreting details as concepts that are significant or meaningful in our reading, thinking, and writing.

- **Reading (Comprehension)**
  As we read the narrative details, we work out the higher levels of meaning by adding up the details and deciding what they signify, show, or prove. Because the details often reinforce the same concepts and theme repeatedly, it can be very helpful to look for repetition. It can also be helpful to write these concepts and themes in the margins as we read through the narrative.

- **Thinking (Interpretation)**
  Next we ask ourselves questions: What is this story about as a whole? What are the key concepts, issues, themes, or ideas that this story illustrates? If someone told us the plot points and details of this story, how would we organize them spatially rather than chronologically, in a way that is meaningful and makes sense?

- **Writing (Summation)**
  Lastly, we summarize the details using meaningful concepts or themes. We also include a few details in the summary to illustrate the whole. The main focus of summarizing narratives is not recounting the plot, but highlighting what the plot and details mean.

Consider the following excerpt from a narrative for children. Most readers will have no difficulty understanding the content. However, as with case studies and interviews, we will need to interpret what the plot and details mean in order to summarize the passage.

1. Reading (Comprehension)

As we read the passage, we include marginal notes that categorize the details into concepts and themes (in bold below) that will ultimately be useful for interpreting and summarizing the narrative.

> Pooh always liked a little something at eleven o'clock in the morning, and he was very glad to see Rabbit getting out the plates and mugs; and when Rabbit said, "Honey or condensed milk with your bread?" he was so excited that he said, "Both," and then, so as not to seem greedy, he added, "but don't bother about the bread, please." And for a long time after that he said nothing... until at last, humming to himself in a rather sticky voice, he got up, shook Rabbit lovingly by the paw, and said that he must be going on.

Pooh and Rabbit visit
→ ***friendship***

Rabbit provides food
→ ***hospitality***

"Must you?" said Rabbit politely. "Well," said Pooh, "I could stay a little longer if it—if you—" and he tried very hard to look in the direction of the larder. "As a matter of fact," said Rabbit, "I was going out myself directly." "Oh well, then, I'll be going on. Good bye."

"Well good bye, if you're sure you won't have any more." "*Is* there any more?" asked Pooh quickly. Rabbit took the covers off the dishes, and said no, there wasn't. "I thought not," said Pooh, nodding to himself. "Well good-bye, I must be going on."

Pooh wants more food → ***hunger/greed***

Pooh leaves when food runs out → ***utility, pragmatism***

Pooh becomes stuck → ***predicament (confinement)***

So he started to climb out of the hole. He pulled with his front paws, and pushed with his back paws, and in a little while his nose was in the open again... and then his ears... and then his front paws... and then his shoulders... and then—

"Oh, help!" said Pooh. "I'd better go back." "Oh bother!" said Pooh. "I shall have to go on." "I can't do either!" said Pooh. "Oh, help *and* bother!"

Now by this time Rabbit wanted to go for a walk too, and finding the front door full, he went out by the back door, and came round to Pooh, and looked at him. "Hallo, are you stuck?" he asked. "N-no," said Pooh, carelessly. "Just resting and thinking and humming to myself." "Here, give us a paw," Pooh Bear stretched out a paw, and Rabbit pulled and pulled and pulled.... "*Ow*!" cried Pooh. "You're hurting!" "The fact is," said Rabbit, "you're stuck." "It all comes," said Pooh crossly, "of not having front doors big enough." "It all comes," said Rabbit sternly, "of eating too much. I thought at the time," said Rabbit, "only I didn't like to say anything," said Rabbit, "that one of us was eating too much," said Rabbit, "and I knew it wasn't *me*," he said. "Well, well, I shall go and fetch Christopher Robin."...

Pooh pretends he's not stuck → ***casual and deceptive***

Pooh defends himself and blames Rabbit → ***self-justification***

Rabbit blames Pooh → ***reprimand***
and gets C.R. to help → ***assistance***

Christopher Robin nodded. "[T]here's only one thing to be done," he said. "We shall have to wait for you to get thin again." "How long does getting thin take?" asked Pooh anxiously. "About a week I should think." "But I can't stay here for a *week*!" "You can *stay* here all right, silly old Bear. It's getting you out which is so difficult." "We'll read to you," said Rabbit cheerfully. "And I hope it won't snow," he added. "And I say, old fellow, you're taking up a good deal of room in my house—*do* you mind if I use your back legs as a towel-horse? Because, I mean, there they are—doing nothing—and it would be very convenient just to hang the towels on them."

C.R. assesses the problem → ***analysis and solution***

Rabbit makes Pooh useful → ***utility, pragmatism***

"A week!" said Pooh gloomily. "*What about meals?*" "I'm afraid no meals," said Christopher Robin, "because of getting thin quicker. But we *will* read to you." Bear began to sigh, and then found he couldn't because he was so tightly stuck; and a tear rolled down his eye, as he said: "Then would you read a Sustaining Book, such as would help and comfort a Wedged Bear in Great Tightness?"

Pooh accepts his lot → ***resignation, patience***

Pooh asks for help → ***humbleness***

So for a week Christopher Robin read that sort of book at the North end of Pooh, and Rabbit hung his washing on the South end . . . and in between Bear felt himself getting slenderer and slenderer. And at the end of the week Christopher Robin said, "*Now*!"

> C.R. reads to Pooh → ***support, consolation as time passes***

So he took hold of Pooh's front paws and Rabbit took hold of Christopher Robin, and all Rabbit's friends and relations took hold of Rabbit, and they all pulled together. . . . And for a long time Pooh only said "*Ow*!" . . . And "*Ow*!" . . . And then, all of a sudden he said "*Pop*!" just if a cork were coming out of a bottle. And Christopher Robin and Rabbit and all Rabbit's friends and relations went head-over-heels backwards . . . and on top of them came Winnie-the-Pooh—free!

> Problem solved with help → ***collaboration, friendship***

So with a nod of thanks to his friends, he went on with his walk through the forest, humming proudly to himself. But Christopher Robin looked after him lovingly, and said to himself, "Silly Old Bear!"

> Pooh proudly on his way → ***freedom, thankfulness***

Milne, A.A. (1992). In which Pooh goes visiting and gets into a tight place. In *Winnie the Pooh* (pp. 22–33). Puffin Books.

2. Thinking (Interpretation)

To figure out what this narrative is about, we need to determine what concepts and themes the details are illustrating, and what those concepts and themes mean as a whole. What might the relationship be between greed and getting stuck? Is there a lesson to be learned, in which over-indulgence leads to confinement and loss of freedom? What is the story illustrating about

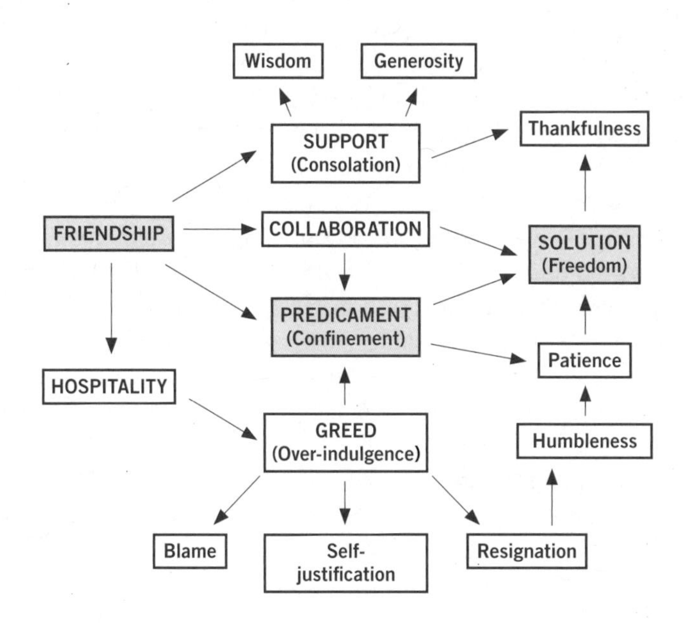

the inclination to blame others and justify oneself in the face of a problem? What about the role of friendship, which both leads to predicaments and solves them? What do we make of the wisdom and generosity of Christopher Robin when he stays with Pooh in the face of his difficulty, offering companionship and support? Or the role of the community that pulls Pooh out of trouble? It may be helpful to work out connections between certain concepts and themes that the details illustrate in a visual way (using different colours to connect key concepts) so as to make sense of the story and present it plausibly to readers. Remember, there are multiple ways to make connections and interpret the story in a reasonable way.

3. Writing (Summation)

In the following summary of this narrative, notice how the concepts and themes drawn from the details make up most of the summary. They appear in bold. Also, note how short the summary is once the details have been interpreted into concepts. To keep the summary brief, all narrative repetitions and any extra verbiage (like adjectives and adverbs) that don't directly add to the clarity of the summary have been eliminated.

> In A.A. Milne's story "In Which Pooh Goes Visiting," **hospitality** goes awry and **friendship** is tested when Pooh goes to visit Rabbit, eats all his food, and becomes stuck in Rabbit's front door on his way out. While the **blame** for this **predicament** could lie with Pooh's **greed** or Rabbit's inhibitive architecture (or both), the two realize that they need the help of friends and the strength of **collaboration** to **solve** the problem and **free** Pooh from his **confinement**. This story ultimately reveals the necessity of **friendship** to **support** one through and rescue one from difficult situations.

Notably, other summarizers might have focused on different concepts or themes drawn from the story and come up with alternative interpretations (Giltrow et al., 2009, p. 98). For instance, an equally plausible summary could consider how one's failings (greed, blame, and self-justification) lead to or exacerbate a problem that can only be solved through humility, resignation, and accepting the help of others. Another possible summary could interpret the story through the lens of utility: when faced with a predicament (being stuck or having the back-end of a bear wedged in one's door), one needs to make the best of the situation by being pragmatic and taking advantage of the benefits it may bring (a towel-horse, being read to, finding comfort in friends). Provided that the summary accounts reasonably for the details and plot in the narrative, its interpretation will be convincing and effective.

EXERCISE 3
SUMMARIZING NARRATIVES

Given the suggestions and example above, read closely, think through, and attempt a short summary on the following narrative excerpt. Keep your summary brief by cutting all the adjectives, adverbs, and repetitions that you can, and review your sentence construction and organization so that your summary flows and makes sense to an outside reader.

> I wandered around in my early twenties, paying rent and reading classifieds and wondering why the lights were not turning green for me. My dream was to be a famous musician (I played the piano), but after several years of dark, empty nightclubs, broken promises, bands that kept breaking up and producers who seemed excited about everyone but me, the dream soured. I was failing for the first time in my life.
>
> At the same time, I had my first serious encounter with death. My favorite uncle, my mother's brother, the man who had taught me music, taught me to drive, teased me about girls, thrown me a football—the one adult whom I targeted as a child and said, "That's who I want to be when I grow up"—died of pancreatic cancer at the age of forty-four. He was a short, handsome man with a thick mustache, and I was with him for the last year of his life, living in an apartment just below his. I watched his strong body wither, then bloat, saw him suffer, night after night, his eyes shut, his mouth contorted in pain.... It was the most helpless I have ever felt in my life.
>
> One night in May, my uncle and I sat on the balcony of his apartment. It was breezy and warm. He looked out toward the horizon and said, through gritted teeth, that he wouldn't be around to see his kids into the next school year. He asked if I would look after them. I told him not to talk that way. He stared at me sadly. He died a few weeks later.
>
> After the funeral my life changed. I felt as if time were suddenly precious, water going down an open drain, and I couldn't move fast enough. No more playing music at half-empty nightclubs. No more writing songs in my apartment, songs that no one would hear. I returned to school. I earned a master's degree in journalism and took the first job offered, as a sports writer. Instead of chasing my own fame, I wrote about famous athletes chasing theirs. I worked for newspapers and freelanced for magazines. I worked at a pace that knew no hours, no limits. I would wake in the morning, brush my teeth, and sit down in the same clothes I had slept in. My uncle had worked for a corporation and hated it—same thing, every day—and I was determined never to end up like him. (pp. 14–16)

Albom, M. (1997). *Tuesdays with Morrie.* Broadway Books.

E. TEMPLATES FOR SUMMARIZING

As we have come to see in the last two chapters, summaries tend to have consistent characteristics and structures. Once we know what those are, writing a summary is relatively straightforward. If in doubt, try the following templates to help you organize the concepts and details of your summary and highlight the authors and texts you're representing.

Abstract Research Articles

In ____________________ (*title of text*) _______ (*add date*), the researcher(s) __________________ (*name researchers*) show that ____________________ (*overarching gist of whole passage*). In the process of this study, the researcher(s) specifically focus on _______________, while also pointing out _______________. For example, _____________. The researcher(s) also suggest that _______________. As a result of these findings, we can see ___________________, which is significant because ____________________.

Note: In most academic contexts, summarizers refer to researchers by last name. If there are more than three researchers being cited, some formats use "et al." after the first researcher's name to signal the whole group of scholars (*et al.* is an abbreviation of the Latin *et alia*, meaning "and others"). For example, Smith et al. observe ________. Smith et al. also note that ________.

Case Studies and Interviews

The case of/interview with ______________ (*names of participants*), reported in __________________ (*title of text*) by __________________ (*name researchers*) _________ (*add date*) shows _____________________ (*main point of case/interview*). This case/interview thus proves ___________________, which is significant because ______________.

Narratives

One of the most significant dimensions of ______________ (*title of story*) by _____________ (*author's full name*) is __________________ (*key theme, idea, or issue*). The main character(s) reveal(s) ___________________ (*notable aspect of key theme, idea, or issue*) in the way they _________________________ (*word, action, idea, or character trait*). Ultimately this story is about _______________________ (*overarching gist of whole story*).

CONCLUSIONS

Summaries are the foundation on which most academic research writing is built. They represent what research scholars or authors have said about a subject, and function as a starting point from which to respond with our own ideas. Whether we are summarizing research information, abstract theories, case studies, or narratives, the process requires our best reading, thinking, and writing skills, as well as patience and practice.

Regardless of the context, the primary goals of summary writing are to interpret and represent the ideas of authors clearly, reliably, and briefly to our readers. Here are some helpful reminders from the last two chapters about summary writing:

- Take the time to understand what you are summarizing. If you don't understand the original text, your readers won't understand it either when they read your summary. Writing reveals rather than conceals our level of comprehension, our capacity to synthesize material, and our ability to express ideas succinctly.

- Incorporate a balance of abstract concepts and concrete details in your summary.

- Organize the summary spatially so that it will make sense to an outside reader who does not know the original text.

- Eliminate adjectives, adverbs, and repetitions from the summary. They end up being verbal clutter that bog down your writing and keep it from being brief.

- Watch sentence construction: Many sentences come out awkwardly when we are trying to summarize someone else's work. Read over your sentences multiple times and edit them to ensure that they actually make sense and that your summary flows.

- Incorporate summaries into your academic writing to reflect the research of other scholars, highlight current views on the subject, and provide evidence for your ideas.

QUESTIONS FOR REFLECTION

1. In academic studies, we recognize that there can be more than one way to interpret or make sense of the information we read. For example, consider the following sentence: *I didn't say she said that.* There are at least five different ways we could interpret this information. See if you can interpret the text in all five ways by highlighting one word at a time: ***I*** didn't say she said that. I didn't ***say*** she said that. I

didn't say ***she*** said that. I didn't say she ***said*** that. I didn't say she said ***that***. What does the information mean in each interpretation? How does it change?

2. What does ethical interpretation involve? How can you hone your ethical interpretation skills as you develop your summary writing?

3. Given the tips and templates in this chapter, interpret and summarize the following passage from an academic article in 100 words or less. In your summary, use a spatial approach and combine concepts with details to make sure the material is clear to readers. Eliminate as much verbal clutter (adjectives, adverbs, and repetitions) as you can and review your sentence construction so the summary points make sense and flow. Be sure to introduce the title of the text and its authors so readers know whose work is being summarized.

Many students enter college in a confused state, confronted with a bewildering mix of choices about classes, majors, social activities, work, teachers, and more. The seeming cacophonous atmosphere in which many of these choices are presented, can be overwhelming; information overload, pressures to make decisions (e.g., to choose a major), and pressures to fit in can lead to many quick and, sometimes, poor choices. The state of confusion that students can experience entering college (and how they manage it) simulates an artist's brushstrokes, some of which can go awry, and is exacerbated given that high school students often lack skills requisite for college success (Gewertz, 2007). Further, frequent musings by students enrolled in college classes also represent potential brushstrokes gone awry (e.g., "I don't think subject X is relevant, why do I have to take it?"). In addition, over time, they may add less rigorous education to their canvas, viewing course learning with too little regard for its long-term value.

Students should not shoulder all the blame for the poor perceptions of college alumni. Other brushstrokes have gone astray. As Anderson (1992) asserted long ago, "There are plenty of people who can be blamed for the decline of the American university" (p. 194). He places the primary burden for the university situation on trustees, overseers and regents; they have the power to act but have been derelict in their duties. Anderson also notes that faculty, as a group, have not exuded excellence, adding undesirable brushstrokes including too few being engaged in the enterprise of teaching.

The student canvas conveys an important underlying assumption in a culture of engagement model, which necessarily begins with faculty taking an initiative to lead the change to positively impact students' work readiness. However, students, employers, alumni and administrators also play key roles. Students should be encouraged to want to learn and taught how to learn, employers and alumni encouraged to provide input to the learning environment, and administrators encouraged to help build a culture of engagement conducive for continuous learning. (p. 98)

Lunt, D., Chonko, L., & Burke-Smalley, L.A. (2018). Creating a culture of engagement in business schools. *Organization Management Journal, 15*(3), 95–109. https://doi.org/10.1080/15416518.2018.1497470

CHAPTER FIVE

COMPOSING A DIALOGUE

Writing as Conversation

So far we have concentrated on the ethical and practical processes involved in summarizing a scholar's research and ideas. Now we are ready to take our research writing to the next level by representing the ideas of research scholars in a full-fledged conversation. Composing a research conversation involves bringing the voices of various scholars together in order to show how their research and ideas intersect. It includes the practices of summary—close reading, interpreting, synthesizing, and representing—that we already know. But it adds two more skills: the ability to distinguish between the different stances researchers have on a topic and organize them into a written conversation and the ability to acknowledge the researchers we are bringing into the conversation through the practice of ethical citation. In this chapter we will focus on the first skill and in Chapter 6 we will turn our attention to the second skill.

A. ORCHESTRATING DIALOGUE

In academic research writing, it is rare to engage with only one scholar's findings and ideas. While we begin by considering one scholar's work at a time, we eventually need to assemble a wide range of research together in a brief and coherent way when we write our research papers. In this process, we summarize who says what about the topic; who agrees with whom; who builds on what others have said; and who disagrees and why. This process of bringing scholars' ideas together in the form of a written dialogue is called ***orchestration*** (Giltrow et al., 2009, p. 103).

The term *orchestration* is most commonly used in music to describe the practice of bringing different instruments together in an orchestra, showcasing their various sounds to create an integrated and meaningful whole. The violins might begin. Then the other stringed instruments may join in. The strings may grow silent while a bassoon and flute play off one another. Different sounds come in and out as the composer has orchestrated them in the musical score.

Like a composer writing a score, a research writer brings together various scholarly voices in a dialogue in order to show readers how his or her knowledge is built collectively and which members of the research community he or she is relying on to build that knowledge. The research scholar showcases this fact by setting up his or her paper as a conversation, "giving voice" to the different members of the research community and showing how their ideas intersect and contribute insights to the discussion.

Giving voice is an ethical practice that allows others their own viewpoints and the ability to speak for themselves about issues that are important to them (Holquist, 1990, p. 164). In research writing we are in the unique position of giving scholars voice as we present their work to our readers. We open spaces in our work for them to speak directly (through quotations), or we represent their stances for them (in paraphrase and summary). But how exactly do we give voice to and orchestrate interactions between scholars in our writing? How do we write dialogically, or compose a scholarly conversation?

B. WRITING A CONVERSATION

We can think of composing a written conversation in the same way we might record a verbal one. Verbal conversations depend on our shared interest about a particular subject at a given moment. We inform each other of what we know about that subject, offering our opinions, insights, concerns, or criticisms as we go. Similarly, in their research writing, scholars convey conversations with each other about subjects that they share an interest in, taking various viewpoints and research findings into account in order to further their understanding and impart it to their readers.

For some scholars the subject may be climate control and the carbon cycle. For others, it may be the various traumas of refugee displacement or the historical complexities of the Stalinist regime. Regardless of the subject, when we write in conversation with others, our starting point is our shared interest and shared desire to develop our knowledge about the topic together through accumulated research and analysis.

Consider the following academic example that reveals a scholarly conversation on the subject of "mass media and childhood obesity in Australia." Notice how the writers of this article (Zivkovik et al.) represent themselves in conversation with other researchers who are studying the same subject. These researchers are emphasized in bold below.

> In our study we were interested in . . . the selection of discourses used in the reporting and public reception of obesity more broadly. The mass media (including television, video games, computers, magazines and other technologies) has an interesting role to play in obesity politics as it is often cited as a major contributor to the global obesity epidemic. The effect of increased sedentary lifestyles and the marketing and consumption of high fat and sugar content foods (and often directly to 'passive' children;

Bonfiglioli et al., 2007) is argued to be a key factor in increased obesity levels. Mass media, however, can also be a public educator, and studies have indicated that the media are often primary providers of science and medical information (**Seale**, 2002; **Hargreaves et al.**, 2003). Studies examining how the media have dealt with obesity are less common, and have been interested in discursive analyses of how obesity is framed as a problem (**Lawrence**, 2004), competing frames, and the subtext of reporting that blames particular individuals or groups and then proceeds to manage and regulate them in certain ways.

Alarmist discourses of risk and threat are often utilized to give meaning to health news stories (**Lupton & McLean**, 1998; **Lupton**, 2004; **Coveney**, 2008; **Nerlich & Halliday**, 2008). In her examination of media coverage of risks associated with food in three Australian newspapers between 2002 and 2003, **Lupton** (2004) established that almost 50 percent of stories on food risks concerned obesity and overweight and, of those, obese or overweight children received the greatest amount of news media attention. Lupton concludes that the discourses expressed in the news accounts on childhood obesity focused on "parental responsibility for their dietary choices" (**Lupton**, 2004, p. 198). Building on Lupton's methodological approach we examined the reporting of obesity over a three-month period in three metropolitan Australian newspapers – *The Advertiser*, *The Australian* and *The Sydney Morning Herald* – between 1 January 2009 and 31 March 2009.... We sourced 181 articles that included our search terms (obesity, parenting, child, eating and diet), made copies of each, and conducted a thematic analysis of text and visual images. We often encountered content overlap as issues of obesity were frequently constructed as a parenting issue and were closely aligned with food consumption. When obesity was constructed in terms of parental responsibility, the onus was on the parent to help their child lose weight for the specific purpose of reducing overweight-associated health problems. (pp. 380–81)

Zivkovik, T., Warin, M., Davies, M., & Moore, V. (2010). In the name of the child: The gendered politics of childhood obesity. *Journal of Sociology, 46*(4), 375–392. https://doi.org/10.1177/1440783310384456

These researchers all care about the same subject: childhood obesity and its representation in the media. Zivkovik et al. orchestrate a conversation in their research writing to show what the different researchers are saying about the subject and where they situate themselves in that discussion. Notice how each researcher is given voice or a say in the matter, and their various positions are highlighted in relation to one another. Zivkovik et al. also show where ideas overlap and differ, and how knowledge about this subject is being built collectively through each member's research findings and conclusions. In fact, we can imagine them all in the same room talking together about their questions, concerns, and findings on this subject, building their knowledge and understanding as they go.

Round Table Discussion on Representations of Childhood Obesity in the Media Happening Today!

If we were to listen in, the verbal conversation might go something like this:

Zivkovik et al.: "Has anyone noticed how mass media affects obesity politics and has been contributing to global obesity?"

Bonfiglioli et al.: "I have! In my research I've been finding that mass marketing and consumption is contributing to passive and sedentary children."

Seale and Hargreaves et al.: "Yeah. That's true. But media doesn't always have a negative effect. Media can also be used to educate, sharing scientific and medical information with the community."

Lawrence: "I think it would be worth studying how the media deals directly with the topic of obesity, frames it as a problem, and blames certain individuals or groups for that problem."

Zivkovik et al.: "Agreed. We've noticed that media uses certain negative language around the issue of childhood obesity."

Lupton, McLean, Coveney, Nerlich, and Halliday: "Yes! Like the alarmist language of threat and risk."

Lupton: "I've been studying this phenomenon for a while and have discovered that half the media stories I've collected on food focus on the risks of obesity, and stories of obese children get the most attention. And you know what's really interesting? A lot of the stories focus on the responsibilities of parents in the matter of their kids' obesity. The onus is on them if their children are obese."

Zivkovik et al.: "That's fascinating! I think we should do a study that looks at how news media reports on obesity for, say, three months to see how the stories talk about child obesity. We could focus on how child obesity is constructed in language and who is blamed for it. I think you're right, Lupton, that the issues of child obesity are often framed as the problem of parents not taking enough responsibility to help their kids lose weight."

As we begin to read research writing more regularly, we notice how it functions as a conversation between the writer(s) of the paper and other researchers interested in the subject. Each scholar responds to and builds on what the others have said, adding his or her voice to the dialogue. In fact, it can be very helpful to record the following information as we read and analyse scholarly materials for a research project or paper:

- With whom is the research writer in conversation?
- What are the different views that the research writer is responding to?
- How exactly does the research writer respond to those views?
- What does the research writer add to the discussion in order to enhance, challenge, or change the way other scholars have understood this topic?

With this information in hand, we have the basic foundation for orchestrating a research dialogue of our own—giving voice to various scholars as they interact with each other.

C. FORMS OF ORCHESTRATION

Research scholars compose different kinds of conversations in their writing, depending on their purpose. Often they represent other scholars speaking together with one unified voice about the subject, like a chorus. This approach is used to represent a viewpoint held by many researchers, or a body of evidence that supports the writer's point. For instance, if we return to the example above, Zivkovik et al. use the "chorus" approach to show that a large number of research scholars all focus on "alarmist discourses" surrounding obesity in the media. They paraphrase that shared idea and document the scholars' names in parentheses to highlight this chorus of voices:

> Alarmist discourses of risk and threat are often utilized to give meaning to health news stories (Lupton & McLean, 1998; Lupton, 2004; Coveney, 2008; Nerlich & Halliday, 2008).

Alongside a chorus approach, research writers often single out a few key scholars as a "duet" or "trio" and give them priority in the dialogue. Research writers give voice to these scholars because they are experts in the field and their work is particularly instructive, applicable, or contentious, or because it is necessary for understanding and reinforcing the writer's own ideas. Alternatively, a research writer may single out key scholars to demonstrate their similarities or differences in order to set up a debate or add to their discussion. As we can see in the example below, Zivkovik et al. single out and draw together the voices of Bonfiglioli et al. with those of Seale and Hargreaves et al. to highlight two distinct views of the effects of mass media on obesity. Bonfiglioli et al. reveal a negative view while Seale and Hargreaves et al. suggest a positive view. Zivkovik et al. signal their differences with the word *however*:

> The mass media...has an interesting role to play in obesity politics as it is often cited as a major contributor to the global obesity epidemic. The effect of increased sedentary lifestyles and the marketing and consumption of high fat and sugar content foods (and often directly to 'passive' children; Bonfiglioli et al., 2007) is argued to be a key factor in increased obesity levels. Mass media, ***however***, can also be a public educator, and studies have indicated that the media are often primary providers of science and medical information (Seale, 2002; Hargreaves et al., 2003).

Finally, a research writer may take a "solo" approach to orchestration, engaging with one specific scholar and setting up a dialogue with them. This dialogue is often used when the research writer wants to highlight and explain an important point that the scholar has made in order to build on it, challenge it, or rely on it as evidence for a point. Often the writer will summarize the scholar's work at length so that readers can understand the full dimensions of the dialogue between them. Returning once more to Zivkovik et al., we can see how they single out Lupton and engage with her work directly in order to build on it:

> In her examination of media coverage of risks associated with food in three Australian newspapers between 2002 and 2003, Lupton (2004) established that almost 50 percent of stories on food risks concerned obesity and overweight and, of those, obese or overweight children received the greatest amount of news media attention. Lupton concludes that the discourses expressed in the news accounts on childhood obesity focused on "parental responsibility for their dietary choices" (Lupton, 2004, p. 198). ***Building on Lupton's methodological approach*** we examined the reporting of obesity over a three-month period in three metropolitan Australian newspapers....

Just as we've seen in the work of Zivkovik et al., our goal is to bring various scholars together in our research writing in order to introduce readers to the current views that exist on a topic and the community of scholars researching it. We also bring scholars together to show readers the similarities and differences between scholarly viewpoints so that we can set the stage to present our own. Finally, we bring scholars together in our work to support our points, showing how we are building on the knowledge of others to establish our own ideas. We will learn how to develop each of these practices in subsequent chapters. For now, try the following exercise to see if you can locate the conversations research scholars are composing, then analyse their form and their purpose.

EXERCISE 1
READING FOR DIALOGUE

Consider the orchestration of the following two research excerpts and answer the following questions:

- Who is brought into the conversation in this excerpt? What are the scholars' names?
- What form of orchestration is used: A chorus, small group, or solo? Why are certain voices given a solo while others only show up in the chorus?
- What seems to be the purpose(s) of the orchestration?
    - To introduce the current research views on the topic?
    - To outline the studies that other researchers are undertaking?
    - To set up a debate, dilemma, or problem?
    - To build on, complicate, disagree with, or resolve an issue?
    - To prove a point or provide expert evidence?
    - To support an idea or show how it is built on the knowledge of others?

Excerpt 1

The apparel industry has concerns about the impact of clothing on sustainability. The approach to sustainability, however, has been largely limited to environmentally friendly material selection (Niinimäki, 2010) or understanding consumers' attitudes and behaviors towards apparel made of organically grown cotton, clothing donation and recycling (Shim, 1995; Hustvedt & Dickson, 2009; Niinimäki, 2010; Goworek, 2011). Although previous studies have revealed important findings, they may be limited because the apparel consumption itself, rather than just selecting and consuming apparel items made of environmentally friendly material, creates much greater impact on the environment as it increases solid waste and depletes resources (Niinimäki, 2010; Hiller Connell, 2011). This calls for more sustainable ways of apparel consumption. (p. 510)

Jung, S., & Byoungho, J. (2014). A theoretical investigation of slow fashion: Sustainable future of the apparel industry. *International Journal of Consumer Studies, 38*(5), 510–519. https://doi.org/10.1111/ijcs.12127

Excerpt 2

The broad effects of climate change are increasingly seen as posing a significant threat to the survival of many plant and animal species, one that joins (and combines synergistically with) habitat destruction, landscape fragmentation, and the spread of invasive species (Hannah et al., 2002; Root et al., 2003; Barnosky, 2009).... Ecologists and conservationists are considering relocating threatened species to new locations before their historical ranges become inhospitable due to climate change (e.g., McLachlan et al., 2007; Hoegh-Guldberg et al., 2008; Richardson et al., 2009). This approach to saving species is defended when animals and plants cannot adapt quickly enough to local, changing environmental conditions and when dispersing to higher latitudes and altitudes on their own is impossible. For example, highways and cities can form inhospitable barriers too extensive for some species to cross unaided. Called "assisted colonization" or "managed relocation" (MR), the idea is controversial, mostly because it may disturb native species and ecosystems when these "climate refugees" establish themselves in new environments.

While some scientists think this is a risk that can be managed, and that the consequences of doing nothing are far worse (e.g., Sax et al., 2009; Schlaepfer et al., 2009), many believe the mere threat of creating invasive species through managed relocation (and the risk of disrupting historical evolutionary and ecological processes) disqualifies it as a viable conservation strategy (Davidson & Simkanin, 2008; Ricciardi & Simberloff, 2009; Seddon et al., 2009). In addition, concerns have been raised about the long-term population genetic ramifications of conservation translocations, including fears of hybridization and introgression of relocated and native populations (Ricciardi & Simberloff, 2009), as well as worries about the introduction of maladapted genotypes into the receiving system and the "swamping" of recipient-system genetic complexes by relocated populations (Vitt et al., 2010). Such concerns would presumably be magnified by proposals to move species across great distances; suggesting, for example, that intercontinental translocations could be particularly risky and therefore strongly resisted by many conservation scientists and managers. (pp. 1801–02)

Minteer, B.A., & Collins, J.P. (2010). Move it or lose it? The ecological ethics of relocating species under climate change. *Ecological Applications, 20*(7), 1801–1804. https://doi.org/10.1890/10-0318.1

D. HOW TO ORCHESTRATE A DIALOGUE BETWEEN SCHOLARS

Seeing how research scholars structure their writing as a dialogue provides a useful starting point to show us how to compose a conversation in our own writing. However, before we can set to work orchestrating a research dialogue ourselves, we first need to determine which scholars are working on the subject we are studying and what each of them is saying about it. In other words, we need to collect the work of scholars in our field of study and read it closely and attentively in order to locate each scholar's research stance and key ideas on the topic.

A ***research stance*** is a declared position or intellectual standpoint that a scholar takes on a research subject. It is where a scholar "stands" on the subject in their field of study. Using the metaphor of sport can help us to understand this concept better. Just like soccer or football players are located in various positions on a playing field, research scholars are intellectually located in various positions in their field of research or study.

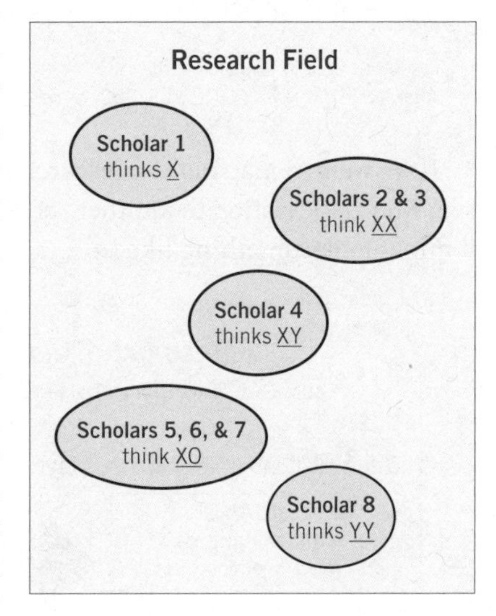

We may think of research fields quite broadly—like the fields of digital media, human rights activism, medical oncology, existential philosophy, environmental ethics, or business communications—and recognize that a lot of research scholars work in each of those fields. However, when it comes to academic research dialogue, the fields of study tend to be small and specialized. For example, if we return to our excerpt by Zivkovik et al., we can see that their field of study and their dialogue within it is very specific: media representations of contemporary childhood obesity in Australia. Despite being so specialized, numerous scholars are involved and locate themselves variously in this field.

To take another example, consider how the research writer below, C. Lafont, introduces a field of study—the philosophy of human rights—and outlines a key dialogue going on in that field between different scholars.

> In recent years philosophical discussions of human rights have focused on the question of whether "humanist" and "political" conceptions of human rights are genuinely incompatible or whether some kind of synthesis between them may be possible.... Defenders of the humanist conception take human rights to be those rights that we have simply by virtue of being human, and try to ground them on some authoritative conception of human nature or human good. By contrast, defenders of the political conception take contemporary human rights practice as providing an authoritative understanding of human rights; by understanding the purposes of the contemporary practice, one can grasp the concept of human rights that is operative within it.
>
> Many participants in this ongoing debate argue that the supposed incompatibility between these approaches is, in fact, not as dramatic as it may seem, and they identify different ways of combining the most fruitful aspects of both (Gilabert, 2011; Liao & Etinson, 2012; Mayr, 2011). However, defenses of this compatibility have been largely one-sided, showing that human rights theories that incorporate the central tenets of humanist approaches can also accommodate the core claims of political approaches.

> But this does not yet answer the question of whether theories using the political approach can incorporate the core claims of humanist approaches without sacrificing their distinctive methodological perspective. Prominent defenders of the political approach answer this question negatively (Rawls, 1999; Beitz, 2009). (p. 233)
>
> Lafont, C. (2016). Should we take the "human" out of human rights? Human dignity in a corporate world. *Ethics & International Affairs, 30*(2), 233–252. https://doi.org/10.1017/S0892679416000101

If we were to map out the research stances of one set of scholars (Gilabert, Liao and Etinson, Mayr) in relation to another set of scholars (Rawls, Beitz) debating in this field of study, it might look something like this:

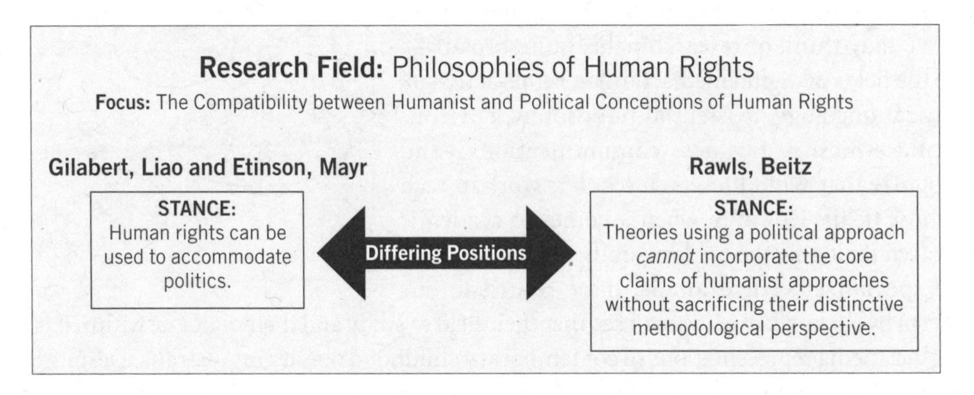

Like this example shows, when we outline a field of study and the research stances of scholars in that field, we don't simply note who says what. We also pay attention to the major points of connection and difference between the scholars' stances. Which scholars are situated close to each other in the field and share a similar stance on the subject? Which scholars are situated far from each other and hold different or opposing stances on the subject? In short, we ask ourselves the following questions:

- Who are the research scholars in this specific or specialized field of study?
- What research stance does each scholar take on the topic of study?
- What similar ideas do the research scholars share about the topic?
- What are the differences between the scholars' stances and ideas?

As we locate this material, we may find it helpful to map out the results visually as in the example above, highlighting the scholars' various positions in the field, the similarities that connect them, and the differences between them. When we map out this material, we are able to see the research relationships between scholars more easily—noticing how they interact with one another—and can begin orchestrating a conversation between them.

As we give research scholars voice in our writing and orchestrate a conversation between them, we need to indicate who says what in that conversation with names and signal verbs, highlighting where researchers stand on the subject in connection with or distinct from one another. For example, consider the following templates that combine research stances with these two types of scholarly interaction:

Orchestrating Connection and Agreement

- According to Researchers X and Y, ___________. Researchers A and B **similarly** suggest that _______________.
- **Like** Researchers A and B, Researcher C **also** holds that ____________.
- A number of researchers (A and B; C; X and Y) **share** the view that _____________.
- **Building on** the views of Researchers X and Y, Researcher Z argues ____________.

Orchestrating Contrast or Difference

- **Distinct from** Researchers A and B, Researcher C points out that _________.
- Researchers X and Y **challenge** Researchers A and B, suggesting that ___________.
- **In contrast to** Researchers X and Y, Researcher Z argues that ______________.
- **Unlike** Researchers D and E, Researcher F proposes ______________.

Depending on the purpose of the orchestration in our writing, sometimes it is enough to show the similarities and/or differences between the various research stances on a subject. Other times, however, we need to delve deeper to spot interactions that are not based on similarity or difference. Sometimes researchers ask questions of each other. Sometimes they point out gaps or limitations in each other's research. Sometimes they distinguish themselves from others in order to present new discoveries or knowledge. With this in mind, we can go deeper into orchestration by asking ourselves the following questions as we read our collection of research material:

- What questions does each scholar ask in the context of his or her study? Do other scholars in the research field answer these questions in their work?

- What gaps in knowledge or limitations in perspective does each scholar point out in the other research material in this field of study?

- What does each scholar contribute to the discussion with his or her research stance? In other words, what new ideas is each scholar bringing to the table in order to help others better understand the topic in this field of study?

We see research writers engage with these kinds of questions often, explaining how scholars in the field are interacting *beyond* their similarities and differences. For instance, consider how the following example shows a wide range of scholarly perspectives on the complex question of whether law should enforce social morality.

> Lawyers and philosophers have long debated whether law should *enforce* social morality. No, says J.S. Mill, unless doing so prevents harm to others. Yes, says James Fitzjames Stephen, so that intentionally inflicted suffering can affirm and validate the community's moral judgments. H.L.A. Hart replies: never, unless doing so attains some good that outweighs the loss of liberty and happiness that come with enforcement. Patrick Devlin rejoins: on the contrary, provided what is at issue is a moral standard whose breach an average person would regard with intolerance, indignation, and disgust, we should enforce it. Ronald Dworkin dissents: but that would be to give force to mere hostilities and prejudices, and those do not even count as moral views. Joseph Raz mediates: it is permissible to uphold social morality when the morality enforced helps constitute a valuable form of life and the 'enforcement' makes no or minimal use of coercion (Mill, 2010; Stephen, 1967; Hart, 1968; Devlin, 1968; Dworkin, 1978; Raz, 1986).
>
> The debate about the enforcement of morality represented in these well-known arguments is far from settled. Disputes continue at the theoretical level, for none of the above doctrines is entirely satisfying and, as with all philosophical arguments, when debate progresses it transforms the questions and our sense of the conditions an adequate answer must meet. And the enforcement of morals is not just a problem that persists for theory; it continues to be controversial in practice. (p. 473)
>
> Green, L. (2013). Should law improve morality? *Criminal Law and Philosophy, 7*(3), 473–494. https://doi.org/10.1007/s11572-013-9248-3

Here scholars are not strictly in agreement or disagreement with each other, but hold a spectrum of views that each contribute to the discussion while also highlighting the limitations of other views. The research writer gives each scholar voice and then steps into the discussion to acknowledge that there is no clear-cut answer to settle the dispute. Often these limitations are expressed directly, as we can see in the next example (highlighted in bold).

> Although the presence of racism within the culture of football has been a feature of scholarly work (see, for example, Back et al., 2001; Burdsey, 2007, 2011; Cleland &

Cashmore, 2013; Garland & Rowe, 2001; King, 2004; Ruddock, 2005), **limited attention has been paid** to how race and racism are discussed on online football fan message boards. As King (2004) points out, the academic literature has primarily focused on racism existing inside stadia and on-the-field, but the advent of social media has opened up new opportunities to examine racism being communicated through other, less overt, channels. (p. 417)

Cleland, J. (2014). Racism, football fans, and online message boards: How social media has added a new dimension to racist discourse in English football. *Journal of Sport and Social Issues, 38*(5), 415–431. https://doi.org/10.1177/0193723513499922

In this excerpt, the research writer J. Cleland draws attention to a range of scholars studying the topic of racism within English football culture and orchestrates their voices as a chorus in this discussion. He then highlights how one scholar in particular (King) points out some limitations in the current discussion. These voices are brought to the reader's attention so that the research writer can introduce a new area for consideration: racism within English football culture as communicated in social media.

As we can see, when research writers orchestrate discussions to show the various stances on a subject in a field of study, they do so in several ways. Often they feature scholars whose stances are similar or those whose stances contrast with each other. However, they may also reveal a spectrum of views that each add something to the discussion or show readers how complex a topic is; or they may reveal questions about or limitations in the views of certain scholars in order to showcase new ways of thinking about the subject. Try the following exercise to see if you can pinpoint these various types of orchestration.

EXERCISE 2
ANALYSING ORCHESTRATION

As you read through the passage below, answer the following questions:

- What is the field of study examined in this excerpt?
- Who are the scholars included in the conversation and what are their stances on the topic?
- What are the similarities and differences between their stances?
- How do the authors orchestrate the scholars' stances into a conversation?

- What questions about or limitations in the field of study are pointed out?
- How do the authors position themselves in the conversation?

The connection between video game violence and youth violence is one that relates to the general connection between exposure to violence and violent behavior. It is empirically supported, for example, that being the victim of violence and engaging in violent behavior are related (Lauritsen & Laub, 2007) and even that victimization tends to follow similar trajectories to known trajectories of offending (DeCamp & Zaykowski, 2015). There are also a number of theoretical arguments and mixed evidence suggesting that exposure to violence merely as a witness can influence violent behavior (Widom, 1989). Some scholars have long been suspicious of impacts from media in comparison to those of family or peers (Sutherland & Cressey, 1960), while other scholars have been arguing that there is such an effect for just as long (Bandura et al., 1963)....

One area of research into the potential effects from video games has focused on an underlying propensity toward violent media. Specifically, these studies recognize and address the issue that children who choose to play violent video games (or are allowed to play them) are already different from their counterparts who do not, even before playing the games. An early study (Ward, 2010) in this area found that controlling for the underlying propensity toward violent media resulted in reduced effects that were only present for heavy gamers, although the measure used for game play did not distinguish between violent and non-violent games and the design had limited controls. Another study (Gunter & Daly, 2012) found that most of the relationships became non-significant or substantially weakened after controlling for this underlying propensity. Although that study did measure only violent games in its design, the measure did not allow for distinguishing the amount of exposure to violent games. Further analyses incorporating alternative predictors of violence indicate that the weak effects from violent games are smaller than effects from various other social predictors of violence (DeCamp, 2015)....

Although there have been a variety of studies examining the relationships between video games and violence, few of these studies have incorporated analytic methods for controlling for the self-selection bias in who chooses (or is allowed) to play violent video games. Those that have done so have only examined violent game play as a dichotomy—that is, comparing children by whether they ever or never play violent video games (DeCamp, 2015; Gunter & Daly, 2012)—or without measuring violence in games (Ward, 2010). Given prior research, this study investigates the following research questions. First, does time spent playing violent games have a positive correlation with violent behavior? Prior research has found evidence of a correlational relationship, but using only dichotomous indicators for game play rather than the degree of exposure (e.g., Ferguson, 2015b; Gunter & Daly, 2012). [Second], does the strength of that relationship decrease substantially with the introduction of violent media propensity as a control? Some studies have suggested that controls reduce or eliminate effects from violent games (e.g., Gunter & Daly, 2012; Ward, 2010), but this also has not been tested using the degree of exposure to violent media. Finally, do other social and environmental factors more strongly predict violent behavior? It has long been argued in criminology that familial and other more proximate effects have a stronger influence on behavior than media (Sutherland & Cressey, 1960) and recent research suggests that this applies to video games as well (DeCamp, 2015), but it is unclear whether a more precise measurement of degree of exposure would find similar results. By treating people who play violent games for a couple hours per year the same as those who do daily, there is potentially a great amount of measurement error that could wash out effects. The present study addresses this gap in the existing literature by using both a control for underlying propensity toward violent media and a measure for game play that taps into the amount of time spent playing violent video games rather than simply whether the individual does or does not. (pp. 389–90)

DeCamp, W., & Ferguson, C.J. (2017). The impact of degree of exposure to violent video games, family background, and other factors on youth violence. *Journal of Youth and Adolescence, 46*(2), 388–400. https://doi.org/10.1007/s10964-016-0561-8

E. ORCHESTRATION IN PRACTICE: WRITING LITERATURE REVIEWS

As we can see, orchestrating a dialogue involves summarizing what scholars think about a subject and showing how their research stances intersect with and diverge from each other. Often the conversations we orchestrate in our research writing are very brief, especially when we represent scholars as a chorus who are unified about an issue or idea. However, we are sometimes asked to orchestrate a more in-depth or involved discussion between a few key scholars or thinkers in the form of a literature review.

A ***literature review*** is an extended orchestration that overviews the key research material found on a particular topic. The word *literature* here does not refer to literary writing, like novels or poems, but more generally to "the material in print on a given subject" (*Canadian Oxford Dictionary*). As such, the main purpose of a literature review is to collect and consider the research material on a specific topic in order to highlight the various stances that research scholars have on it. How exactly have the experts dealt with this topic? By highlighting these areas, we show what has already been studied in the field as well as where the gaps in knowledge or areas for further study might be located.

We write literature reviews, then, to figure out what research scholars have written about a topic, analyse how their ideas interact, discover what knowledge emerges from their combined viewpoints, and, ultimately, situate ourselves in dialogue with them. Because we need to understand what other scholars have written about a topic *before* we can step into a discussion with them, we usually write a literature review as a precursor to a research paper, at the beginning of a research article, or as a preliminary chapter in a scholarly book. They tend to be used most commonly in the research writing of the social sciences, but they have their place in the humanities and the sciences as well.

At first glance, we might wonder what sets a literature review apart from a research summary. Don't they both summarize the work of research scholars? In fact, they differ in three main ways: Firstly, a literature review covers a wider range of research material than a typical summary, drawing different scholarly viewpoints together and showing how they interact. Secondly, a literature review is framed as a dialogue in which each scholar is given voice to weigh in on the subject and take part in the conversation with other scholars. Thirdly, a literature review involves analysis and evaluation. As writers draw scholarly viewpoints together, they interpret how different scholars understand the topic and assess their connections and distinctions. Writers also need to be able to discern which areas of knowledge have become well established on the subject and which ones need further investigation. Consequently, writers of literature reviews provide commentary about the research material they are reviewing and may also briefly state how their own views fit into the conversation.

When we write a literature review, we can structure it chronologically or thematically. When we use a ***chronological structure***, we organize and discuss our research sources according to *time*. We use this structure to highlight how research material has changed or developed over a period in history or from the past to the present. For example, a chronological review on the topic "theories of mental illness" might present how the understanding of mental illness has changed over time by tracing research across a number of decades and ending with current theories on the subject.

When we use a ***thematic structure***, we organize and discuss our research sources in terms of the themes, concepts, or issues they cover. We use this structure to highlight the different aspects of a topic or to compare different viewpoints on one aspect of a topic. For example, a thematic review on the topic of "theories of mental illness" might organize research findings by theory, discussing the behavioural, social-cognitive, and biological approaches to mental illness one at a time. Or it might compare and contrast different researchers' views on one particular theory of mental illness, like the social-cognitive theory.

Consider the following condensed literature review that researchers Filho, Silva, and Ferreira include as part of a larger research paper on waste water management. Note how it uses a chronological structure, summarizing the changes of nuclear magnetic resonance over time with words and phrases suggesting temporality (in bold below). We can also see how the writers analyse the research material as they proceed, using words and phrases like *for this reason*, *thus*, and *hence* (underlined below) to indicate its significance for their purposes.

Currently, new trends to afford lower limits of detection and to obtain information for complex systems without arduous sample preparation are available. Nuclear magnetic resonance (NMR) is possibly the most powerful tool for the determination of molecular structures, dynamics and interactions for simple to complex molecules and systems and in various physical phases (solids, gels, liquids and gases). For this reason, NMR has been the object of several improvements for directional and multidimensional analysis. **In the late 1970s** (Wantanabe & Niki, 1978; Albert, 2002), the very first experiments of high-performance liquid chromatography (HPLC) coupled with NMR were performed. **Since then**, technological advances, including cryomagnets, cryoprobes, new coil designs and complex and effective pulse sequences, have allowed NMR to advance knowledge to new frontiers. For example, high-resolution magic angle spinning (HR-MAS) (Sacco et al., 1998; Simpson et al., 2001; Farooq et al., 2013; Kelleher et al., 2006) and, **more recently**, comprehensive multiphase probes (CMPs) (Courtier-Murias et al., 2012) permitted the use of a single hybrid NMR probe to obtain solution-state, gel-state (HR-MAS) and solid-state experiments that are **available today** (Simpson et al., 2012; Lam et al., 2007). This technology allowed for the study of both structures and interactions as well as between phases in the native state to fully understand unaltered complex systems. Thus, the ability of NMR to provide information on the molecular scale for analytes of different physical states, while employing little or no pretreatment, makes it highly suitable for environmental studies. Hence, the aim of this text is to summarize several applications of NMR and LC-NMR in studies of the inputs and outputs of sewage treatment plants.... (p. 649)

Filho, E.G.A., Silva, L.M.A., & Ferreira, A.G. (2015). Advancements in waste water characterization through NMR spectroscopy: Review. *Magnetic Resonance in Chemistry, 53*(9), 648–657. https://doi.org/10.1002/mrc.4158

Another concise literature review can be found in the second paragraph of the excerpt provided in Exercise 2 (Section D). There the research writers use a thematic organization to highlight different kinds of studies that have looked at the relationship between video gaming and violence. This example, like the one above, is very short and functions as a small part of a larger research paper.

Most literature reviews are longer, though, as writers take into account a wider range of research material or delve deeper into each study. The number of studies, the level of analysis of each study, and the interactions between the studies are often detailed and involved, as we will see more clearly in the exercise below. Research writers also tend to include commentary on the importance, influence, and/or effectiveness of the studies as they relate to each other or to the topic at hand. As they do this, they set up a research discussion between scholars which they later plan to join with their own research stance.

EXERCISE 3
REFLECTING ON LITERATURE REVIEWS

As you read the literature review below, consider the following questions:

- Which scholars are brought into the conversation and why?
- What position do they each take on the concept of aggression?
- How is this literature review organized? Chronologically, thematically, or both?
- What commentary do the research writers include as they orchestrate this dialogue?

In the psychological literature, aggression is generally taken to be a purposeful act intended to cause harm to somebody (or some animate being) who does not wish to be harmed. The somebody is usually somebody else, although of course some people inflict self-harm. The act should be intentional, given that accidental harm is not considered aggressive. For some decades, the literature on aggression focused on direct, in-person kinds of aggression, including direct physical attacks, such as hitting, kicking, punching, and direct verbal attacks, such as threats, taunts, or insults.

But in the early 1990s, the focus was broadened to include other kinds of aggression. Bjorkqvist, Lagerspetz, and Kaukiainen (1992) introduced the concept of *indirect aggression*, which is aimed at someone but is not perpetrated face to face. It is often accomplished via a third party; for example, spreading nasty rumors about someone. Indirect aggression can also include instances in which a deliberate harmful act took place but the victim was not present during the attack; hiding, stealing or damaging someone's belongings are usually done when the victim is not present and can be considered indirect physical bullying.

Crick and Grotpeter (1995) proposed the term *relational aggression* to refer to aggressive behaviour that is intended to damage someone's relationships. This also includes rumor spreading and social exclusion. Although relational aggression is often indirect (e.g., spreading rumors targeting someone's relations and reputation with others; never choosing a mate to work or play with, never talking to him/her), it can be direct, face to face as well ("You can't play with us"). Galen and Underwood (1997) introduced the similar term *social aggression*, referring to aggression intended to damage another's self-esteem or social status. Some evidence suggests that the pain of relational aggression can be more influential than the pain stemming from physical aggression (Chen et al., 2008; Van der Meulen et al., 2003).

It is not generally accepted that aggression should embrace the indirect and relational forms, in addition to the more straightforward hits and insults studied in earlier decades. Especially in adult life, aggression can occur in the workplace, including more sophisticated means such as where someone sets totally unrealistic goals and undermines another's confidence and work satisfaction. And in this century, cyber-aggression includes attacks via mobile phones and the Internet. (pp. 26–27)

Smith, P.K., Del Barrio, C., & Tokunaga, R.S. (2013). Definitions of bullying and cyberbullying: How useful are the terms? In S. Bauman, D. Cross, & J.L. Walker (Eds.), *Principles of cyberbullying research: Definitions, measures, and methodology* (pp. 26–40). Routledge.

CONCLUSIONS

When we engage in research, we investigate how scholars and research experts have dealt with a particular topic, issue, or problem in a specific field of study. When we share this research with our readers we give each scholar voice, carefully representing how their ideas interact by composing a conversation between them. This conversation highlights similarities between the scholars' research stances and brings them together, often in the form of a chorus. It also highlights differences between scholarly stances or reveals a wide spectrum of positions to show the complexity of the subject and the range of viewpoints pertaining to it. In fact, a conversation may be orchestrated to show how scholars question one another's ideas or point out limitations in one another's research in order to introduce new ways of thinking about a subject.

Composing or orchestrating conversations relies on our ability to summarize different research scholarship as well as our capacity to organize and integrate various scholarly voices together. We orchestrate conversations throughout our research writing, whether in the form of short interactions or in-depth literature reviews, so that the stances and findings of scholars are clear to readers, and, ultimately, so that our own research stance will make sense in relation to theirs. In this way, we show that research scholarship is a practice of mutual interaction, of many viewpoints coming together to develop our knowledge and understanding.

QUESTIONS FOR REFLECTION

1. Consider the kinds of conversations you have every day. If you were to write down one of those conversations, how would you make the different viewpoints clear to your readers, giving each person voice? If you were to represent yourself in that conversation, how would you link your ideas to others in the conversation? How would you distinguish your ideas from others?

2. Analyse the following excerpt and write a short summary of it in which you orchestrate the various researchers' stances on the subject. Use the strategies and templates included throughout this chapter to help you.

Excerpt from "Factors Contributing to the Early Failure of Small New Charity Start-Ups" by Roger Bennett

Human capital theory (Becker, 1975) posits that the individual characteristics of the founder of an organisation represent critical prerequisites for survival. Major human capital characteristics include the founder's educational background, career history, and industry-specific experience. Educational background is said to be important because, allegedly, it can affect the productivity of a founder in terms of the person's efficiency and effectiveness in organising resources. Also, the well-educated may be better at collecting and analysing relevant information; obtaining start-up capital, hence enabling the establishment of better equipped operations; and establishing useful networks. Experience plays a prominent role in human capital theory *vis-à-vis* enterprise survival and as such merits further discussion.... Duchesneau and Gartner (1990), Nikolaeva (2007), and Huang et al. (2012) have noted the importance of experience as a determinant of favourable outcomes for new business start-ups, [however,] Oe and Mitsuhashi (2013) reported "very mixed results" regarding whether start-ups are more successful when founders have "experience in related areas" (p. 2193). Oe and Mitsuhashi (2013) attributed inconsistencies in research findings to the need for a founder to distribute his or her experience throughout a newly founded organisation and to have it interpreted appropriately. A founder may have learned routines that were experienced in previous employment, but this knowledge needs to be passed on to other people and incorporated into the new organisation's activities and structure. Thus, according to Oe and Mitsuhashi (2013), founders need to work hard in order to convert their past experience into organisational assets.

Nevertheless, for the founder of a charity, experience of having helped run an organisation could result in the person holding more realistic expectations with respect to fundraising targets and the kinds of behaviour necessary to deal with financial and organisational crises. Prior management experience may have equipped an individual with strong communication and/or leadership skills, self-confidence, resourcefulness, and the ability to learn from mistakes (Gaskill et al., 1993). It might also have provided certain operational skills needed to manage a start-up; notably those relating to marketing, organisation, managing staff and volunteers, and communication with outsiders (Nikolaeva, 2007). Skills and resources, according to Harmancioglu et al. (2009), need to fit closely with the skills and resources actually required. Effective deployment of skills and resources is insufficient for success, Harmancioglu et al. (2009) continued, if the skills and resources involved are not the ones that are needed. Experience of having started a business from scratch could be especially valuable for the founder of a new charity. (pp. 334–35)

Bennett, R. (2016). Factors contributing to the early failure of small new charity start-ups. *Journal of Small Business and Enterprise Development, 23*(2), 333–348. https://doi.org/10.1108/JSBED-11-2013-0173

3. By nature our viewpoints and perspectives are always limited. For example, when we stand in a room, our perspective of that room will be partial: we can only see what is in front of us because we do not have eyes in the back of our heads! We need someone else in the room to comment on what is going on behind us. We determine the full picture of the room by bringing our various perspectives together to see the whole. One of the key ways scholars engage in academic conversation is to address the limitations of one viewpoint or perspective and add to it in order to develop our understanding of the whole. Consider the following examples. In what ways do you think these viewpoints on the topic are limited? What other stances and what kinds of research would genuinely help us fill out our understanding of the topic?

   - Research on living animals has been practised since at least 500 BCE. Animal testing has enabled the development of numerous life-saving treatments for both humans and animals. There is no alternative method for researching a complete living organism.

   - As of 2018, the majority of North Americans use social networking sites such as Facebook, Instagram, Twitter, LinkedIn, and Pinterest. Social networking sites promote increased interaction with friends and family; offer teachers, librarians, and students valuable access to educational support and materials; facilitate social and political change; and disseminate useful information rapidly.

- Vegetarians do not eat meat (including poultry and seafood) in their diets because eating meat can harm health, waste resources, cause deforestation, and create pollution. Moreover, killing animals for food is cruel and unethical since non-animal food sources are plentiful.

- The minimum drinking age in the United States is 21, although exceptions exist on a state-by-state basis. Teens have not yet reached an age where they can handle alcohol responsibly, and thus are more likely to harm or even kill themselves and others by drinking prior to 21.

All examples are drawn and adapted from ProCon.org.

4. Choose a specific topic that interests you in a field of study in which you would enjoy doing research. Collect five academic research articles on that topic and read them carefully. Map out the various research stances the scholars take on this topic and orchestrate a short literature review that accurately reveals their viewpoints in relation to and in distinction from one another.

CHAPTER SIX

ETHICAL CITATION

Acknowledging Others in the Conversation

Now that we know how to orchestrate a dialogue among research scholars, we need to make sure we acknowledge each of these researchers to our readers. In other words, we need to show readers which researchers said what, where, and when in the conversation we have orchestrated. This practice of acknowledgement is called citation. In this chapter we will discover how to cite the scholars we have brought together in conversation. In particular, we will consider the ethical dimensions of citation, learning how to show respect and responsibility towards other researchers as we acknowledge them in our research writing.

A. ACKNOWLEDGING OTHERS

Citation is a practice of verbally acknowledging the scholars in our academic community whose research and ideas we are bringing together into conversation in our writing. When we cite research scholars in our work, we acknowledge that our knowledge is developed in relation to others. As we participate in a research community, we cite our interactions to show our readers exactly whose ideas we are engaging with and responding to.

Citation is often described as "giving credit where credit is due." We want to show our readers that we are not stealing ideas that originally belonged to someone else or pretending someone else's ideas are our own. The language of "giving credit" and "stealing," however, are economic terms that don't get to the heart of what it means to truly acknowledge others. When we acknowledge other scholars through citation, we show our appreciation and respect for their research and affirm their role in our thinking process. Our citation indicates to readers that we are reliable representatives of research and they can trust what we say.

Our acknowledgement, then, is primarily ethical rather than economic in nature. It is an ethical stance of being open to others, affirming their knowledge and ideas, and giving them recognition for their research. As communications scholar Michael Hyde (2011) defines it,

> Acknowledgement is a capacity of consciousness that enables us to be and remain *open* to the world of people, places, and things so that we can "admit" (Middle English: *acknow*) its wonders into our minds and then "admit" (Middle English: *knowlechen*) to others the understanding that we have gained and that we believe is worth sharing. This entire "admission" process is mandatory for establishing the truth of anything and the knowledge that comes with it. (p. 37)

The knowledge that research scholars share with us in their writing makes it possible for us to "know together" as we mutually pursue a question or issue within our community (p. 37). Whether we are writing a short summary or a literature review, a research essay or a scholarly article, we participate with a group of scholars in dialogue about an issue that mutually interests us and demonstrate that interaction ethically to our readers through citation.

B. PRACTISING ACKNOWLEDGEMENT: DEMONSTRATING RESEARCH INTERACTIONS

Citation acknowledges the research and ideas of other scholars in the very *structure* of our academic writing. Whenever we interact with scholars' research and ideas, we introduce them, represent their ideas faithfully, indicate where they originally said them, and explain those ideas so that they make sense to our readers. In other words, we structure citation in our prose through four particular actions:

1. Introducing	Introduce the researchers and their work.	*This is Fred.*
2. Representing	Accurately state the researchers' relevant material using quotation or paraphrase.	*Here's what Fred said.*
3. Documenting	Highlight where and when the researchers originally stated these ideas.	*Here's where/when Fred said it.*
4. Explaining	Indicate how you understand these ideas or make sense of them.	*Here's what I understand Fred to be saying.*

We are already well familiar with the first two practices, as we used them to develop our research summaries and literature reviews. In this chapter we will go a step further to see how academic acknowledgement extends to other forms of research writing, and learn how to incorporate all four actions of acknowledgement in our own writing. To start, then, let's consider how these four actions are structured in the following example. This example has been highlighted to emphasize each action: ***introducing*** (underlined), ***representing*** (shaded), ***documenting*** (bold), and ***explaining*** (double underlined).

According to Lewis **(2010)**, there has been an anthropological turn in ethics, focusing on "lived ethics." Writers are now investigating in depth the way "ethical teachings are appropriated, lived and transmitted by broader segments of the population" **(p. 399)**. This approach aligns with the rise of communitarian themes, and is research driven. The concern is with building rich and thick descriptions of the lived experiences of moral agents. Lewis **(2010)** argues that this move is counter to what many normative ethicists practice, where the focus has "largely ignored what people alive today and outside the academy think about these matters" **(p. 396)**; it invests real normative significance in a wider range of understandings than is typically the case in normative theorising. (p. 140)

Macklin, R., & Mathison, K. (2018). Embedding ethics: Dialogic partnerships and communitarian business ethics. *Journal of Business Ethics, 153*(4), 133–145. https://doi.org/10.1007/s10551-016-3431-0

Notice how the researchers Macklin and Mathison introduce the research scholar by last name (Lewis) and document *where* (pp. 399, 396) and *when* (2010) Lewis talks about "an anthropological turn in ethics." They represent Lewis's views in the form of paraphrase and direct quotation and explain how Lewis's ideas fit into the larger conversation on ethics that they are addressing in their text.

Regardless of the topic or field of study, scholars structure their academic writing to acknowledge their research interactions to readers. Each discipline or field of research will use different forms of citation to highlight those interactions, but this structure of acknowledgement with its four practices—introducing, representing, documenting, and explaining—tends to be consistent across all academic fields.

EXERCISE 1
STRUCTURING ACKNOWLEDGEMENT IN ACADEMIC WRITING

Consider the following three excerpts from academic papers across different fields of research. Locate all four practices of acknowledgement—introducing, representing, documenting, and explaining—in each passage and highlight them.

Excerpt 1

In *On the Different Forms of Insanity, in Relation to Jurisprudence* (1842), Prichard identified two types of disease affecting the will and emotions: moral insanity and impulsive insanity. By "moral insanity" Prichard explained that he meant "a disorder which affects only the feelings and affections, or what are termed the moral powers of the mind, in contradistinction to the powers of the understanding or intellect" (p. 19). The disease, he noted, typically produced a profound alteration in the temper and habits of a person such that an individual who was esteemed for "probity and high respectability" would suddenly become "depraved, reckless, and devoid of all moral principle" (p. 59). Moral insanity overlapped with the second "class of mental affections," which, Prichard acknowledged, was "very important in a legal point of view, and of very difficult investigation":

> These are distinguished in the following treatise, by the name of Insane impulse, or Instinctive madness. The character of the disease is a liability to sudden impulses to commit acts which bespeak madness, or are not those of a sane person. Such acts are often of an appalling and atrocious kind.... (p. 20)

As this definition reveals, Prichard found it impossible to describe impulsive insanity without lapsing into tautology. He admitted that it was "often very difficult to determine whether...persons [liable to such impulses were] criminals or lunatics" (pp. 20–21).... But he insisted on the validity of these diseases. (pp. 370–71)

Ganz, M.J. (2015). Carrying on like a madman: Insanity and responsibility in *Strange Case of Dr. Jekyll and Mr. Hyde*. *Nineteenth-Century Literature, 70*(3), 363–397. https://doi.org/10.1525/ncl.2015.70.3.363

Excerpt 2

Historians like Jean Barman (2005) and Sean Kheraj (2013) have noted the incongruity of widely shared perceptions of [Vancouver's] centrally located Stanley Park as pristine wilderness, Eden-like in its suggestion of a time before the land was touched by human activity. The park, they note, is as much a constructed space as the rest of the city, moulded by generations of inhabitation, industry, landscaping, and contentious displacements. Yet its historicity remains widely unrecognised by proponents of an idyllic Vancouver who, like the well-known author and artist Douglas Coupland, imagine a Stanley Park where "there is nothing—just the trees and animals. As it should be" (p. 140). Coupland was recently commissioned to produce a gold-lacquered replica of Stanley Park's famed 800-year-old hollow tree. The tree was badly damaged in a 2006 windstorm, and Coupland has noted his desire to preserve its memory for future generations and new immigrants before it is lost to time. In commenting on the project, Coupland further mused on his city's relationship with its past: "Vancouver is a city with so little history compared to most other cities...does it feel like a blank piece of paper to newcomers? Maybe it does, and that's one of the city's attractions—the feeling that it's a place where one can start over, or perhaps reinvent oneself" (Judd, 2014). The liberating promise of this lack of history, the opportunity it affords to turn the page, to start anew, is seductive. It certainly fits well with the energetic and exciting image of Vancouver promoted by the constructors of the shimmering glass condo towers where Coupland's golden tree will offer a gilded glimpse of the past to consumers of the city's countless shopping and entertainment amenities prominently featured in the project's advertising material. (pp. 184–85)

Kenny, N. (2016). Forgotten pasts and contested futures in Vancouver. *British Journal of Canadian Studies, 29*(2), 175–197. https://doi.org/10.3828/bjcs.2016.9

Excerpt 3

Atlantic salmon utilize foraging areas in Arctic and Subarctic waters both in the western and eastern North Atlantic; these provide the conditions for an exceptional increase in size at age during the second post-winter season at sea. The Arctic regions of the North Atlantic undoubtedly are presently subject to increasing environmental change (Lindsay et al., 2009) and, for example, Wang and Overland (2009) include predictions of a sea ice-free Arctic in September by the year 2037. Such large-scale and pervasive changes in the physical environment will inevitably exert major influences at all levels of the pelagic food web in Arctic seas, including top predators such as Atlantic salmon. The exceptional size that MSW fish can achieve between their first and second sea-winter (Allen et al., 1972) is related to the availability of high-energy content prey. These food resources are exploitable by salmon because they have evolved the ability to migrate to distant Arctic habitats and return to their natal river to spawn (Dadswell et al., 2010). The nature of the migration control and specific routes taken by differing stocks is still under debate, but an anadromous life-history strategy clearly confers a fitness advantage to salmon because the remote feeding areas in the Arctic are typified by low species diversity but high seasonal productivity, which affords salmon feeding opportunity with little competitive challenge (Quinn, 2005). It is therefore intuitive that variation in salmon growth may be a function of productivity at the base of the food chain in the Arctic, albeit perhaps with lag effects given that salmon prey upon larger zooplankton and forage fish. (p. 594)

Friedland, K.D., & Todd, C.D. (2012). Changes in northwest Atlantic arctic and subarctic conditions and the growth response of Atlantic salmon. *Polar Biology, 35*(4), 593–609. https://doi.org/10.1007/s00300-011-1105-z

Throughout the rest of this chapter, we will learn how to acknowledge other research scholars openly in our academic writing through the four activities of citation: introducing, representing, documenting, and explaining. As we will see, these activities bring together the skills we have learned in the last three chapters.

C. INTRODUCING SCHOLARS: PLAYING THE HOST

"Introducing" is the practice of presenting to our readers the scholars whose research and ideas we're discussing. Like a talk show host introduces a speaker to the audience by name and often shares some information about the speaker before he or she begins talking, we host communication between our scholars and the audience reading our work. We introduce one to the other and sometimes explain a little bit about the scholars' work so our readers can understand the scholars' background and where they are coming from.

As we saw in Chapter 3, we usually refer to research scholars by last name. Only when we first introduce them do we refer to them by full name or by first initials and last name. We also use signal verbs so that readers can distinguish between what we are saying (as host) and what the researchers have said. These introductions can take various forms, but here are some common ways to introduce researchers and their work in our writing:

- In his article, ___________, **Researcher X** asserts that _______________.
- **Researcher X**, a prominent psychologist in the field of trauma studies, argues that _______________.
- In their study of ___________, **Researchers X, Y, and Z** note that ____________.
- As **Researcher X** puts it in her article, ___________, _________________.

These templates introduce research scholars individually, acknowledging one study or aspect of their work. But we can also introduce researchers as a group. We use collective introductions when we want to introduce a general idea or common point held by many researchers across different studies. These group introductions cite the researchers' last names in brackets *after* the point of their studies has been stated. For example:

- **As many studies have shown,** _________________ (Researchers A, B, and C; Researcher D; Researchers E and F; Researcher G).
- **Researchers seems to agree that** _________________ (Researchers A and C; Researcher B; Researchers D, E, and F; Researchers G and H).

➢ **In a number of cases, research findings point to** ______________ (Researcher A; Researchers B, C, and D; Researchers E and F; Researcher G).

➢ **While some research findings suggest** ______________ (Researchers A and B; Researcher C; Researcher D), **other findings reveal that** __________________ (Researcher E; Researchers F and G).

Depending on our purposes for introducing scholars and their research in our work, we will either use "chorus" citations or direct and individualized introductions. In order to determine which introductory technique to use in your own writing, examine how the research writing in your field introduces its research scholars. Take note and follow suit.

D. REPRESENTING SCHOLARS: QUOTING AND PARAPHRASING

"Representing" is the practice of communicating scholars' ideas and findings to our readers. As we saw in Chapter 3, when we represent scholars' ideas and findings we function as their *representative*, standing in for them or writing on their behalf. We give scholars voice, re-presenting their research to others in dialogue with our own work. In the process, we are careful to convey what scholars have said about their research as neutrally and respectfully as we can. In this way we "do justice" to their ideas.

In Chapter 3 we also learned that we can represent the research of scholars in two ways: by *quoting* what they have written word for word or by *paraphrasing* what they have written in our own words. Now let's consider the purpose and craft of quotation and paraphrase more closely to see how they function beyond the context of summary, and how they apply to research writing more broadly.

1. Quotation

We quote research scholars word for word when we want to do one of the following:

- engage in a close reading and analysis of a researcher's exact words
- compare a researcher's specific words with those of another researcher
- apply a researcher's exact definition or terminology to our own research context
- draw upon a researcher's exact descriptions or observations to make a point
- use the researcher's direct words as evidence to support our stance
- emphasize a researcher's word or phrase that we want to agree or disagree with

There are two critical things to remember when we incorporate quotations. The first is ***accuracy***. We need to make sure that we have copied the scholar's words correctly and have not taken them out of context in our writing. Accuracy also involves signalling to readers that these words are not our own but belong to someone else; we do this by enclosing their words in quotation marks or by setting them apart from the rest of our text as indented block quotations.

Alongside accuracy we need ***integration***, the practice of incorporating quotes seamlessly into our prose. Whenever we quote a scholar, we take his or her words out of their original context and drop them into a new context—*our* writing. So we need to integrate those words "into their new textual surroundings" (Graff & Birkenstein, 2014, p. 43). It is as if we are making a new home, space, and context for those words to communicate in, showing readers how the material we are quoting interacts with that of other researchers as well as with our own.

We integrate quotes by framing them in our writing. ***Framing*** means connecting a quotation to whatever comes directly before and after it. On a structural level, we make sure a quote applies to the point we are making. We also discuss the quote, showing readers how it connects with our own ideas or the work of other researchers. On a semantic level, we combine our introductory material with the quotation to create a grammatical sentence, using clear punctuation (like a comma or colon) if required and quotation marks or spaces to distinguish the researcher's words from our own:

- As Researcher X observes, "______________________."
  Introductory Clause *Quotation*

- Researcher X defines this term as follows: "__________________."
  Introductory Sentence *Quotation*

We also use ellipses (...) to indicate when we have left material out of a quotation as we incorporate it into our writing context. While these elements may look different depending on the research community we are writing in, the necessity of framing and grammatically integrating quotations is consistent across the disciplines.

Next, we follow the quote with a sentence or two that explains how we understand it or shows how we are making sense of it for our context. We'll consider this process of explanation in more detail when we come to Section F. But for now, have a look at the following templates to help you get started on framing a quotation.

- As Researcher X observes, "____________." This observation connects to the work of Researcher Y in that ____________.

- Researchers X and Y note that "____________." What I understand them to be saying is ____________.

- From Researcher Y's perspective, "__________." Basically, what she is proposing is __________.

- Researchers X and Y describe their most critical finding as follows: "__________." In effect, they show that __________.

In the exercise below, consider the ways that academic writers introduce and integrate the words of other scholars into their own writing as quotations.

EXERCISE 2
QUOTATION

Consider the following passages from academic writing across different fields of research. How is each quotation introduced and integrated in order to represent each scholar's words accurately in a new context?

Excerpt 1

A telling example in their book, *Let Us Now Praise Famous Men*, James Agee and Walker Evans (1941) adjure their readers: "Above all else: in God's name don't think of it as Art" (p. 14). These words communicate a sensed need to disassociate their practice of photography from the aesthetic. (p. 245)

Cubitt, S., & Politoff, V. (2011). Visual communication in traditional and digital contexts. In G. Cheney, S. May, & D. Munshi (Eds.), *The handbook of communication ethics* (pp. 241–257). Routledge.

Excerpt 2

The identification of authorial signature with the narrator, by contrast, is a distinguishing mark of autobiography, argues Philippe Lejeune in his seminal essay "The Autobiographical Pact." Lejeune usefully defines the relationship between author and reader in autobiographical writing as a contract: "What defines autobiography for the one who is reading is above all a contract of identity that is sealed by the proper name. And this is true also for the one who is writing the text" (p. 19).... With this recognition of the autobiographical pact, Lejeune argues, we read differently and assess the narrative as making truth claims of a sort that are suspended in fictional forms such as the novel. (p. 11)

Smith, S., & Watson, J. (2010). *Reading autobiography: A guide for interpreting life narratives* (2nd ed.). University of Minnesota Press.

Excerpt 3

Finally, the question is posed which Habermas holds to be fundamental, namely: "How can we justify the principle of universalization itself, which alone enables us to reach agreement through the argumentation on practical questions?" (p. 44). It is this final question that is of interest to us. (p. 281)

Ricoeur, P. (1992). *Oneself as another* (K. Blamey, Trans.). University of Chicago Press.

2. Paraphrase

We paraphrase a researcher scholar's work in our own words when we want to do one of the following things:

- highlight a researcher's stance, general concepts, findings, or conclusions
- express an idea or observation that various research scholars agree upon
- exemplify a number of different views on the same subject
- outline a range of research ideas that lead up to the work we're doing now
- use a researcher's ideas as evidence to support our stance

As with quotation, when we paraphrase a researcher's words it is important to practise accuracy and integration. However, accuracy and integration look a bit different in this context. Because we focus on concepts rather than the nitty-gritty details when we paraphrase, accuracy has to do with how precisely we can portray the gist of a researcher's or group of researchers' material and ideas. As we saw in Chapter 3, to be accurate in representing material and ideas, we need to make sure we understand them for ourselves before we can synthesize them in a coherent way for our readers. We also present the research material as neutrally as possible. We may go on to critique or affirm it, but not before we represent it fairly and respectfully.

Integrating paraphrased material is similar to integrating quotations in our academic writing. We begin by introducing the research scholar(s) whose material we are paraphrasing. Scholars' names can either be stated in the text itself with signal verbs or included alongside their research ideas in parentheses. The following templates show various ways to connect researchers' names with their paraphrased ideas.

➢ Researcher X views this dilemma as a matter of ____________. However, this perspective is limited by ____________.

- Researchers agree that _______ (Researchers A and C; Researcher B; Researchers D and E). Together they show the significance of _________.

- As many studies have shown, ______________ (Researchers A, B, and C; Researcher D; Researchers E and F; Researcher G). Although these studies differ in their approach, they connect on the matter of ________.

- In a number of cases, research findings point to ______________ (Researcher A; Researchers B, C, and D). These findings are important because _________.

In the exercise below, consider the ways academic writers craft their paraphrases, integrating the ideas and research of other scholars into their own writing.

EXERCISE 3
PARAPHRASE

Consider the following two passages of academic research writing. How are researchers' ideas paraphrased and integrated in a new context? How is/are the writer(s) using the paraphrased material in each example?

Excerpt 1

Because of their impact on woody vegetation in mountain areas, snow avalanches have been recognized as a major disturbance factor (Khapayev, 1978; Johnson, 1987; Veblen et al., 1994; Larocque et al., 2001). Despite considerable data on snow avalanche occurrence and frequency, especially in alpine sites where historical records are available, the ecological impact of avalanches on treed slopes remain poorly documented. (p. 2103)

Germain, D., Filion, L., & Hétu, B. (2005). Snow avalanche activity after fire and logging disturbances, Northern Gaspé Peninsula, Quebec, Canada. *Canadian Journal of Earth Sciences, 42*(12), 2103–2116. https://doi.org/10.1139/E05-087

Excerpt 2

It is difficult to write on photography today without entering into debates on the concept of archive, as theorized by such luminaries as Michel Foucault, Jacques Derrida, Paul Ricoeur and Giorgio Agamben.... Although each differ in their approach, there is an emphasis on how the complexities of the past and the present—that is what can be thought, said and seen is dependent on the idiosyncrasies of what remains in all sorts of archives. It is through them that we recall and revisit individual and collective memories, where what is and is not recorded in images, objects, documents and traces becomes a relation between the sayable and the unsayable. (p. 137)

Carrabine, E. (2014). Seeing things: Violence, voyeurism and the camera. *Theoretical Criminology, 18*(2), 134–158. https://doi.org/10.1177/1362480613508425

E. DOCUMENTING RESEARCH SCHOLARSHIP

Beyond introducing and representing the research scholars with whom we are interacting, citation involves documenting where and when those researchers wrote that material. Documentation is important because it gives credibility and authority to our representations. Just like in news reports, where journalists report the facts and details of an event—indicating what happened to whom, where and when—in order to demonstrate that their reports are reliable, academic writers represent who said what, where and when to prove their representations of research are reliable. Consider the following example, comparing how news reports and research writing similarly document the facts of one's findings: *who* (bold); *what* (underlined); *when* (shaded in blue), and *where* (shaded in grey).

News Report Excerpt

Canadian Olympic snowboarder Max Parrot announced on Thursday he has been diagnosed with Hodgkin's lymphoma.

Parrot, a 24-year-old from Bromont, Que., captured slopestyle silver at the 2018 Winter Olympics in Pyeongchang, South Korea. He was diagnosed with the cancer on Dec. 21, 10 days after undergoing a biopsy.

CBC Sports. (2019, January 17). *Canadian snowboarder Max Parrot announces Hodgkin's lymphoma diagnosis.* CBC. https://www.cbc.ca/sports/olympics/canadian-snowboarder-max-parrot-1.4981689

Research Writing Excerpt

In *On Photography*, **Susan Sontag** (1977) points out that the "aestheticizing tendency" of photography is also seen to neutralize the distress that photographs of suffering can effect in the viewer (p. 108). **Caroline Brothers** (1977) similarly describes, in relation to photojournalism, how the aestheticization of death becomes a "means of deflecting its impact and sheltering the public from scenes considered too gruesome" (p. 172). (p. 245)

Cubitt, S., & Politoff, V. (2011). Visual communication in traditional and digital contexts. In G. Cheney, S. May, & D. Munshi (Eds.), *The handbook of communication ethics* (pp. 241–257). Routledge.

Each academic field of study or discipline uses a particular documentation style to acknowledge where and when scholars have written their research and made their claims. For example, in the humanities many scholars use the **MLA** (Modern Language Association) documentation style. In most social science disciplines, scholars use the **APA** (American Psychological Association) documentation style. In disciplines like business, history, music, and the fine arts, scholars use **Chicago** style to document resources, while scholars in the sciences use a range of other styles.

While each style documents who said what, where and when, it does so in its own way in keeping with the priorities of the discipline or scholarly community. For example, in literary studies *who* and *where* are privileged in the representation of research scholarship using MLA style, while in psychology *who* and *when* are privileged using APA style. Compare how these priorities are revealed in the following example:

MLA Style

In extreme cases, as **Charles Taylor** points out, "non-recognition . . . can inflict harm, can be a form of oppression, imprisoning someone in a false, distorted, and reduced mode of being" (25).

Stumm, Bettina. "Witnessing Others in Narrative Collaboration." *Biography*, vol. 37, no. 3, 2014, p. 763.

APA Style

In extreme cases, as **C. Taylor** (1994) points out, "non-recognition . . . can inflict harm, can be a form of oppression, imprisoning someone in a false, distorted, and reduced mode of being" (p. 25).

Stumm, B. (2014). Witnessing others in narrative collaboration. *Biography, 37*(3), 763. https://doi.org/10.1353/bio.2014.0069

As we document the researchers whose work we quote or paraphrase, we use the citation method common to the field of study in which we are working, or the one recommended to us by our professors. The specific documentation requirements for each method can be found in writers' reference guides and writing centres as well as on most university and college library websites.

Alongside documenting the words and ideas of other research scholars *within* our academic writing—what academics call in-text citations—we also acknowledge the research scholars whose work we have referred to throughout our document by providing our readers with a list of our sources. This list is located at the end of our document and is known variously as our *Bibliography*, our *Works Cited*, or our *References* (depending on the documentation style we are following). Here, in catalogue form, we show readers at a glance the range of research we've drawn on in our work. This detailed catalogue allows readers to locate for themselves the research material we've referred to, in case they want to check our findings or look into the subject more deeply themselves. We will discuss how to compose academic bibliographies in more detail in Chapter 10. For now, we want to recognize that full documentation includes both the presence of in-text citations in the body of our work and a catalogue of research sources located at the end of our work.

F. FROM REPRESENTATION TO EXPLANATION

Finally, we acknowledge a scholar's research and ideas by explaining or making sense of them for our readers. When we practise explanation, we are acknowledging, "Here's what I understand Researcher X to be saying." We explain research to our readers because they may not be familiar with the scholar's work we are referring to. We also explain research to our readers to show how we are making sense of a scholar's ideas in connection with our own and those of other researchers. Explanations can thus be seen as bridges of understanding, connecting researchers together by means of their ideas and connecting readers to research ideas they may not yet know, but want to understand.

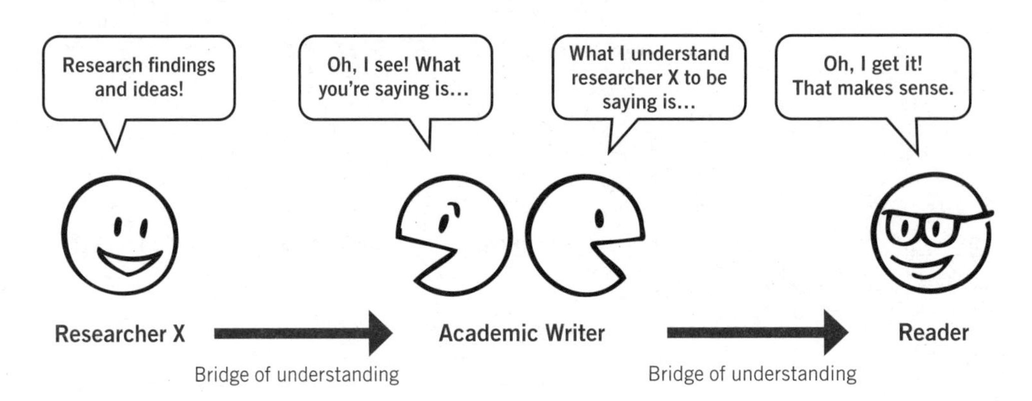

We regularly explain our understanding of a researcher's ideas to readers after we have represented those ideas in quotation or paraphrase. Consider the following three examples of explanation (emphasized in bold), and note how each one follows a quotation or paraphrase of the researchers' work. How does each research writer below explain his or her understanding of the research represented?

Many authors, including Hans Morgenthau, one of the founding fathers of modern Realism, are convinced that what we are depends on how we appear in the eyes of others. Both in domestic and in international politics, Morgenthau writes, "the desire for social recognition is a potent dynamic force determining social relations and creating social institutions.... The image in the mirror of our fellows' minds...determines what we are as members of society" (Morgenthau, 1985, p. 87). **However, when Morgenthau speaks of social recognition, he does not mean moral relationships of mutual affirmation, but "prestige." Prestige is a sign of asymmetrical power and thus by definition monopolized by the few at the expense of the many.** (p. 214)

Heins, V. (2012). The global politics of recognition. In S. O'Neill & N.H. Smith (Eds.), *Recognition theory as social research: Investigating the dynamics of social conflict* (pp. 212–229). Palgrave Macmillan.

Literal exegesis of Scripture is an enterprise in which the basic tasks, such as consultation of the best manuscripts and accurate construal and translation of passages in the original, enable a reader to know what the text actually says and means. The early Christian writer Augustine (354–430 CE) sets this out as his influential manual of biblical and doctrinal exposition:

> ...With the assistance of reliable texts derived from manuscripts with careful attention to the need for emendation, [the student of scripture] should now approach the task of analyzing and resolving the ambiguities of the scriptures. When in the literal usages that make scripture ambiguous, we must first of all make sure that we have not punctuated or articulated the passage incorrectly. Once close consideration has revealed that it is uncertain how a passage should be punctuated and articulated, we must consult the rule of faith, as it is perceived through the plainer passages of the scriptures and the authority of the church. (*De Doctrina Christiana* iii.1)

What Augustine sets out here is basically what is often described as "lower criticism." This is contrasted with the "higher criticism" that characterizes modern historical exegesis, one that is less concerned with what the text tells us about doctrine and morals, and more with the history and the circumstances of its writings and its sources. (pp. 18–19)

Rowland, C. (2009). The literature of the Bible. In R. Lemon, E. Mason, J. Roberts, & C. Rowland (Eds.), *The Blackwell companion to the Bible in English literature* (pp. 10–21). Blackwell.

Dori Laub's reflections on his work with Holocaust victims also illuminate witnessing as against the simpler experience of empathy or vicarious trauma (1995). For Laub, what makes the Holocaust so horrifying is that, "during its historical occurrence, *the event produced no witnesses*" (p. 65). **Here Laub is not saying that there were no observers but**

as noted earlier, observing is not witnessing. Arguably the difference involves distance. Inside the camps, there was no distance, no ability to situate what was happening against some other reality. (pp. 274–75)

Kaplan, A.E. (2011). Empathy and trauma culture: Imaging catastrophe. In A. Coplan & P. Goldie (Eds.), *Empathy: Philosophical and psychological perspectives* (pp. 255–276). Oxford University Press.

It takes time and practice to make sense of other scholars' research material for ourselves and be able to explain it to our readers. However, using templates like the ones below can get us in the habit of explaining our understanding of a researcher's ideas after we have represented them in a quote or paraphrase.

- What I understand Researchers X and Y to be saying is ____________.
- If I understand Researchers X and Y correctly, they are proposing that ____________.
- In other words, Researcher X is asserting that ______________.
- Researcher X is not saying __________, but ______________.
- In effect, Researchers X, Y, and Z are showing that ______________.
- As I see it, Researcher X is refuting the claim that ________________.

G. STEPPING TOWARDS SIGNIFICANCE

In certain academic genres, like summaries and literature reviews, our acknowledgement of scholarly research culminates in our explanation of it. We introduce scholars, represent their work, document it, and explain it to our readers. We demonstrate that these scholars are in conversation with one another in a particular field of study, give them voice, and orchestrate a dialogue between them. We do this to show our readers the current research views on a subject, the varying stances on it, the key similarities and differences between those stances, and the particular aspects of the research that stand out.

However, as we begin to write larger and more involved research documents, we discover that we need to go a step further. Readers don't just want to know who says what, where, and when, or even what we think Researcher X meant when she said Y. They want to know what is important or significant about the research that we are sharing with them and what our stance is on it. Anticipating our readers' expectations, we indicate the *significance* of the research material and it's importance for our study. In doing so, we take a stance and put ourselves into the conversation.

In the following example, notice how Michael Hyde represents the ideas of David Bohm in quotation, documents them, explains his understanding of those ideas, and then *puts himself in dialogue* with Bohm in the form of disagreement (emphasized in bold).

> Perhaps, like his fellow physicist David Bohm, he believes that it is not rhetoric but "dialogue" that enables the scientist to engage in rational collaborative deliberation with his or her colleagues. Writes Bohm:
>
> > Conviction and persuasion are not called for in dialogue. The word "convince" means to win, and the word "persuade" is similar. It's based on the same root as are "suave" and "sweet." People sometimes try to persuade by sweet talk or to convince by strong talk. Both come to the same thing, though, and neither of them is relevant.... If something is right, you don't need to be persuaded. If somebody has to persuade you, then there is probably some doubt about it. (27)
>
> Bohm, in short, is denying that rhetoric (certainly depicted in a narrow-minded and uninformed way) has a role to play in scientific dialogue. **I, however, must disagree, especially in light of the literature on the "rhetoric of science," which makes it clear how scientific dialogue constitutes a rhetorical process that presupposes a history of both great and small minds being persuaded and convinced by arguments unfolding in the face of uncertainty.** (p. 90)
>
> Hyde, M.J. (2006). *The life-giving gift of acknowledgement: A philosophical and rhetorical inquiry.* Purdue University Press.

While we may not fully understand the content of Bohm's viewpoints above, we can readily see that Hyde lays them out for us in order to respond to them with his stance of disagreement. Over the next few chapters, we will learn the various skills needed to recognize the stances of other scholars, assess their research and ideas, and respond to them with our own stance in the form of a dialogue. For now we can begin to envision this dialogue—connecting our explanation of a researcher's ideas to an interaction with them—with the following templates:

- What I understand Researchers X and Y to be saying here is ______________. Their observations connect with my findings that ______________.
- In essence, Researchers X, Y, and Z are showing that ______________. We build on their ideas to demonstrate that ______________.
- As I see it, Researcher X is refuting the claim that ______________. However, what Researcher X does not take into account is ______________.

- Basically, Researcher X is asserting ________________. This claim needs to be taken one step further in order to address our concern that ____________.

- In short, Researchers X and Y are proposing ____________. I agree/disagree with their proposition because ____________.

CONCLUSIONS

Citation is the way we structure our acknowledgement of other scholars and their research in our writing. It includes the specific activities of introducing researchers and their work, representing their research and ideas by means of quotation or paraphrase, documenting where and when that research took place (its original context), and explaining our understanding of the research. Ultimately, it also involves interacting with the research in the context of our own work as we will come to see in the following chapters. In sum, citation is an ethical way of showing that our knowledge is formed in community with other scholars, giving recognition to the members of the community whose ideas we draw on and respond to in our writing.

QUESTIONS FOR REFLECTION

1. Why are scholars obligated to acknowledge their interactions with other researchers in their academic writing? How is this acknowledgement ethically responsible?

2. Find an academic research article in a field that interests you. Analyse the article for ethical citation. In your analysis consider the following questions:
    a) How does the writer introduce the researchers they interact with?
    b) How does the writer represent the research ideas of others and document them?
    c) How does the writer explain those ideas to readers?
    d) How does the writer interact with those ideas and connect them to his or her own research?
    e) Are there ways in which you think the research scholar could be more ethical in acknowledging other researchers and citing his or her ideas?

3. In a paragraph or two, interact with one of the ideas from the research article you have chosen for the question above.
    a) Begin your interaction by introducing the research scholars who wrote the article, representing an idea that you want to interact with in quotation or

paraphrase, and documenting this idea in MLA, APA, Chicago, or another recommended style.

b) After acknowledging the idea with ethical citation, explain your understanding of the idea and engage with it, connecting it to your own ideas about the subject. Use the templates outlined in this chapter to help you. If in doubt, you can model your interaction on the final example in this chapter, where Michael Hyde interacts with the work of physicist David Bohm.

PART 3
DEVELOPING SKILLS OF RESPONSE

CHAPTER SEVEN

CLAIMS, REASONS, AND REASONING

Making Sense of Research Stances

Over the last few chapters, we have learned the basic steps for composing a research dialogue in our academic writing. We have discovered how to be open and receptive to the research we read; how to summarize and orchestrate the views of researchers into a dialogue, giving them voice in relation to one another; and how to acknowledge researchers' work through the practice of citation. With this foundation in place, we are ready take the next step. In the next three chapters, we will learn how to engage meaningfully with the research we've collected and respond intelligently to it with our own stance.

In this chapter we will examine the concept of *stance* and learn how scholars present their stances in their research writing in order to open readers to new or deeper ways of understanding a subject. We will describe the three elements of a stance—its claim, reasons (evidence), and reasoning—and see how scholars position their stances in response to those of other scholars. Our goal in this chapter is to be able to recognize and track with a scholar's claim, reasons, and reasoning. That way we will be well equipped to analyse and assess a research stance (Chapter 8), and to learn how to craft our own stance in response as we join the research dialogue (Chapter 9).

A. UNDERSTANDING STANCES

In the chapters we have read so far, we have learned that a ***stance*** is a standpoint or position on a subject. It refers to *how we see* and *what we think* about a subject, and highlights where we stand when we give voice to our ideas. The language of "standing" and "position" suggests that our seeing and thinking is rooted in a location—a particular place and time period (like our history, culture, environment, etc.). This location is not just physical. It is also social and political. We see and think about the world according to our gender, race, class, age, and other identity positions. Academic scholars call this our *positionality.* If I were a Black transgender woman in my late twenties living in urban California I would see the world differently than if I were a white cisgender man in my mid-sixties living in rural Ukraine. My knowledge and ideas about the world would be different too. Our stance, then, is rooted in our location and positionality, from which we see and understand the world around us.

In an academic context, our stance or standpoint is drawn from our particular location in a research environment. We might call this our *research location*: the field of study we are in, the ideas and theories we have been introduced to, the knowledge we have gathered from thinkers and scholars, etc. Our research stance, then, is *how we see* and *what we think* about a research topic in light of our location and our work in a particular field of study and community.

When scholars take a stance in their research writing, they communicate where they stand on a particular research topic. This stance may take the form of an *assertion* of their views on the topic or a *hypothesis* to test their views on the topic. When we ***assert*** something, we develop an argument to prove our case and provide evidence or reasons to back up our claim (Searle, 1979, p. 62). This kind of stance is regularly used in humanities disciplines where researchers aim to convince others of a specific standpoint that they deem valid and/or beneficial in their field of study. Their goal is not to prove that their own standpoint is right while everyone else's is wrong, but to persuade readers that their stance is a viable position in the dialogue by means of careful analysis of primary documents and established research in the field. This kind of research writing is often called *argumentative* or *persuasive research writing* because it uses assertive persuasion to interact with other viewpoints and encourage further dialogue on the subject.

When we ***hypothesize*** something, we consider whether something is the case, asking questions and making suppositions about its possible truth and drawing out its implications in order to accept or reject them (Fisher, 1989, pp. 402–03). This kind of stance is found in many social science and natural science disciplines where researchers test and develop theories, models, or hypotheses that build research knowledge on a subject. A hypothesis is different from an assertion in that it takes the form of a proposition to be analysed rather than an argument to be proved. Hence, the writing that emerges from this practice is often called *analytical research writing*, in which researchers explore, observe, and evaluate primary evidence and established research in the field in order to reach valid conclusions that benefit the community and encourage further exploration and discussion.

A research stance, then, is not about declaring opinions or imposing ideas on others. In fact, it is not an aggressive or combative position at all. Nor is it an independent statement of opinion that stands apart from the crowd. As we will see in this chapter, when research scholars voice their stances, they do so in a diplomatic and dialogic way, in response to the standpoints of other researchers within a conversation and a community.

B. ARGUMENTATIVE RESEARCH WRITING: RECOGNIZING STANCES AS ARGUMENTS

In many humanities disciplines, as well as in some other research communities, scholars are concerned with the meanings, characteristics, symbols, definitions, and descriptions of human expression and activity. In their research writing, their stances often take the form of arguments that make claims about how to interpret and understand a piece of literature, visual data, a historical event, a philosophical idea, a religious text, a cultural artifact, etc. These claims are then supported with expert reasons and reasoning.

In everyday situations, we tend to think of arguments as quarrels or disputes between two or more people. With this context in mind, we naturally assume that a research argument is a stance that opposes, attacks, or criticizes other researchers. In fact, a ***research argument*** is a logical reasoning process that scholars use to demonstrate their views on a topic. It functions as a receptive response to the research findings and ideas that other scholars have established or affirmed. Consequently, we think of research writers as *making* arguments rather than *having* arguments.

Watterson, B. (1994). *Homicidal psycho jungle cat.* Kansas City, MO: Andrews McMeel Publishing,. p. 117.

Making an argument involves a complex thinking and writing process in which scholars prove a claim through logic and evidence to show readers that their stance is a valid and viable way to understand the subject. Having an argument, let's be honest, is usually about throwing emotionally charged opinions around. As sociolinguist Deborah Tannen puts it in her book *The Argument Culture: Moving from Debate to Dialogue* (1998), "public discourse requires *making* an argument for a point of view, not *having* an argument—as in having a fight" (p. 4). One is productive, meant to further our knowledge collaboratively with others; the other is reductive, geared towards winning a battle.

Making an argument has its roots in ancient Greek culture, where proficient orators engaged in public dialogue with one another or with a general audience in an assembly, court of law, or other communal event. These orators would use rhetorical strategies—such as reason, emotion, and language style and structure—to persuade listeners of their argument. They would also convince their audience by highlighting their credibility and their moral conduct as trustworthy and reliable: "Take my word for it, I'm a good and honourable person!" ***Rhetoric***, as the Greek philosopher Aristotle described it, refers to the means and methods of persuasion we can use in a given situation to convince others of our standpoint (*On Rhetoric* 1.2; Abrams & Harpham, 2009, p. 311). Aristotle focused on three means of persuasion—***logos*** (logic/reasoning), ***ethos*** (ethics/integrity), and ***pathos*** (emotional impact)—that we still use today in order to convince others of our standpoint. For example, lawyers rely on logic, reason, and precedent to make a convincing case for a jury and judge. Companies often foreground their reliability or moral conduct to convince clients or consumers to do business with them. Advertisements use certain images to appeal to our emotions, compelling us to buy an item or support a cause.

In academic writing, however, rhetoric is not used to convince people to "buy" our argument, to take sides, or even to see the world as we do. Instead, its purpose is to "show forth" subject matter in such a way that others can see it with new eyes, gain knowledge, and respond constructively. As Michael Hyde (2011) puts it: "rhetoric is at work whenever language is being employed to open people to ideas, positions, and circumstances that, if rightly understood, stand a reasonable chance of getting people to think and act wisely" (p. 39). The goal, then, of research arguments is to open readers to information and ideas that they haven't thought of before, building their knowledge and promoting responsibility in the research community and beyond.

With this in mind, the most convincing form of argument in the context of research writing is *logos*, or logic. A logos argument provides evidence, critical thinking, and reasoning about a topic in order to contribute new knowledge and understanding about it. There are a number of ways that researchers can make a logical argument, depending on the research genre and discipline in which they are writing. Philosophy uses argumentation differently than history. Law uses argumentation differently than literary studies. However, there are two basic characteristics inherent in all logical arguments: a convincing *claim* and expert *reasons and reasoning* to support that claim. Researchers state a claim to their readers and use expert reasons and reasoning to prove it. Let's examine these two characteristics more closely:

1. Logical arguments make a convincing claim about an issue from a particular stance.
   A ***claim*** is a statement or assertion put forward as true. When we make a claim, we assert that we have something important to say that needs to be heard. Making a claim depends on *agency*—our ability to voice ideas in the academic community—and *conviction* that we have a new way to understand something or put it into practice.

2. This claim is proved by means of expert reasons and reasoning.
   Reasons are the evidence or proof on which a claim is based. They are the grounds on which scholars "stand" to support their claims and the means scholars use to test or prove the legitimacy of their claims. Alongside reasons, scholars use ***reasoning***—the mental processes of inquiry, deduction, analysis, etc.—to persuade readers of the value and validity of their claims.

Research scholars often begin an argument by stating their claim directly at the outset of a research paper. They do so to introduce readers to their argument and the line of reasoning they intend to use throughout the rest of the paper. If we examine the first few paragraphs of an argumentative or persuasive research article, we can often spot the claim because scholars state it with a personal pronoun (*I* or *we*) and provide a specific verb that indicates they are making a case for something:

- I argue...
- This paper claims...
- I contend...
- We assert...
- I am convinced that...
- I reason...
- I am persuaded that...
- We maintain...
- We make the case that...
- I insist that...
- We affirm...
- I uphold that...
- I think...
- It can be argued that...

For example, we can see how the claim is put forward as an argument in the following research introduction (in bold below):

> It is widely believed that working on the built environment is increasingly becoming a predominant condition of the contemporary architectural practice. As many authors point out, this can be related both to the decreased capacity of urban territories to accommodate new buildings in a full urban fabric as well as to a new approach toward an environmental, economic, and socially sustainable development. Assuming, with Attiwill, "the concept of interior" "as a question and problematic within contemporary culture" (2009, p. 2), **I will argue** here that the centrality of adaptive reuse for contemporary architectural theory and practice can also be associated with the shifting social and cultural conditions of modern European cities. (p. 3)
>
> Lanz, F. (2018). Re-inhabiting. Thoughts on the contribution of interior architecture to adaptive intervention: People, places, and identities. *Journal of Interior Design, 43*(2), 3–10. https://doi.org/10.1111/joid.12121

Here, the research writer, F. Lanz, introduces a "widely believed" idea in the field of architecture that she addresses and revises by means of her claim. In doing so, Lanz highlights that she is participating in an ongoing dialogue on the topic. Since most research topics in the humanities are *multifaceted*, they are open to questions and discussion, inviting researchers to explore them with various views or stances.

To illustrate, imagine we are exploring the topic "depictions of female beauty in American advertisements." We could easily find various stances on this topic that would result in a number of different claims. Some of these claims could be stated as follows:

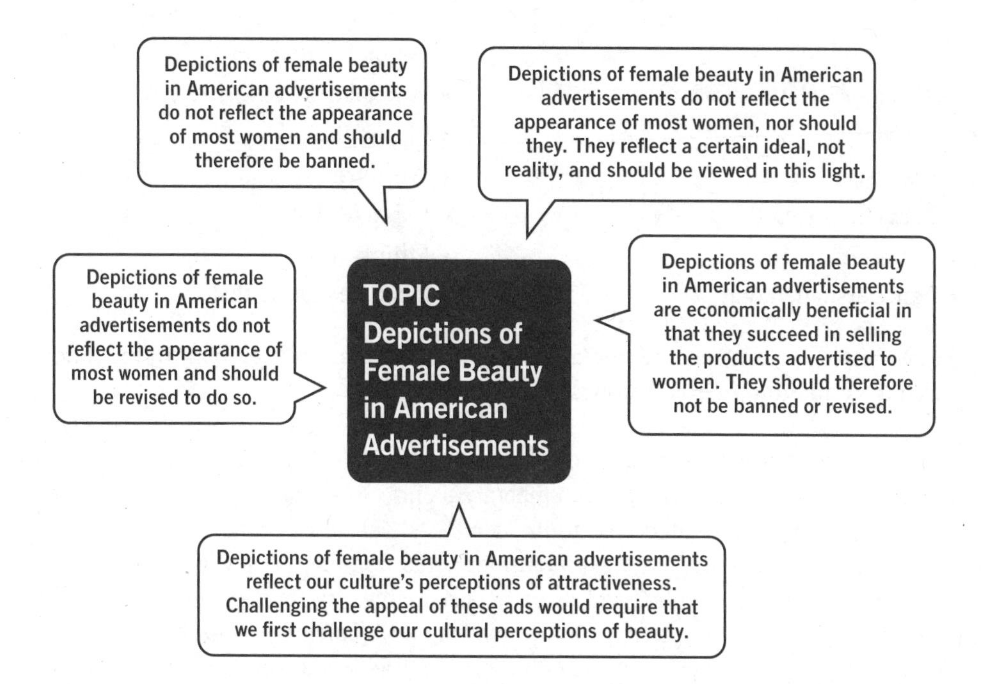

Notice how each of these claims takes a particular stance on the subject of female beauty in American advertisements. Some take a stance of approval and support for current media practices; others suggest clarification and development; still others challenge or critique it. The multifaceted nature of this topic encourages dialogue and discussion. There is no one right answer for addressing this issue, but there are multiple positions from which to view and analyse it. If we were to combine all the insights (reasons and reasoning) for each stance, we would end up with a fuller and deeper understanding of the topic.

In approaching a research topic, then, scholars take different stances, each rooted in reasons and reasoning to support their claims. They may agree, partially agree, or wholly disagree with one another. They may ask questions, answer questions, complicate matters, fill gaps, address limitations, build on one another's claims, or challenge those claims. Ultimately, this mutual exchange of ideas—or dialogue—in their research writing develops our collective understanding of the topic.

C. ANALYTICAL RESEARCH WRITING: RECOGNIZING STANCES AS HYPOTHESES

While argumentative or persuasive research writing tends to use an *argument model* to take a stance on a subject, analytical research writing tends to use an *exploratory model*. Analytical research writing can be found across the disciplines. However, it tends to be most common in contexts where scholars draw on *qualitative research* (observations, interviews, and case studies) or *quantitative research* (statistics, lab experiments, and empirical evidence) to analyse human and natural phenomena. Here, scholars, test hypotheses against facts and findings in order to reach new knowledge or a deeper understanding of a subject. This exploratory stance depends on *inquiry*—the ability to voice questions and possibilities in the academic community—and a *methodology* with which to test ideas and produce new knowledge or implement new practices.

In analytical research writing, a scholar's claim usually takes the form of a hypothesis to investigate rather than an argument to prove. Depending on the research community in which it is used, this claim may be referred to as a *hypothesis*, *thesis*, *proposition*, *position*, or *supposition*. It is the scholar's "best guess" or prediction of what they think they will discover in their findings. Even if a hypothesis turns out to be misguided or incorrect when tested, the research community will still have learned something from the experiment and its findings.

Like a research argument, a research hypothesis depends on expert reasons and reasoning to succeed. In this case, ***reasons*** are the evidence and findings discovered when a hypothesis or theory is tested. They are the ground on which scholars "stand" to ascertain whether their hypotheses are valid or need modification. Alongside reasons, scholars use ***reasoning***—the mental processes of inquiry, induction, analysis, etc.—in order to develop and test their hypotheses and make sense of their findings.

Scholars often begin an analytical research paper by proposing their claim directly. They do so to introduce readers to their hypothesis and their method for testing that hypothesis before they delve into their findings. When we examine the first few paragraphs of an analytical research paper, we can spot the claim by reading closely: scholars often introduce it with a personal pronoun (*I* or *we*) or with a direct reference to the paper (*this paper*; *this study*) alongside a verb that indicates they are proposing or testing something:

- This paper proposes...
- This study tests...
- We hypothesize...
- We suppose...
- I speculate...
- This essay analyses...
- We infer...
- I predict that...
- I suggest...
- This study investigates...
- We theorize...
- We expect...

For example, notice how the research claim is put forward as a hypothesis in the following research introduction (in bold below):

> **We hypothesize** that in the absence of any intervention, exposure to thin media images compared to control images will lead to decreased state body satisfaction and state body esteem amongst adolescent girls. However, after a brief media literacy intervention, **we**

predict that there will be no differences in levels of state body satisfaction and state body esteem between girls who viewed thin models or control images. (p. 398)

Halliwell, E., Easun, A., & Harcourt, D. (2011). Body dissatisfaction: Can a short media literacy message reduce negative media exposure effects amongst adolescent girls? *British Journal of Health Psychology, 16*(2), 396–403. https://doi.org/10.1348/135910710X515714

We can immediately see that the claim is specific—we know exactly what the topic is (media images and body satisfaction/esteem) and who is being studied (adolescent girls). We can also see that this topic invites discussion. Because the writers frame their claim as a *hypothesis*—a theory or supposition—and make predictions, it is clear that they intend to investigate the matter, add to the current conversation on this topic with a new idea, and invite researchers to respond with further exploration. Given the differences we've just learned between claims asserted as arguments and claims proposed as hypotheses, try the following exercise to confirm your understanding.

EXERCISE 1
PINPOINTING A CLAIM

Read the two research introductions below and see if you can pinpoint the scholar's claim in each. Next, analyse the introductions with the following criteria:

- What exactly is the writer's claim? State it in your own words.
- Is the claim specific? What does it tell you about the research context—who and what is being researched where and when?
- Does the claim respond to other stances and/or invite discussion? How so?

Excerpt 1: Argumentative Stance

Several scholars argue that blackmail is morally wrong because it is coercive (Shaw, 2012; Berman, 1998; Berman, 2011; Fitzpatrick, 1998; Gorr, 1992; Lamond, 1996). These coercion-based views focus on the blackmail proposal, the blackmailer's offer or threat to act in a certain way (paradigmatically, to disclose information whose revelation would harm or embarrass the target of blackmail) unless the target agrees to the blackmailer's demands. On James Shaw's *simple account*, the typical blackmail proposal wrongs the target by unjustifiably impinging his authority to decide what to do.

Coercion-based views are a genuine breakthrough for explaining the immorality of blackmail, which is one of the most-discussed questions in criminal law. Yet although coercion-based views capture a core aspect of why blackmail is wrong, they are incomplete. They do not explain everything that is wrong with blackmail, nor do they offer a fully convincing explanation of why blackmail should be criminalized. Meeting these challenges requires analyzing the blackmail agreement as well as the blackmail proposal.

In this article I defend the *complex account* of why blackmail is wrong. [In] this view, blackmail is typically wrong because the blackmail proposal is coercive and the agreement contemplated in that proposal is fraudulent. The complex account is a friendly amendment to coercion-based views like Shaw's simple account. Compared to alternatives, the complex account provides a more complete explanation of why blackmail is immoral and a stronger case for why blackmail should be criminally prohibited. (pp. 22–23)

Galoob, S. (2016). Coercion, fraud, and what is wrong with blackmail. *Legal Theory, 22*(1), 22–58. https://doi.org/10.1017/S1352325216000082

Excerpt 2: Exploratory Stance

The mass media and the general public are captivated by findings of gender differences. John Gray's (1992) *Men Are From Mars, Women Are From Venus*, which argued for enormous psychological differences between women and men, has sold over 30 million copies and been translated into 40 languages. Deborah Tannen's (1991) *You Just Don't Understand: Women and Men in Conversation* argued for the *different cultures hypothesis*: that men's and women's patterns of speaking are so fundamentally different that men and women essentially belong to different linguistic communities or cultures. That book was on the *New York Times* bestseller list for nearly four years and has been translated into 24 languages (AnnOnline, 2005). Both of these works, and dozens of others like them, have argued for the *differences hypothesis*: that males and females are, psychologically, vastly different. Here, I advance a very different view—the *gender similarities hypothesis* (for related statements, see Epstein, 1988; Hyde, 1985; Hyde & Plant, 1995; Kimball, 1995).

The gender similarities hypothesis holds that males and females are similar on most, but not all, psychological variables. That is, men and women, as well as boys and girls, are more alike than they are different. In terms of effect sizes, the gender similarities hypothesis states that most psychological gender differences are in the close-to-zero ($d \leq 0.10$) or small ($0.11 < d < 0.35$) range, a few are in the moderate range ($0.36 < d < 0.65$), and very few are large ($d = 0.66–1.00$) or very large ($d > 1.00$).

> Although the fascination with psychological gender differences has been present from the dawn of formalized psychology around 1879 (Shields, 1975), a few early researchers highlighted gender similarities. Thorndike (1914), for example, believed that psychological gender differences were too small, compared with within-gender variation, to be important. Leta Stetter Hollingworth (1918) reviewed available research on gender differences in mental traits and found little evidence of gender differences. Another important reviewer of gender research in the early 1900s, Helen Thompson Woolley (1914), lamented the gap between the data and scientists' views on the question: The general discussions of the psychology of sex, whether by psychologists or by sociologists show such a wide diversity of points of view that one feels that the truest thing to be said at present is that scientific evidence plays very little part in producing convictions (p. 372). (p. 581)
>
> Hyde, J.S. (2005). The gender similarities hypothesis. *American Psychologist, 60*(6), 581–592. https://doi.org/10.1037/0003-066X.60.6.581

D. REASONS AND REASONING

Taking a stance requires research scholars to support their claim with reasons and reasoning in order to test or prove its validity on its own terms as well as its value for advancing knowledge in the research community. When scholars test or prove a claim with reasons and reasoning they create an *informed position* that has credibility in the academic world, a claim that is not rooted in opinions or assumptions but in research findings and logic. They use reasons and reasoning to help readers understand their viewpoints, make sense of their conclusions, and embrace their stance.

1. Reasons

Reasons refer to the evidence that research scholars use to test, develop, support, or advance their claims. Different fields of study use different kinds of evidence. In the sciences, researchers tend to use lab findings, field experiments, established theories, and statistical evidence to test and verify their claims. In the social sciences, researchers tend to rely on interviews, testimonies, case studies, and historical trends, as well as field experiments, established theories, and statistics to make and analyse their claims. In the humanities, researchers usually use textual or visual evidence as well as established theories and historical data to support or advance their claims. In other contexts, legal documents and precedents, authorized resources, expert assessment, polls, and personal experience may function to validate a claim.

The most common forms of evidence include the following:

- **Authorized Resources**: Evidence drawn from dictionaries, encyclopedias, governmental documents, legal documents, financial documents, etc.

- **Case Studies**: Evidence drawn from documenting the development of a particular person, group, or situation over time

- **Expert Assessments**: Evidence drawn from experts in the field of study

- **Field Experiments**: Evidence drawn from findings observed in their natural setting

- **Historical Data**: Evidence drawn from documents, records, letters, newspapers, diaries, drawings and other data left by people and/or cultures of the past

- **Interviews**: Evidence drawn from oral or written interviews with others

- **Lab Findings**: Evidence drawn from findings observed in a controlled setting

- **Legal Documents**: Evidence drawn from legal treaties, agreements, declarations, records, codes, proceedings, etc.

- **Legal Precedents**: Evidence drawn from previous court decisions in order to resolve similar questions of law

- **Personal Experience**: Evidence drawn from first-hand experience

- **Polls**: Evidence drawn from canvassing people to obtain information or opinions on a particular topic

- **Statistics**: Evidence drawn from logical, numerical data demonstrating a degree of certainty for a proposition or a hypothesis

- **Testimonies**: Evidence drawn from first-hand witnesses of an event

- **Textual Evidence**: Evidence drawn from primary texts like pieces of literature, scripts, scores, archives, anthologies, etc.

- **Theories**: Evidence drawn from rational, abstract thought used to explain common or concrete phenomena

- **Visual Data**: Evidence drawn from fine art, photography, film, television, video games, advertisements, comic strips, posters, cartography, etc.

EXERCISE 2
PINPOINTING REASONS, RECOGNIZING FORMS OF EVIDENCE

Consider the following examples of evidence used in different fields of study and pinpoint which kinds of reasons from the list above are being used.

Excerpt 1

The most common role attributed to dignity in relation to human rights is as their foundation. This attribution is abundantly evident in the various human rights documents that together constitute a common ground and touchstone for both theorists and practitioners. For instance, the preamble to the Universal Declaration of Human Rights (1948), arguably the most central document for the practice of human rights, refers to the "inherent dignity...of all members of the human family", and Article One claims that "All human beings are born free and equal in dignity and rights." The International Covenant on Civil and Political Rights (1966a), and the International Covenant on Economic, Social, and Cultural Rights (1966b), are even more explicit about attributing a foundational role for dignity, with both preambles "Recognizing that these rights derive from the inherent dignity of the human person." (pp. 1087–88)

Killmister, S. (2016). Dignity, torture, and human rights. *Ethical Theory and Moral Practice, 19*(5), 1087–1101. https://doi.org/10.1007/s10677-016-9725-6

Excerpt 2

According to Biasco, Goodwin, and Vitale (2001), in the general college population, 47% report having witnessed bias on campus. However, that number increases to above 50% among other groups, such as African Americans (D'Augelle & Hershberger, 1993; Fisher & Hartman, 1995). Bias toward homosexuality seems especially prevalent, with 60% of students having heard negative remarks about homosexuality on campus (Malaney et al., 1997). Sexism occurs on campus as well. One study indicated that college women tend to experience sexism once or twice a week (Swim et al., 2001). (p. 507)

Boysen, G.A. (2012). Teachers' responses to bias in the classroom: How response type and situational factors affect student perceptions. *Journal of Applied Social Psychology, 42*(2), 506–534. https://doi.org/10.1111/j.1559-1816.2011.00784.x

Excerpt 3

Many of the participants also shared personal stories in relation to how their experiences in residential school affected their ability to parent, and the negative intergenerational impacts that followed. Here are two examples from Survivors who participated in the study:

> We came out of residential school with all this shame and guilt and everything. I held it in for so many years—that's how I lived. Like her [pointing to another focus group participant], I turned to alcohol and intravenous drugs. You know, it was horrible. (Regina FG participant)
>
> I know when I finished residential school after year [i.e., age] 16 I was full of anger and bitterness. When I started having my children, I turned to alcohol. I didn't know what love was all about. Now I can hug and love my children, but then I couldn't hug them at all. We didn't even like ourselves, you know. For me, I didn't like myself one bit. (Regina FG participant) (p. 7)

Hanson, C. (2016). Gender, justice, and the Indian residential school claims process. *International Indigenous Policy Journal, 7*(1), 1–16. https://doi.org/10.18584/iipj.2016.7.1.3

2. Reasoning

Reasoning refers to the mental processes scholars use to analyse a subject and reach meaningful conclusions about it. Logical reasoning in an academic context involves organizing thoughts in a rational way to develop a stance. Scholars use reasoning to show readers why they are making the claim they are; why they are convinced this claim is valid; and what meaningful conclusions they draw from their argument or exploration to apply to a wider population, other contexts, or a future state. In order to develop a stance, scholars across the disciplines rely on two key forms of reasoning: *deductive* and *inductive* reasoning.

Deductive reasoning is the process of taking a general theory, idea, system, or rule and applying it to a specific case, instance, or situation. It is, as the *Canadian Oxford Dictionary* defines it, the practice of "inferring particular instances from a general law." We can think of deduction as a method of confirming or validating what we have found to be true or believe to be true with actual facts and findings.

This definition sounds confusing in the abstract, but we actually use deductive reasoning all the time. Every time we take a general idea, norm, rule, concept, or theory to be true and then apply it to a specific situation or experience, we have used deductive reasoning. Consider the following everyday examples of deduction:

General Idea Taken to Be True	Specific Situation	Conclusion
Sugar is bad for your health.	This ice cream has a lot of sugar in it.	→ I probably shouldn't eat very much of it.
Plants need water and light to flourish.	My plant is out in the sun, but it's dying.	→ It must not be getting enough water.
Airlines recommend arriving at the airport sixty minutes before departure for check-in and baggage drop-off.	My flight leaves at 2 p.m.	→ That means I should be at the airport by 1 p.m.
A cluttered and messy space is the sign of a creative mind.	My room is a mess.	→ I must have a creative mind!

Similarly, in an academic context, deductive reasoning often begins with a theory, concept, or idea that we believe to be true. Thinkers in logic call this a *premise*. We assert our premise and work to validate it in a specific context by means of reasons (facts and findings). For example, we may assert that "life is nasty, brutish, and short" (as the philosopher Thomas Hobbes did) and work to prove this premise with data in a particular context, like in a society ruled by a corrupt government or in a slum plagued with deprivation and disease. Alternatively, we may have a theory about how best to interpret the novel *Dracula*, and then show how different parts of the text work to prove that theory.

Deductive Reasoning

Many scholars use deductive reasoning when they are writing argumentative or persuasive research papers. Here they rely on a premise to pose their claim and work towards proving it throughout their paper with specific textual examples, historical or cultural data, philosophies, legal documents, or other forms of evidence. They convey their deductive reasoning by using words such as *thus* and *therefore*, showing readers how the specific data validates their claim.

Consider the following example in which the researcher's claim (underlined) and language of *thus* and *therefore* (bold) have been emphasized:

> Understanding the law, it is argued, requires more than simply assessing whether it is effective in accomplishing its intended aims. Such analyses of legal regimes are incapable of accounting for individual experience with the law and thus overlook the decentered nature of power. The law, it is claimed, cannot be understood simply as an external brush acting upon a blankly receptive canvas. Indeed, "individuals come to the law (and the law comes to them) with a body of knowledge, assumptions, ideology, and experience with the law and legal actors that affects whether or not they will assert their legal rights" (Nielsen, 2004, p. 69). **Therefore**, to understand how the law actually works, we require an analysis of the law's actual effects on ordinary people. Looking at, and thinking about, the law in this manner shifts our focus from an instrumental view of legal processes toward trying to understand the actual effects of the law (Engel, 1995, 1998). How does the law affect people? How can we study the way that the law is embedded in social life, normative systems, and social institutions? How is the law experienced in people's everyday realities? (Sarat & Kearns, 1995).
>
> One way to go about this is to study the "legal consciousness" of ordinary people, examining how they think about the law and their understandings of the way that the law actually "works" in their daily lives. In this view, ordinary people provide a point of access to privileged knowledge of the operation of law. **Thus** if we wish to gain knowledge about the actual practice of the law, we must seek to "understand how legality is experienced and understood by ordinary people as they engage, avoid, or resist the law and legal meanings" (Ewick & Silbey, 1998, p. 35). (pp. 826–27)

Berti, M. (2010). Handcuffed access: Homelessness and the justice system. *Urban Geography, 31*(6), 825–841. https://doi.org/10.2747/0272-3638.31.6.825

Notice how the research writer, M. Berti, begins with the general idea that legal regimes cannot account for individual experiences with the law. Nor can the law simply be seen as a set of rules imposed on people. Berti relies on these two premises to deduce his claim: "to understand how the law actually works, we require an analysis of the law's actual effects on ordinary people." In other words, the law must be analysed as it applies to specific situations and individuals. This deduction is reinforced by Berti's use of *therefore* and *thus* to articulate his claim, which he states twice in this short section (see underlined portions). The rest of the paper goes on to support this claim by means of specific evidence and detailed analysis.

Inductive reasoning is the process of looking for an overarching theory, pattern, or trend that makes sense of specific cases, collected instances, or particular findings. It involves putting together information that has been observed (what we already know) to arrive at a conclusion that has not yet been realized (what we don't know). For this reason, it is often called "cause and effect" reasoning or "if/then" reasoning. Inductive reasoning is used to form *inferences* (if this is the case in this instance, then we can expect it to be the case in other instances) and to make *predictions* (if this is the past trend, then we can expect X in the future). Every time we make sense of details in order to construct a big picture, make a prediction, notice trends, or develop expectations, we have used inductive reasoning. Consider the following everyday examples:

Details/Observations	Meaning
Lately I've seen many new and unusual ice cream flavours—like Basil Lime, Blueberry Balsamic, and Mint Curry.	➔ We have developed a strong foodie culture that values innovative and adventurous cuisine.
It's been sunny and hot every day for two months straight.	➔ I predict this heat wave will continue into autumn.
Matt picked me up from the airport the last three times I travelled.	➔ I expect he'll pick me up this time too.
I've got books, papers, pens, and art supplies stacked so high that I can't even see my desk underneath!	➔ So much clutter is surely the sign of a creative mind.

When scholars reason inductively, they make many observations, collate those observations, and trace a pattern or extrapolate a theory from the data they have collected. As they do so, they cannot necessarily know for sure whether their pattern or theory is true, but they hypothesize that it is. As research scholars use this method of reasoning, they may identify trends among specific data in order to formulate a hypothesis that explains these trends; they may propose a general theory to make sense of observations they've made in a specific context; or they may make predictions for the future or inferences for other populations or contexts based on their findings.

Inductive Reasoning

For example, if a group of sociologists observes higher mortality rates from drug overdose in homeless communities compared to other more affluent communities, they might make a hypothesis such as, "We suggest that economic poverty has a greater influence on drug-related deaths than other factors." The sociologists would have based this hypothesis on having closely studied the relationship between poverty, overdose, and death in homeless communities versus those in affluent ones. Over the course of a research paper, they would show readers the validity of their hypothesis by demonstrating how their studies and findings confirm it.

Many scholars use inductive reasoning when they are writing analytical research papers. Here they present their claim as a hypothesis, one they have come to by examining a wide range of cases, data, or trends. They may also use cause and effect language like "if/then" as well as modal verbs like "could" or "should" to indicate their inferences or predictions. Consider the following example in which the researcher's claim and language of "if/then" and modality are emphasized with underlining and bold respectively.

> Both obesity and educational attainment have increased dramatically in the last 40 years. In the United States, the prevalence of obesity (body mass index or BMI 30 and greater) increased from 15% in the 1970s to over one third in 2012 (Ogden et al., 2007; Flegal et al., 2012), whereas the proportion without a high school degree decreased from 45% to less than 10% (author's calculation based on the 1970 Census and 2010 American Community Survey). Obesity is associated with a host of metabolic complications and chronic conditions (e.g., diabetes, cardiovascular disease and cancer), and elevates disability and mortality (Willett et al., 1999; Yu, 2016), whereas post-secondary education is conducive to favorable health outcomes (Smith, 2007; Cutler, 2008). Despite the obesity epidemic, the most educated people are least likely to be obese (McLaren, 2007). Early trend analyses found that the most educated groups have experienced the greatest increases in obesity, and the negative education-obesity association has weakened over time (Zhang & Wang, 2004; Wang et al., 2008; Himes, 2005; Ford et al., 2011); however, recent studies found that although obesity has increased for all educational groups, the education-obesity linkage has remained unchanged or become stronger (Yu, 2012; Ljungvall & Zimmerman, 2012; Krieger et al., 2014; An, 2015)....
>
> The persistent or increased educational inequalities in obesity **suggest** that health programs targeting the less educated groups **could** reduce national obesity levels.... Presumably, **if** the negative education-obesity association prevails throughout the educational spectrum, [**then**] population improvements in education (e.g., by shifting more people to higher educational levels) **should** slow down the obesity epidemic, even without altering educational inequalities in the obesity risk. (pp. 1–2)

Yu, Y. (2016). Four decades of obesity trends among non-Hispanic whites and blacks in the United States: Analyzing the influences of educational inequalities in obesity and population improvements in education. *PLoS ONE, 11*(11), 1–13. https://doi.org/10.1371/journal.pone.0167193

Notice how the research writer, Y. Yu, begins with specific observations about the relationship between obesity and education. He identifies current trends in the area of study with the phrase, "Early trend analyses found...." He also presents a hypothesis about the relationship between obesity and education which he plans to explore in his paper: "The persistent or increased educational inequalities in obesity suggest that health programs targeting the less educated groups could reduce national obesity levels...." Finally, he makes predictions in light of this hypothesis: "Presumably, if the negative education-obesity association prevails throughout the educational spectrum, [then] population improvements in education... should slow down the obesity epidemic...." Here he uses the cause and effect formulation "if/then" to highlight his inferences. He also uses modal verbs that express possibility—"*could* reduce" and "*should* slow down"—to make predictions to his readers based on the trends he sees.

Inductive reasoning can be relatively easy to pinpoint because of the suppositional or speculative language writers use to express trends, inferences, and predictions. Researchers *expect, anticipate, suppose, infer, propose, venture, surmise*, or *predict* that something is true in light of certain observations. As we've seen, "if/then" language is commonly used as well to suggest the cause and effect of a certain phenomenon or to show a particular relationship between things, like obesity and education for instance.

In sum, inductive reasoning tends to be used in research writing where the process is exploratory and researchers develop hypotheses based on research observations and findings. Deductive reasoning tends to be used in research writing where the process is controlled and researchers prove their assertions with research evidence. That said, when scholars engage in analysis, they often bring these two forms of logical reasoning together, building bridges between general ideas and specific data, between hypotheses and observable facts. For instance, a research paper may be presented as an inductive study, but have deductive reasoning embedded throughout. Conversely, a research paper may be shaped as a deductive analysis, but have inductive reasoning posed in its conclusion: What next? Where do we go from here? What can we expect in the future as a result? We will look more closely at how to analyse and think critically about a researcher's reasoning in Chapter 8. For now, let's see if we can locate these two forms of reasoning in the following exercise.

EXERCISE 3
DISCERNING INDUCTIVE AND DEDUCTIVE REASONING

Consider the following two excerpts. Determine whether the research writers are using deductive or inductive reasoning to develop their claims. Give reasons to support your answers.

Excerpt 1

In 1973, John Creech, a physician employed by B.F. Goodrich in Louisville, Kentucky, noticed a strange and alarming coincidence at one of the company's main polyvinyl chloride polymerization factories, for which he served as plant physician. Three years before, in 1970, a patient under Creech's care, a thirty-six-year-old who had worked at the Goodrich facility for fourteen years, was diagnosed with an exceptionally rare liver tumor. The cancer was typed as *angiosarcoma*, a malignancy that arises from cells associated with blood vessels. It is hard to diagnose, both because it is so uncommon and because attempts at biopsy can easily lead to copious bleeding. Furthermore, treatment options are no impetus for early diagnosis. Angiosarcoma, at any stage, carries a very poor prognosis. Creech's first patient died of the disease in 1971, fourteen months after his diagnosis. Even if Creech had a suspicion that the vinyl chloride played a role in the cancer, he would have had nothing solid to go on. A single animal study implicating vinyl chloride as a cancer-causing agent had only just been published in 1971; the cancers identified were not of the same cell type of angiosarcoma. Nevertheless, it was presumed that vinyl chloride could cause liver damage, if not cancer....

The death of the single 1971 angiosarcoma victim seemed to be an isolated event at first. Then, in 1973, Creech became aware of a second and then a third additional death from angiosarcoma of the liver. All were among employees of the same plant. This might have been unusual for even a more common type of cancer. The odds against this as a chance occurrence for angiosarcoma were staggering.... An initial case report by Dr. Creech, coauthored with the Goodrich corporate medical director, [went to] press as a brief "special communication" to the *Journal of Occupational Medicine*, with a summary header acknowledging "the probability that this condition, in some instances, may be causally related to...polyvinyl chloride resins" (Creech & Johnson, 1974). (pp. 71–72)

Blanc, P.D. (2007). *How everyday products make people sick: Toxins at home and in the workplace.* University of California Press.

Excerpt 2

There are many things in the world. We can use some of these things to achieve various ends of ours. Along with many other things that we can use, we can use each other.

We can use each other's bodies. I can use your mass to lift me skyward on the see-saw. I can use your body as a shield as I run away from the opposing team. I can use your body, held in stocks or in prison, to deter those contemplating crime. In a bad spot, I can use your body for food....

We can use people's minds and what those minds contain: ideas, emotions, memories, attitudes of love, trust, respect. I can use your idea as an inspiration for my own, or I can plagiarize you—using your idea as my own.... I can use your love to support me through difficult times. I can use your love to get you to lend me money....

There has been a great deal of philosophical discussion about using people, using people intentionally, using people as a means to some end, and using people merely (or just, or only) as a means to some end. In this paper, I will defend the following claim about using people:

> Not Always Wrong: using people—even merely as a means—is not always (*prima facie* or *pro tanto* or all-things-considered) morally objectionable.

Having defended that claim, I tentatively suggest that the following claim is also correct:

> No One Feature: when it is morally objectionable to use people (either as a means or merely as a means), this is for many different kinds of reasons—there is no one wrong-making feature that every morally objectionable using has in common.

After discussing these claims, I will use them to present and motivate what I call the "precaution" theory of norms against using people. I will conclude by considering a few cases from the criminal law context—cases that are naturally described as using people—to assess the moral appropriateness of this kind of use in these cases, and to demonstrate how the theory applies to the real world. (pp. 777–78)

Guerrero, A.A. (2016). Appropriately using people merely as a means. *Criminal Law and Philosophy, 10*(4), 777–794. https://doi.org/10.1007/s11572-014-9346-x

E. RECOGNIZING STANCES AS RESPONSES

Stances do not exist in isolation. Scholars make claims to engage with and respond to the ideas of others—to show that their stances make a valid and valuable contribution to the scholarly dialogue and knowledge in the field of study. When we examine academic research writing, we realize that each claim a research scholar puts forward is formulated as a response to what other scholars have already said about the topic. In most contexts, scholars begin their writing by affirming what other researchers have said about a subject in a neutral or positive way, sometimes in a summary and other times in a literature review. In doing so, they highlight the range of current research viewpoints on a topic and rely on them as a jumping-off point from which to present their own stance in response.

We can see this movement very clearly in the excerpt by S. Galoob that we looked at in Exercise 1. In his research article, Galoob begins by orchestrating a conversation that shows what research scholars have been saying about blackmail:

> Several scholars argue that blackmail is morally wrong because it is coercive (Shaw, 2012; Berman, 1998; Berman, 2011; Fitzpatrick, 1998; Gorr, 1992; Lamond, 1996). These coercion-based views focus on the blackmail proposal, the blackmailer's offer or threat to act in a certain way (paradigmatically, to disclose information whose revelation would harm or embarrass the target of blackmail) unless the target agrees to the blackmailer's demands.

Galoob focuses on one stance upheld by a number of scholars: that blackmail is morally wrong because it is coercive. In a neutral and unbiased way, he outlines the "coercion-based views" upheld by these scholars. He even goes on to affirm these views:

> Coercion-based views are a genuine breakthrough for explaining the immorality of blackmail, which is one of the most-discussed questions in criminal law.

Next he points out a gap or limitation in the current research that he wants to address. Specifically, he points to limitations in the "coercion-based views" of blackmail (emphasized in bold) and shows how they can be addressed:

> **Yet although** coercion-based views capture a core aspect of why blackmail is wrong, **they are incomplete. They do not explain** everything that is wrong with blackmail, **nor do they offer** a fully convincing explanation of why blackmail should be criminalized. Meeting these challenges requires analyzing the blackmail agreement as well as the blackmail proposal.

So far, Galoob has suggested that the current coercion-based views are beneficial in analysing why blackmail is wrong, but also that they are limited. They don't explain everything that is wrong with blackmail or why blackmail should be criminalized, because (as is suggested in his earlier explanation) they only focus on the "blackmail proposal." Galoob insists that a fuller understanding of why blackmail is wrong requires that researchers look not just at the "blackmail proposal" but also at the "blackmail agreement." With this gap and suggestion in mind, he is now ready to present his claim:

> In this article I defend the *complex account* of why blackmail is wrong. [In] this view, blackmail is typically wrong because the blackmail proposal is coercive and the agreement contemplated in that proposal is fraudulent. The complex account is a friendly amendment to coercion-based views like Shaw's simple account. Compared to alternatives, the complex account provides a more complete explanation of why blackmail is immoral and a stronger case for why blackmail should be criminally prohibited.

Notice how Galoob's claim responds to the limitations he sees in the "coercion-based views" upheld by other scholars. It's not that he thinks their views are wrong or have failed in some way. They simply don't explain or account for the whole picture of why blackmail is wrong. He presents his argument as a "friendly amendment" to these other views, one that adds to the "simple account" upheld by Shaw and others. In response to them, he argues for a "complex account" that focuses on the wrongs of *both* the blackmail proposal *and* the blackmail agreement. He then follows up his claim by indicating two good reasons why his complex view is a valuable addition to the discussion: it "provides a more complete explanation of why blackmail is immoral and a stronger case for why blackmail should be criminally prohibited."

Because research writing functions as a dialogue among scholars, we consistently see researchers presenting their stances as claims in response to the work of other researchers. This is exactly what we do when we dialogue with others in everyday contexts. In ordinary conversations we can respond to what someone else has said in many different ways:

- We can wholeheartedly agree with it.
- We can agree with it and build on it.
- We can partially agree with it, but modify or change it in some way.
- We can generally agree with it, but challenge a certain aspect that doesn't make sense to us or fit with reality as we know it.
- We can think it too simplistic a view and show that the subject is more complex or multifaceted.
- We can point out a shortcoming or limitation in it that needs to be addressed.
- We can disagree with it or challenge it.
- We can question it.
- We can provide solutions for it or offer suggestions to fix it.

Just like in everyday conversations, research responses take a number of different forms. A response-based claim may agree with, modify, complicate, challenge, question, or even oppose current stances on the topic. Below are the most common ways that scholars articulate a claim as an argument or hypothesis in response to other researchers working in the field.

Kind of Response	Typical Formulations
"Yes! And also..." **Agreeing (with modification)** **Building on (with a twist)**	• We agree with these positions; however... • Although I agree with this view, I would add that... • While we agree with this proposition, we also suggest ... • Building on these views, I hypothesize... • Following this trajectory, we predict...
"Hmm. But what about...?" **Addressing limitations and filling gaps**	• Given these limitations, we argue... • One area that has not been addressed is X. As a result, I argue... • In light of this shortcoming, we suggest... • Because this dimension has been overlooked, I suggest... • Despite these findings, I am left with the question...
"Yes, but..." **Complicating a simplistic view**	• This issue is more complex than the research shows, because... • We argue that this is not simply an issue of X, but also of Y. • From another perspective, I propose... • We want to complicate this issue by suggesting...
"Perhaps we could try..." **Posing a solution to a problem**	• The best way to address this problem is... • The key issue in this problem is... • While others have recommended X, I argue that... • There are many solutions to this problem, but I propose...
"No, because..." **Opposing or challenging claims**	• Although others have suggested X, I propose that... • In contrast to these claims, I hypothesize... • As opposed to X, we argue... • I challenge this claim by suggesting... • As an alternative to this view, I propose...

We will consider these templates in more detail in Chapter 9, where we will learn how to present our own stances and craft our claims as responses in a research dialogue. For now, see if you can discern the kind of response used in the following academic excerpts.

EXERCISE 4
STANCES AS FORMS OF RESPONSE

1. Find the claim in each excerpt and underline it.

2. Consulting the chart above, name the kind of response you think each scholar or team of scholars is using to state their claim. (Note that the scholars may be using more than one kind of response or combining different kinds of responses to state their claim.)

Excerpt 1

What is less known about compassion fatigue is the concept's history. Originally a term referring to society's increasing avoidance of social problems (Link et al., 1995) and reluctance to intervene in international conflict (Mestrovic, 1997), compassion fatigue was once thought of as a collective apathy. At what point did compassion fatigue become a healthcare concept? And what might this history reveal about the current use of the term? This viewpoint paper revisits compassion fatigue in light of its historical roots, so as to problematize an otherwise taken-for-granted concept. The argument is made that theorizing compassion fatigue requires an eye toward both history and the unconscious, two dimensions currently neglected in the contemporary healthcare literature. Both of these dimensions can be accounted for and rendered coherent by taking a psychodynamic perspective. Moreover, such a perspective can help better explain compassion fatigue's perpetuation in healthcare settings. (pp. 363–64)

Gerard, N. (2017). Rethinking compassion fatigue. *Journal of Health Organization and Management*, *31*(3), 363–368. https://doi.org/10.1108/JHOM-02-2017-0037

Excerpt 2

The question is whether organic food quality should be defined only according to single food constituents or whether these compounds can be seen as indicators for some of the *product*-oriented quality criteria of organic food. For several years, FQH (Organic Food Quality and Health Association) members, who are experts from different disciplines, have been working on these organic food quality criteria issues. A major challenge is the need to define food quality concepts and methods for determining quality (Kahl et al., 2010). Organic food quality still needs to be developed further; concepts, definitions and evaluation methods may change during this development. Therefore it is not the aim of this paper to present a final statement about organic food quality but to give arguments for a substantial debate on this topic. The goal of this paper is to describe and discuss the topic of organic food quality by focusing on concept development, definition and a framework for evaluation. (pp. 2760–61)

Kahl, J., Baars, T., Bügel, S., Busscher, N., Huber, M., Kusche, D., Rembialkowska, E., Schmid, O., Seidel, K., Taupier-Letage, B., Velimirov, A., & Zalecka, A. (2012). Organic food quality: A framework for concept, definition and evaluation from the European perspective. *Journal of the Science of Food and Agriculture, 92*(14), 2760–2765. https://doi.org/10.1002/jsfa.5640

Excerpt 3

For a number of years, scholars of Jewish history have successfully used postcolonial concepts in their studies. This is particularly true for the history of Middle Eastern and Mediterranean Jewry, but in the field of European Jewish history researchers have also undertaken to bring together postcolonialism and Jewish Studies.... In this essay, I will build on and expand the scope of a postcolonial approach to the history of Central European Zionism by looking at central elements of Buber's political thinking. In addition to his view of the Orient and its significance for Jewish self-perception, I will discuss Buber's ideas on the social and economic constitution of the Arab-Jewish commonwealth in Palestine, as well as his attitude toward the evolving national conflict between Jews and Arabs. On this basis, I will determine the peculiarities of Buber's own nationalism. I will argue that this nationalism, while deeply rooted in European nationalist ideologies, had much in common with the nationalism of anticolonial movements in terms both of its emancipatory intent and of its ambivalent content. It is best understood as a subaltern nationalism that participated in and contributed to the hegemonic nationalist discourse, albeit from a position at the margins of this discourse. (pp. 162, 163)

Vogt, S. (2016). The postcolonial Buber: Orientalism, subalternity, and identity politics in Martin Buber's political thought. *Jewish Social Studies, 22*(1), 161–186. https://doi.org/10.2979/jewisocistud.22.1.05

Excerpt 4

A more nuanced, less didactic understanding of identity may be required if successful challenges to the increasingly punitive criminal justice agenda are to be made. Moreover, the binary distinction of victim/offender is problematic when we listen to the life stories of ex-prisoners as these counternarratives involve more complex identities than analysis through the lens of binary opposites can provide. By incorporating prisoner and ex-prisoner narratives into the wider human rights paradigm, [I propose that] a more responsive and effective paradigm of action, based on restoring justice, repairing harm, and making peace, can be achieved. (p. 119)

Farrant, F. (2014). Reimagining the criminal, reconfiguring justice. In M. Jensen & M. Jolly (Eds.), *We shall bear witness: Life narratives and human rights* (pp. 118–133). University of Wisconsin Press.

CONCLUSIONS

Stances, or research standpoints, function as the basis for most research papers. A stance typically takes the form of a claim—an argument or a hypothesis—that is developed and supported by reasons and reasoning. Research writers take stances to think outside the box, test research findings, prove theories, and contribute to the collective knowledge about the subject. Once we know what to look for, we can pinpoint researchers' claims quite easily and discern the kind of reasons and reasoning they use to engage with the ideas and research of others. As we've come to see, research claims don't stand on their own as solitary assertions or rootless propositions; nor are they combative critiques aimed at tearing apart the work of other researchers. Instead, they build on and respond insightfully to the work of others in the form of a dialogue. Ultimately, researchers develop their work within the research community in order to introduce their insights to the world beyond, applying their research to practical situations and prompting readers to think critically and creatively, respond insightfully, and act wisely in the wider community.

QUESTIONS FOR REFLECTION

1. What kind of research writing have you been reading in your courses? Is it mostly argumentative (or persuasive) research writing that works to prove an argument, or analytical research writing that explores a hypothesis? What are the main differences between these two forms of research writing?

2. When you collect research evidence for a project, what kind of reasons or evidence do you normally rely on? Are you a fan of statistics? Are you drawn to personal stories and testimonials? Are you inclined towards authoritative texts? Or do you prefer lab-

oratory results or findings? Consider the field of study that you are pursuing or the degree you are in the process of completing. What kind of evidence is valued and convincing for *this* research community? How can you add this kind of evidence to your repertoire?

3. In this chapter we have learned how research scholars use deductive and inductive reasoning in order to test, support, or advance a claim. Deductive reasoning is often used to prove a stance or theory with supportive evidence, while inductive reasoning is often used to analyse collected findings in order to explain them or extrapolate from them. What are some daily activities or ordinary contexts in which you use deductive and inductive reasoning?

4. Choose a selection of research articles on a topic of interest (or return to the five articles you chose to answer the reflection questions in Chapter 5). Pick out the research claim in each article and determine the kinds of reasons the scholars are using to make their case. Do the scholars rely mainly on deductive or inductive reasoning to create a convincing argument or explore their hypothesis? How do they present their stance *in response* to the stances of other scholars on the subject? Take notice of the techniques and language they use so you can apply them in your own research writing.

CHAPTER EIGHT

CRITICAL ENGAGEMENT

Analysing Content and Assessing Ideas

In Chapter 7 we learned how to pinpoint researchers' stances and how to distinguish between the types of reasons and reasoning they use to test or prove their claims. In order to be able to respond to them with our own stance, however, we need to go one step further. It's not enough to be able to identify the aspects of a researcher's stance; we also need to be able to analyse the research material and reasoning strategies they present in order to decide what and how to respond to them. In this chapter we will develop our analytical reading and critical thinking skills so that we can participate meaningfully in our written research conversations.

A. CRITICAL THINKING

We often assume that ***critical thinking*** means criticizing or finding fault with someone else's ideas. However, the word "critical" originally comes from the Greek *kritikós*, which means to judge or discern, to make sense of, to evaluate, and to weigh evidence. In academia, we define critical thinking as making sense of ideas, weighing evidence, and making careful judgements in order to reach valid conclusions. These practices are neutral, intellectual activities rather than negative or positive assessments.

In fact, we use critical thinking every day. We engage in logical mental processes, asking ourselves questions in order to reach reasonable conclusions: What will I wear today? What will I eat for lunch? When will I meet up with my friend? These decisions seem simple enough and don't take much critical thought. But they do take mental effort when their context or circumstances become more involved: What will I wear *to my job interview to make my best impression*? What will I eat *in the food court that fits with my dietary restrictions and avoids my gluten allergies*? When will I meet up with my friend *to tell her that I'm dating her ex*? Now our seemingly simple decisions take some analysis and insight to reach.

Critical thinking involves making "the best possible choice from a range of possibilities" (Henderson, 2011, p. 15). In order to reach the "best possible choice," we need to examine and weigh our options, considering the benefits and shortcomings of each. We also need to make inferences about the short- and long-term effects (on ourselves and others) of each option. Depending on what the situation is, we may need to ask hard questions, compare data or experiences, analyse evidence, and reason through the possibilities in order to reach the best one.

Sometimes we don't use our full mental capabilities when making a choice or reaching a conclusion. Our decisions may be rooted in impulse and emotion, which cause us to make snap decisions or jump to conclusions, assuming that what we see in the moment is all there is (Kahneman, 2011, p. 86). In contrast, when we aim to think critically, we don't take information at face value or base our judgements on appearances or assumptions. Instead, we examine the underlying meaning of what we see and scrutinize our opinions and presuppositions.

Critical thinking is a slow and rigorous mental process. In his book *Thinking, Fast and Slow* (2011), psychologist and economist Daniel Kahneman locates the mental processes of critical thinking—such as attention, analysis, comparison, and evaluation—in his "slow" category, meaning that they involve significant mental effort to achieve (pp. 20–24). It takes mental effort to deliberate, to weigh evidence, to ask pointed questions, to discern connections and distinctions between ideas, to evaluate material, and to make fair judgements.

In an academic context, these mental practices are highly valued. Since the focus of academic research is to build new knowledge and to develop a deeper understanding of a subject of study, we must regularly attend to and evaluate the information and ideas proposed by other researchers in our field: What new views or findings do they bring to the dialogue? Are we convinced by their evidence? Do we track with their reasoning? Are we compelled by their conclusions? In this chapter we will discover four key dimensions of critical thinking—*attentiveness, analysis, assessment*, and *fair judgement*—and work through the kinds of questions we need to ask in order to help us engage critically with the research material and scholarly reasoning we read.

B. READING TO UNDERSTAND: DEVELOPING OUR ATTENTIVENESS

Critical thinking begins with our ability to understand research material, concepts, and data (Henderson, 2011, p. 8). As we noticed in Chapters 3 and 4, understanding research writing can feel daunting, especially if we are not accustomed to reading it. Given its specialized prose, the concepts can be difficult to grasp and the material can be confusing. In fact, we likely won't understand the research content fully on our first reading. That's normal. We can, however, deepen our understanding with time and practice and the skill of attentiveness. ***Attentiveness*** involves giving our full attention to what we're reading and asking questions about it so that we can make sense of the material.

The "journalist's questions" are a good place to start. When journalists investigate an event or issue, they ask six basic questions: *What? Where? When? Who? Why?* and *How?* As readers, we can use these same questions to gather the basics of the research material we're reading. Perhaps the three most effective journalist's questions for our context are *what, who*, and *how*. The question "What?" helps us decipher the research content and reasoning strategies in a text. The question "Who?" helps us to attend to the scholarly conversations and contexts surrounding the content. The question "How?" helps us notice the way research ideas are being organized and presented. These key questions can be broken down into sub-questions that guide us into a deeper understanding of what we're reading, as outlined in the following lists.

What: Understanding the Content

- What is the specific topic of the research paper?
- What is the purpose of this research study?
- What are the key terms of the topic? How are they defined and developed?
- What is the researcher's stance on this topic?
- What claim (argument or hypothesis) does the researcher state to reveal his or her stance?
- What other stances does the researcher respond to in making his or her claim?
- What reasons (evidence) does the researcher provide to support this claim?
- What kind of reasoning does the researcher use to convince readers of the accuracy and validity of this claim? Is it deductive, inductive, or a combination of the two?
- What is significant about the researcher's stance? What new knowledge or understanding is being added with his or her research material?
- What conclusions does the researcher reach about this topic of study?
- What areas of this research could use more exploration, explanation, or elaboration?

Who: Understanding the Conversation

- Who is the researcher (or group of researchers) writing this paper?
- Who are the other experts on the topic, according to the research writer?
- Whose work has the research writer consulted, relied on, and brought together in conversation on this topic?

- Whose work does the research writer respond to directly in order to make his or her claim?

- Whose work does the research writer build on, challenge, complicate, question, or modify throughout this paper?

- Who is the intended audience for this research paper?

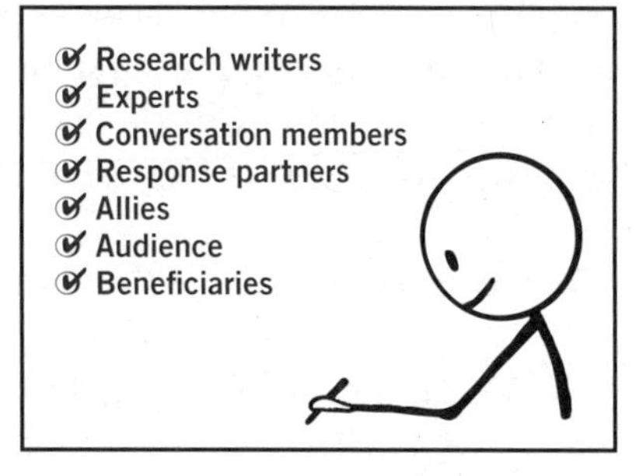

- Who will benefit most from this research material? What communities could be helped or supported?

As we work to understand the content and conversations of a research text, we also analyse its construction: How has it been put together? We trace how a text is constructed by looking at its introduction, body, and conclusion. How are the topic and stance introduced? How are the research points established and explained? And how effective is the conclusion for wrapping up the study? We can also analyse whether the text is clear, organized, and effective for presenting the research material to its intended readers.

How: Understanding the Construction

- How is the introduction constructed?
    - What material is included in the introduction?
    - How are the topic, stance, and research conversation introduced?
    - Is the introduction logical, coherent, and easy to follow?
    - Is the introduction effective for introducing the topic to its intended readers?
    - Is more information needed at the outset of this paper that hasn't been provided?

- How is the body of the paper constructed?
    - How are the main points arranged? Are they in a logical and effective order?
    - Does the research writer include headings? Do these headings help readers follow the researcher's train of thought?
    - Is each point clear and well explained? If not, can you pinpoint the problem?
    - Is each point supported by relevant research evidence and logical reasoning?
    - Is the language and tone suitable for the intended readers of this paper?

- How is the conclusion constructed?
    - How does the conclusion wrap up the research material and ideas?
    - Does the conclusion include a summary of the research stance?
    - Is the conclusion clear about the purpose for the research material presented in

this paper? For example, does it discuss implications, applications, or actions that need to be taken in light of the research presented?
  - Does the conclusion present any research limitations of this study or pose questions for future exploration or experimentation?

Once we've read our collection of research texts with what, who, and how in mind, we can focus on which ideas overlap and which ones differ across the texts. As we saw in Chapter 5, we use these connections and distinctions to better understand and map out the various research stances across different papers.

Connections between Ideas

- What ideas overlap across the texts?
- Which researchers are in agreement with one another?
- What specific viewpoints do they share?

Distinctions between Ideas

- At what point do researchers diverge in their views? List the different stances.
- How does each researcher distinguish their stance from other stances?
- Which stances are most conflicting?

As we can see, asking good questions and reading attentively can help us tackle the difficult material in research texts and bring us to a deeper understanding of them. We have now set the groundwork for interacting critically with what we've read. In fact, we may already have found areas that we want to analyse further; we may have questions about the research evidence that we want to ask; we may have reservations about a line of reasoning that seems inconsistent or incomplete on first glance; or we may have found ideas presented in a disorganized or ineffective way that we want to address.

C. READING TO RESPOND: ANALYSING AND ASSESSING CLAIMS, REASONS, AND REASONING

Once we understand the content, conversation, and construction of what we are reading, we are ready to take our critical thinking skills to the level of analysis and assessment. When we ***analyse*** something, we break it down to examine its essential elements or components in detail. When we ***assess*** it, we evaluate its quality. In this section we will focus on how to analyse and assess the most important dimensions of a research paper—the claim, reasons, and reasoning—in order to be able to respond to them.

As we saw in Chapter 7, a researcher takes a stance on a topic in the form of a claim that he or she tests (a hypothesis) or proves (an argument) by means of reasons and reasoning. For example, a researcher might make the claim, "Eating sugar is worse for your health than eating fat." This issue has been widely debated with keen participants on all sides. We find some participants wholly *for* consuming sugar. We find other participants wholly *against* sugar and pro fat. Other participants may take the stance that neither sugar nor fat is good for the body. Still others may claim that sugar and fat are both necessary in moderation. Regardless of the stances they take, participants join the ongoing dialogue with expert reasons and logical reasoning for making their claims. Why? Because they want to show others that their stance is valid and valuable to the discussion. For example, an invested participant might make the following case:

> Fat is healthier than sugar because of X, Y, and Z. I base my claim on these statistics and those research studies (*expert evidence*). I compare how fat and sugar are taken up differently by the digestive and metabolic systems (*comparative reasoning*), with fat being more effective for optimal functioning. I show how detrimental sugar is to human health and anticipate all potential questions with reasons why it is (*explanation*). I am myself a medical practitioner who has found that a fat-based diet helps aid this, that, and the other disease (*experienced expert = credibility*). Now you should be fully convinced of my claim that fat is healthier than sugar!

When we analyse and assess a research paper, then, we are taking apart a researcher's claim, reasons, and reasoning in order to examine them thoroughly so we can ascertain whether they are logical, credible, and convincing. In short, do they make sense, and do they hold up under scrutiny?

Considering the Claim (Argument/Hypothesis)

- Is the claim specific and compelling?
- Does the claim contribute something new to the ongoing dialogue about this issue?
- Does the claim rest on any underlying assumptions, unstated definitions, generalized ideas about certain people, places, or things, or an unsubstantiated belief?
- In what ways is the claim limited by the context, time period, location, and lens of the researcher?

Weighing the Evidence

- How does the researcher test or prove the claim? What is his or her *methodology*?
- Is there enough evidence to test and prove the claim?
- Is the evidence scholarly and up to date?
- Is the evidence suitable for this context or issue?
- Does the researcher rely heavily on one type of evidence at the expense of others?
- How does the researcher deal with evidence that doesn't fit with his or her claim?

Tracking with the Reasoning

- Does the researcher use deductive logic, proving a claim with specific cases or data?
- Does the researcher use inductive logic, bringing specific cases or data together to develop a general principle or hypothesis?
- Does the researcher explain patterns and clarify details in the findings?
- Does the researcher compare and contrast ideas meaningfully?
- Does the researcher examine the underlying meaning of statements, systems, ideas, relationships, or events in connection with his or her claim?
- How does the researcher explain limitations in his or her research that contradicts his or her claim?
- Are there any gaps or inconsistencies in the researcher's line of reasoning?
- Are the researcher's conclusions relevant and convincing?

Questions like these can help direct us in our analysis and assessment. However, working through lists of questions can also feel overwhelming. Let's step back from the lists, then, and consider what these critical processes look like in practice. In his famous "Letter from Birmingham Jail" (1963) Martin Luther King, Jr. demonstrates excellent critical analysis and assessment skills in responding to a public statement by eight members of the clergy who were troubled by his public protests against racism and his acts of non-violent resistance in Birmingham,

Alabama. He presents these analyses and assessments dialogically, writing *in conversation* with the clergy he is responding to. As we examine the following excerpts, we will see how critical thinking can work in practice and how to begin applying these practices ourselves.

An easy way to get started in our critical analysis is to examine the key words someone uses to make a claim or support a point. Words are slippery things. We often take a word's meaning for granted (especially if we know the word well) or forget that it can have multiple meanings. With this in mind, we begin by asking, "What does this word really mean?" or, "What does the writer mean by this word?"

In his letter, Martin Luther King, Jr. illustrates this practice when he examines the meaning of the word *law*. King indicates that *law* is a general term that needs to be unpacked and carefully defined. How we define our words, he argues, shapes our actions:

> You express a great deal of anxiety over our willingness to break laws. This is certainly a legitimate concern. Since we so diligently urge people to obey the Supreme Court's decision of 1954 outlawing segregation in the public schools, at first glance it may seem rather paradoxical for us consciously to break laws. One may well ask: "How can you advocate breaking some laws and obeying others?" The answer lies in the fact that there are two types of laws: just and unjust. I would be the first to advocate obeying just laws. One has not only a legal but a moral responsibility to obey just laws. Conversely, one has a moral responsibility to disobey unjust laws. I would agree with St. Augustine that "an unjust law is no law at all." Now what is the difference between the two? How does one determine whether a law is just or unjust? A just law is a man-made code that squares with the moral law or the law of God. An unjust law is a code that is out of harmony with the moral law.... Any law that uplifts human personality is just. Any law that degrades human personality is unjust. All segregation statutes are unjust because segregation distorts the soul and damages the personality. It gives the segregator a false sense of superiority and the segregated a false sense inferiority. Segregation...ends up relegating persons to the status of things. Hence segregation is not only politically, economically, and sociologically unsound, it is morally wrong.... (pp. 169–70)
>
> King, M.L., Jr. (1994). Letter from Birmingham jail. In *A time to break silence: The essential works of Martin Luther King, Jr., for students* (pp. 163–183). Beacon Press. (Original work published 1963.)

Rather than get into an argument with the clergy about his willingness to break the law, King takes a step back to consider what exactly is meant by *law*. He suggests that there are at least two kinds of laws: "just laws" that square with moral or natural law and "unjust laws" that are rooted in a particular tradition or culture. King advocates obeying just laws and breaking unjust laws with non-violent resistance. He also implies that simply obeying a law without considering whether it is just or unjust, is a mechanical and uncritical practice that should be questioned.

While we may or may not agree with King's definitions of *law*, we can see from his example that critical thinkers ask what something means in order to respond to it. The clearer and more specific a definition is, the better we can understand the terms we are dealing with, tackle the ideas they represent, and engage intelligently with them. When we think critically, then, we don't take terms, concepts, or customs—like *law*—for granted. Instead, we uncover their underlying meanings and re-examine their conventional uses.

We also engage in critical thinking when we assess a researcher's reasoning. We do this by examining each idea and considering the connections between them. In particular, we ask: "How does one idea logically relate to the next?" Moving logically from one idea to another in a process or sequence is commonly referred to as ***causal reasoning***. In his letter, King assesses the causal reasoning that the clergy put forth. He demonstrates how sound reasoning upholds a logical relationship between the cause of something and its effect or the practice of an action and its result, while faulty reasoning muddles them. Let's take a look at his assessments.

In the excerpt below, King responds to the clergy's disapproval of the non-violent demonstrations taking place in Birmingham by critically assessing their concerns. He observes that while they deplore the demonstrations, they ignore the underlying racist conditions that triggered them. In King's words, the clergy are looking only at the *effects* and not the *causes* or underlying *conditions* of the demonstrations:

> You deplore the demonstrations taking place in Birmingham. But your statement, I am sorry to say, fails to express a similar concern for the conditions that brought about the demonstrations. I am sure that none of you would want to rest content with the superficial kind of social analysis that deals merely with the effects and does not grapple with the underlying causes. It is unfortunate that demonstrations are taking place in Birmingham, but it is even more unfortunate that the city's white power structure left the Negro community with no alternative. (p. 165)

King, M.L., Jr. (1994). Letter from Birmingham jail. In *A time to break silence: The essential works of Martin Luther King, Jr., for students* (pp. 163–183). Beacon Press. (Original work published 1963.)

Here, King points to the importance of being able to assess the relationship between the effect of a given issue or idea and its underlying causes. In causal reasoning, we critically assess how well—logically and accurately—a research writer explains the link between what happens first and what happens next: Does A inevitably cause B? Does B necessarily result from A? As critical thinkers, we must dig into the data we see in order to ask, "What is the root of this problem? What are the underlying causes of this issue? What is the backstory that led to this outcome?" We must also go beyond the data to ask, "What does this data show? What patterns does it reveal? What trends does it produce?" We examine research writing with these questions in mind and assess how the writer has addressed them.

Similarly, King shows us that critical thinking examines the relationship between the *means* (the method or process) and the *end* (the goal or outcome) of an activity. He addresses the clergy's condemnation of the peaceful demonstrations in Birmingham on account of the violence they precipitate. The *end* (violence) does not justify the *means* (peaceful demonstrations), the clergy seem to be saying. But King uncovers their faulty reasoning:

> In your statement you assert that our actions, even though peaceful, must be condemned because they precipitate violence. But is this a logical assertion? Isn't this like condemning a robbed man because his possession of money precipitated the evil act of robbery?... We must come to see that, as the federal courts have consistently affirmed, it is wrong to urge an individual to cease his efforts to gain his basic constitutional rights because the quest may precipitate violence. Society must protect the robbed and punish the robber. (pp. 172–73)
>
> King, M.L., Jr. (1994). Letter from Birmingham jail. In *A time to break silence: The essential works of Martin Luther King, Jr., for students* (pp. 163–183). Beacon Press. (Original work published 1963.)

King questions the reasoning behind the clergy's assertion by suggesting that the *means* (non-violent demonstrations to protest racial segregation) do not logically connect to the *end* (violence) the clergy are condemning. To show that this reasoning is faulty, King uses a simile for comparison: Condemning peaceful demonstrations because they could precipitate violence *is like* condemning a robbed man because his having money could precipitate his being robbed. The peaceful demonstrations, just like having money, are neutral in and of themselves. Neither of them *necessarily* leads to violence. To suggest that one inevitably leads to the other or that one should be condemned in light of the other is not logical thinking.

As King demonstrates in this passage and in the previous one, critical thinkers need to analyse a line of reasoning in order to engage with it and respond to it. We analyse a line of reasoning by asking questions: "Does A necessarily lead to B? Is A meant to produce B? Is B the goal or intended outcome of A? Does A justify B? Does B justify A?" As we analyse these relationships, we ask ourselves whether the connections a research writer has made between A and B make sense logically and prove consistent across other contexts and conditions.

King also assesses the "means and end" relationship in another way. In the case where the clergy *do* logically connect the means and the end of an action, King uncovers the negative intentions behind their logic and the "either/or" thinking that tends to accompany *means-end* reasoning. As King observes,

> You commend the Birmingham police force for keeping "order" and "preventing violence".... It is true that the police have exercised a degree of discipline in handling the demonstrators. In this sense they have conducted themselves rather "nonviolently" in public. But for what purpose? To preserve the evil system of segregation. Over the past few years I have consistently preached that nonviolence demands that the means we use must be as pure as the ends we seek. I have tried to make clear that it is wrong to use immoral means to attain moral ends. But now I must affirm that it is just as wrong, or perhaps even more so, to use moral means to preserve immoral ends. Perhaps Mr. Connor and his policemen have been rather nonviolent in public... but they have used the moral means of nonviolence to maintain the immoral end of racial injustice. (pp. 180–181)
>
> King, M.L., Jr. (1994). Letter from Birmingham jail. In *A time to break silence: The essential works of Martin Luther King, Jr., for students* (pp. 163–183). Beacon Press. (Original work published 1963.)

In this passage, King asks a pointed question about the purpose behind a seemingly moral action: police keeping order and preventing violence. This action may *seem* moral, King reasons, but it is actually being used to support a corrupt agenda and maintain the status quo of racism. As a critical thinker, King refuses to take actions at face value and focuses on their underlying purposes or intentions.

Taking our cue from King, we engage in critical thinking when we question what *seems* to be the case and work to get to the bottom of an issue or idea. This means we look for the underlying assumptions that research writers have when they make their claims and notice when they are simplifying a complex issue or protecting the status quo with their research and ideas. We also take note of whether their purposes suit their methods and whether their methods fit their goals.

Returning to the passage above, we can see that King shakes up the "either/or" logic normally associated with the end and the means of an action. Typically, we *either* hold that (a) a noble goal justifies immoral means, *or* that (b) moral means justify an ignoble goal. In other words, we *either* privilege the end goal (and care less about what we have to do to get there) *or* privilege a meaningful process (and care less about the goal or the outcome). While "either/or" thinking is logical, it divides issues into opposing sides that are mutually exclusive. One can either choose A or B, but not both. If A, then not B. If B, then not A.

King challenges this "either/or" logic as the basis for making sense of complex issues like social justice or racism and opts for "both/and" logic instead. Rather than choose *either* moral ends with immoral means *or* moral means for an immoral end, he suggests, "the means we use must be as pure as the ends we seek" (p. 180). *Both* the means *and* the ends must be moral, King asserts. As a critical thinker, King avoids the "black-and-white" thinking and the rigid reasoning that occurs when we put ideas or actions into either/or categories. Similarly, when we engage in critical analysis, we examine the kinds of connections that are typically made between ideas, issues, or actions, and which contexts or conditions make them problematic or inadequate. We also aim to steer clear of "either/or" thinking in order to consider the multifaceted nature of complex research material.

In sum, we can see that critical analysis and assessment involves the following practices:

- analysing the meaning of words and considering whether terms could be redefined or understood differently

- studying the way ideas are connected to determine if the writer's line of reasoning or the relationships between ideas are logical and coherent

- digging deep to assess the root of a problem, the cause of an issue, the meaning of the data, or the intention behind an action

- questioning commonplace assumptions, attitudes, or actions and suppressing the impulse to take ideas or information at face value

- examining rigid or binary oppositions (like "either/or" thinking) and imagining how they could be revised to account for complex situations and practices

With these practices in mind, let's take note of the dialogic writing strategies that King uses to make his critical thinking clear. He often *affirms* or concedes to an aspect of the clergy's assertions before he challenges them; he *asks* numerous questions as he probes the logic of the clergy's assertions; he regularly uses the word *but* as he *rebuts* the ideas of the clergy that concern him; and he consistently *explains* his reasoning as he subverts that of the clergy's. These are handy strategies to use as we communicate our critical thought to others. Keeping these strategies in mind, see how well you can pinpoint the different aspects of King's critical thinking in the following exercise.

EXERCISE 1
ANALYTICAL REFLECTION

Analyse the excerpt below from Dr. King's "Letter from Birmingham Jail" and determine what aspects of critical thinking he uses. Also, highlight the writing strategies he uses to make his critical thinking clear to his audience.

> You may well ask: "Why direct action? Why sit-ins, marches and so forth? Isn't negotiation a better path?" You are quite right in calling for negotiation. Indeed, this is the very purpose of direct action. Nonviolent direct action seeks to create such a crisis and foster such a tension that a community which has constantly refused to negotiate is forced to confront the issue. It seeks so to dramatize the issue that it can no longer be ignored. My citing the creation of tension as part of the work of the nonviolent-resister may sound rather shocking. But I must confess that I am not afraid of the word "tension." I have earnestly opposed violent tension, but there is a type of constructive, nonviolent tension which is necessary for growth. Just as Socrates felt that it was necessary to create a tension in the mind so that individuals could rise from the bondage of myths and half-truths to the unfettered realm of creative analysis and objective appraisal, so must we see the need for nonviolent gadflies to create the kind of tension in society that will help men rise from the dark depths of prejudice and racism to the majestic heights of understanding and brotherhood. (pp. 166–67)

King, M.L., Jr. (1994). Letter from Birmingham jail. In *A time to break silence: The essential works of Martin Luther King, Jr., for students* (pp. 163–183). Beacon Press. (Original work published 1963.)

As we develop our critical analysis and assessment skills it can be helpful to begin with easier material than academic research writing. Try out your critical thinking skills on advertisements, online articles and blogs, or news reports. Then apply your skills to more difficult prose like research writing. The following exercise is a good starting point to begin your practice.

EXERCISE 2
ANALYSIS AND ASSESSMENT

Analyse the material below with the following questions in mind:

- Are key terms directly defined or just assumed? Are any word choices questionable?
- Is the line of reasoning logical? Are there any gaps or inconsistencies between ideas?
- Does the message respond to or challenge other ideas clearly and coherently?
- Are the conclusions valid?
- Does the text rely on assumptions or overgeneralizations?
- Does the text raise any questions for you?

Excerpt 1

Being in a car changes who we are. We dehumanize other drivers. We refuse to let them merge; we tailgate and block. We forgive our errors and overestimate our competency: the vast majority of drivers believe they have above-average skills. We prefer large cars or SUVs because they feel safer, though studies indicate that the safer we perceive ourselves to be, the less sensibly we drive. (SUV drivers are more likely to not wear seatbelts and to drive drunk. And sitting up high makes us think we're going slower than our actual speed.) We are each the centre of our own traffic universe.

Gillmor, D. (2016, July 20). Stuck: Traffic is ruining our lives—but we can be saved. *The Walrus.* https://thewalrus.ca/stuck/

Excerpt 2

The race to become the greenest city in the world is a friendly but fierce competition. It's friendly because when one city succeeds, we all benefit from the shared knowledge, improved health of our planet and new opportunities for the green economy. The race is fierce because the stakes are high. In fact, the earth requires a world full of greenest cities if we hope to maintain our collective standard of living for generations to come.... Together, Vancouver's communities, businesses, and organizations have shown the world what it means to build a healthy, connected and sustainable future. We will continue to show the world that Vancouver is leading in the global movement for a more sustainable world. (p. 3)

Greenest City: 2020 Action Plan, Part 2. (2015). Hemlock Printers.

D. MAKING FAIR JUDGEMENTS

As we have seen, thinking critically about someone else's research and ideas demands attentiveness, analysis, and assessment. We engage in these practices in order to make fair judgements about their work. Fair judgements begin with an open mind. This open-mindedness helps us to avoid the misjudgements or judgementalism that can result from quick and careless reading or biased personal opinions. Fair judgements also involve weighing evidence and seeing multiple sides of an issue in order to reach conclusions about the work. In fact, the word ***judgement*** denotes the ability to use our critical faculties to discern and decide on the merits of a thing in question (*Canadian Oxford Dictionary*). When we think of fair-minded judges in a court of law, for example, we expect them to make just and equitable judgements through a careful examination of the facts, testimonies, and evidence, alongside intelligent reasoning and insightful questions, in order to reach a verdict. We all want our ideas to be judged fairly with equity, justice, and care, so we extend that same consideration to others.

How, then, do we make fair judgements about a researcher's work? The first thing to remember is that making judgements doesn't mean finding fault with or poking holes in the research we read. Instead, it is a fair-minded process geared to help us reach a conclusion about a work of research. It involves at least four practices:

- **Setting the Criteria for Assessment**
  Fair judgements begin with a clear set of criteria by which to judge a work of research. We've already seen the most important criteria to consider: a clear claim, a logical line of reasoning, convincing evidence, insightful analysis, engagement with other research, coherent organization, meaningful conclusions, etc. We can judge the merits and quality of these elements by applying the questions from Sections B and C to the research text

we're evaluating. They represent our set of criteria. Ultimately, we want to judge how accurate, valid, reasonable, and convincing the research is that we are examining.

- **Assessing the Research Context and Conversation**
  A fair judgement involves gathering a wide range of research texts that demonstrate various perspectives on the topic in order to discern where the particular text being evaluated fits into the conversation. We judge each researcher's material and ideas fairly by examining how he or she responds to and engages with other research material. No one's research material or stance can stand alone. Looking at a specific research paper within a broader context helps us to discern where there may be gaps in a researcher's evidence, missing material, limited analysis, or areas for further study.

- **Discerning the Research Purpose and Value**
  Fair judgements are also a matter of discerning the purpose and value of the research text we're reading. We can judge the text's value by examining its effects, importance, or usefulness in the research community as well as in the wider community: What is the purpose of this research? What does this research add to the current discussion on this topic? Are its conclusions fitting for the given situation and audience? Where does its trajectory lead? What is the upshot of this research, its outcomes or effects? What can it do in the world? Who does it help? What does it change?

- **Taking a Stance**
  Finally, making a fair judgement means taking a stance on the research material and deciding how we will respond to it with our own claim. Like a fair judge reaching a verdict, we must weigh the evidence, listen carefully to all the data, and examine the lines of reasoning in order to reach our stance with equity, justice, and care. Ultimately, we will need to decide which aspects of the research we support, which aspects we will build on, which aspects we find limited, which aspects we deem questionable or problematic, and which aspects we disagree with, in order to respond with our claim. We will learn strategies for doing so in the following chapter.

It takes time and care to make fair judgements because doing so involves bringing together all the other aspects of critical thinking in order to draw conclusions about someone's research and to reach a stance. Many of us struggle to engage deeply in this way because we are so used to making snap judgements in other contexts of communication. For example, we are invited to share our instant reactions to blogs, videos, posts, images, media statements, and online articles in ways that don't utilize our critical thought. The results may be provocative or humorous, but they don't resemble the kind of responsible and fair-minded engagement called for in academic contexts. When it comes to reading and responding to academic research, we have to think differently—slowly, methodically, perceptively, and equitably.

EXERCISE 3
FAIR JUDGEMENTS

Read through the following research writing excerpt and determine the set of criteria you would use to make a fair judgement about this work. Also, consider the following questions:

- What wider body of evidence would you need to examine in order to identify how the research writer is responding to the surrounding research on this topic?
- What value might this work have? For whom?
- What reasonable and fair-minded stance might you take in response to it?

My seven-year-old daughter came home from after-school club, sat down at the computer and found a website called kizi.com, which she had been playing on at school. A banal, colourful click-and-drag hairdressing scenario appeared and she settled down. About 15 minutes later, I noticed a very different scene. The background was bright pink and the scene was a hospital bed with a pregnant cartoon female. She was staring worried and wide-eyed from the screen, with a black eye and tears brimming, covered in bruises and scratches, and spiked with what looked like large thorns.

That was my introduction to the world of online pregnancy games for girls. www.mafa.com, a games hub, is home to 'the best free girl games' online. Styled in bright pink and purple, the site has hundreds of cooking, makeover, baby-care, dressing-up, bridal and party-prep games, featuring big-eyed, lustrous-haired, mainly Caucasian teens with a large contingent of cartoon celebrities from Disney and television, including Elsa (*Frozen*), Rapunzel (*Tangled*), Ariel Sofia (*Princess Sofia*) and Dora (*Dora the Explorer*). In amongst these are slightly less-expected scenarios, including dentistry, surgery and pregnancy.

At first glance, as an adult female and mother, whose work involves digital media production and learning, my semiotic sirens went off loudly. The excessive pink was one thing; the ultra-fem characterisation (a Barbie/anime mash-up) was another. The context was something else. I do not necessarily recognise all the Disney princesses out of context (in the emergency room as opposed to the enchanted forest), so to me the graphics immediately suggested teen pregnancy and domestic violence. A young woman beaten by the boyfriend who had knocked her up? But was this an overreaction to a simple fantasy-land aesthetic with some (probably copyright-infringing) characterisation thrown in as an easy hook?...

Parental anxiety around screen time and digital content is high and increasing (Byron, 2008; Palmer, 2007). Young girls feeling pressured to conform to body images, gender stereotypes and sexualised selves from a young age, juxtaposed with the contradictory identities of childhood, is also well reported (Coy, 2009; Robinson, 2013). As the images (and communities) that our children have access to online are proliferating, the feeling of losing control or influence (and the associated guilt) has to be balanced with the reality that each older generation has fretted about unsuitable cultural influences or technologies with regard to their children. (pp. 163–64)

Sinker, R., Phillips, M., & de Rijke, V. (2017). Playing in the dark with online games for girls. *Contemporary Issues in Early Childhood, 18*(2), 162–178. https://doi.org/10.1177/1463949117714079

E. CRITICAL ENGAGEMENT IN PRACTICE: WRITING A CRITICAL ANALYSIS

In certain fields of study, we use and develop our critical thinking skills by writing critical analyses. A ***critical analysis*** is a formal and objective assessment of a text that examines the writer's communication style and effectiveness—the *means* and *methods* a writer uses to convince us of his or her standpoint and the benefit of his or her research. These analyses are found particularly in the humanities disciplines, like literature, religion, philosophy, art, film studies, cultural studies, etc., where a researcher's ability to argue and convince readers of a claim is central to the research dialogue.

As we learned in Chapter 7, the *means* and *methods* by which we convince others is called *rhetoric*. For this reason, a critical analysis may also be called a ***rhetorical analysis*** in certain research communities. This kind of analysis takes apart a research text to examine its content, construction, and effect. We ask, "*How* and *how well* does this research writer communicate his or her stance or claim, evidence, reasoning, and conclusions?" Depending on the context, we may also include our reasons for assessing the text as we do and the stance we take in response to it.

We write critical analyses in order to understand how a research text is constructed, to evaluate its stance for clarity and effectiveness, and to assess the importance of its stance in the research community. We also write critical analyses to become skilled at articulating our own assessments and our reasoning to others.

Writing a critical analysis of a research text is a two-part process. First, we carefully read, analyse, and assess a text for the following elements:

- the scholar's purpose in communicating the research from his or her particular stance
- the research context and community in which the scholar is participating

- the effectiveness of the text's claim, reasons, and reasoning
- the effectiveness of the scholar's organization, language, and tone to communicate the claim, evidence, and conclusions
- the overall effects of the research on/for the intended audience
- the limitations of the research for fully understanding the subject of study

Second, we write critical analyses using essay structure as well as a neutral and objective tone. We may use the pronoun *I* as we write but we do so sparingly, since the analysis is not a personal opinion piece but a critical assessment of someone else's research and ideas. Consider using the following structure as you compose your critical analysis:

- **Introduction**
  - Name the text and research writer(s) as well as any relevant background and publication information.
  - Give a brief summary of the text's stance and approach.
  - Compose a short thesis that addresses the text's main features and explains what makes the text important (or limited) and effective (or ineffective) for the study of the topic and/or the scholarly dialogue in which it is engaged. Note that you may find the research text significant and effective in some ways and limited in others. Your goal is to be honest and direct about both the convincing and unconvincing elements of a text rather than frame it as either all positive or all negative.

- **Body**
  - Support the thesis by drawing on all the analytical information you gathered when reading and assessing the text. For example, perhaps your thesis is that the research text offers a persuasive argument that is well supported with research evidence but doesn't contribute any new knowledge to the research community in this field. You would then use your body paragraphs to support this thesis with reference to the text itself to provide evidence for this analysis and assessment.

- **Conclusion (Optional)**
  - Reiterate the thesis and your reasons for making it, and offer a final thought: What do your reasons add up to?

To see how these elements fit together, consider the following critical analysis. While this analysis assesses a mental health reference guide rather than a research text, it reveals the key components of this genre: it analyses how the text is constructed and the effects of that construction on the audience, and it assesses the influence, value, and validity of the text for building the academic community's knowledge and expanding their viewpoints. For clarity, the introductory paragraphs, body paragraphs, and conclusion are signalled in the margin and the thesis is underlined.

Introduction: Text named, relevant background and publication information discussed

I received the "Quick Reference Guide: Assisting Students in Distress" at the end of 2014 (UVic, 2014b). Every faculty member was given one as part of a three-year initiative (2014–2017): the University of Victoria (UVic) Student Mental Health Strategy, a "framework that provides direction for the Division of Student Affairs and the broader university community for a holistic and comprehensive approach to student mental health" (UVic, 2014a). The somewhat vague wording of this UVic initiative seemed to reflect the uncertainty that continues over issues of mental health on campus, and beyond—a once-tabooed topic, stigmatised (still stigmatised), a subject to be awkward and unsure about, even fear. The Strategy also reflected any number of similar initiatives across university campuses in North America and Europe, which are struggling to deal with a rising incidence of mental health problems among students. It was good to see an attempt to address student mental health...and the four glossy pages of the UVic Reference Guide seemed appropriately timed to allay some of that fear and offer a resource that might be helpful to both faculty and students....

Introduction: Thesis articulated and outline of paper provided

Over three years later, the same Guide is still in use and can be found as a pdf online. What intrigued—and concerned—me was a conflict in the rhetoric of the Guide that nicely reflects a historical dichotomy of care and fear that has long governed our uncertain response to mental illness. A simple resource of information for faculty suggests awareness and care for those with mental health issues (and for this, institution and resource should be praised); but this sense of care, and arguably the resource itself, is undermined by a recourse to fear, so that not mental illness but rather Madness is glimpsed on the page—Madness which has traditionally been seen and represented as a threat that must be contained. In the remainder of this article, I conduct a brief rhetorical analysis of the UVic Guide to "Assisting Students in Distress," to highlight the continuing sense of fear that surrounds issues of mental illness and troubles a university response to the crisis on campus. My aim is not to simply criticise the resource; rather, I seek to generate discussion that will help us further improve services and resources for students, staff and faculty....

Body: Thesis supported with analysis and assessment of the text

On its cover, the Guide sets out a passive, non-confrontational visual and written rhetoric to represent a sensitive issue: an appeal to pathos, to an emotional calm; yet it suffers from being too passive, so appearing to avoid rather than clearly address its topic. A neutral purple and yellow colour scheme sets the tone on the cover, with a stock computer image of three light-green centric circles at its centre; within these sit three purple flowers and three purple leaves. The image reassures—its simplicity and 'threes' offer balance and symmetry, reminiscent of a zen pool with floating blossom; in other words, this Guide is a calm response to the "distress" of the student highlighted in the title. But what is this distress? A student stuck up a mountain, drowning at sea? The title is unclear, its logos poor. Subtitles introduce the "Mental Health Initiative," clarifying focus a little, and then the resource offers, on the first inside page, lists of "Possible Signs of Student Distress" and then "Tips for Assisting a Student in Need"—again, in vagaries of description. Like any public service piece, the information suffers from having to be brief, so oversimplifying, and from offering almost banal advice, such as if a student seems to have a problem, then talk to him/her.... The signs of distress as listed also remain rather vague, and include signs of social withdrawal, alcohol and drug use, expressions of violence and feelings of hopelessness—not necessarily signs of mental illness.... We remain uncertain as to what it is we are dealing with here—mental health is not mentioned, and although alluded to ("hopelessness"), depression is conspicuous by its absence, considering it is the main mental health issue on campus right now. The careful, thoughtful passivity ultimately says less than it should (a failure in logos, in information), trying to avoid a topic it is perhaps uncomfortable addressing, instead creating further uncertainty—referring to something that cannot be named, misdirecting its pathetic appeal and even creating a subtle sense of fear.

This fear is more pronounced on page three, entitled "Recognising Concerning Student Behaviour".... Three options are given to the reader: (1) observe, "Uncharacteristic Behaviour" and respond, "Gather Information and Seek Advice"; (2) observe, "Disruptive or Distressed" behaviour and respond, "Timely Consultation Required" (but with whom?); and (3) observe, "Dangerous, Threatening or Violent Behaviour" and respond, "Immediately Report." The choices are (necessarily?) reductive, and speak to a tradition of psychiatry that reduces complex individual experiences to symptoms, rather than—as advocated by Mad Studies—consider the various social contexts of the individual (Menzies et al., 2013)....

Body:
Thesis supported with analysis and assessment of the text

More troubling is the visual rhetoric of the page, particularly option 3: "Dangerous, Threatening or Violent Behaviour," which is positioned central to a two-page spread and coloured red. Red for danger. This dominates the inside pages—this is where your eyes immediately go when you open the Guide. The diagram seems to highlight information relating to the threat the student poses, not the help we might provide—the focus seems wrong. An arrow then points from "Immediately Report" to telephone numbers for emergency services and campus security. Indeed, the 9-1-1 number for emergency services is given six times in the Guide, four times on page three alone. Campus Security, however, is the most cited number at seven times, far more than the number for Counselling Services (twice) and Health Services (twice). Why do we require these numbers so many times? Again, the emphasis highlights "threat" and not "help".... The lesser threats of options 1 and 2 on the diagram connect to the more useful telephone numbers of Counselling and Health Services, but this list entitled "See Something, Say Something" offers a rhetoric reminiscent of war-time safety propaganda...that remind us to be vigilant for terrorist threats. Is this an unintentional emotional appeal to fear due to the poor wording of information; is it a logical appeal cloaked in pathos to emphasise the importance of this information? Or does the writer really want to instil fear of mental illness into the reader? The Guide then positions—unwittingly or not?—the distressed student as a threat, akin to a terrorist or bomb that might explode at any moment on campus....

Ultimately, the Guide portrays student "distress" (mental illness) as a threat to class, campus and more immediately to the member of faculty dealing with the student/threat. The drive to care, which can be read in the production of this Guide and its intent to offer helpful information, is overpowered by a stigma of fear long attached to mental illness. Considering that depression is the main concern on campus—an illness not generally associated with violent outburst and attacks (in fact, most common mental illnesses are not)—the rhetoric...of the Guide appears misfocused. In our drive to aid those with mental illness, and be more mindful of the stresses faced by university students, it seems that we still cannot escape a reading of Madness. What, then, is the effect of the Guide on the reader? What response to a student with mental illness does it encourage from the faculty or staff member? Perhaps the reader is unconsciously just a little more unsympathetic, a little more tense, fearful, when "confronted" by a student with mental health problems, and left wondering which telephone number is best to call. Madness, here, breaks free of its medical redefinition as mental illness, escaping through the vagaries of "distress" and a fear for personal safety, remaining something that we do not understand. The Guide reminds us that we need to look closely at how we read and represent mental illness on university campus; we must leave behind a rhetoric of fear (so ingrained that it manifests unintentionally?), if the mental health crisis is to be looked at, not only in a more caring, compassionate manner, but in—perhaps more importantly—an original and creative (indeed, dare I write, critical) way, so that we might at least begin to understand the crisis on campus. (pp. 1–7)

Conclusion: Thesis and reasons reiterated; what the reasons add up to

Hawkes, J. (2019). A quick reference guide to mental health on university campus: A brief rhetorical analysis of fear. *Disability & Society, 34*(1), 1–7. https://doi.org/10.1080/09687599.2018.1536841

CONCLUSIONS

Critical thinking involves a set of complex mental processes that do not come naturally to most of us. It takes time and practice to make sense of ideas, weigh evidence, analyse and assess material, and make fair judgements. We can learn these skills by examining how other thinkers do it, reading attentively and asking key questions about a text, and writing critical or rhetorical analyses. Through our processes of critical thinking, we learn to hold our opinions and snap judgements loosely in order to examine and engage with the ideas of others as thoroughly and objectively as possible. Critical thinking is not just a skill we hone in academic contexts. It is a life skill we cultivate in order to make good decisions; to understand ourselves and others; to make sense of our social, political, and economic systems; and to recognize flaws and inconsistencies in the media. Critical thinking is not our automatic default position when we take in and process information. We have to choose it every time. But it's worth choosing if we want to engage meaningfully with others and be equitable in our responses.

QUESTIONS FOR REFLECTION

1. We each have strengths and weaknesses when it comes to our critical thinking skills; some aspects of critical thinking come more easily to us than to others. Which aspects of critical thinking—attentiveness, analysis, assessment, or fair judgement—do you find come easiest, and which ones do you find more challenging? What are some practical steps you can take to hone the critical thinking skills that you find more difficult to practise?

2. As we delved into Martin Luther King, Jr.'s exemplary model of critical thinking, what did you find most striking in his responses to the clergy and in his manner of responding? Why? What can you draw from his model to use in your own critical thinking practices?

3. In the spring of 2017, Martin R. Schneider tweeted about a workplace experiment he and his female co-worker Nicole tried after he accidently signed off on emails to a client using her signature. When he indicated to the client that he was actually Martin and not Nicole, the client's tone changed considerably and became much more respectful and agreeable. Concerned that men and women were not receiving the same respect in the workplace, Martin and Nicole decided to switch signatures for a week to see what would happen. Martin tweeted the following about his experience:

   I was in hell. Everything I asked or suggested was questioned. Clients I could do in my sleep were condescending. One asked if I was single.

   Nicole had the most productive week of her career. I realised the reason she took longer is because she had to convince clients to respect her.

> By the time she could get clients to accept that she knew what she was doing, I could get halfway through another client.
>
> I wasn't any better at the job than she was, I just had this invisible advantage.
>
> Schneider, M.R. [@SchneidRemarks] (2017, March 9). *So here's a little story of the time @nickyknacks taught me how impossible it is for professional women to get the respect they deserve* [Tweet]. Twitter. https://twitter.com/SchneidRemarks/status/839910253680553988

This ordinary experiment reveals how easily we can make assumptions about other people without even being aware of it. All it took was a simple name change for Martin and Nicole to receive different treatment. Making snap judgements about others (and being disrespectful as a result) happens when we don't think critically about our assumptions and our ways of engaging with others. What are some practical ways that you can critically analyse and challenge common assumptions about certain people, places, activities, or beliefs?

4. Critical thinking involves making fair judgements about what we see, hear, and read. In an academic context, we make fair judgements by evaluating research findings and ideas by means of a clear set of criteria and a wide range of research evidence. That way we can discern the value of the work and take a reasonable stance in response to it. Consider the following research excerpt and determine how you would go about judging the work fairly. What specific steps would you take?

> Free societies employ a variety of institutions in which speech is heavily regulated on the basis of its content in order to promote other desirable ends, including discovery of the truth. I illustrate this with the case of courts and rules of evidence. Of course, three differences between courts and the polity at large might seem to counsel against extending that approach more widely. First, the courtroom has an official and somewhat reliable (as well as reviewable) arbiter of the epistemic merits, while the polity may not. Second, no other non-epistemic values of speech are at stake in the courtroom, whereas they are in the polity. Third, the courtroom's jurisdiction is temporally limited in a way the polity's may not be. I argue that only the first of these—the 'Problem of the Epistemic Arbiter' as I call it—poses a serious worry about speech regulation outside select institutions like courts. I also argue for viewing 'freedom of speech' like 'freedom of action': speech, like everything else human beings do, can be benign or harmful, constructive or pernicious. Thus, the central question in free speech jurisprudence should really

be how to regulate speech effectively—to minimise its very real harms, without undue cost to its positive values. In particular, I argue against autonomy-based defences of a robust free speech principle. I conclude that the central issue in free speech jurisprudence is not about speech, but about institutional competence. (pp. 407–08)

Leiter, B. (2016). The case against free speech. *Sydney Law Review, 38*(4), 407–439.

CHAPTER NINE

RESPONSE-ABLE STANCES

Developing a Dialogic Research Position

By this stage in our research process, we know that scholars are in conversations all around us. We can identify where they stand, what they claim, and how they support and reason out their ideas dialogically in a research community. As we've interacted with their work, we've become skilled at listening, interpreting, representing, acknowledging, analysing, and evaluating their research and ideas ethically. Now comes the exciting part, where we get to represent our own ideas in response to what we've researched and read: What do I see? What do I think? How do I understand these research findings? What can I add to this dialogue? We raise our voices to assert where we stand on a subject, and we join the research dialogue with our stance, communicating our ideas and the reasons behind them to others.

In this chapter, we will learn how to position our research stance as a claim that responds to the ideas and findings of other researchers. We will also examine two models commonly used in academic research writing for developing this response-able stance—a *debate model* and a *discussion model*. Drawing on these models, we will be able to communicate our research position and line of reasoning dialogically when it comes to our own research writing.

A. TAKING A RESPONSE-ABLE STANCE

When we take a stance on a research topic, we assert our *agency*—our ability to speak and act in the world—in order to represent our views and findings. At the same time, we realize that our standpoints are never stand-alone points. They are always responses to other standpoints that we agree or disagree with, build on or challenge, question or affirm. We call these ***response-able stances***. When we take a response-able stance, we communicate our views and findings as they relate to and respond to the views and findings of other researchers. In the process, we demonstrate how we have come to our views and how they build on established research knowledge (Arnett et al., 2009, p. 55). Our academic readers need to know who and what we are responding to when we take our stance so that our ideas make sense and have significance. With this in mind, let's take a few moments to review our research context and community.

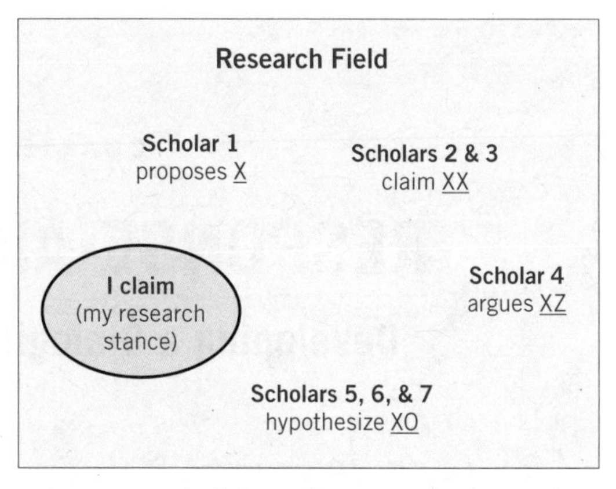

As we know, whenever we research a topic we step into a field of study and join an academic community interested in that subject. To take a stance within that community, we need to figure out where we stand in relation to where the other researchers stand on the topic. To figure out where we stand, we ask ourselves, "Which aspects of this research are most compelling to me?" and, "What do I want to contribute to this discussion?" We join a dialogue by focusing on the research we find most interesting or insightful on the topic: "Whose ideas draw me in and inspire me to think in new ways?" We also contribute to this dialogue by taking note of what researchers haven't yet said about the topic: "What is missing from the conversation?" "What gaps exist in the research?" "What ideas haven't been considered in depth or addressed fully?" Every time we question a point a researcher has made—wishing that the material was addressed from a different angle, time period, or viewpoint; wondering who and how the research is helping; or noticing that a certain demographic (race, class, ethnicity, gender, age, etc.) has been left out of the research—we have just discovered an opening in the dialogue where we can step in with our stance.

For this stance to be credible and convincing in our academic community, we present it as a compelling claim that is grounded in research evidence and reasoning. A groundless claim is called an *opinion*. Since we share our opinions constantly in ordinary conversations and on social media, we may assume that our opinions are suitable for readers in academic communities as well. However, opinions hold little credibility in research writing because they tend to be reactive responses rooted in snap judgements rather than in critical analysis. Opinions also lack verifiable research evidence to back them up, evidence that is accepted and respected by researchers in the field of study. To convince readers of our stance, then, we must have "ground" under our feet on which to "stand" (Arnett et al., 2010, p. 118). Our research is the ground that gives depth and validity to our stance and helps our ideas stand up under scrutiny.

To write dialogically and benefit the community with our stance, we must not only be aware of our research context but also be mindful of our research relationships. We become truly *response-able* to others in our research writing when we see ourselves as *responsible* for our claims and interactions. To be response-able means that we take responsibility for our voice and use it to contribute beneficially to the conversations we are in. In other words, we are responsible for our responses.

How, then, do we communicate our response-able stance in a responsible way? First, as we've already seen in the previous chapters, we begin by acknowledging and affirming what other researchers have said about a topic before we assert our stance. We also interact with the research of others respectfully as we establish our points, so that each one of our ideas is rooted in the current research dialogue on the topic. This means our response-able stances are receptive and responsive at every turn.

Second, we ensure that our response-able stances are active. We assert our agency and represent our ideas and findings with confidence and conviction. But we do so without being combative. We do not approach research knowledge as a power struggle between ideas or between researchers, but as a multi-sided discussion in which we work together to seek out how best to understand a topic. This means that even though we assert our stance from our particular standpoint, we always do so with openness towards other views. We represent new theories or concepts in relation to old ones, combine current ideas to offer deeper insights on a subject, and revise outdated or inadequate research findings respectfully. In the process, we make sure our voice does not dominate or drown out anyone else's voice. Ultimately, we assert our stance as one plausible, well-researched position among others, one that participates in the research dialogue responsibly without arrogance or antagonism.

Third, we work hard to craft our language and line of reasoning in order to show readers the value and validity of our stance. We call this "rhetorical competence." As we saw in Chapter 7, *rhetoric* refers to the means and methods we use to persuade others of our stance. And *competence* refers to how skilfully we can do that. We may think this means using language and logic to win readers over to "our side" or to render them speechless with our brilliance; but actually, in research writing we aim for rhetorical competence in its best possible sense: using language and logic to open our readers to new ways or more nuanced ways of understanding a subject, and taking responsibility for what we say so that readers can trust our words and our work (Hyde, 2011, p. 39). Ultimately, we want to bring readers to an "Aha!" moment, where they see something in the research that they hadn't seen before, or where they come to think about the topic in a new way.

Our goal in crafting a response-able stance, then, is to build up the research community, seeking to develop knowledge in connection and dialogue with its other members. We also seek to move our ideas outward from the research community to the world we live in, applying our research to real-life contexts and drawing readers in to think and act wisely in response. In short, we not only aim to create compelling and well-crafted stances, but to take responsibility for what our stances do in the academic community and beyond.

B. CRAFTING A RESEARCH CLAIM

How, then, do we take a response-able stance and develop it in our research writing? As we might imagine, it's easier said than done. While we regularly take stances on topics in ordinary conversation, we often struggle to translate those into our research writing. How do we take a position on something that strikes us as purely factual and doesn't seem to invite multiple perspectives? How do we argue for or against something without attacking the "other side" or trying to win readers to "our side"? How do we hypothesize something new to add to a discussion among expert scholars? Then there's that very practical question: When professors say, "Take a stance in your research writing," what exactly are they wanting us to do? Let's start there.

A research stance, as we saw in Chapter 7, has three key components: a *claim* about a topic from our particular standpoint that we prove by means of expert *reasons* and *reasoning*. Let's begin by looking at how to craft a claim, and then turn to some common ways to support, test, or prove that claim with reasons and reasoning later in this chapter.

A claim is an argument or hypothesis that we put forward to prove or test in our research writing. It refers to *what we see* and *how we think* about a topic, and highlights where we stand when we give voice to our research and ideas. Crafting a claim begins by making specific observations about the topic at hand, based on the research we have collected on it. ***Observations*** are the things we *observe* or *see* as we examine what other researchers have discovered, theorized, or concluded about a topic. They are the backbone of our research claim. In fact, we regularly set up our claims with an observation. Consider the following two example observations that are used to set up a research claim:

> The frequency of cyberbullying is less than that of traditional bullying, but is rapidly increasing because of the rising use of technological devices among youth (Modecki et al., 2014). (p. 16)
>
> Tural Hesapcioglu, S., & Ercan, F. (2017). Traditional and cyberbullying co-occurrence and its relationship to psychiatric symptoms. *Pediatrics International, 59*(1), 16–22. https://doi.org/10.1111/ped.13067

> Banking crises are more frequent in comparison to other crises involving currency or debt, both for emerging and advanced economies (Reinhart & Rogoff, 2013). (p. 305)
>
> Hasanov, R., & Bhattacharya, P.S. (2019). Do political factors influence banking crisis? *Economic Modelling, 76*, 305–318. https://doi.org/10.1016/j.econmod.2018.08.010

In the first example, we can see that the writers' observation comes directly out of research done by Modecki et al. If we look at the second example, we see that the observation stems from work done by Reinhart and Rogoff. What we observe about a topic, then, is always rooted in a research context, in what other scholars in the community and conversation are saying.

While we begin our claim with observations—*what we see*—we can't stop there. We must then use those observations as a launching point for *what we think*. This means turning our observations into an argument or hypothesis—*what we think about what we see*—that is open for discussion and contributes something new to the research dialogue. However, it's easy to get stuck in this shift from *seeing* to *thinking* and find ourselves mistaking our observations for our full claim. For example, we might *see* in our research findings that cyberbullying is on the rise and then assert: "I hypothesize that cyberbullying is increasing." Or we might observe that banking crises are more frequent than other financial crises in emerging and advanced economies and then state: "I argue that banking crises happen more often than other financial crises." However, the problem with these statements is that they aren't dynamic claims that introduce a new way of looking at something. They are simply facts about cyberbullying and observations about banking crises. Such facts and observations may work to reinforce our current knowledge about the topic, but they do not offer new or meaningful contributions to the research conversation.

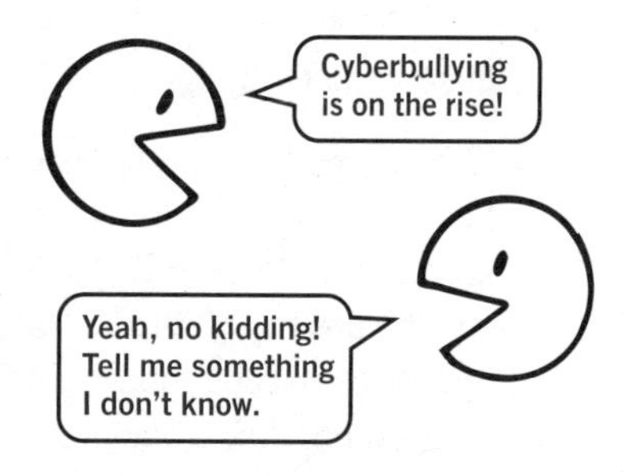

As research writers, it is our job to *do something* with our observations, to make them into meaningful claims that respond to other researchers and contribute new ideas and findings to our research community. We can transform an observation into a claim by answering one of the following questions as specifically as possible:

- What does the observation prove or show about this issue?
- What does the observation mean for the future of this issue?
- What is the most critical, concerning, or important effect of the issue I've observed?
- What is the most likely result or outcome of the issue I've observed?
- What is the most likely cause of the problem I've observed?
- What is the best solution to the problem I've observed?
- Why is this observation important to the study of this topic?
- Why does this observation matter for understanding this issue?

For instance, notice how the two observations below are turned into claims by answering one of the above questions:

Observation within a Research Context

Relying on the research of Smith (2016), Taylor (2012), Sharp et al. (2015), and Roosen (2017), I observe that there are fewer grey whales breeding off the coast of California than there used to be.

Observation + Claim

The decline in grey whales breeding off the coast of California has been attributed to a number of concerning factors (Smith, 2016; Taylor, 2012). While Sharp et al. (2015) and Roosen (2017) suggest that the main reason for this decline is shifting ocean currents due to climate change, I hypothesize that the most likely cause is the increased pollution in and human activity around the Baja lagoons, the primary destination of southbound grey whales.

Please note that the researchers and research material in this example are invented. Any connections between invented examples and actual circumstances, people, or other resources are coincidental.

Observation within a Research Context

Thanks to the research findings of Petkau and Jones (2010), Atinson et al. (2016), and Ozumi (2015), I observe that poverty is on the rise in Canada.

Observation + Claim

Poverty is on the rise in Canada for various reasons (Ozumi, 2015), including precarious employment (Petkau & Jones, 2010) and poor earnings (Atinson et al., 2016). Because these issues cannot be easily resolved, I argue that Canadians need to become better equipped to live within their means and use the funds they do have more wisely.

Please note that the researchers and research material in this example are invented. Any connections between invented examples and actual circumstances, people, or other resources are coincidental.

As we analyse these examples, we can see that the observation states a particular fact rooted in the current research on the topic that becomes the launching point from which to develop a claim. In both cases, the claim builds on the observation: the claim in the first example addresses the *most likely cause* of the issue stated in the observation; the claim in the second example points to the challenging causes of the issue and offers a *solution* to the problem posed in the observation. We can also see in both cases that the claim responds to the research of others in the field of study. In the first example, the claim responds to the views of Sharp et al. and Roosen in the form of a contrast. In the second example, the claim responds to the reasons for poverty provided by Petkau and Jones, and Atinson et al. in the form of a solution to the problem they raise.

In both examples, the observation and the claim are stated in separate sentences. But we can also combine a claim with our observation in a single statement. In order to do so, we need to begin by outlining the research context that has resulted in our observation to show readers where we're coming from in making our claim. Then we can connect our observation to our claim with phrases such as:

- proves that...
- demonstrates that...
- means that...
- shows that...
- is most likely caused by...
- is best solved by...
- is significant because...
- is important because...

For example:

Outline the Research Context

There is a decline in grey whales breeding off the California coast (Smith, 2016; Taylor, 2012; Sharp et al., 2015; Roosen, 2017).

Observation + Claim

- ➢ The decline of grey whales breeding off the California coast *means* _____ (my claim).
- ➢ The decline of grey whales breeding off the California coast *is most likely caused by* ______ (my claim).
- ➢ The decline of grey whales breeding off the California coast *is significant because* ______ (my claim).

Example Claim

I hypothesize that the decline of grey whales breeding off the California coast *is most likely caused by* the increased pollution in and human activity around the Baja lagoons, the primary destination of southbound grey whales.

Outline the Research Context

Poverty levels are rising in Canada (Petkau & Jones, 2010; Atinson et al., 2016; Ozumi, 2015).

Observation + Claim

- The fact that poverty is on the rise in Canada *proves that* ______ (my claim).
- The rise of poverty in Canada *is best solved by* ______ (my claim).
- The rise of poverty in Canada *demonstrates that* ______ (my claim).

Example Claim

I argue that the rise of poverty in Canada *is best solved by* Canadians becoming better equipped to live within their means and using the funds that they do have more wisely.

Whichever way we choose to state our claim, we ensure that our observations are rooted in research and that they work to launch our hypothesis or argument.

EXERCISE 1
TURNING OBSERVATIONS INTO CLAIMS

To practise turning observations into claims, we might find it helpful to start with invented material or imagined data. Using your imagination, turn the following observations into claims by adding invented material. Don't worry at this stage about whether your claim is factual or researched (it can be entirely made up). Focus instead on the craft and structure of your claim. Use the questions and examples above to help you.

Observation 1
People living in urban locations struggle more with isolation and loneliness than those living in rural environments.

Observation 2
All across the interior of Greenland, glacial ice is melting at a rapid pace.

Observation 3
The *Lord of the Rings* trilogy reveals strong female protagonists in the characters of Éowyn and Arwen.

Observation 4
Many Torontonians travel to cottages in Muskoka on the weekends.

Observation 5
Therapy animals have a natural tendency to bond with clients, seeking affection from and interaction with them.

Once we have formulated our claim, we are ready to hone and strengthen it so that it becomes meaningful to our research community. There are two key ways to do that:

1. Precision

The more precise we can make our claim, the more accurate and compelling it will be. We develop a precise and focused claim in order to reflect the specificity of where we stand and what we see from there. For example, notice the difference in the following two claims in terms of their precision:

- ***General claim***: "I argue that everyone should have equal rights."
- ***Specific claim***: "I argue that equal employment rights for men and women ought to be protected under the Canadian Charter of Rights and Freedoms in current battles over women holding management and CEO positions."

As we can see, the general claim is less convincing than the specific claim because it is not located. In its attempt to be all inclusive, the general claim doesn't actually represent anyone in particular. To be convincing, it would need to focus on *someone*—a specific community within a specific context—rather than on *everyone*. A general claim like the one above also doesn't represent a unique standpoint on the subject within a research context; instead, it reflects a commonly-held belief. While it may be true, it doesn't bring anything new or compelling to the research discussion. At best, it reiterates something we already know.

To create a specific claim we would need to ask ourselves fact-based questions about equal rights in order to specify our location. If we return to the second claim, we see that it is precise and located because it has answered the fact-based questions *what* (employment rights), *where* (in Canada), *when* (currently), and *who* (women in management and CEO positions). We can do the same for our general claims in order to make them precise and convincing, reflecting our specific views from where we stand. As we do this, we will have a much better chance of showing other members in the community the validity of our claim and its contribution to the dialogue and field of study.

2. Modality

Using modality also helps us clarify our claim by being honest about the particular location where we are standing. We want to be clear that our standpoints are necessarily limited by certain factors: our field of study, the research materials we've gathered, our framework, our context/background, etc. To do that, we often use modality in the form of modal verbs when stating our claim. Examples of modal verbs are:

- may
- might
- must
- should
- could
- can
- would
- will
- ought to
- able to
- need to
- have to

Using modality highlights that we have a limited view from our research location, but it also signals the potential for our claim to contribute new knowledge to our field of study. For example, notice the terms of modality highlighted in bold below:

> This essay... [suggests] that a gendered approach to disability **could** advance the broader feminist project of fully accounting for individual differences by shifting antidiscrimination law's ethic of rights to an ethic of care. (p. 840)
>
> Travis, M. (2017). Gendering disability to enable disability rights law. *California Law Review, 105*(3), 837–884. https://dx.doi.org/10.15779/Z38599Z13G

> [A]dequate subtyping of IGD (Internet Gaming Disorder) through the proper identification of attributing vulnerabilities and motives for excessive gaming **may** facilitate a more accurate diagnosis of IGD and enable us to provide more targeted and personalized treatment for patients with each subtype of IGD. (p. 481)
>
> Lee, S., Lee, H.K., & Choo, H. (2017). Typology of internet gaming disorder and its clinical implications. *Psychiatry and Clinical Neurosciences, 71*(7), 471–491. https://doi.org/10.1111/pcn.12457

The researchers in these examples state their claims as hypotheses drawn from their particular standpoints. They do not hide the fact that there are different ways to interpret the same findings from other standpoints. Instead, they use modality to highlight the contribution that their research stance makes to the dialogue, suggesting the value of viewing things as they do.

C. POSITIONING OUR STANCE DIALOGICALLY: TEMPLATES FOR RESPONSIVE CLAIMS

When we put ourselves in dialogue with other researchers, we take a stance in response to what they are saying about the topic at hand. When it comes down to it, there are only a few ways to position a stance and state our research claim as a response. As we saw in Chapter 7, a response-able stance may agree with, modify, complicate, challenge, question, solve, or oppose current stances on the topic. This means our claim can respond to others in one of the following ways:

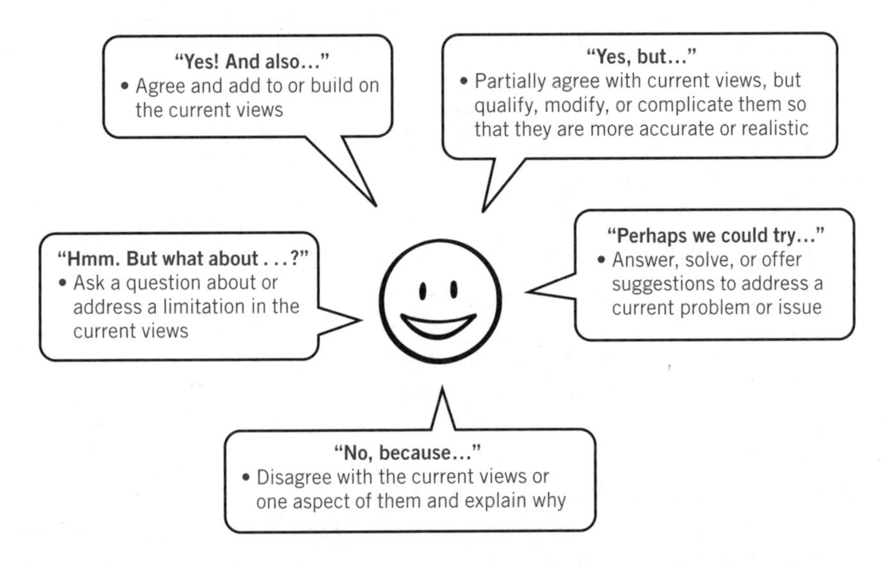

Once we are aware of these different styles of response, we can choose from the following templates to position our claim in our research writing:

1. Templates for Agreeing and Adding: "Yes! And also ..."

Our claim may build on the work of other researchers by adding a new dimension to the discussion, a new application of a theory, or a new context for the ideas.

- ➢ We build on Researchers X and Y's idea that __________ to suggest __________.
- ➢ My research adds to the work of Researcher X by showing ___________.
- ➢ We develop the view posited by Researchers X and Y, proposing __________.
- ➢ I argue that Researcher Y's theory has very useful applications for _________.
- ➢ Our view that ________ confirms Researcher Y's hypothesis ________.

2. Templates for Honing: "Yes, but ..."

Our claim may agree with the work of other researchers to a certain extent, but qualify, modify, or complicate an aspect of those ideas in order to make them more accurate, realistic, or precise.

- I agree with Researcher X that ________, but it would be beneficial to also consider ________ in this analysis.
- One area that Researchers X and Y have not addressed in this important discussion is ________. In order to fill this gap, we argue ________.
- This issue is a good deal more complex than Researcher Y claims due to ________ and needs to be addressed as follows: ________.
- We opt for the middle ground of ________ between the extreme positions of Researcher X and Researcher Y.
- A number of complications arise when applying Researcher Y's proposition, such as ________. I address these complexities by suggesting ________.

3. Templates for Questioning: "Hmm. But what about...?"

Our claim may question the work of other researchers, highlighting a shortcoming or limitation that must be addressed to further the community's understanding about the topic.

- Given that this dimension has been overlooked by Researchers X and Y, among others, I propose ________.
- Given the limitations of Researcher X's experiment, I hypothesize ________.
- While Researchers X and Y have addressed this issue expertly, I am left with the following question: ________.
- The findings of Researchers X and Y raise a number of questions. The most important one that I want to address here is ________.
- I question this notion put forth by Researcher Z because ________, and argue for ________ as an alternative.

4. Templates for Solving: "Perhaps we could try..."
Our claim may offer a solution, answer, or suggestion for resolving a particular problem that other researchers have raised in their work.

- The best way to address the problem posed by Researchers X and Y is _______.
- Bringing together the research of Researchers X and Y with that of Researcher Z, we address this problem by recommending ___________.
- While Researchers X and Y suggest that ___________ would solve this problem, I am convinced that ______________ would be more productive.
- As Researchers X, Y, and Z observe, there are a number of solutions to this problem, but we propose ______________ as the most viable option.
- In our research, we have found that the most beneficial answer to the problem raised by Researcher Z is ___________.

5. Templates for Disagreeing: "No, because..."
Our claim may disagree with, diverge from, problematize, or counteract the work of other researchers and provide clear reasons for doing so.

- We oppose Researcher X's claim that ________ on account of _________.
- Despite the positive outcomes, I am not convinced of Researcher Y's position because ____________.
- In contrast to the hypothesis proposed by Researchers X and Y, I propose that ________ because ___________.
- As an alternative to Researcher X's stance, we suggest that _________ because ___________.
- Contrary to Researcher Z's claim that ________, we hypothesize ______ due to _________.

From the templates above we can see that there are many different ways to state our claim and assert our standpoint in response to the research of other scholars. Now we are ready to complete our claim by showing how our stance contributes to the research conversation in which we are engaged and the field of study in which we are located. In what ways does our stance build knowledge, promote understanding, expand ideas, support others, or benefit the community?

To ensure we are contributing to the conversation, we need to consider two questions our readers will inevitably ask when they read our claim: "So what?" and "Who cares?" In other words, what is important about our research stance and who will it impact in a positive way? The following templates help us to address these questions as we assert our stance and state our position.

- This standpoint changes how we see ______________.
- This position is crucial in light of the contemporary concerns about _________.
- This argument challenges the work of researchers who have held that ___________.
- This hypothesis is important because _____________.
- This study brings to light the issue of __________, which earlier studies have not addressed.
- This position has significant implications for ________________.

Without identifying the significance (*who cares* and *so what*) of our research stance or stating the contribution it makes to the conversation, our readers may not understand *why* we are making our claim and may be quick to lose interest in our facts, findings, and ideas. Research writers must directly state how valuable their position is to the community in order to persuade readers to listen to, engage with, and respond to it.

D. PULLING IT ALL TOGETHER: RESPONSE-ABLE STANCES IN DIALOGUE

We have now looked at five basic templates for responding to researchers with our claim. We have also considered ways to show how our claim contributes to the research conversation. What follows are two different templates that bring these aspects together so that we can articulate our stance in the context of a dialogue.

Template 1

According to Researchers A and B, ___________. Researchers X and Y similarly suggest that _________________. While I agree with their point that ____________, their research has yet to consider ___________. In this paper, I argue that it would be beneficial to bring __________ to bear on this analysis because __________. My hope is that this new dimension will flesh out our current research practices and offer some practical applications for ______________.

Template 2

A number of researchers (Researchers A and B; Researcher X; Researchers Y and Z) share the view that ________________. In contrast to this view, Researchers C and D suggest that ______________. I am not convinced that either of these extremes is realistic or beneficial. Instead, I opt for a middle ground position of _________. This standpoint requires that we adapt how we see ____________, which is necessary for understanding ____________ more fully.

Notice how both templates make observations about the current research on the topic, bringing into conversation a number of its key thinkers and pointing out a gap or limitation in the discussion. The stances are positioned responsively, each claim honing the other ideas in the dialogue. Both templates also include a sentence that indicates the value of the stance straightaway so that readers are clear about its importance for the research community.

E. TWO DIALOGIC MODELS FOR DEVELOPING A STANCE

We now know that when we state our stance, we do so by presenting a claim in response to those of other researchers. But how do we advance our stance beyond stating our initial claim? How do we develop our reasons and reasoning to make our stance credible and compelling across our whole paper? In order to answer these questions, we first need to consider *what kind of stance* we are taking when we make our claim. Are we arguing for or against something? Are we trying to prove that something is right or wrong? Are we hypothesizing the outcome of an issue, action, or experiment? Are we recommending one interpretation of a text above another? Are we proposing a combination of research ideas that will result in a more accurate view of the topic? How we develop our stance depends on what we want to test or prove through our research and what we want to contribute to the research dialogue on the topic.

There are two common models for developing a stance dialogically in a research paper: a debate model and a discussion model. A ***debate model*** is often used in argumentative research writing, especially when there are clear sides to an issue. Here we assert our claim in response to another side or alternative position in the dialogue and rely on reasons and reasoning to prove that claim. A ***discussion model*** is used when there are not clear sides to an issue. It is thus typically found in analytical research essays, but certain argumentative essay styles may use it as well. Here we propose our claim in response to other viewpoints on the topic as one good possibility among others. We may also present our claim as a hypothesis responding to a question or problem raised by other researchers. Notably, in a debate model, a claim functions as an assertion of truth that is verified or proven by reasons and reasoning. In a discussion model, a claim functions as a proposition of truth or a quest for truth that is tested and developed through reasons and reasoning.

The model we use to develop our stance will depend on the discipline in which we're writing, the research community we're writing for, and the purpose of our communication. A debate model is often used in political writing, legal deliberations, and philosophical discussions, where one may take sides on an issue. A discussion model tends to be used in social and scientific contexts (to solve complex problems or make sense of findings) and may also be used in literary and cultural contexts (to interpret texts or images). Let's look at how to use these two models in our research writing.

1. A Debate Model

A debate model works well if we are studying an issue that has two clear sides. When we use a debate model, we make an argument *for* or *against* something, a case that holds up under scrutiny and counter-argument. In this form of argumentation our goal is to persuade others of the truth of our claim and to convince them of its value and validity through strong evidence and persuasive reasoning. For example, a researcher in urban planning could take a stance for or against creating new bike lanes in Vancouver and offer valid reasons and reasoning for doing so.

When using a debate model, we provide readers with a research context, a debatable claim, and reasons and reasoning for making that claim. In addition to these elements, we offer *rebuttals* or *counter-arguments* to address oppositions to our claim. Because research claims are never beyond dispute, we must address any oppositions to our claim so as to leave no doubt in the reader's mind that we have carefully explored each side thoroughly before taking our stance.

Consider how these four elements—a research context, a debatable claim, reasons and reasoning, and rebuttals—work in the following invented example:

Urban Planning Research: New Bike Lanes in Vancouver

1. **Research Context**: Consulting the research of Lark and Pasteroff (2011), Spick (2015), Turan and Chau (2012), and Kwok et al. (2016), I observe a divide in stances regarding new bike lanes in Vancouver.

2. **A Debatable Claim**: Drawing on the views of Turan and Chau (2012) and Spick (2015), I argue that we should not create new bike lanes in Vancouver.

3. **Reasons and Reasoning** (to support the claim):
   - New bike lanes will further congest already congested traffic areas (*with examples*).
   - New bike lanes privilege bikers over drivers, but drivers make up a larger percentage of the city's population. They require the lanes for easy commute and cannot bike long distances to work (*with deductive reasoning, analysis, and testimony*).
   - Bike lanes have not, so far, created a greener Vancouver (*with statistics*).

4. **Rebuttals** (to address the oppositions to the claim):
   - I realize that the addition of more bike lanes would encourage commuters to use bikes rather than cars, ***but*** most commuters live too far from their jobs to travel to them by bike.
   - Granted, we have many people who travel by bike; ***however***, there is still a greater portion of the population travelling by car and becoming more impatient and reckless on the roads due to extra congestion.
   - ***While recognizing that*** we are aiming for a greener city with less exhaust pollution, I am convinced that having more bike lanes doesn't stop most drivers from continuing to use their cars.

Please note that the researchers and research material in this example are invented. Any connections between invented examples and actual circumstances, people, or other resources are coincidental.

When we use a debate model to develop our stance, we need to ensure that all four of these elements are incorporated strategically within our research paper. With these elements in mind, try the following exercises:

EXERCISE 2
RECOGNIZING A DEBATE MODEL

Locate the writer's *research context*, *debatable claim* and the *alternative sides* of racial profiling outlined below. While this excerpt is drawn from the introduction of the article, you should also be able to discern preliminary signs of *reasons*, *reasoning*, and *rebuttals* that will be developed in the body of the article.

A police officer sees a suspicious bulge in the pocket of a passing pedestrian and deliberates whether to stop and search. While the bulge is not necessarily proof of carrying an illegal firearm, it is certainly a legitimate indication. The pedestrian is also a young, black man, and from past searches and convictions, the police arguably know that such men are much likelier than other people to carry an illegal firearm. Should the police officer be instructed to take this information into account? The issue is not limited to policing, as some Muslims who are regularly selected for an 'enhanced security check' at airports could testify (Johnson, 2004; Glaser, 2014; Blackwood, 2015). Nor is it necessarily limited to searching for weapons and bombs; if, one day, the tax authority notices that Jews are much likelier to cheat on their tax returns, should more Jews be selected for random investigation?

Search practices which are based on racial profiling are deeply controversial. On the one hand, racial profiling has become immensely popular in some police and security forces both inside and outside the United States (UN Doc A/56/49, 2002), and this popularity is not without academic support (Levin, 1992; Risse & Zeckhauser, 2004). Racial profiling is often advocated as a means of maximizing the effectiveness of scarce resources in controlling crime and preventing terrorist attacks (Persico, 2002; Gross & Livingston, 2002). On the other hand, some criticize the reliability of profiling methods, drawing attention to difficulties involved in collecting, analyzing, and presenting the data underlying such search practices (Smith & Alpert, 2002; Durlauf, 2005; Tamir, 2006). Others emphasize that racial profiling is offensive even if statistically reliable (Harris 2003), adding that profiling methods stigmatize not only the profiled individual but also the entire profiled group, most of which is law-abiding (Carter, 2004; Daly, 1999)....

This article seeks to expose an additional problem with racial profiling, arising from its reliance on the following type of *inference*: from the individual's membership of a certain racial group, the searcher is invited to infer that the individual is likelier to exhibit some *culpable* behaviour (hereinafter referred to as 'inference to culpable behaviour'). The article seeks to show that inference to culpable behaviour requires contradictory presuppositions. Unlike existing objections, the argument thus focuses on the epistemic qualities of racial profiling rather than on its social costs. Racial profiling is unsuitable for policing because it is *irrational* for the criminal justice system to deploy profiling in order to detect a person who engages in criminal activity and then put that person to trial (Gardner, 1998)....

The crux of the argument is that racial profiling requires contradictory presuppositions about the freedom of the suspected behaviour.... On the one hand, racial profiling and the inference to culpable behaviour it involves take the suspect's behaviour to be determined by his race, age, and gender, none of which is within his control. Racial profiling thus presupposes that the suspect's behaviour is unfree. On the other hand, [similar] to criminal trials, search practices ought to presuppose the exact opposite—namely, that the individual is free to determine his own behaviour. If the suspected behaviour is in fact free, the involved inference to culpable behaviour is not probative of the individual suspect's behaviour, rendering profiling methods which rely on it useless. Alternatively, if the suspected behaviour is unfree, the inference is probative, but the suspect is not culpable and should thus not be put to trial as long as criminal trials seek to avoid punishing those who are not culpable. (pp. 175–77)

Pundik, A. (2017). Against racial profiling. *University of Toronto Law Journal, 67*(2), 175–202. https://doi.org/10.3138/UTLJ.3883

EXERCISE 3
THE OTHER SIDE

Take the example above—"New Bike Lanes in Vancouver"—and make a case for the opposite claim: "I am *for* creating new bike lanes in Vancouver." Use your imagination (or do a little research) to offer valid reasons and reasoning for this claim and thoughtful rebuttals against the opposition to show how you could develop this stance convincingly within a research paper.

When using a debate model to develop a research stance, keep these strategies in mind:

- Situate your observations about the issue within a research context.
- State your claim for or against the issue clearly and directly.

- Provide reasons and use reasoning to support and prove your claim. Emphasize your logic, analytical ability, and the significance of your evidence.

- Anticipate opposition and know the other side so thoroughly that you can rebut it with your reasoning. Consider stating the counter-arguments in your paper directly to show how your reasoning exposes their limitations or debunks their claims.

2. A Discussion Model

A discussion model highlights multiple ways of looking at a problem, question, issue, or text, but focuses on the *one way* we think is most beneficial, useful, or fruitful for addressing it. When we use a discussion model, we don't make a case for or against something but consider the many sides of an issue before proposing a particular direction, interpretation, cause, or solution as the basis for our stance. Researchers who use a discussion model tend to be interested in working together with others to solve problems, reconcile opposing sides, or engage with multiple perspectives in the community.

For example, social geographers might write about the problem of homelessness in Vancouver using a discussion model. They may suggest that there are many ways to address homelessness that have positive impact, but choose to focus on *one way* that they think would be most helpful or beneficial. If they want their stance to have credibility in the academic community, they need to do significant research to determine that their strategy is, in fact, the most beneficial way of addressing homelessness in Vancouver. In the process, they would need to gather evidence to support their stance and rely on inductive and/or deductive reasoning to show readers how it is a viable way to address the problem.

When we use a discussion model, we provide readers with key elements that develop our stance: We begin with a *problem* or *issue* and then provide *multiple research positions* on that problem or issue. We *validate* the legitimacy of these positions before proposing a compelling *claim* as the most viable interpretation of or solution to this problem or issue, followed by *reasons* and *reasoning* to support that claim. Consider how these five elements work in the following invented example:

Social Geography Research: Addressing Homelessness in Vancouver

1. **A Problem or Issue**: Homelessness has been on the rise in Vancouver since 2010.

2. **Multiple Research Positions** (to address the problem):
   - To address the rising number of homeless people, we need to build more affordable social housing (Smith, 2011).
   - To address the rising number of homeless people, we need to first address the addictions that are contributing to their homelessness (Sio & Partridge, 2015).
   - To address the rising number of homeless people, we need to encourage families to take responsibility for their homeless relations (Chu & Ang, 2013).
   - To address the rising number of homeless people, we need to help the homeless gain and maintain jobs, support themselves, and procure their own housing (Aloue, 2015).

3. **Validation** (legitimating other positions):
   - I find these solutions plausible and support each of them as viable ways to address the homeless crisis in Vancouver. However, I propose... (*claim*)
   - While building more affordable social housing (Smith, 2011) and promoting employment counselling and self-sufficiency (Aloue, 2015) can be very beneficial ways to deal with the homeless crisis in Vancouver, I suggest... (*claim*)

4. **A Compelling Claim**: I propose that the best way to address the rise of homelessness in Vancouver is to confront the underlying issues of mental illness and addiction that afflict many homeless people by providing more mental health facilities and addiction management sites in the area.

5. **Reasons and Reasoning** (to support the claim):
   - Members of the community who struggle with mental illness and addiction cannot seem to "climb out" of homelessness in the way that those who are struggling solely with unemployment often can (*with statistics, case studies*).
   - Homelessness in Vancouver grew tremendously when psychiatric hospitals closed in the Lower Mainland and patients were released into the public. Such patients were encouraged to integrate into mainstream society but ultimately could not. Many have ended up homeless and need special care (*with historical documentation*).

- Housing this population may help in the short term but does not deal with the underlying issues with mental health and addiction that keep people on the streets (*with deduction and analysis*).

- Currently, many homeless people with mental illnesses self-medicate and become addicted to drugs. This drug addiction makes it impossible for them to become stable enough to gain employment (*with statistics, case studies, research documentation*).

- Mental health facilities and addiction management sites would benefit this community through consistent care, counselling, and monitored drug use (*with inductive reasoning, case studies, and research documentation*).

Please note that the researchers and research material in this example are invented. Any connections between invented examples and actual circumstances, people, or other resources are coincidental.

When we use a discussion model to develop our stance, we need to incorporate these five elements strategically within our research paper. With these elements in mind, try the following exercises.

EXERCISE 4
RECOGNIZING A DISCUSSION MODEL

Locate the *problem or issue*, *multiple research positions*, *validation*, and *claim* in the passage below. While this excerpt is drawn from the introduction of the article, you should also be able to discern preliminary signs of *reasons* and *reasoning* that will be developed in the body of the article.

Clinical empathy is an essential element of quality care, associated with improved patient satisfaction, increased adherence to treatment, and fewer malpractice complaints (Burns & Nolen-Hoeksema, 1992; Raken et al., 2009, 2011; Hojat et al., 2011; Del Canal et al., 2012) as well as increased physician health, well-being, and professional satisfaction (Mercer & Reynolds, 2002; Benbassat & Baumal, 2004). However, despite all these clear advantages to both patients and physicians, empathy in medicine remains an undervalued and understudied topic (Riess, 2010; Schattner, 2012). Maintaining appropriate levels of clinical empathy is challenging because medical practitioners routinely deal with the most emotionally distressing situations—illness, dying, suffering in every form—and such situations can rapidly make an empathic person anxious, perhaps too anxious to be helpful (Neumann et al., 2011; Halpern, 2012). This painful reality may take its toll on these individuals and can lead to compassion fatigue, burnout, professional distress, and result in a low sense of accomplishment and severe emotional exhaustion (Figley, 2012; Gleichgerrcht & Decety, 2013). Thus, physicians may experience difficulty empathizing with their patients (Feighny et al., 1995; Bonvincini et al., 2009). For instance, a study which coded interviews between physicians and lung cancer patients found that, out of 384 empathic opportunities—defined as patients' statements including an explicit description of emotion or patients' statements or clue that indicated an underlying emotion—physicians responded empathically to only 39 of them (10%), most often responding with little emotional support and shifting to biomedical questions and statements instead (Morse et al., 2008). Although the reasons for such difficulties are likely complex and multifaceted, one possible explanation may be that physicians lack the cognitive and emotional resources to engage in empathic processing. The vast majority of doctors have the capacity for empathy (Handford et al., 2013). However, particular skills such as attention, self-regulation, and emotional awareness are needed to reliably respond empathically to distressed patients while making difficult decisions and performing potentially high-risk, high-demand interventions. Added to this are organizational demands for ever increasing caseloads, which reduce the time doctors can spend with patients or use to manage their own emotions. Maintaining person-oriented connections during such high stress conditions requires a great deal of attention and self-regulation, which taxes a limited supply of cognitive and emotional resources (Feighny et al., 1995; Haque & Waytz, 2012). (pp. 1–2)

Gleichgerrcht, E., & Decety, J. (2014). The relationship between different facets of empathy, pain perception and compassion fatigue among physicians. *Frontiers in Behavioural Neuroscience, 8,* 1–9. https://doi.org/10.3389/fnbeh.2014.00243

EXERCISE 5
ANOTHER POSITION

Take the example above—"Addressing Homelessness in Vancouver"—and make a case for one of the other positions listed as possible solutions to this problem. Use your imagination (or do a little research) to offer a set of valid reasons and reasoning to show how you could develop this claim convincingly within a research paper.

When using a discussion model to develop a research stance, try these strategies:

- State the problem or issue clearly.
- Offer current research positions that have been proposed to solve this problem, or expert perspectives that have been established about the issue.
- Grant the validity of these other positions. Under which circumstances are they legitimate and beneficial?
- State your own claim in relation and response to these other positions.
- Support your claim with reasons and reasoning.
- Complete the picture by showing how the other positions would benefit if your claim were considered and implemented.

CONCLUSIONS

When we craft a response-able stance, we voice our standpoints and take responsibility for our research and ideas in relation to those of other scholars. As we discovered in this chapter, formulating a stance means taking our research observations and doing something with them—turning them into a claim that we can test or prove with reasons and reasoning. As we develop our claim, we add to, modify, question, solve, or disagree with the work of other scholars. In the process, we choose a dialogic model that makes sense given the purpose of our stance, the style of research essay we are writing, the conversation we are in, and research community we are writing for: Is a debate model or a discussion model more appropriate for presenting our views and research findings? As we develop these aspects of our stance, we become confident academic writers, able to assert, test, and prove our claim in relation and in response to other researchers, and to contribute to the dialogue on the subject.

QUESTIONS FOR REFLECTION

1. One of biggest challenges for new research writers learning how to develop a response-able stance is distinguishing a claim from an observation about a topic. Observations are statements that acknowledge facts or research findings, while claims are

assertions or hypotheses that take a stance on those facts and findings. With this distinction in mind, reflect on the following statements drawn from the Canadian general interest magazine *The Walrus* and determine which ones you think are specific observations and which ones are actual claims. Justify your choices.

- "In Canada, the maximum sentence for making and selling child pornography is ten years" (p. 51).

  Kolker, R. (2017, September). Project spade. *The Walrus, 14*(7), 44–57.

- "Canada's economic history was defined by the need to tame its vast tracts of land through trade and transportation networks—canals, railways, and highways" (p. 14).

  Taylor, P.S. (2016, October). Once we were builders. *The Walrus, 13*(8), 14–15.

- "Compassion, like politics, is opportunistic" (p. 13).

  Al-Solaylee, K. (2016, March). Suffering's second act. *The Walrus, 13*(2), 13–14.

- "Though there are likely several reasons for [the decline of employment rates and earnings of university graduates]...one in particular matches perfectly with the type of change I've observed on my watch: the eradication of content from the classroom" (p. 35).

  Srigley, R. (2016, April.) Pass, fail. *The Walrus, 13*(3), 34–43.

2. In ordinary conversations and on social media we are quick to respond to the ideas and activities of others with our opinions. In fact, we are invited to opine constantly. Why do stances rooted in opinion hold little to no credibility in the context of academic research writing?

3. When we communicate with others, we tend to use certain patterns of response that fit our level of comfort in the conversation. Think about your default responses in conversation with friends and family: Do you typically agree with them? Add a useful point that builds on theirs? Refine their ideas with qualifications or complexities? Ask questions? Try to solve their problems? Challenge their ideas? Do you disagree with them? How might your typical patterns of response in ordinary conversation influence how you state your research stances in an academic dialogue?

4. Consider the topics of research below. Which ones might you expect to use a debate model of development and which ones might you expect to use a discussion model? Why? Give reasons for your decisions.

- capital punishment
- freedom of speech
- cyberbullying
- university education
- ancient mythology
- fast fashion
- climate change
- wars on terror
- childhood obesity
- John Milton's sonnets
- organic farming
- deforestation
- religious pluralism
- social health care
- genetic cloning
- urban poverty
- histories of colonization
- doctor-assisted death

PART 4
PARTICIPATING IN ACADEMIC DIALOGUE

CHAPTER TEN

RESEARCH TOPICS AND PROPOSALS

Preparing to Write

In academic courses we are often asked to develop a research project and write an essay that stems from our work. When we "do research," we gather selected resources in order to investigate the current knowledge about a topic. We engage with the findings and ideas we have discovered in the form of a research essay. In fact, we could define a ***research essay*** as a written investigation into a specific topic, wherein we take a stance on what we've discovered in order to contribute something valuable to the research discussion on that topic.

In the following chapters, we will see how this written investigation takes the form of a dialogue, both with other research scholars and with our readers: we assert our views in relation to those of other researchers in order to compel readers to engage with and respond to us. In these final chapters, we will apply the dialogic skills we've developed in the previous chapters in order to learn how to write an effective and ethical research essay.

Before we can sit down to begin writing, we need to do some preparatory work to develop our project. We first need to choose a research topic and collect the findings of expert scholars on this topic to determine their various stances. Next, we need to think through the research material we have discovered, generating our own ideas and organizing our thoughts in response to what we've read. Finally, we must take a stance and make a claim about the research we have gathered, so we can contribute something meaningful to the dialogue on the topic. In this chapter, we will work through each of these practices in order to prepare for writing our research essay. We will also learn how to compose a ***research proposal*** and ***bibliography***, which we are commonly asked to write before starting our essay. We use research proposals and bibliographies to persuade readers of our project's value, communicate our initial stance and findings, outline our writing plan for the essay we will produce, and provide an organized list of resources that we've collected for our project.

A. CHOOSING A RESEARCH TOPIC

Choosing a research topic fills some of us with dread and others with delight. Many of us have no idea what subject we'd like to investigate in depth or what interests us to the degree that we would want to study it in detail. Others of us are thrilled with the possibility of developing our own topic. We are excited to investigate something we care about rather than having to choose a topic from a list our instructor has prepared. Regardless of what camp we find ourselves in, this section is geared to help us choose a topic and research that topic with confidence.

Choosing a research topic begins with self-reflection. To research something and write about it well, we have to care about it. It may come as a surprise that scholars engage in research because they care about their chosen subject—however abstract or obscure. They are deeply invested in studying their topic and committed to a community of other researchers who also care about it. With this is mind, we choose our topic by asking ourselves, "What do I really care about?"

We tend to care about the issues, questions, or problems that concern us. According to the late literary theorist and critic Northrop Frye (1990), we are all concerned beings. We are concerned about *primary needs* such as food, shelter, procreation, and freedom of movement. These are the generic concerns of life that we share with animals on a physical level (p. 42). We are also concerned about *secondary needs* that arise from our interconnections with other human beings. These include "patriotic and other attachments of loyalty, religious beliefs, and class-conditioned attitudes and behaviour" (p. 42). Things like power, civic duty, ecological sustainability, economic disparity, stories and histories, and spiritual practices are concerns we share with other human beings.

Many of our concerns have both a *primary* and a *secondary* dimension. For example, we may be concerned about the effects of climate change on glacial melt. This has both a physical dimension (ice is melting; certain animals are struggling to survive) and a societal dimension (climate change is affected by human pollution, marked by unsustainable environmental practices, influenced by political and economic power, etc.). In our concern for the environment, we could look into any of these aspects to develop a research project. To begin reflecting on what our concerns might be, we can ask ourselves the following questions:

- What do I like to read about in my free time?
- What topics do I get into deep and meaningful conversations about?
- What problems in my community really bother or upset me?
- What matters do I struggle with personally?
- What issues on the news catch my attention or disturb me?
- What activities do I participate in that are life-giving to me?

- Where do I spend my money, my time, and my energy?

When it comes to developing a topic in the context of a college or university course, we often do not have the freedom to choose *any* topic we care about, but have to choose something within the parameters of our course, subject, or discipline. With this in mind, we may need to be more specific with our self-reflection questions:

- What did I most enjoy reading about in this course?
- What sorts of conversations in the classroom or online got me excited?
- What material in this course did I struggle with or find troubling?
- What ideas introduced in this course were valuable to me?
- What areas of the course were most interesting for me to learn about?

EXERCISE 1
SELF-REFLECTION

To discern what you care about, sit down with a blank piece of paper and a pen for ten minutes and jot down all the things you can think of that excite you, bother you, interest you, or affect you, as well as the things that you most value. Depending on the parameters of your research project, you may want to be general or course specific in your reflections.

Note that our minds are stimulated differently when we use pen and paper than when we type on the computer. To stimulate your reflective abilities, put aside your laptop for this exercise and return to old-fashioned scribbling.

Once we know what concerns us, we can decide which concern to investigate more deeply in a research context. To do that, it is often helpful to turn our concern into a research question that we can actually investigate. For example, we might care about social media and find ourselves spending a lot of time on it. We could turn that interest into any number of research questions:

- Why is social media addictive?

- How does social media affect personal relationships?

- How do we balance our social media presence with actual life responsibilities?

- What is the relationship between social media and ADHD?

- How does increased time on social media affect mental focus and productivity?

- Why should we "unplug" from social media on a regular basis?

We frame our concern as a research question or set of questions in order to give us a clear direction for our investigation. Some scholars call this ***inquiry-based research***: a systematic study of the genuine question(s) we have in order to tackle an issue, problem, or concern that we care about. As we develop our research questions, we need to keep two things in mind. Our questions should be *analytical* and our questions should be *specific*. Let's look at each of these in turn.

1. Analytical Research Questions

Analytical research questions are the kinds of questions we ask in order to take a meaningful stance on a topic. They are questions that cannot be answered with simple facts or a straightforward "yes" or "no." Instead, they elicit multiple answers to explain the issue, depending on the standpoint we take. To ask an analytical research question, we begin with the question words, "Why?" "How?" or "What is the relationship between ...?" as we dig into the issue, problem, or concern that we want to research. These question words help us delve into the deeper and more complex aspects of a subject, as well as encourage us to use our critical analysis skills as we engage in our research practice. For example, analytical research questions on the topic of social media might include the following:

- ***Why*** is social media addictive?

- ***How*** does increased time on social media affect mental focus and productivity?

- ***What is the relationship between*** social media and ADHD?

These are considered analytical research questions because they don't have a simple or single answer. They could each be answered in multiple ways, depending on the standpoint that we take. For instance, if we were to investigate the question, "Why is social media addictive?" we would find that different research scholars answer this question differently, each with their own explanation based on their standpoint, focus, and field of study.

When we choose *one* explanation or answer to our analytical research question and value it above others, we take a stance on it and make a claim: "I argue that social media is addictive because __________ " or "I hypothesize that social media is addictive because __________." This stance will invoke discussion because not all scholars will share our standpoint or value the same explanation that we do. As a result, we have the opportunity to develop our stance over the course of an essay, convincing other scholars of its validity and contributing our views to the research dialogue.

2. Specific Research Questions

In addition to being analytical, a research question needs to be specific. Specific questions narrow our concern into an investigable topic with a particular focus. When we develop an analytical research question, we often start broad and general. For instance, if we are concerned about the negative effects of social media, our preliminary research question might be:

- ***How*** does social media negatively affect people?

This question is a good starting point. But we would quickly find that it is too broad to investigate in any depth.

In order go deep, we need to narrow our focus and locate our question in a concrete context—a certain time, place, and community. Here, fact-based questions, like *who*, *what*, *where*, and *when*, can help us narrow down our analytical research question so that it can be explored in detail in an essay. For example, if we return to our question above, we can ask fact-based questions to narrow down the term *social media*, specify the "negative effects" we mean, and identify which "people" we want to focus on:

- **What** form of social media am I focusing on?

- **What** negative effects am I referring to?

- **Which** people are being negatively affected?

As we answer each of these fact-based questions, we end up with a concrete and focused analytical research question:

> ***How*** does spending extensive time on Facebook (*the form of social media*) fuel body image concerns and negative emotions (*the negative effects*)—like envy, discontent, or shame—in adolescent girls (*the people affected*)?

Rather than tackle a general subject with a broad question, we hone our analytical research question into a manageable size so we can dig deeply into it, take a stance, and add something valuable to the research dialogue on the issue.

We also locate our analytical research question in a specific scholarly context and research community. Which field of research are we situated in to begin our exploration? And what research community do we expect to dialogue with and contribute to as we investigate our question? Given our analytical research question above, we may well be situated in the field of psychology, media studies, gender studies, or health, and may plan to contribute to a discussion in any one of those fields.

EXERCISE 2
PRACTISING ANALYSIS AND SPECIFICITY IN ANALYTICAL RESEARCH QUESTIONS

1. To begin crafting a research topic, turn one of your concerns into an analytical research question by framing it as a "Why," "How," or "What is the relationship between…" question.

2. As you develop your analytical research question, ensure that it is genuine (you don't already know the answer to it), meaningful (you are excited to research it and feel you could get invested in discussions about it), and worthwhile (it takes up an issue that a research community is concerned with and has already raised some dialogue about).

3. Make your analytical research question specific and concrete by honing it with fact-based questions—"What," "Who," "Where," and "When." These questions help to focus your topic and locate your research investigation in a specific context.

B. COLLECTING RESEARCH ON THE TOPIC: WHERE INVESTIGATION MEETS DISCERNMENT

Now that we have an analytical research question, we are ready to delve into our research investigation. While we may be excited to get started, the actual process of investigation can often feel daunting. In our digital age, we are virtually swimming in a sea of information. At some level, we think this should make our research process easier. However, having so much information can actually challenge our ability to research. We can become overwhelmed by the sheer number of articles, books, and other sources we find about our topic. How do we choose? What do we choose? How do we distinguish between general information and "good research" that is valued in our academic community?

Let's consider two questions to start our investigation off on the right track: *Where should we look* to find reliable resources for our topic? And *what should we look for* in choosing the best research material for our topic?

1. Where Should We Look?

To look for reliable resources on a topic, we need to begin with the academic context we're in. We are already situated in an academic field of study—a course, a community of scholars, a research environment, etc.—when we begin our investigation. Where we search is determined by this location and by the kind of resources and material valued by the scholars in our field of study. In an academic context, we cannot rely on general search engines like Google or Yahoo to locate the best resources for our topic. While internet searches are an easy go-to to find all manner of information meant for general consumption, academic scholars tend not to use them for two reasons.

Firstly, *they are too broad*. Internet search engines draw on material that is universal and wide-ranging. Everything that has been published on the World Wide Web is available to us. Using an internet search to find specific scholarly conversations on a topic is like examining the entire Pacific Ocean for a particular school of fish usually found near the shores of Hawaii. We may well find our particular school of fish in the Pacific Ocean, but why not just go to the shores of Hawaii to search for it, since that is usually where it is sighted? Similarly, we may well find some solid academic resources using a broad internet search, but why not just search an academic library website that specializes in scholarly research instead?

Secondly, *they have no guarantee of scholarly credibility*. The resources that show up on our internet feed when we conduct a search are inevitably those that have received the most hits, or those that are promoted by companies with the deepest pockets. As a result, we are receiving a biased list of resources based on popularity, algorithms, and marketing, not on quality. Even Google Scholar does not guarantee reputable academic resources. It is vulnerable to spam and lacks screening for quality. It does not necessarily detect search fields correctly or pull up the most relevant material for our topic. This means we have to figure out for ourselves which results are credible, well researched, or relevant. Wading through numerous results and trying to discern the good research in the mix can be a frustrating and time-consuming affair.

To ensure quality research and to truly discover what other scholars in our field are saying about a topic, we need to turn to academic search options that focus our investigation and locate the most relevant and reliable resources. Let's consider, then, our academic search options.

Our most valuable search option is our university or college library. Academic research is housed in academic libraries, and each library has reference librarians who can personally guide us towards the most effective research on our topic. In fact, visiting an academic library and gaining the expert recommendations of a reference librarian can save us a lot of time in tracking down resources. These librarians know where to find the most useful material within a field of study in the shortest time frame, and they can show us how to use academic search engines, electronic databases, and the library's catalogue to find quality resources. Most libraries also offer online chat reference services, so we can benefit from the research recommendations of a reference librarian remotely.

Alongside the support of a reference librarian, it is helpful to learn how to navigate our academic library website ourselves in order to find the most valuable sources. Academic library websites will normally have a general search engine on their home page that allows us to do a ***library-wide search***, that is, a search of all of the library's resources: books, e-books, reference materials, academic journals, media, and other documents housed in the library or subscribed to online. Unlike a general search engine on the internet, a library search focuses on academic resources that have been confirmed as credible and scholarly research.

When we explore the library's website, we find links to the following resources:

- The library's ***catalogue***, where we can search for books, e-books, government reports, maps, microforms, musical scores, etc. Scholarly books and collections are especially useful for extended or comprehensive studies that have looked at a topic's many facets, often from multiple perspectives.

- The library's ***journal collections***—scholarly print journals, microform journals, and e-journals (as well as newspapers and magazines)—that the academic library subscribes to. We do a journal search when we want to scan all the journals in a specific field of study—like archaeology, print media, landscape architecture, or internal medicine. Searching fields of study can prove effective for pinpointing the most relevant journals on our subject, which we can then search for research articles.

- A variety of ***indexes*** and ***databases*** where we can search for academic articles directly from scholarly and technical journals, newspapers, conference proceedings, etc. Some indexes and databases are interdisciplinary (like *Academic Search Premier*, *JSTOR*, *LexisNexis*, and *ProQuest*) and others focus on a particular field of research (like *ERIC*, *PsycINFO*, and *PubMed*). Indexes and databases are very useful for finding scholarly articles on our topic across a wide range of journals.

With this background in mind, let's consider how we might go about searching an academic library website for resources on a specific topic. Returning to our research question from Section A, let's imagine we are seeking resources that analyse the negative effects of social media (e.g., Facebook) on the body image and emotional state of adolescent girls. Because this subject is current, we would probably begin our search by looking for recent academic articles written on the topic.

When we want to search for articles topically, we begin with a *library-wide search* or an *index and database search*, choosing the keywords in our question as our search terms. For example:

The best keywords to use in a preliminary search are the ***nouns*** that signal the main categories of our research topic. Notably, the keywords we're using may not be the same ones that are programmed into a database. We may have to use synonyms for our keywords to get the results we want. For example, if the database doesn't recognize "Facebook," we may have to use the broader category "social media" instead. If the database doesn't pull up many resources on "adolescent girls," we could try the more general terms "adolescents" or "teenagers."

On the other hand, if we find too many articles with our keyword search *Facebook + Adolescent Girls*, then we can limit our search by adding other keywords from our question.

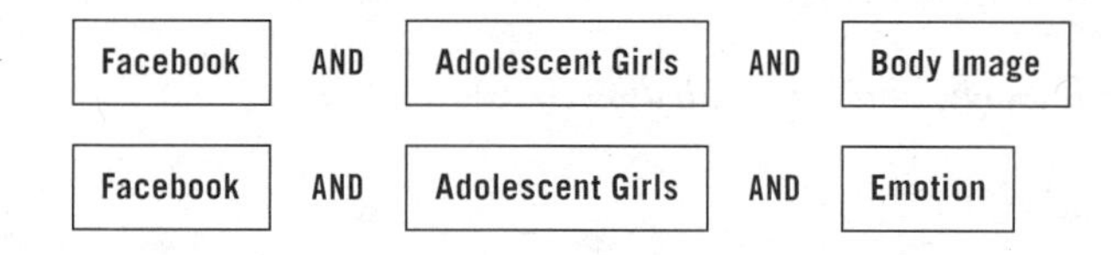

Doing a library-wide search or an index and database search may yield all the academic articles we need and more. But for those of us who prefer a subject search rather than a topical search, we may find it easier to peruse our library's *journal collections* and find our articles that way. To search the journal collections in a library, we need to determine what field of study our topic fits into and the various subjects it involves.

For example, if we return to our research question, we see that it fits nicely in the field of *psychology*. But it also crosses over into *sociology*, *child and youth development*, *media studies*, and *health*. We will find numerous journals in each of these fields of study. We can then choose the most likely journals to have articles on our topic, such as the following:

- *Journal of Youth and Adolescence*
- *Cyberpsychology, Behavior, and Social Networking*
- *Computers in Human Behaviour*
- *Media Psychology*
- *Body Image*

Depending on our topic, we may also need to consult books, e-books, or other reference materials alongside our journal articles. While we may stumble across this material in a library-wide search, it is more likely that we will find relevant sources by doing a *catalogue search* that only pulls up the books, e-books, and reference material in the library. In a catalogue search, we can narrow our results by searching for subject terms and keywords (and their synonyms) again.

Because books are extended studies of a topic, we may find we need to use broader categories—like "social media" or "mass media" and "adolescence" or "youth"—and related subject terms to find relevant sources. For example, a catalogue search with these broader terms may yield such books as the following:

- *Adolescence, Girlhood, and Media Migration* (2018)
- *Adolescents and Their Social Media Narratives: A Digital Coming of Age* (2018)
- *Global Youth in Digital Trajectories* (2017)
- *Emotions, Technology, and Social Media* (2016)
- *Youth and Media* (2015)
- *Digital Youth: The Role of Media in Development* (2011)
- *International Handbook of Children, Media and Culture* (2008)

We consult our collected books to gain a strong understanding of the context of our topic and to find relevant information for our specific study.

2. What Should We Look For?

The kinds of resources we seek as we investigate our topic are determined by our field of study. What counts as "good research" depends on what the community of scholars in that field find credible and convincing. The resources that make for a convincing research essay in the field of English literature differ from those that make for a credible research essay in zoology, anthropology, or geography. We begin our investigation, then, by observing what resources and research practices are considered valuable in our community—what do other scholars use in order to make their claims and develop their reasoning? We have our best chance at contributing to a research dialogue if we rely on the kinds of resources that scholars in that dialogue use, recognize, and respect.

That said, there are some general principles of "good research" that scholars across the disciplines use to select quality resources. We can use these principles to help us choose our resources regardless of our field of study:

- ***The research is quality controlled.*** Academic journals that publish scholarly articles have a system of quality control in place in order to ensure that the research they publish is first-rate. Each research article that is submitted goes through an extensive process of review by experts in the field. If the research lacks credibility, insight, or relevance, it will be rejected or require revisions before being reconsidered for publication. This review process is called "peer-review." Academic journals that are peer-reviewed are considered the most reliable and trustworthy sources of quality research. Luckily, most academic library websites have the option of selecting "peer-reviewed" research as a search parameter. When we use it, we automatically get the highest quality sources.

  When it comes to researching books, we tend to find that the most prestigious material is published by university and academic presses. Among the most respected publishers are Oxford University Press, Cambridge University Press, Routledge, Blackwell, and Palgrave Macmillan. That said, there are many other university presses and reputable publishers of academic scholarship beyond these five. If in doubt, ask a research librarian or course instructor about the academic quality of a selected book.

- ***The research writer is engaged in dialogue.*** We can also recognize quality by the number of references a research writer cites. Generally speaking, the more research writers interact with other scholars in their work the better. We want to choose the resources that reference other research extensively. Research writers who engage with the research of other scholars to frame, develop, test, and support their work show that they have read and understood the research in their field. Because they know this research in depth and in detail, they can be trusted as qualified scholars.

- ***The research is current.*** We also look for quality by considering whether our resources are current. Current research is not necessarily better than older research, but for many topics it is more relevant. Current research offers the latest findings, most recent contributions, and most up-to-date knowledge on a particular topic. For investigating topics in the sciences and social sciences especially, it is critical that we have the latest information so that our own study has currency and credibility, and so we can contribute to the existing dialogue on the topic rather than weigh in a few years too late on outdated research.

When we choose our resources, we can discern these three principles of "good research" quickly and easily. As we scan a research document, we can see how recently it was published, how many references it draws upon, and whether it was published by a reputable press or a peer-reviewed journal.

While we keep these principles and the values of our research community in mind when we choose our resources, we also need to realize that "good research" has a personal dimension: What resources are most compelling *to me*, drawing me in to investigate this topic further? What resources get my thoughts brewing and motivate me to engage in a research conversation on the topic? When we find resources that make us sit up and pay attention, that challenge us or transform our views, we have just encountered "good research." Discovering good research can cause us to invest ourselves in a topic in ways we could not imagine before. In fact, in light of such discoveries, we may find ourselves adjusting our topic, changing our preliminary research question, or redirecting our investigation.

If we discover a compelling resource, we can check out other material written by the same research scholars. It may be that we like their work more broadly, not just this particular article. Alternatively, we may want to follow up on the resources they cite and interact with in their work. Often, consulting the researchers' bibliography or references at the end of their article or book will lead us to more valuable material and give us a sense of the conversation they are participating in, a conversation that we would also like to join.

EXERCISE 3
FINDING RESOURCES

Once you have a research topic and the question(s) you want to investigate in hand, visit your academic library website. Consult a reference librarian to help you navigate the library website and gain the most out of its search engines and resources. Then try the following searches:

1. A *library-wide search* using your topic's keywords (and synonyms).
   - How many sources does this search yield?
   - Find a few sources that are directly applicable to your topic.

2. A *catalogue search* for books and references by subject or keyword.
   - How many sources does this search yield?
   - Find a few sources that are relevant to your topic.

3. A search of your library's *journal collection* by field of study.
   - How many journals does the library have in your field of study?
   - Which ones would likely have the most relevant articles for your topic?
   - Find a couple of articles in these journals that directly relate to your topic.

4. An *index or database search* by keyword (and synonyms).
   - How many journal articles does this search yield?
   - Find a couple of articles in a database that is relevant to your topic.

Collect eight to ten scholarly resources in total. Ensure they are current, quality controlled, credible in the research community, and compelling to you.

C. THINKING THROUGH THE RESEARCH: GENERATING AND ORGANIZING OUR IDEAS

Perhaps we now find ourselves sitting at a desk piled high with resources, wondering what to make of the research we've collected and how to begin formulating our ideas for our essay. We know that the more we've thought through our resources and made sense of our ideas, the easier it will be to take a stance and start writing. But thinking through research material can be difficult if we don't know how to direct our focus or navigate our thoughts.

One way to help us make sense of our research and focus our thinking is to learn *what kind of thinker* we are and use that to our advantage. There are at least two kinds of thinking we use to process research information and organize our ideas: ***linear thinking*** and ***lateral thinking*** (De Bono, 1967). We usually tend towards one or the other in our mental processing. Recognizing what kind of thinker we are can help us work through our research material productively, stimulate our best thoughts, develop our reasoning, and approach our research essay with confidence; so let's look at these two processes in detail.

1. Linear Thinkers

Many of us work through our ideas in a systematic, sequential, or linear way. We like to organize our research information and analyse it in a logical manner. And we tend to make lists, outlines, tables, or charts to order our thoughts. We also rely on internal dialogue to formulate our ideas. That is, we "talk to ourselves" to make sense of our thoughts. Until we have made sense of something in our minds, we don't usually share it with others. If this sounds like you, try the following tips as you approach your research project.

Use your strengths to your advantage. You have strong organizational skills and are good at staying on task. And you benefit from logical and orderly processes and procedures. With this in mind, start assembling your research findings and organize your thoughts by ***asking*** the journalists' questions (who, what, where, when, why, how) to make sense of your research information; by ***listing*** the various research positions, key ideas, and conclusions you find; and by ***outlining*** your ideas in relation to this information.

ASKING THE JOURNALISTS' QUESTIONS

Let's return to our sample topic and imagine we are writing our research essay about the negative effects of Facebook on adolescent girls. We might begin by asking the journalists' questions to think logically through this topic:

What? The negative effects of Facebook—particularly negative body image and negative emotions resulting from unrealistic comparisons between adolescent peers on Facebook.

Where? In North America.

When? Currently (I will focus on the last decade).

Who? A cross-section of adolescent girls ranging from thirteen to sixteen years old.

Why? To understand how an image-based social environment like Facebook shapes adolescent girls' perceptions of themselves in relation to their peers and to determine whether adolescent girls using Facebook are more at risk for negative self-evaluation than those who do not use Facebook.

How? By exploring research about Facebook and its adolescent users, centring on its negative psychological effects. I will rely on psychological research—specifically theories of identity formation and developmental psychology—to help me understand how adolescent girls may be at risk.

By beginning with the journalists' questions, we can often formulate the basic aspects of our research project that we want to develop in our essay.

LISTING

These basic aspects can be developed by listing our key research findings in relation to each of the areas we have outlined above. After we list our key findings, we should be able to discern which research material is most promising and where some of the gaps in research are. We should also be able to formulate a preliminary response to the research we've found. For example:

1. Numerous researchers are studying the negative effects of social media on adolescents. The articles and books I collected exploring this issue in the last decade include ______________________________.

2. I found six resources on negative psychological and emotional outcomes for adolescents who use Facebook as their primary means of social interaction. They are ______________. These sources focus specifically on the following negative outcomes: ____________________.

3. I found two resources that deal specifically with negative comparisons and self-perception. These focus on adolescents across genders. The main findings in these two articles are: ______________________.

4. I found two resources that highlight the connection between negative body image and Facebook use. They focus on adolescent girls. The main findings in these two articles are: __________________________.

Promising Findings: The resources I have found are great for establishing a psychological framework for my study. I have also found lots of evidence that excessive Facebook use has negative effects on adolescents—particularly for creating negative image-based comparisons and self-perceptions.

Limitations: I haven't found many studies about Facebook that focus specifically on adolescent girls.

Preliminary Response: Since few studies have focused on adolescent girls specifically, this seems to be an important gap to address in the research conversation on this topic. The findings across genders apply to adolescent girls, but I want to know if girls in particular have different negative self-perceptions and self-judgements than other gender identities.

Listing can help us categorize and organize our research findings, figure out where the gaps might be, and determine which findings to focus on. While we often feel the need to incorporate all of our findings into our research essay, we actually want to be strategic and choose only the most relevant areas of research that fit our focus. In other words, we want to select the aspects of the scholarly research conversation that we would like to contribute to directly. Working though our research with lists can help us to focus our attention, choose relevant evidence, and begin to flesh out our ideas.

OUTLINING

Based on the research findings we have categorized and organized, we can now sketch a preliminary outline for our essay. In our outline we can include our topic and research question, the most current and relevant research material, a research gap we've found, and a tentative stance to address that gap. We can also begin to organize our key ideas into points that we'd like to make in the body of our research essay.

Outline

Focused Topic: The negative impact of Facebook on young adolescent girls in North America

Research Question(s): How does excessive Facebook use affect the self-perceptions and body image of young adolescent girls? Which girls are most susceptible to negative self-perceptions and comparisons?

Current Research: Scholars confirm that social media has a significant impact on adolescent personal development and self-perception. In particular, some scholars have observed that adolescents who use Facebook as their primary means of social connection are likely to struggle with negative self-comparison, body dissatisfaction, and increased depression and anxiety.

Research Gap: There is limited research about the way Facebook affects adolescent girls specifically. The current scholarship about Facebook focuses on adolescents in general.

Tentative Stance: I hypothesize that adolescent girls who use Facebook as their primary means of social connection are more likely to struggle with negative psychological effects than their peers who do not.

Point 1: ______________
Research material to discuss:

Point 2: ______________
Research material to discuss:

Point 3: ______________
Research material to discuss:

Point 4: ______________
Research material to discuss:

As we can see, linear thinking works through ideas in a systematic and logical way. It helps us to order our research material into useful categories and select the findings that are most applicable to our discussion. By using the journalists' questions, lists, and outlines, we can create the basic framework for our research essay before we begin writing.

2. Lateral Thinkers

When approaching research material, some of us are more instinctive and unsystematic in our thought processes. We have piles of good ideas, but sometimes they feel jumbled together like a drawer of mismatched socks. We feel constricted by too many rules, formulas, and plans, and find they impede our ideas and hamper our flow of thought. We are process oriented, preferring to start writing before all our ideas are set in stone and seeing where the journey takes us. We tend to verbally process ideas too, throwing a thought out there to others before we've had time to think it through and making sense of it through external dialogue. If this sounds like you, try the following tips as you approach your research essay.

Use your strengths to your advantage. You have strong intuition and are good at generating new and creative ideas. You also benefit from externally processing to reach your conclusions. With this in mind, externalize your thoughts with techniques such as ***free writing*** (to release your thoughts and generate ideas); ***mind mapping*** (to draw your ideas visually in order to see key points); and ***looping*** (to focus your ideas and narrow them into a workable stance). These are useful processing techniques to help you express your thoughts and begin to organize them meaningfully.

FREE WRITING

A good way to generate ideas about a topic is to free write about it. In a free write, we get our ideas out on paper without censoring them with grammar or semantic rules. Because our minds make connections more easily when we write longhand than when we type, it is important to do a free write with pen and paper. It's also helpful to choose a quiet space. When we avoid distractions we give our minds a chance to engage fully with the topic rather than forcing them to divide their attention between various stimuli. Finally, we choose a time frame, like ten or fifteen minutes, and write out thoughts continuously without checking ourselves (or the time) and without judging our writing and ideas. For example, a free write on the negative effects of Facebook on adolescent girls might look something like this:

Negative Effects of Facebook on Adolescent Girls

I'm a big fan of Facebook and like to connect with my friends on it. I love being able to create myself in the way that I want others to see me—like I can choose my best self and present it. It's a real ego boost to get lots of likes. I mean, I know it's mostly meaningless but I like that people are looking at my profile and stuff. Um yeah. What else to say. I like looking at other people's profiles too and it's a good way to stay connected with friends from high school but I think that using Facebook a lot could be negative on younger teens. They don't really know who they are yet so they're more susceptible to images without um without the capacity to separate what they see from the reality of people's lives. Like Facebook is all about creating a self that others see and want to connect with and to share ideas and stuff. So it's really image based. And everyone else's pictures look so good so if we compare ourselves to the pics and the lives people show on Facebook, then we don't measure up because our reality isn't as great as what we present. It's hard not to get caught up in the images and teenage girls need approval and are really self-conscious about themselves so they will probably be sucked in by the images of others and feel like bad about themselves in comparison. I think it would be good to see what studies show about Facebook affecting the way girls see themselves and how it may be negative. If girls are using Facebook as the main way to connect to friends, then it may create a weird tension between what she sees on Facebook and what she sees in real life. And if she can't tell the difference between images and reality then she may end up with image issues—like body dissatisfaction and self-dislike or whatever.

When we free write, we allow our thoughts to run loose without structure or judgement. We can think of it as "stream of consciousness" writing. We let the stream flow to see what ideas are generated in the process.

MIND MAPPING

Once we have generated some ideas about our research topic, we can start drawing connections between our ideas, laying them out visually through the practice of mind mapping.

Mind mapping helps us externalize our thoughts and approach them visually. On paper we can organize and coordinate our ideas by using certain colours, shapes, and lines. When ideas are visually laid out before us, we are often able to make connections that we didn't necessarily think of at first. For example, a mind map exploring the negative effects of Facebook on adolescent girls might look as follows:

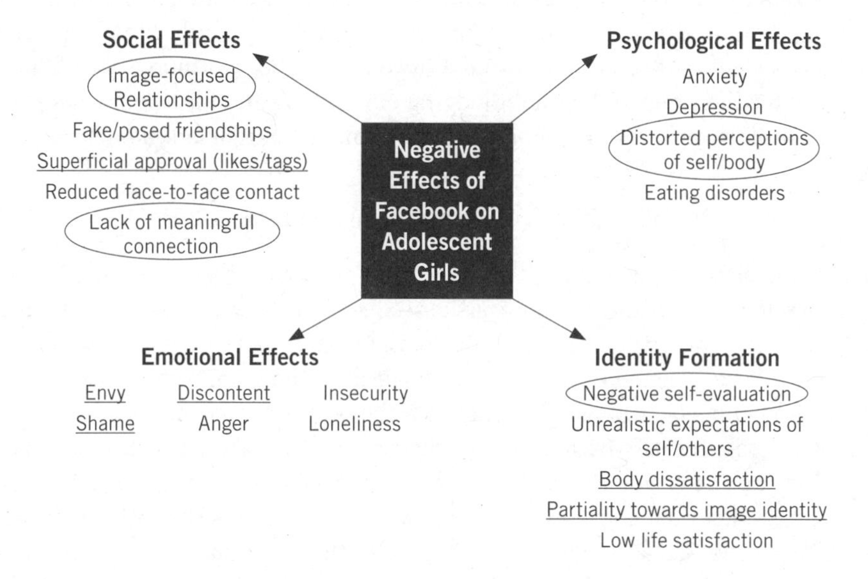

Mind mapping helps us develop our ideas and lay out all the aspects of our topic. We can colour coordinate similar ideas, highlight connections and outcomes with arrows, and underline or circle the issues that most interest us. Our mind map may look incoherent to others and our ideas may be quite broad at this stage, but as we organize our ideas under key headings, we can start to visualize the main areas where we could delve deeper in an essay.

LOOPING

To begin focusing and narrowing our ideas into a stance for our paper, we can try a mental process called "looping." Looping involves choosing the ideas that are most compelling from our free write or mind map and summarizing each of them in a single sentence. This is our first "loop." For example, two key ideas that we could draw from our work so far on the negative effects of Facebook might be:

- I think the images posted on Facebook could negatively affect how adolescent girls see themselves and compare themselves to their friends.

- I think adolescent girls struggle to distinguish between the images of beauty and fun posted by their friends on Facebook and the ordinary realities of life.

In our first loop, our ideas will probably be observational and general. In order to make them more specific and focused, we take the sentences from our first loop and do a short free write on them. We then take our best ideas from this free write and summarize them. This is our second "loop." As we keep working through loops, we will discover a focal point that interests us. Perhaps it's one that keeps repeating itself or seems to be the main connecting point between our ideas. For example, another loop or two might lead to a focus like:

- I think adolescent girls who use Facebook as their primary means of connection with friends are more susceptible to negative comparisons and self-perceptions (like body dissatisfaction) than girls who don't use Facebook as a key source of social connection.

Once we have a focus or tentative stance that we'd like to test or prove in our essay, it is a good time to return to the research we've collected on our topic to see what the experts are saying. Do their research and ideas fit with our direction and the stance we're thinking of taking? If we aren't finding evidence to support our stance or if we see that researchers are going in a different direction than we are, we will need to take note and work to refocus or reframe our ideas so that they can fit into the current dialogue on the topic.

As we can see, lateral thinking stimulates our creative ideas so we can work through them in spatial and visual ways. We give all our ideas voice as we let them flow out and we save judgement until later, when we choose our focus from those ideas and consider the research findings that connect with them.

In sum, when we know our typical pattern of thinking—whether it's linear or lateral—we can play to our strengths, directing our energy productively, and making the most of our research and ideas to begin the writing process. That said, we recognize that other ways of thinking can be helpful too, even if they don't come as easily to us. For instance, linear thinkers may benefit from the flow of free writing and lateral thinkers may find it useful to list ideas or ask journalists' questions. Since different thinking processes each have their own advantages, we benefit from drawing on various techniques so as not to become rigid in our mental processing.

EXERCISE 4
MENTAL PROCESSING

Now that you have considered the two different approaches to thinking through research material, do you tend to be a linear thinker or a lateral thinker?

- Choose one of the techniques that fits your natural preference—journalists' questions, listing, outlining, free writing, mind mapping, or looping—and use it to begin planning your research essay.

- Now challenge your norm with one of the processing techniques that is less natural to you. How does using an alternative approach help to think outside the box and hone your ideas?

D. WRITING A PROPOSAL AND A BIBLIOGRAPHY

As we work through our research findings, generating and organizing our ideas, we begin to develop our stance and the direction we want to go in our study. Inevitably, our ideas will expand and change as we write our research essay. But we have laid the groundwork and now have a solid foundation to begin our writing. We are ready to try out our stance and preliminary ideas on readers in the form of a research proposal and bibliography.

As students, we often write research proposals and bibliographies as "test runs" for our research essays, with course instructors as our primary readers. As scholars, we continue to propose new research projects to specialized readers—members of scholarly committees, research-funding agencies, publishers, related corporations, etc.—in order to gain their interest, support, and funding. In fact, a research proposal can be seen as a pitch to convince readers of the value of our research project so that it will be published or funded. Whether we are students or scholars, we write research proposals and bibliographies to show readers how we are responding to the research of others with our project, stance, and initial findings.

A ***research proposal*** is a logical plan for our research essay or project in which we communicate our preliminary material and ideas, and convince readers of the value and feasibility of our work. It introduces our topic and research question(s)—the issue, problem, or concern we plan to pursue in our essay. It shows our readers *why* we are investigating this issue and *how* we are making sense of the research material we've collected so far. In a research proposal, we assert our preliminary stance, the approach we will use to prove that stance, and how our ideas will contribute to current knowledge on the subject. A research proposal is accompanied by a ***bibliography***—an organized list of the resources that we've collected as the basis for our proposal.

The way we format a research proposal and bibliography will depend on our context—the field of study we're writing in and the readers we're writing for. Different research communities use different formats to organize their proposals and bibliographies. It is important to follow the standard format for the field of study we're writing in or the format that our instructor has requested. That said, research proposals do share some key characteristics across the disciplines. Once we know what they are, we can modify them to fit our context:

- **A Title**: We compose a fitting title to capture the essence of our work.

- **An Introduction**: We introduce the topic, the current research knowledge about the topic, and the major issues and key research points surrounding it.

- **A Problem and Purpose**: We highlight a problem, issue, or concern about the topic that has stimulated our research question(s) and exploration. We provide a reasonable explanation for why this problem (issue or concern) should be explored and why our particular study needs to be done in order to explore it.

- **A Literature or Resource Review**: We show the current knowledge and research dialogue on our topic by outlining the key ideas in the resources we have collected, explaining how we are making sense of those ideas in regard to our research question(s), and noting any gaps or limitations we have discovered in the process. Sometimes this element is incorporated in the introduction.

- **A Stance**: We take a stance on the research we have found, presenting our claim as an argument or hypothesis in response to the views of other scholars. We also provide important details that may help us test or prove our claim (including testable theories that support our stance) or challenge our ability to prove it (limited findings, inconclusive data, alternative viewpoints).

- **A Methodology or Approach**: We highlight the methodology or approach we will use to test our hypothesis or prove our argument. We can think of a methodology as the "best practice" for approaching our research questions and developing our case. In this section, we often include the parameters of our study (what we will and will not be analysing in our research process) and where we expect to find the materials we need to support our stance. We also indicate whether we see any limitations to our approach that may affect our viewpoints or influence the reliability of our study.

- **Significance or Impact of Research**: We discuss the potential impact or significance of our research, focusing on the gaps in knowledge we will be filling or the beneficial contributions we will be making to the research community and beyond.

While these characteristics do not apply to every field of study, they do typify the areas that researchers focus on to communicate the direction and value of their initial research and ideas. To see how to formulate a research proposal using these elements, let's return to our research topic about Facebook and adolescent girls.

The Unhappy Side of Social Media: How Facebook Fuels Negative Comparisons and Self-Perceptions in Adolescent Girls

Introduction: Spending time on social media is one of the main ways that adolescents connect with their peers. Social media connections have an impact on their personal development and self-perceptions (Walsh, 2018; Košir et al., 2016). While some of these impacts are positive, scholars have also observed problems. In particular, they have noticed that adolescents who use Facebook as their primary means of social connection and their measure of self-worth are likely to struggle with negative self-comparisons (Frison & Eggermont, 2016b), body dissatisfaction (Rousseau et al., 2017), decreased life satisfaction (Frison & Eggermont, 2016a), and increased depression and anxiety (Muzaffer et al., 2018).

Problem and Purpose: While scholars have focused on the negative effects that Facebook can have on adolescent users in general, I am interested in the negative effects that Facebook has on girls in particular. In this essay, I will explore how spending extensive time on Facebook fuels negative comparisons and self-perceptions (especially in regard to body image) in young adolescent girls. On Facebook, adolescent girls can create an image and persona of themselves that they think others will like and accept. In the process, however, they can easily confuse the "likes" and "tags" of others for genuine acceptance and mistake the images of others for their actual reality. For adolescent girls, visual comparisons can produce negative self-perceptions that can lead to body dissatisfaction and result in emotional distress. In this study I ask: Which girls are most susceptible to negative self-evaluation and resulting emotional distress due to Facebook use? And how might a precarious social standing (or lack of belonging) in a peer group affect a girl's Facebook use and her susceptibility to negative comparisons?

Stance: In this paper, I hypothesize that adolescent girls who use Facebook as their primary means of connection are more susceptible to the "social media visual fables" (Walsh, 2017, p. 69) presented by their peers than those who do not. By buying in to the reality of the images they see, adolescent girls are more likely to struggle with negative self-perceptions and body dissatisfaction, as well as negative emotions like envy, discontent, or shame, drawn from their visual comparisons. In concentrating my attention on adolescent girls, I recognize that my findings will be gender-limited. I trust, however, that my particular focus will help to develop a basis for comparing the self-perceptions of teenage Facebook users who identify as male, transgender, or non-conforming.

Methodology: To frame my study, I rely on theories of identity formation in developmental psychology (Erikson, 1968; Côté & Levine, 2016) and focus on gendered identity in social media (Walsh, 2018). To establish the fact that adolescent Facebook users are more susceptible to negative comparisons and self-perceptions and decreased life satisfaction than non-Facebook users, I draw on the two-wave studies undertaken by Frison and Eggermont (2016a; 2016b). I add to their discussion by comparing self-reported data of adolescent girls who use Facebook avidly to those who do not use Facebook regularly. At this stage, the most useful self-reported data I have found is drawn from Walsh (2018). However, I hope to locate more studies that use self-reported data as well as studies that focus on identity formation in social media to help flesh out my initial findings. I expect that the two-wave studies and self-reported data from other published studies will yield results that prove my hypothesis.

Significance: I build on the current studies examining the negative effects of Facebook on the identity formation of adolescent girls. In doing so, I hope to encourage effective strategies to reduce these negative effects. Perhaps the easiest strategy is to limit Facebook use. However, it may be more productive to encourage alternative identity narratives, ones that are more realistic or multifaceted than the image-based personas produced on Facebook. My study will aid in developing the groundwork we need to help teenage girls recognize and deal with their negative self-perceptions that stem from "social media visual fables."

Notably, not all research proposals are this length. Some are shorter and others are longer, depending on the context they are written in and the readers they are written for. Nor do all research proposals use these specific headings. Some are written in paragraph form without headings and others use alternative headings. However, this example gives us a good sense of the key areas that interested readers need to know if they are going to approve and support a research project.

EXERCISE 5
PROPOSING TO READERS

As you begin composing a research proposal, consider your research context and write with your readers in mind by using the following questions:

- What field are you situated in?
- Which research material are you responding to?
- Who are your readers?
- What do they need to know in order to support and approve your project?
- How would they like you to format your proposal?

A research proposal is followed by a bibliography, formatted according to the reference style used by our research community or preferred by our instructor. A bibliography lists the resources we have cited directly in our research proposal. It may also include other resources we have consulted that did not make their way into our proposal but will likely be used in our research essay. The following bibliography lists the resources used in the sample research proposal above. It follows APA style in its organization and listing of references, since this project would likely be situated in the field of psychology, which uses APA style to acknowledge the research of others. Please note that while the bibliography below is single-spaced, most referencing formats (including APA style) use double-spacing.

References

Heading is centred

Côté, J. E., & Levine, C. G. (2016). *Identity formation, youth, and development: A simplified approach*. Psychology Press.

Erikson, E. H. (1968). *Identity, youth and crisis*. W. W. Norton.

Frison, E., & Eggermont, S. (2016a). Exploring the relationships between different types of Facebook use, perceived online social support, and adolescents' depressed mood. *Social Science Computer Review, 34*(2), 153–171. https://doi.org/10.1177/0894439314567449

Frison, E., & Eggermont, S. (2016b). "Harder, better, faster, stronger": Negative comparison on Facebook and adolescents' life satisfaction are reciprocally related. *Cyberpsychology, Behavior and Social Networking, 19*(3), 158–164. http://doi.org/10.1089/cyber.2015.0296

Resources are listed in alphabetical order by author's last name

Each new resource begins at the left margin; subsequent lines are indented

Košir, K., Horvat, M., Aram, U., Jurinec, N., & Tement, S. (2016). Does being on Facebook make me (feel) accepted in the classroom? The relationships between early adolescents' Facebook usage, classroom peer acceptance and self-concept. *Computers in Human Behavior, 62*, 375–384. https://doi.org/10.1016/j.chb.2016.04.013

Muzaffar, N., Brito, E. B., Fogel, J., Fagan, D., Kumar, K., & Verma, R. (2018). The association of adolescent Facebook behaviours with symptoms of social anxiety, generalized anxiety, and depression. *Journal of the Canadian Academy of Child and Adolescent Psychiatry, 27*(4), 252–260.

Rousseau, A., Eggermont, S., & Frison, E. (2017). The reciprocal and indirect relationships between passive Facebook use, comparison on Facebook, and adolescents' body dissatisfaction. *Computers in Human Behavior, 73*, 336–344. https://doi.org/10.1016/j.chb.2017.03.056

Walsh, J. (2018). *Adolescents and their social media narratives: A digital coming of age*. Routledge.

CONCLUSIONS

A research essay is perhaps the most common academic writing genre that we use to interact with the research and ideas of other scholars and respond with our own. In order to write one, we first need to develop a topic and investigate the academic resources we find on that topic. Developing a topic involves choosing an issue that interests us or a problem that concerns us and turning it into a specific analytical research question that we can investigate. In our investigation, we find the most reputable scholarly resources by using the search engines found on our academic library's website. Once we have a collection of relevant resources, we read them carefully to discern what other scholars have said about our topic. We draw on our linear and lateral thought processes to develop, focus, and organize our ideas. In effect, we are using our reading and thinking processes to engage in a dialogue with other scholars on the topic. But the dialogue doesn't end there. We also set up a dialogue with our readers when we create a research proposal and bibliography. Here we share our preliminary research and ideas to show our readers the value and validity of our project.

QUESTIONS FOR REFLECTION

1. When we choose a research topic, we usually begin with general questions of concern to help us figure out what we want to research. We call this *inquiry-based research*. We then narrow our broad topic into a workable research project by developing an *analytical research question* (*how, why, what is the relationship between*...) to direct our study and develop our stance. We make this analytical research question as specific as possible by using *fact-based questions* (*who, what, where, when*) that help us locate our study in a particular context. Using your imagination, turn each of the following general questions into a specific analytical research question that could be investigated for a research project. For example:

   General question: What is confirmation bias?

   Reframed as a specific analysis question: Why is it problematic that internet searches pull up material that confirms our biases?

   - What exercises are good for losing weight?
   - Where are the effects of climate change having the worst impact?
   - What makes an indoor space beautiful?
   - What is the Universal Declaration of Human Rights?

2. When we collect our research materials, what should we be looking for in each resource to determine whether it is reputable or quality research? Consider the research material you have collected for your research project and evaluate it according to these criteria.

3. Imagine you are writing a research essay about the social and emotional dimensions of childhood development. As you work on your research proposal, you refer to a particular article that now needs to be cited in your bibliography. Using a writers' reference guide, cite the publishing information below in APA style. Now try it in MLA style. Finally, try it in Chicago style. How do these formats differ? Which format will you need to use for your own research essay?

Article Title: Addressing Children's Social Emotional Needs with Children's Literature
Research Writer: Melissa Allen Heath
Name of Journal: School Psychology International
Volume: 38
Issue: 5
Date of Publication: 2017
Pages: 453–457
DOI: 10.1177/014303431770447

CHAPTER ELEVEN

INTRODUCTIONS

Joining a Scholarly Dialogue

Imagine you are travelling by car from Vancouver to Calgary to visit your family for Thanksgiving. This is the first time you've done this trip on your own and, as luck would have it, your GPS is broken. You could rely on the maps app on your phone, but you decide to go out on a limb and do the trip old-school style, with an up-to-date Google map printed off your computer. As you look at the map, you notice that there are a couple of routes to Calgary. You opt for the shortest route, up towards Kamloops and over through Revelstoke and Banff. You have not personally taken this route before, but you know of friends who have, and your parents went this way when they came to visit you last summer. You consult them and get their advice. All told, it is the most direct route between the two cities.

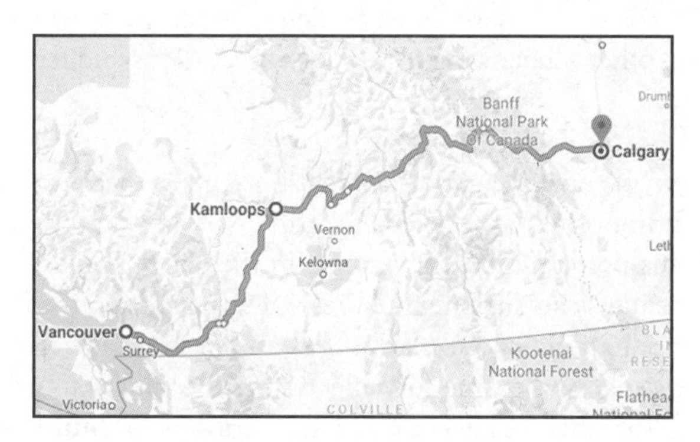

Early Friday morning, you get up, throw your bags into the car and drive off with your map beside you. You know the trip takes about ten hours and you want to make good time. The traffic moves relatively well until just outside Kamloops, where you hit a jam seemingly out of nowhere. You start analysing what could be causing it: A car accident? Roadwork? A fallen tree across the road? A mudslide? Finally, after an hour, you begin moving again, and realize that the most rational possibility—roadwork—was the cause of the delay. You go on your way without further traffic interruptions.

As you drive past bare spots in the landscape, you wonder what exactly the logging industry is up to. You consider whether the monetary gain is worth the blight on the scenery and the damage to the ecosystem. As you drive through the Rockies you marvel at the majesty of the mountains and consider when to do your next hike in Banff National Park. You imagine doing Skoki Loop with your best friend. Finally, you reach Calgary a little after 9:00 p.m. Your parents open the door and greet you excitedly, asking, "How was the trip?" You give them some of the highlights and also announce that you've decided to drive through Kelowna on the way back, to avoid the Kamloops roadwork. After a few minutes, you raise the logging question with your parents, proposing how the industry might change its tactics so as not to destroy the natural ecosystems in its wake.

In many ways, writing an academic research essay is like taking a well-planned road trip:

- **Introduction**
  The introduction is like sitting at a computer and mapping out a route for the trip. In an introduction, we tell readers where we are going (the topic), who has "taken this trip" before and what their directions and viewpoints were (the current research conversation), our standpoint on the "trip" (a stance and claim), and how exactly we plan to "get there" (a trajectory) in our essay.

- **Body Paragraphs**
  The body paragraphs are like taking the road trip itself. On the way, we make observations and analyse those observations in order to make sense of them. On a road trip, we may gather evidence of stopped cars, cut trees, and beautiful landscapes by means of pictures on our camera or phone. Similarly, in an academic paper, we draw on evidence or the research findings of other scholars to discuss our observations and test or prove our claim.

- **Conclusion**
  The conclusion is like arriving at our destination. This is the moment for a short overview of the most important aspects of the "trip." No one wants a detailed recap of the full journey at this point. Unlike the parents in the above scenario, the readers of our research essay are like road-tripping buddies. They have just done the trip with us, so it doesn't make sense to pull out our map at the end to retrace the route we just took with them. Instead, we take some time for reflection and evaluation. In our conclusion we offer applications for what we have learned, implications for future studies, or lingering questions that could stimulate further dialogue.

In this chapter and those following, we will look at each of these three areas of essay writing in detail—introductions, body paragraphs, and conclusions—for an academic research context. In this chapter we will focus on how to write a research introduction, combining the writing skills we have developed so far. With examples, tips, and templates, we will explore how to introduce readers to our research directly and compellingly, and how to set up our stance as a claim in dialogue with other researchers at the outset of our papers.

A. THE FIVE ELEMENTS OF AN ACADEMIC INTRODUCTION

Like organized travellers who meticulously plan a road trip before they hop into the car, academic writers lay out what they intend to do and how they intend to do it in their research introductions. They introduce their specific topic of study, summarize the current research conversation taking place about that topic, step into that conversation with their stance (in the form of a claim), and plot their trajectory or intended line of reasoning with which they will test or prove their claim. While research introductions leave little to the imagination, they are ideal for presenting research material directly and compellingly to interested readers.

Most research introductions rely on the following five elements of composition to enter the scholarly conversation and orient readers at the outset of an essay.

- **Introducing the topic and creating common ground**
  We introduce readers to our topic and create common ground between us to ensure that we are beginning "on the same page."

- **Establishing the current research context and conversation**
  We acquaint readers with the current research context and conversation by highlighting the key research ideas and viewpoints of expert scholars in the field of study.

- **Pointing out a research gap**
  We indicate a specific aspect of the topic that has not been explored in current research or discussed thoroughly in the research dialogue.

- **Taking a stance**
  We step into the dialogue with our stance in the form of a claim that contributes to the conversation and builds knowledge within the scholarly community.

- **Providing a trajectory**
  We briefly outline how we will explore or prove our claim in the body of our essay.

These practices should look familiar to us, as we've considered how they function in various academic genres in the previous chapters. Let's focus now on how they work together as we begin to write our research essays.

1. Introducing the Topic and Creating Common Ground

A research essay begins with one or two clear statements that set the stage for the academic dialogue that follows. These statements introduce the topic to our readers and create "common ground" between us. ***Common ground*** refers to the basic knowledge that we hold in common with others about a topic of conversation. As we saw in Chapter 2, common ground puts us and others on the same page or within the same communication situation so that we can understand one another easily. When we hold basic knowledge in common with others, we can depend on that shared foundation between us to communicate effectively with one another.

We ensure shared knowledge at the outset of our research essays with introductory statements that situate readers in our research context and get the conversation going. As we craft our introductory statements, it is important to keep two things in mind: we need to imagine readers who already know something about our research topic, and we need to create common ground that fits the specificity of our topic. To see how these two aspects—knowledgeable readers and specificity—are involved in our introductory statements, let's imagine a topic that a literary researcher might write about: the subversive feminism of Desdemona in Shakespeare's *Othello*.

With knowledgeable readers and specificity in mind, the writer might begin a research essay with the following statements to ensure common ground:

> Studies of Shakespeare's *Othello* have often considered Desdemona a caricature of the ideal woman of the seventeenth century: docile, virtuous, and submissive to her husband (Stems & Tailor, 2009; Fosterman, 2013). However, a close reading of the play reveals that Desdemona exhibits a subversive feminism, challenging both her father's control over her and Othello's accusations of infidelity (Ong & Tse, 2010).
>
> Please note that the names and material used in this example are invented and any correspondence to actual research or researchers is purely coincidental.

Notice how this example specifically introduces the topic and fosters common ground between the research writer and readers who are interested in and acquainted with Shakespeare's *Othello*. Readers who haven't heard of *Othello* or don't care about Shakespeare's plays will not likely be reading this essay or benefit from this researcher's interpretations. However, with a knowledgeable and interested readership in place, this example begins very specifically: it directly introduces the play, the character of Desdemona, and two scholarly interpretations of her femininity.

This directness and specificity may come as a surprise to some of us. We may have the impression that research essays begin by introducing a topic generally or indirectly, relying on platitudes like "women throughout history," "feminism across the centuries," or "drama throughout the ages" before actually getting to the topic itself. In fact, research writers tend to get straight to the topic. As we introduce our topic and create common ground, we avoid sweeping generalities that don't clearly

introduce the topic or provide a research context for our readers. Notice how the following platitudes fail to create common ground, because they offer no context or substance:

- Throughout history, humans have sought to understand themselves.
- Consumerism is an influential force in everyday life.
- Powerful monarchies have always oppressed people.
- The world is in crisis.

While each of these statements may contain an element of truth, none of them makes for an effective beginning to a research paper; they all leave readers unclear about the actual topic, the subjects of the study (what and who are we talking about?), the location of the study, and the time period being examined. We create common ground by introducing our topic specifically to readers who are interested in and already know something about the subject, readers who we expect to respond to us and ultimately join the dialogue about the topic.

Starting our research paper with specific common ground meant for knowledgeable readers, however, can be tricky. One way we can ensure that our beginning is specific enough is to include the keywords of our topic directly in our first sentence. For example, if we happen to be writing on the topic, "heroin overdose in Vancouver's Downtown Eastside," then our first sentence might read as follows:

> Since 2003, **heroin overdose** in **Vancouver's Downtown Eastside** has been on the decline due to the work of Insite, the first legal supervised injection site in North America.

Notice how the key aspects of the topic—heroin overdose and Vancouver's Downtown Eastside—make their way into this sentence. We ensure our common ground is specific by highlighting the *what*, *who*, *where*, and *when* of our topic. Doing so creates a clear starting point and context for our readers.

EXERCISE 1
CREATING COMMON GROUND

Imagine that your research topic is "AIDS awareness and prevention in Kenya" and that you have come up with the following five possible introductory statements. Rank the statements from best to worst for use in an essay on this topic.

- People in developing countries struggle with many diseases.
- AIDS prevention is currently a serious concern in Kenya.
- Global awareness and aid for AIDS prevention in Kenya has been rising since 2008.
- AIDS is a disease that kills many people in Africa.
- The world is experiencing more and more disease.

2. Establishing the Current Research Conversation

Once we've set the stage with our introductory statements, we are ready to acquaint readers with current research knowledge about our topic, showing them the field of study in which we're situated and the scholarly conversation we are joining. As we do, we demonstrate that we know what expert researchers are saying about our topic and that we are qualified to contribute to the research conversation with our own work.

There are a few ways to share current research with our readers in an introduction. Each one involves the skills of orchestration that we learned in Chapter 5, using the "chorus," "trio/duet," or "solo" approaches. First, we may decide to introduce the general views that researchers have established on our topic in the form of a chorus. We call these established views ***secured generalizations***—statements about a topic that have become accepted by the research community as common knowledge or fact (Giltrow et al., 2009, p. 255). Rather than make our own generalizations, we attribute them to the experts. For instance, instead of saying, "Mouthmint is the best toothpaste" (which sounds like our opinion), we secure that generalization by pointing to the experts and statistics: "Ninety-eight per cent of dentists agree that Mouthmint is the best toothpaste." An audience is more apt to be convinced by what dentists say about the best toothpaste than by the average person's opinion.

The same goes for building credibility in our research introductions. When we introduce the general views of expert researchers and secure these views with citations, we show our readers that what we are saying is already confirmed and valued in the research community. Notice how the following example takes a generalization about the topic and secures it with citations:

Example 1: Using Secured Generalizations

[P]rolonged or repeated exposure to stress and trauma can have serious negative consequences for physical and mental health (Schneiderman et al., 2005), particularly when stress is experienced early in development (Lupien et al., 2016). (p. 111)

Cross, D., Fani, N., Powers, A., & Bradley, B. (2017). Neurobiological development in the context of childhood trauma. *Clinical Psychology: Science and Practice, 24*(2), 111–124. https://doi.org/10.1111/cpsp.12198

We might assume that this generalization—prolonged and repeated exposure to trauma has negative physical and mental health outcomes—is common knowledge. However, by securing this generalization with citations, the writers have ensured that it has authority in the research community: valued researchers have said it and verified it. By drawing on other established scholars' words, the writers of this article have introduced the conversation on this subject with authority and research credibility.

A second way to introduce the current research on our topic is to summarize the main standpoints that expert researchers hold. Using a "duet" or "trio" approach, we introduce two or three positions held by experts on the topic. Like secured generalizations, this approach shows our readers that we know the established standpoints on our topic and, further, that we are aware of the differences between those stances. In a few short sentences, we not only reveal our competence as researchers, but also our ability to distinguish between research stances in the conversation. For this reason, many research writers who begin their introductions with a secured generalization will also add a succinct dialogue between experts, outlining the key stances about the topic.

Example 2: Highlighting Key Standpoints

> Most of the work on counterfactual thinking in children has been undertaken by developmental psychologists who have tried to ascertain when these thoughts start and their link to moral development. Research suggests that pre-school children rarely produce spontaneous counterfactual assertions but can generate them on request. However, by the age of six, children demonstrate automatic counterfactual thoughts (Kuczaj & Daly, 1979). Yet this was contradicted in a more recent study which showed that even a majority of 11-year-old children did not engage in counterfactual thinking (Rafetseder et al., 2013). Evidence also indicates that, from the age of seven, the emotions of guilt and regret, which are often referred to as "counterfactual emotions" also begin to emerge (Guttentag & Ferrell, 2004). (p. 207)
>
> Hill, J. (2017). Counterfactual thinking and educational psychology. *Educational Psychology in Practice, 33*(2), 206–223. https://doi.org/10.1080/02667363.2017.1288086

Here the research writer outlines three established standpoints in the dialogue about the age when counterfactual thinking begins in children. From these few sentences, we learn that there is a range of research evidence exploring this topic and that the stances do not necessarily agree. This format can be a strategic way to emphasize the dialogue as we introduce the current research on our topic.

A third way to share current research in our introduction is to engage directly with one specific expert in the field, using a "solo" approach and setting up a dialogue between us. This expert is usually someone whose work we appreciate and want to build on or whose work we find limited and want to develop. Engaging with one specific researcher at the outset of our work suggests that we are invested and detail-oriented scholars, able to look deeply into the ideas of others and grapple with them in conversation.

Example 3: Engaging with One Specific Expert

> Within autobiography studies, it is generally taken for granted that most autobiographies appear in the shape of a book. However, American historian Michael Mascuch provides another view. In *Origins of the Individualist Self* (1997), he suggests a relation between the history of the book and the autobiographical genre. He argues that the idea of the "author" as a model of individual identity is related to the physical book, which became accessible to more people from the end of the eighteenth century onwards—to readers as well as to publishers.... As an author, one could master one's own life narrative in the public eye of readers. In addition, being the author of a published book could lead to public rewards such as recognition and money. (pp. 117–18)
>
> Huisman, M. (2010). Selling the self: Publishing and marketing autobiographies in the nineteenth century. In A. Hornung (Ed.), *Auto/biography and mediation* (pp. 117–130). Universitätsverlag.

Here the research writer engages with one expert, the American historian Michael Mascuch, to introduce a critical issue in her own research on publishing and marketing autobiographies: the relationship between authorship and publication.

Whether we focus on one expert view to highlight a specific research area, a group of experts to outline a range of viewpoints, or secured generalizations to assert an established idea held by many experts in the research community, we introduce and orchestrate the current research conversation on our topic at the outset of our work in order to join the dialogue. When we have limited experience in our field of study we rely on experts to secure our credibility as researchers. But even when we become established scholars, we continue to point to well-known ideas and engage with other viewpoints in dialogue, reinforcing the fact that building knowledge is not a solitary or individualist pursuit, but a shared activity among committed thinkers.

3. Pointing Out a Gap

When we introduce the research and ideas of other scholars, we show our readers the current knowledge on our topic. We use the term "gap" to indicate what *hasn't* been studied or said about the topic, what pieces of knowledge are missing or need to be developed. As we saw in previous chapters, a ***gap*** is an opening in the conversation between researchers. It is a point of entry where we can join the dialogue, situate our stance on the topic by means of a claim, and offer something new to the field of study. Inevitably, there are always openings in research conversations, spaces for new discoveries and areas for further analysis. New findings or insights can be adopted. Practices in one community can be applied to another. Old conventions can be revisited and updated; and limited standpoints can be revised.

In our introductions we indicate a gap in the current knowledge *explicitly*. For example, notice how clearly the knowledge gap is articulated (emphasized in bold) in the following excerpt:

> While companies linking political positions with brands has become increasingly prevalent, **surprisingly little research explores the issue**. This is despite the knowledge that political orientation influences a battery of behaviors and cognitive processes (e.g., Carney et al., 2008). In fact, papers studying "lifestyle politics" have found political meaning in consumption decisions across an array of categories such as fashion, recreation, and entertainment. Specifically, a number of factors influence political consumerism, which represents the notion of purchasing only from companies with shared values (Shah et al., 2007). With a now sizable literature examining the implications of brands being associated with causes (Andrews et al., 2014; Kerr & Das, 2013; Varadarajan & Menon, 1988) and social responsibility (Biehal & Sheinin, 2007; Briggs et al., 2016; Brown & Dacin, 1997), the **lack of attention** to brands and politics is even more unexpected. (p. 125)
>
> Matos, G., Vinuales, G., & Sheinin, D.A. (2017). The power of politics in branding. *Journal of Marketing Theory and Practice, 25*(2), 125–140. https://doi.org/10.1080/10696679.2016.1270768

Researchers use specific language to represent gaps in knowledge. Conjunctions like *while, however, although, yet, despite, besides*, and *beyond* are coupled with phrases like *only beginning, incomplete, lacking, little, limited*, and *under-developed* to highlight research limitations. We draw attention to gaps in existing research in order to show how our stance can fill the gap and contribute to the current research dialogue on the topic.

4. Taking a Stance

In most research writing we join the dialogue directly in our introduction with our stance, letting readers know up front what our claim is and how we plan to test or prove it in our essay. As we learned in Chapters 7 and 9, our claim takes the form of an argument or hypothesis about the topic that responds to other standpoints and contributes to the research conversation. Because stances are meant to fill current gaps in knowledge and further our collective understanding, it makes sense to locate our claim right after we point out a knowledge gap. This two-step process is very common in research introductions to show how our stance builds on, modifies, complicates, challenges, questions, or opposes the established stances of other researchers. Consider how this approach is used in the following examples:

With the growth of new digital sources of big data, such as loyalty cards, business analytic solutions providers such as SAS and IBM are promoting cost-effective, cloud-based tools and services for small firms to exploit their flexible and intuitive MO [market orientation]. However, there is an analytical gap within the literature regarding our current knowledge of digital marketing generally, and the place of big data specifically. Previous studies of loyalty cards have focused on the consumer perspective in exploring the link with loyalty, or on development history and the technology involved (Everett, 2009; Smith & Sparks, 2009; Turner & Wilson, 2006; Wright & Sparks, 1999; Ziliani & Bellini, 2004). Gaps exist regarding loyalty cards and their impact (Cortinas et al., 2008), with implications for marketing planning within smaller firms (Donnelly et al., 2012). With the central proposition of this study being that loyalty card data should not create a digital divide between large and small firms, [we suggest] a complementary relationship between the informal nature of small-firm MO and the formalised nature of digital loyalty card data.... (p. 423)

Step 1: Gap

Step 2: Stance (Claim)

Donnelly, C., Simmons, G., Armstrong, G., & Fearne, A. (2015). Digital loyalty card 'big data' and small business marketing: Formal versus informal or complementary? *International Small Business Journal, 33*(4), 422–442. https://doi.org/10.1177%2F0266242613502691

To our knowledge, little research has been performed on the relationships between working environment, workaholism and work–family conflict among this group of workers.... The aim of this study was to investigate relationships between working environment factors, workaholism and work–family conflict among academics working in universities. We had three hypotheses: (1) Academics are more workaholic and will report more work–family conflicts than other university personnel. (2) Workaholism and work–family conflict among academics are primarily driven by the demands of the job. (3) Workaholism mediates the effects of work factors on work–family conflict among academics. (p. 1073)

Step 1: Gap

Step 2: Stance (Claim)

Torp, S., Lysfjord, L., & Midje, H.H. (2018). Workaholism and work–family conflict among university academics. *Higher Education, 76*(6), 1071–1090. https://doi.org/10.1007/s10734-018-0247-0

With this two-step approach in mind, we can state our claim clearly and with purpose—showing readers what our stance is on the topic and how it fills a gap in current research knowledge as we join the dialogue. There are many ways we can communicate our stance (see Chapters 7 and 9); we now have the resources, exemplars, and templates to articulate it in the context of our introduction.

5. Providing a Trajectory

Finally, a research introduction includes an outline or overview of the main areas of discussion that will follow in the body paragraphs. Most research writers state up front how they will test or prove their claim in their introduction, outlining their line of reasoning and key points before jumping into their body paragraphs. For example, L. Green includes the following trajectory at the end of his introduction:

> **I begin with** some general observations about social morality. **Next**, I consider how such a thing could change, and—what is different—how it could *be changed*, including through the instrumentality of law. If morality can be changed, we need to consider whether it *should* be changed, and if so how. There is, obviously, no general answer to this last question, save the formally correct but empty one: law should attempt to change social morality for the better. But to exemplify the sort of analysis I think worth pursuing, **I conclude with** some less empty, but more conjectural, reflections on a case for changing aspects of our social morality about sex. I choose the example because it is the area in which the debates about the enforcement of morals were fought out, and also because it is where we now find some of the sharpest conflicts between liberal and more 'traditional' moralities. (p. 475)
>
> Green, L. (2013). Should law improve morality? *Criminal Law and Philosophy, 7*(3), 473–494. https://doi.org/10.1007/s11572-013-9248-3

As we can see, the trajectory of our main points can be stated simply and succinctly in two or three short sentences:

- First, I will ___. Second, I will ___. Third, I will ___, and fourth, I will ___.
- In this study, we begin with ___. Next, we consider ___. Then, we conclude with ___.
- In section one I will focus on ___. Then, in section two, I will address ___.

Depending on our research context and community, we may be encouraged to write a very short trajectory that indicates our key points, or we may be asked to develop a methodology that explains how we will explore our research claim. Regardless of the form our trajectory takes, we aim to be direct about our path of analysis. Since our goal in research writing is to show readers the value and validity of our stance in the current research dialogue, it is better to state our trajectory directly than to hint at it and hope readers figure out our line of reasoning as they go along.

An effective research introduction includes each of these five elements of composition in one form or another, depending on the research context and the established parameters of the essay. Generally, though, research introductions tend to be brief and to the point. A good rule of thumb for determining the length of an introduction is to think of it as approximately one tenth of the full essay. For example, if an essay is 1,000 words long, the introduction should be about 100 words. If the essay is 2,500 words long, the introduction should be around 250 words. This rule of thumb is helpful for keeping our writing on track and including only the most important elements in our introduction, saving the development and exploration of our research for our body paragraphs.

B. INTRODUCTIONS ACROSS THE DISCIPLINES

As we've worked through the scholarly examples in this textbook and read research writing in our various courses, we've probably noticed that scholars engage in research, develop knowledge, and deepen understanding in their research communities in different ways. They have different goals and interests as well as different research techniques that make their way into their writing: Scholars in the social sciences research people—their beliefs, behaviours, traditions, interactions, and institutions. They study what people do and why they do it, how people engage with each other and the world around them. Scholars in the humanities research human understanding and expression in its various forms—languages, literary texts, histories, philosophies, religious documents, ancient manuscripts, art, and music. Scholars in the sciences research data collected about the material world (matter)—like biology, the environment, ecology, astronomy, and physics—as well as its abstract forms and systems, such as mathematics and its various applications.

These differences shape how scholars introduce their research in their writing. Notably, they incorporate the five elements of composition outlined above, but they do so differently depending on their discipline. To see how, let's look closely at example introductions from the social sciences, the humanities, and the sciences.

1. Social Sciences: Considering an Introduction in Feminist Geography

Online spaces with user-generated content (e.g. weblogs, online social networks, list-servs, *YouTube*, the comments sections of news sites) may constitute the next frontier in qualitative human subjects research, as they offer seemingly "unrestricted access to infinite amounts and types of data... worldwide access to a larger and more diverse participants pool and ease of data collection that can save time and cut costs" (Keller & Lee, 2003, p. 211). Yet these data are not treated as products of human subjects research, an epistemological and ethical stance that we argue merits closer scrutiny, particularly from feminists. This [imagery] of online spaces as vast tracts of untapped data is at odds with our own experiences of these spaces as virtual yet still material extensions of our everyday lives that shape our research subjectivities, the kinds of questions we ask, and our relationships to both data and online subjects. While online research has grown tremendously in human geography (Madge, 2007), our understanding of the particular epistemological, methodological, and ethical challenges, and the political implications of these emerging research practices, has not kept pace.

Topic & Common Ground

General Gap

In this article we contribute to filling this gap by developing a critical dialogue on interpreting politics and visibility in online spaces, researcher positionality across virtual and material study sites, and subjectivity and power in online research ethics.... Our searches led us to a number of methodological guidelines that have recently sprung up around online research methods (Pittenger, 2003; Keller & Lee, 2003; Buchanan, 2004). While full of practical advice, many of these texts deal with ethics only through the relatively narrow lens of institutional ethics protocols, which often lag behind technological developments. Moreover, institutional approaches tend to reinforce (or ignore the messiness of) problematic distinctions between categories such as private/public, personal/political, and virtual/material. As researchers familiar with the important contributions of feminists to research methods and ethics (e.g., Fonow & Cook, 1991; Moss, 2002; England, 1994; Sharp, 2005; Pratt, 2004; Rose, 1997), we responded to these guidelines by wondering how we might translate the kinds of research ethics that we typically encounter in feminist geography to online research practices. While not all feminist geographers engage in human subjects research, feminist social science and feminist geographical research ethics typically revolve around a relational, situated, and place-based stance that tends to assume face-to-face contact and 'field' settings (Moss, 2005; Katz, 1994; Dyck, 1993). It is not immediately clear how this ethical stance can be transposed to online spaces, nor how online research might complicate the key insights of feminist research ethics. Our objective in this paper, then, is to argue that the insights of feminist ethics and a feminist geographical lens are crucial for bringing much-needed reflexivity and reciprocity into online research; simultaneously, online research opens up exciting new ways of conceptualizing central ideas within feminist research ethics, including politicization, positionality, and power.

Current Research

Focused Gap

Stance (Claim)

Through a combination of individual reflections and collective interpretations, we seek to question the political possibilities offered by online spaces that allow for the 'personal' to be made 'political,' yet exclude certain bodies and voices. We wonder about the ways in which we interpret the virtual and material as interacting (or not) with one another and how this affects our positionality as researchers, our data collection, and our analyses. Finally, we reflect on the ethical and practical decisions that we are asked to make as online researchers and how these necessitate a questioning of subjectivity and power. (pp. 526–27)

Explicit Trajectory

Morrow, O., Hawkins, R., & Kern, L. (2015). Feminist research in online spaces. *Gender, Place, and Culture, 22*(4), 526–543. https://doi.org/10.1080/0966369X.2013.879108

2. Humanities: Considering an Introduction in English Literature

The work of Charlotte Brontë intersects with two fundamental elements in nineteenth-century psychological thought: the practice of moral management and the pseudo-science of phrenology. Both derive from the larger theory of faculty psychology, and both connect the dangers of imaginative daydreaming and reverie with the threat of insanity (Rylance, 2000, p. 27). Recent criticism emphasizes the role of phrenology and/or traditional faculty psychology in Brontë's novels and in her philosophy (Dames, 2001; Elliott, 2008; Shuttleworth, 1996; Manyard, 1984;

Topic & Common Ground

Current Research

Showalter, 1985; Gilbert & Gubar, 2000; Gettleman, 2007; Barker, 1994; Gérin, 1967). While the critical alliance of her novels with the tenets of these theories is illuminating, I contend that it is ultimately misleading. These critics tend to sustain the traditional Victorian binaries that put self-control in conflict with imaginative states (Caldwell, 2004, p. 109). Brontë's writings depict her inversion of the theories typically espoused by nineteenth-century psychologists, who instigated a materialist reanimation of Descartes's metaphysics in the form of a binary set up between the waking, rational mind and the imaginatively induced derivatives of sleep, such as somnambulism, trance, and waking dreams. Brontë shows how it is the unrelenting *regulation* of the imagination through incessant self-control that creates various forms of insanity and becomes ultimately devastating to the self, depicting instead the moral basis of a complex dialectic between self-control and ecstatic self-loss. (p. 1)

Gap & Stance (Claim)

Stance & Implicit Trajectory

Tressler, B. (2015). Illegible minds: Charlotte Brontë's early writings and the psychology of moral management in *Jane Eyre* and *Villette*. *Studies in the Novel, 47*(1), 1–19. http://doi.org/10.1353/sdn.2015.0002

3. Sciences: Considering an Introduction in Microbiology and Immunology

The ability to specifically modify individual loci in the genomes of patients' cells (gene editing) provides an ideal method to correct inherited disorders. Although gene editing can be done using adeno-associated virus (AAV) vectors or even synthetic nucleotide templates (Khan et al., 2011), for the purposes of this review we will focus on gene editing that is mediated through an engineered nuclease. In nuclease-mediated gene editing, an engineered nuclease, from any nuclease platform technology, is used to create a specific double-strand break (DSB) in the genome of a cell (Boissel et al., 2014; Scharenberg et al., 2013). This DSB activates the cells' DNA repair machinery, and if the break is repaired in a mutagenic fashion by nonhomologous end joining (NHEJ), insertions/deletions can be generated at a specific genomic location, thereby giving precise spatial resolution to the modification. If, on the other hand, the DSB is repaired by homologous recombination (HR; also called homology-directed repair [HDR]) using a provided donor template that can enter into the HR process and input new genetic information into the target genome, specific nucleotide changes can be made to the genome at a specific genomic location thereby giving precise spatial and nucleotide resolution to the modification. In HR-mediated genome editing, single nucleotides can be changed or whole multigene cassettes can be inserted into the genome in a precise location.

Topic & Common Ground

Current Research

The use of genome-editing technologies to modify various types of blood cells, including hematopoietic stem cells (HSCs), has emerged as an important field of therapeutic development for hematopoietic disease (Porteus, 2015; Corrigan-

Curay et al., 2015). Although these technologies offer the potential for generation of transformative therapies for patients suffering from myriad disorders of hematopoiesis, their application for therapeutic modification of primary human cells is still in its infancy. Consequently, development of ethical and regulatory frameworks that ensure their safe and effective use is an increasingly important consideration. Here, we review a number of issues that have the potential to impact the clinical implementation of genome-editing technologies, and suggest paths forward for resolving them so that new therapies can be safely and rapidly translated to the clinic. (p. 2553)

Gap in knowledge

Stance (Claim)

Trajectory

Kohn, D.B., Porteus, M.H., & Scharenberg, A.M. (2016). Ethical and regulatory aspects of genome editing. *Blood, 127*(21), 2553–2560. https://doi.org/10.1182/blood-2016-01-678136

C. STUDENT EXAMPLES

When we start writing research essays at college or university, they tend to be relatively short documents with short introductions. However, when we look to academic research articles as our guides, we notice that they are long documents with long introductions. We need to see some short student introductions to really get a sense of how to craft our own. The following two introductions are written by undergraduate students at the first- and second-year levels. As you read them, notice how they include the five components of a strong introduction—common ground, current research, a gap in knowledge, a stance in the form of a claim, and a trajectory—in different but equally effective ways.

Over the last few years, the use of dietary vitamin D supplements has become more common in Canada (Lips, 2010), yet the number of Canadians suffering from substandard vitamin D levels remains remarkably high. With more studies revealing vitamin D's potential to prevent a variety of health problems such as cancer (Bergren & Heuberger, 2010), cardiovascular disease (Sarkinen, 2011), depression (Penckofer et al., 2010), and bone disease (Lapp, 2009), it has become clear that the maintenance of sufficient vitamin D levels is of great importance. In "Addressing Vitamin D Deficiency in Canada: A Public Health Innovation Whose Time Has Come," Schwalfenberg et al. analyze the current state of vitamin D research and expose a serious problem in the low levels of vitamin D in Canadians, reporting that 70–97% of the population is living with insufficient levels despite the increased availability of vitamin D supplements (p. 351). If so, are supplements able to sufficiently restore vitamin D levels, or is the real problem that Canadians are not getting enough? I will argue that supplements are a safe and effective source of vitamin D, and that it is necessary for more Canadians to take them regularly in order to maintain adequate levels. To support this argument, I will review the current state of vitamin D deficiency in Canada, and determine exactly how much vitamin D is necessary for optimal levels. I will then reveal the efficacy of modern vitamin D supplements, and evaluate the potential benefits and side-effects that have been addressed in scholarship.

The novel *Jane Eyre* by Charlotte Brontë and the essay *A Room of One's Own* (hereafter referred to as *A Room*) by Virginia Woolf deal with the main idea of women's courage to overcome class and gender-based cultural norms (Ayyildiz, p. 146). The topic is worth investigating because both Brontë and Woolf use female protagonists—Jane and Mary respectively—to challenge society's oppression of women displaying both internal and external struggles regarding physical space, financial independence, and freedom of expression. However, Brontë and Woolf focus on the external more than the internal, possibly subconscious, aspects of the struggle. Despite being in the first person, Jane and Mary's emotional conflict in both texts remains somewhat of a mystery since they refrain from straightforwardly exposing it. Although both texts are deemed courageous for challenging the patriarchy, there is a strong underlying current of internalised female inferiority that is prevalent behind the exterior of each narrative. I argue that Jane and Mary both appear to challenge the external limits of the patriarchy, but remain modest and objective to disguise their internal struggles of self-doubt. In other words, even though they question patriarchal society, they still abide by it in certain circumstances. I will explore this tension by examining the literary devices, narrative voice, diction and ambiguity in both texts to support my interpretation and analysis.

Despite the fact that these papers are about different topics, both of them begin with a focused sentence that states exactly what the paper is about. Both students situate themselves in a research conversation, the first one securing generalizations about the importance of Vitamin D for illness prevention and the second one providing grounds for a gender-based approach to interpreting *Jane Eyre* and *A Room of One's Own* with reference to one key scholar. Both students point to a gap in the dialogue in order to present their respective claims. Both students also offer a trajectory, indicating how they will explore or prove their claim in the context of the paper. If we are struggling to write our research introductions, these strong exemplars can point us in the right direction.

D. STARTING OUR INTRODUCTIONS

No matter how many exemplars we look at, we will still find that writing our own introduction is a daunting task. The white page looms before us. The due date creeps up on us. And the clock is ticking. We each stare at the blinking cursor on our computer screen, not knowing how or where to begin. We often feel stuck before we start.

There are two things that may help to relax us and get us going. First, it is important to realize that there is more than one way to start writing an essay and that we do not necessarily need to begin at the beginning. In fact, how we launch into our writing process depends on our mental processing—how we make sense of our research and ideas. Let's go back for a moment to the concepts of linear and lateral thinking introduced in Chapter 10.

- If we are linear thinkers, then it is usually helpful to frontload our work. We use our preparation notes—journalists' questions, lists, and outlines—to figure out what we think and want to say about the topic *before* we begin writing. Once we've laid everything out in our notes, we begin our essay *at the beginning* by introducing our topic and current research, articulating a knowledge gap, composing our claim, and offering a clear trajectory for our essay. Figuring out what we think before we write our introduction (and the rest of our essay) will take some time. But once we've finished the mental grunt work, we'll know what we want to say and where we're headed in our essay. Writing the essay itself should flow quite easily as a result.

- If we are lateral thinkers, then it is usually helpful to backload our work. We use the process of writing *itself* to figure out what we think and want to say. This means we jump right into a rough draft of our essay, using our preparation notes and visual diagrams to help us compose a provisional stance and a set of points we would like to cover. We draw on our research findings as we go along, discovering who thinks what about the topic and how their work fits into each point we're making. The result will be a messy draft of our thinking and research process, but this draft will lead us to a set of conclusions and a strong research claim. Once we have this material together, we are ready to write our *actual* introduction—clearly stating the topic and current research, a knowledge gap, our claim, and the paper's trajectory. Later, we can return to the body paragraphs, organizing them, cleaning them up, and making them persuasive and effective. This means a lot of back-end writing, so we give ourselves ample time to rewrite and edit our work.

Second, as we can see from the range of examples above, there is no one right way to organize or format a research introduction. While introductions share key characteristics, they vary in form and style depending on the field of study, the research conversation, the readers, and the writer's goals and thought processes. However, as we start to develop our introduction-writing skills, it can be helpful to try a few templates. These are not meant to take the place of our own thought processes, but they can make us feel more confident as we navigate the research essay genre and make it our own. With this in mind, give the following templates a try:

The topic of ________________ has gained considerable attention in recent years due to ________________. As researchers observe, ____________________________ (*cite researchers*). While a number of studies have explored ____________________ (*cite researchers*), they have not gone far enough in addressing ________________. One reason for this oversight may be _____________. In order to fill this gap, I examine

__________ and hypothesize ____________. This area is critical to address because __________. In order to explore my stance, I will first consider__________. I will then turn my attention to ________ and ________. Finally, I will close with __________.

In analysing the literary text _________ (*title*) by __________ (*author*), a number of researchers have foregrounded the issue of ______________ (*cite researchers*) as critical to our understanding of the work. Specifically, Researchers X and Y have suggested _________ (*cite researchers*). While this issue is an important one, it appears that a key dimension of this issue has been overlooked: ___________. In this paper, I argue that _________ in order to add to/build on the current scholarship. I support my interpretation in three main ways: ___________, ____________, and ___________. Clearly this is a key area to address in the text because ____________.

In the past decade, researchers have shown increasing concern about __________ (*cite researchers*). This problem has a number of key factors including ________, _________, and __________ (*cite researchers*). In an attempt to solve the problem, Researchers X and Y have suggested ____________ (*cite researchers*). Researchers A, B, and C have alternatively argued for ______________ (*cite researchers*). Despite the viability of both solutions, a third alternative _____________ has been missed. In this paper, I propose implementing _____________ as the most beneficial response to this problem because _____________. To support my case, I will explore four key areas in which it proves beneficial: _________, __________, ___________, and __________. My hope is that by contributing this alternative to the discussion we might be able to move forward in the following way(s): ____________.

CONCLUSIONS

Writing a research introduction is easier than we think once we realize that it includes the five key elements of composition that we have already practised earlier in this textbook: (a) a specific topic introduced by means of common ground; (b) the current research context and conversation; (c) a gap in knowledge about the topic; (d) a stance in the form of a claim that fills this gap and joins the research dialogue; and (e) a trajectory that outlines how the claim will be explored in the essay. Now that we know what to include in a research introduction, we are well on our way to writing one! However, it is also important to recognize the kind of thinkers we are in order to use our strengths and organizational preferences to write the best introductions possible. Those of us who are linear thinkers tend to begin our essay writing by composing a clear and well-established introduction directly, and then work in a systematic way to complete the rest of the paper. Those of us who are more lateral in our thinking begin with a tentative stance and get straight to writing the body of our paper to figure out what we think. Then we return to the beginning of our essay to write a clear and compelling introduction that reflects where our ideas have ended up. Whatever way we choose to write it, an academic introduction is meant to show how we are joining the research dialogue on a topic and contributing our ideas to build the collective knowledge of the research community.

QUESTIONS FOR REFLECTION

1. Review the five key elements of a research introduction and analyse why each one is essential for setting up a research essay. Why might research writers across different fields of study all strive to incorporate these elements in their introductions?

2. Read the academic introduction below and highlight each of the five key elements of composition that we've learned. Where is each one located in the introduction? What might the reasoning be behind using this particular order or organization?

The legal framework for consultative land and resource regulation in Brazil is considered exemplary. Nevertheless, the lack of local compliance led to international pressure in the late 1980s and 1990s regarding high deforestation and related greenhouse gas emission rates (Kolk, 1998). In 2004, after ten years of experience with (mostly internationally funded) environmental protection programs (PPG7), the Brazilian government decreed additional far-reaching rules to curb deforestation by protecting almost half of the Brazilian Amazon and by cutting off market access of whole municipalities that would not obey strict deforestation standards. Today, Brazil is being celebrated as the country of successful anti-deforestation policies with continuously falling deforestation rates (Boucher et al., 2014).

We agree with the recently published empirical results that the enforcement and implementation of anti-deforestation policies are a precondition for further land-use planning (Börner et al., 2015). However, by assessing the viability of the different land-use management approaches and governmental implementation capacities, we argue that by far more holistic and integrated policies than currently practiced are needed *after* an effective control of deforestation. To evaluate the chances of becoming successful in land use management, we refer to the concept of a developmental state (Woo-Cumings, 1999) and its cornerstones, namely clear political priorities and mature institutions. As empirical background, we use extensive research on actor perspectives regarding the highway BR-163 taking course from Cuiaba/Mato Grosso to Santarém/Pará. We will highlight the outcomes of three recent regulation attempts in regional and land-use planning at different governmental levels and show the possibilities and pitfalls of those approaches. (pp. 119–20)

Schonenberg, R., Hartberger, K., Schumann, C., Benatti, J.H., & Fischer, L.C. (2015). What comes after deforestation control? Learning from three attempts of land-use planning in Southern Amazonia. *GAIA, 24*(2), 119–127. https://doi.org/10.14512/gaia.24.2.10

3. Choose one of the introduction templates in Section D that makes the most sense given your field of study, topic, and research findings, and try it on for size. Fill in the gaps and make any necessary adjustments in order to suit your specific communication needs.

CHAPTER TWELVE

BODY PARAGRAPHS

Giving Structure to the Conversation

In Chapter 11, we compared writing a research paper to taking a well-planned road trip. In our introduction we "map out a route," taking into account who has travelled this way before and what their viewpoints were, as well as our own stance and how we plan to reach our goal. In our body paragraphs we "take the trip" itself. When we travel, we see interesting things, reflect on them, talk about them with our fellow travellers, and draw conclusions about them. Similarly, in our body paragraphs we make observations, reason with other researchers, examine and analyse research evidence, and reach conclusions. We even have terms that suggest travel when it comes to thinking and writing ideas: we talk about our *train* of thought, our *line* of reasoning, our *direction*, *trajectory*, or next *steps*.

Body paragraphs represent a journey of knowledge in which we bring our research and ideas into dialogue with other research scholars. Here, we have the opportunity to test or prove our claim in the context of a research community and contribute new knowledge or understanding to the topic at hand. To do that well, we engage directly with expert researchers in the field to make our points and to lead readers through our reasoning process so that they are convinced by our ideas and recognize the contribution we are making. In this chapter, we will learn how to structure our body paragraphs dialogically and how to develop them to reflect our analysis and reasoning, using established patterns of arrangement and transitions to direct readers through our work.

A. RESEARCH DIALOGUES IN BODY PARAGRAPHS

When we write our body paragraphs, we are engaged in two dialogues simultaneously—one with other research scholars and one with our readers. We interact with the work of other scholars in the content of our writing and we share our research and ideas with interested readers, inviting them to engage with our evidence and reasoning. We can visualize these two conversations as follows:

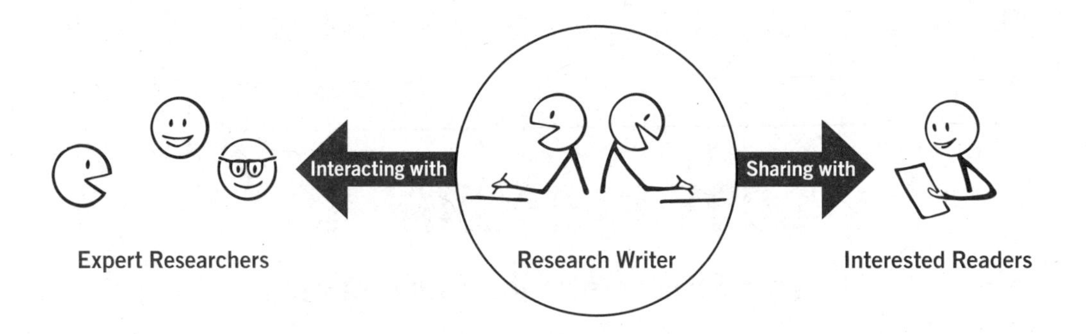

It is our goal to recognize and acknowledge both of our interlocutors—the researchers and readers with whom we are engaged—in writing our body paragraphs. So let's reflect on these relationships for a moment.

Every point we make in our body paragraphs needs to relate and respond to the points of other researchers writing on our topic. This involves ensuring that their research is openly and accurately represented in our paragraphs. We may feel an impulse to ignore research evidence that doesn't validate our stance, or we may be inclined to oversimplify the work of other researchers in order to prove our claim. However, neither of these impulses fosters genuine dialogue, advances knowledge, or reflects the complexity of most subject matter. If our goal is to deepen our shared understanding of a subject, then we seek out rather than suppress a variety of perspectives. This is why researchers engage with other scholarship, consider a range of findings, and discuss those findings dialogically in their body paragraphs. They are showing how other ideas intersect with and diverge from their own.

Alongside our dialogue with other researchers, we also write our body paragraphs to engage with our readers. All the content we include in the body of our work is meant to communicate our research and reasoning to an interested, knowledgeable audience. We share this material with our readers and invite them to think through it and respond. In doing so, we set up a dialogue between us. The better we can visualize our readers—who they are and what they know—the more effective our communication will be. We will be able to predict their level of understanding about the subject, the questions they'll ask, and the explanations they'll need. If our stance, research material, reasoning, or train of thought isn't clear to our readers, we will hinder their ability to engage and respond.

To write our body paragraphs dialogically, then, we do two things simultaneously: First, we structure our paragraphs as a dialogue between ourselves and other researchers. Second, we direct readers through our research and ideas using specific patterns of development to help them track with our reasoning and to encourage their engagement and response. In the following sections, we will first learn how to ***structure*** our body paragraphs dialogically and then we will consider how to ***develop*** them using conventional patterns of arrangement.

B. DIALOGIC STRUCTURE: BUILDING BODY PARAGRAPHS

Let's start by tackling the dialogic structure of our body paragraphs. Body paragraphs are structured differently depending on the kind of research we are undertaking and the discipline or research community for which we are writing. In the argumentative and analytical research essays typically found in humanities disciplines, our body paragraphs are made up of key points, each one developed in dialogue with the research of other scholars. We thus engage in multiple dialogues throughout our body paragraphs, each one centred on the point we are making. Alternatively, in the analytical research essays typically found in science and social science disciplines, our body paragraphs are divided into key categories that reflect our investigative activities. We begin the body of our essay with the research of other scholars (what they show), then turn to our own findings (what we see), and finally discuss how the two intersect. In this way, we engage in one overarching dialogue structured across our body paragraphs as a whole, with the bulk of our discussion occurring near the end. To understand these differences, let's look at each of these dialogic structures more closely.

1. Dialogic Structure in Humanities Research Essays

In most humanities disciplines, we use research essays to make sense of human ideas, expressions, or events in their various forms. In our research essays we analyse texts, events, art, or ideas and assert our interpretation of them by means of an argument or hypothesis: "Here's how I think this text (image, event, idea, etc.) should be understood in light of my research on it." We spend our body paragraphs making points to support our claim or prove our case, showing readers how we've reached our standpoint by means of analysing the text (image, event, idea, etc.) in its context and engaging with the theories of other researchers about it.

There is no set rule about how many points of analysis we need to include to support our claim or prove our case in the body of our essay. However, each point we do make needs to draw on the research of experts in order to be viable and convincing to our readers. For this reason, we structure each point dialogically in relation to the research and ideas of the experts we are relying on. This dialogical structure is made up of four components:

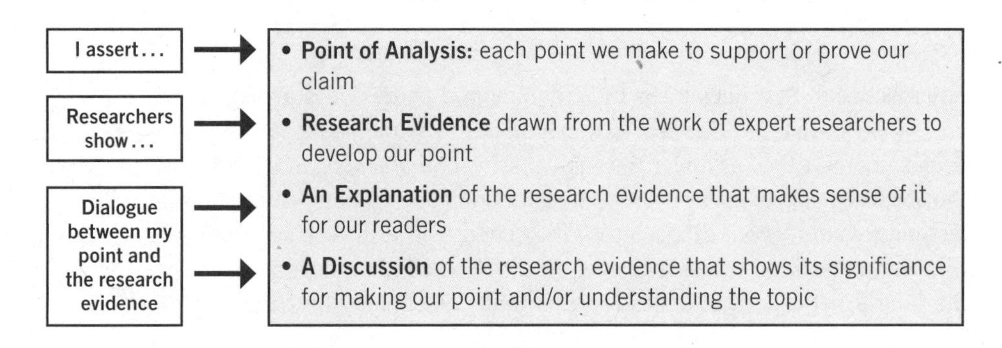

While each component is necessary for developing our research dialogue with other researchers and helping readers understand our points, new research writers often fixate on the first two components at the expense of the second two. They make good points and support them with research evidence, but they don't explain that evidence or discuss its significance (why it matters) for making their point. Only when we explain and discuss the research evidence *in relation to our point* do we engage in dialogue with it. Otherwise, we are just recapping the research of others. We need to make our dialogue explicit so readers recognize how our points build on, intersect with, or challenge the research and ideas of others.

There are two ways to structure our body paragraphs with these four components in mind. The first is to incorporate all four components in each body paragraph. In this ***paragraph-based*** format, each paragraph is dedicated to one point of analysis with its relating evidence, explanation, and discussion. For example, notice how the following paragraph, drawn from an article in media and cultural studies, includes all four components:

> That media coverage of atrocities has not [prevented] their recurrence suggests that we must frame bearing witness as something that *exceeds* seeing, because seeing does not necessarily compel responsibility. This requires interrogating what *responsibility* might mean within the context of bearing witness, and whether news media are equipped to produce texts that express and facilitate responsibility. Describing bearing witness in the context of survivor testimony, Shoshana Felman (2000) writes:
>
> > To bear witness is to take responsibility for truth: to speak, implicitly, from within the legal pledge and the juridical imperative of the witness's oath. To testify ... is more than simply to report a fact or an event or to relate what has been lived, recorded and remembered. Memory is conjured here essentially in order to *address* another, to impress upon a listener, to *appeal* to a community.... To testify is thus not merely to narrate, but to commit oneself, and to commit the narrative, to others: to *take responsibility*—in speech—for history or for the truth of an occurrence. (2000, 103–04)
>
> Any practice of bearing witness thus requires two parties: it is a mode of address that consists of an appeal to the audience to share the responsibility for an event, and is thus a site for the *transmission of moral obligation*. Critically, the speaker's appeal goes beyond the communication of facts, and thus what testimony is (for) is not exhausted by the concept of truth. The survivor bears witness to that which cannot be seen; the embodied knowledge of suffering; the limit-experience that defies representation. Testimony thus involves the

Point of Analysis

Point Developed

Research Evidence

Explanation of Evidence

Discussion

> attempt to translate affect into discourse in order to perform a response to trauma, and elicit an effective response that moralizes the audience's future action. (pp. 1226–27)

Tait, S. (2011). Bearing witness, journalism, and moral responsibility. *Media, Culture, & Society, 33*(8), 1220–1235. https://doi.org/10.1177%2F0163443711422460

As we can see from this example, when we develop our point of analysis in a single body paragraph, we begin by stating our point directly so that readers know immediately what the paragraph is about. We then turn to research evidence, drawing on the work of other scholars to support or prove our point. In the process, we dialogue with that evidence, explaining and discussing it in relation to our point in order to show readers how our ideas engage with and respond to the research of other scholars on the subject.

We can also see from this example that research writers use certain words to signal their shift from providing research evidence to explaining and discussing that evidence as it relates to their point. Notice how S. Tait uses the word *thus* four times to link her ideas with Felman's and to highlight the significance of her point. As we write our own body paragraphs, we can use the following signal words and phrases to make the shift from stating our research evidence to explaining and discussing it:

Signalling Explanation

- Thus...
- To clarify...
- In other words...
- That is to say...
- As we can see...
- This evidence shows...
- This evidence indicates...

Signalling Discussion

- Therefore...
- Hence...
- Consequently...
- Accordingly...
- As a result...
- This evidence proves...
- This point is significant because...

A paragraph-based structure can work well if our points of analysis are brief or our research essay is short. However, most points of analysis in a research paper require several paragraphs to be fully developed. Our points are usually made up of several sub-points that can each be quite involved. Consequently, it may take four or five paragraphs to cover *one point* of analysis, depending on how many sub-points it comprises and the range of evidence and explanation we need to support those sub-points. The result is a dialogic essay structure that is ***point-based*** rather than paragraph-based.

This second way of structuring our body paragraphs is much more common than the first in humanities research writing. When we use a point-based structure, we focus on fully developing each point of analysis rather than concerning ourselves with the number of paragraphs it takes to make a point. We may need to develop our point and support it with research evidence over a number of paragraphs before we can engage in a discussion about it and show its significance.

Consider the following excerpt from a research article in literature and popular culture. Here we can see how a point of analysis is developed over a number of paragraphs, with evidence included and explained across paragraphs and significance posed at the end.

> Anyone who doubts the power of books to root themselves in the developing psyche has only to consider the impact of J.K. Rowling's Harry Potter series. Adult alarm over children's responses to these books has led to extraordinary acts of censorship and even public book burnings. For educated adults it is easy to dismiss such occurrences with smiles and disbelieving shrugs at the naivety of those who believe books have any real impact on their readers, but in fact those who respond less temperately may have a more instinctive understanding of the power of stories to bypass the barriers we all erect against memes that challenge cultural assumptions. Reading about Harry Potter may not lead child readers into satanic debauchery, but I would argue that it may well encourage them to question power relations and easy assumptions of privilege.
>
> **Point of Analysis**
>
> **Point Developed**
>
> For instance, on his first visit to the Ministry of Magic, the locus of power in the wizarding world, Harry Potter finds himself confronted by an ornate fountain:
>
>> A group of golden statues, larger than life-size, stood in the middle of a circular pool. Tallest of them all was a noble-looking wizard with his wand pointing straight up in the air. Grouped around him were a beautiful witch, a centaur, a goblin and a house-elf. The last three were all looking adoringly up at the witch and wizard. (Rowling, 2003, p. 117)
>
> **Narrative Evidence**
>
> This sycophantic grouping makes visible the embedded power relations that many critics feel underpin much of Rowling's narrative. Farah Mendelsohn, for instance, argues that "[t]he structure of J.K. Rowling's books is predicated upon a status quo and a formal understanding of authority in which hierarchical structures are a given" (2002, p. 181). Thus the dominance of the witch and wizard is clearly established by their centrality, relative height and exaggerated good looks. Even more significantly, the reader is told that their raised wands function as visible indicators of imperial privilege since clause three of the Code of Wand Use categorically states: "*No non-human creature is permitted to carry or use a wand*" (Rowling, 2000, p. 119). This restriction is bitterly resented, as Griphook, the goblin, later reveals:
>
> **Research Evidence, Explanation, and Discussion**
>
>> "The right to carry a wand," said the goblin quietly, "has long been contested between wizards and goblins."
>>
>> "Well, goblins can do magic without wands," said Ron.
>
> **Narrative Evidence**

> "That is immaterial! Wizards refuse to share the secrets of wandlore with other magical beings, they deny us the possibility of extending our powers!" (2007, p. 395)

...Certainly, the subordination of wandless magical creatures such as centaurs, goblins and house-elves within Rowling's magic world...evokes patterns of exploitation found in contemporary life. While the alien qualities of centaurs, goblins and house-elves are most obviously indicated by the equine lower bodies of the centaurs, the long fingers of the goblins and the bat-like ears, enormous eyes and diminutive size of the house-elves, they are also defined as 'other' by more subtle and yet also more familiar markers of difference. While Firenze, the friendliest of the centaurs is dazzlingly blonde (1997, p. 187), Ban, his antagonist is "black-haired and -bodied" as well as being much "wilder-looking" (1997, p. 185).... Similarly, goblins, including Griphook, have swarthy faces and "dark, slanting eyes" (2000, p. 387) that Jackie Horne finds suggestive of the "stereotype of the Jewish moneylender or perhaps even of an Italian Mafioso" (2010, p. 81) and Dobby, the house-elf, not only has "an ugly brown face" (Rowling, 1998, p. 249) but also speaks in a way which Brycchan Carey argues is strongly "reminiscent of 1930s and 40s Hollywood misconceptions of African-American dialects" (2003, p. 103). Given these indicators of racial profiling it is difficult to argue that characters such as Firenze, Griphook and Dobby do not function within a complex dialectic of appropriation and resistance that mirrors enduring patterns of colonial and postcolonial interaction.

Research Evidence, Explanation, and Discussion

Effectively then, it is possible to argue that Rowling's wizarding world positions all non-human magical beings as subalterns, a standard designation for the colonial subject constructed both by a dominant discourse and his or her internalization of that discourse (Spivak, 1992). Crucially though, this positioning is not accepted by everyone within Rowling's fictional world. Hermione Granger, for instance, describes the house-elves as 'slave labour' (2000, p. 162) and contemptuously dismisses Ron Weasley's claim that servility is natural to these creatures by arguing that it is people like Ron "who prop up rotten and unjust systems" because they are simply too lazy to question their society's assumptions (2000, p. 112). By offering conflicting perspectives on complex issues, Rowling may be seen to open up a safe space in which her young readers are encouraged to develop their own responses to questions of power and disempowerment that reach far beyond the imagined walls of Hogwarts. (pp. 16–18)

Explanation of Evidence

Brown, M. (2017). Children's literature matters (?). *English Academy Review, 34*(1), 8–22. https://www.doi.org/10.1080/10131752.2017.1333207

Developing a point of analysis across a number of body paragraphs means that we have more space to engage in interactive dialogue and develop each aspect of our point with explanation, discussion, and significance. Notice, for example, how M. Brown goes back and forth between Rowling's texts, scholarly viewpoints on those texts, and her own explanation and analysis in the excerpt above. The result is an animated dialogue that she uses to make her point and convey its significance across multiple paragraphs.

With this dialogic structure in mind, try the following exercise in order to practise developing a point of analysis across a number of body paragraphs yourself.

EXERCISE 1
PRACTISING A POINT-BASED STRUCTURE ACROSS BODY PARAGRAPHS

Return to the sample argument in Chapter 9 (Section E) about creating new bike lanes in Vancouver. Imagine that you are taking a stance *for* creating new bike lanes (instead of against it) with the claim "Vancouver should create more bike lanes." You decide that one of your points of analysis to support this claim will be, "having more bike lanes will encourage commuters to travel by bike rather than by car." Relying on the four components of body paragraphs discussed above, you outline your point as follows:

Point of Analysis
Having more bike lanes will encourage commuters to travel by bike rather than by car.

Research Evidence
- Choose evidence that is relevant to this point in order to support it.
- Use evidence that is reliable and authoritative in order to be convincing.
- Show that this evidence is representative of the research that is available.

Reasoning: Explaining, Discussing, and Analysing the Evidence
- Explain the research evidence to show how you understand it.
- Consider how the evidence relates to the views of other scholars.
- Discuss how the research evidence supports or proves the point.

Significance: Showing the Importance of the Point
- State why this point and its evidence are important to the dialogue on this topic.

Relying on actual research evidence for support, develop this point into a three- or four-paragraph analysis, covering all four necessary components in the process.

2. Dialogic Structure in Social Science and Science Research Essays

In the sciences and social sciences, most of our research relies on investigation and experimentation in order to develop new knowledge and contribute to the research dialogue on the subject. Our research essays are organized to reflect this focus: writers provide an objective picture of the qualitative and quantitative research that has been collected about a subject in order to draw meaningful conclusions about it that engage with those made by other scholars. We usually begin our research essay with a claim that takes the form of a hypothesis. In our body paragraphs, we test our hypothesis by using the established theories and methods of other researchers as well as our own experimentation or data accumulation to reach a conclusion.

This process is, of course, structured as a dialogue. We situate our investigation and the hypothesis we are testing in a research conversation, beginning with a ***literature review*** of what other researchers have said about our topic. This review may be located in our introduction or developed in our early body paragraphs. We then explain how we will test our hypothesis—the ***methods*** we will use to collect our data and our reasons for using these methods—as well as our purpose for testing our hypothesis. What knowledge do we hope will be gained? What do we hope to contribute to the research conversation with our investigation?

Next we summarize the ***results*** of our test—the findings we have discovered and the numerical data we have accumulated—and explain them to our readers with supporting information. We often spend the bulk of our body paragraphs on this section in order to make sure that our readers not only see the data but also understand what it means. Finally, we provide a ***discussion*** of our findings in relation to the findings of other researchers. In what ways do they coincide? In what ways do they differ? Why do these similarities and/or differences matter for understanding the topic? What new knowledge do our findings contribute to the research conversation? And why is that knowledge significant for our understanding of the subject?

As we can see, our dialogic structure begins with what other researchers say (a literature review), turns to what we say (our methodology and results), and culminates in a discussion of our results as they relate to the findings of others and contribute to the research knowledge on the topic. This structure can be categorized as follows:

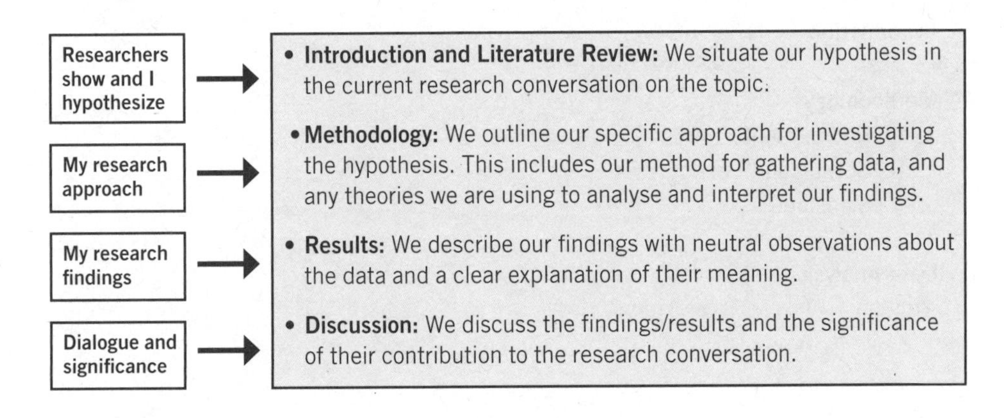

Note that although this is a four-part structure, our research essays are not limited to four body paragraphs—one for each category. Rather, each category is made up of many paragraphs so the material in each can be fully developed.

Using this approach is such a common way to structure research papers in the social sciences and sciences that it has come to be known by the acronym **IMRaD** (**I**ntroduction, **M**ethods, **R**esults, **a**nd **D**iscussion). In fact, if we were to randomly select two research essays from different fields in the social sciences, we would quickly see these structural categories by scrolling through the essay's headings.

Introduction
(a) Theoretical Perspective
(b) Literature Review

Methods
(a) Data Collection
(b) Data Analysis

Results
(a) Overview
(b) Definitions

Discussion

Ploeg, J., Lohfeld, L., & Walsh, C.A. (2013). What is "elder abuse"? Voices from the margin: The views of underrepresented Canadian older adults. *Journal of Elder Abuse & Neglect, 25*(5), 396–424. https://doi.org/10.1080/08946566.2013.780956

Introduction

Methodology
(a) Recruitment
(b) Setting and Participants
(c) Measures

Data Analysis

Findings

(a) Alignment of Power Holder Values
(b) Perceived Purpose
(c) Working Practice
(d) Orientation to Change and Ideas

Discussion

Bigby, C., & Beadle-Brown, J. (2016). Culture in better group homes for people with intellectual disability at severe levels. *Intellectual and Developmental Disabilities, 54*(5), 316–331. https://doi.org/10.1352/1934-9556-54.5.316

Similarly, if we were to examine two scientific papers from different fields of study, we would also see the IMRaD structure:

Introduction

Materials and Methods

(a) Brown rot infection in stone fruit orchards
(b) The model
(c) Model application to the peach-brown rot system
(d) Model simulations and yield sensitivity...

Results

(a) Basic reproduction number, disease progress trajectories and yield losses
(b) Sensitivity of yield to the variation in the parameter estimate
(c) Sensitivity of the yield to agricultural practices

Discussion

Bevacqua, D., Quilot-Turion, B., & Bolzoni, L. (2018). A model for temporal dynamics of brown rot spreading in fruit orchards. *Phytopathology, 108*(5), 595–601. https://doi.org/10.1094/PHYTO-07-17-0250-R

Introduction

Study Area

Methods

(a) Shoreline Mapping and Analysis
(b) Vulnerability Assessment
(c) Analysis of Modeling Results

Results

(a) Shoreline Movement
(b) Hazard Assessment

Discussion

(a) Shoreline Dynamics
(b) Coastal Evolution
(c) Geohazard Mapping

Radosavljevic, B., Lantuit, H., Pollard, W., Overduin, P., Couture, N., Sachs, T., Helm, V., & Fritz, M. (2016). Erosion and flooding—threats to coastal infrastructure in the Arctic: A case study from Herschel Island, Yukon Territory, Canada. *Estuaries and Coasts, 39*(4), 900–915. https://doi.org/10.1007/s12237-015-0046-0

If we are writing in the sciences or social sciences, then, these categories help us to structure and arrange our body paragraphs dialogically. However, given that there are distinctions between disciplines and certain structural preferences as well (like opting for "Findings" rather than "Results" or adding other headings to the IMRaD structure), it is important to use the categories common to our field of study or specified by our instructor as we delve into our body paragraphs.

C. PATTERNS OF DEVELOPMENT: LEADING READERS THROUGH OUR REASONING

Alongside structuring our paragraphs as a dialogue with other researchers, we lead readers through our thought processes by using particular patterns of development to help them understand our reasoning and respond to our work. If we think about research writing as a journey of knowledge, we take readers on that journey by means of our "train of thought" and make sure they "track" with us by developing our research and ideas in clear and logical ways. To direct readers through our thoughts and reasoning processes, we put ourselves in their shoes and consider what they need in order to make sense of our work.

In their book, *Landmarks: A Process Reader* (2003), R. Birks, T. Eng, and J. Walchli highlight eight established patterns of development for communicating our reasoning clearly to our readers in our body paragraphs:

- Description
- Narration
- Example
- Definition
- Process Analysis
- Comparison & Contrast
- Classification & Division
- Cause & Effect

We use these patterns to organize our thought processes and show readers the purpose of each point we are making or result we are sharing. For example, if our purpose is to show how different breeds of dogs fare on one particular diet, then we will probably use a "comparison and contrast" pattern to develop our analysis. We will compare and contrast how each breed of dog fares on the diet using research evidence to support our reasoning. Let's look at these eight patterns closely to see how they work and to determine which patterns make sense in which contexts and for what purposes.

1. Description: A Spatial or Sensory Development of Ideas

Purpose: We use description to convey the specific characteristics of a person, place, or thing, helping readers to picture them in order to establish a point or explain a result.

Context: Researchers often use description to discuss a piece of art or a character in a literary text; to detail a case study; to review a particular human practice or biological process; to illustrate a historical event; or to survey a geographical location.

Example: *Describing a literary scene*

> Extending the dystopianism out from the factories and literal machinery, Dickens **represents** the weather of Coketown as dreary and dark as the factories enveloped by it. In the previous **description** of the setting of Coketown, the factories are set against a natural **backdrop** of a "black wet night" that absorbs the dystopian buildings into dystopian weather and darkness to create layers of dreariness that bury the characters inside.... Pipe steam and chimney ash combine with relentless mist and rain, washing out the **landscape** in gray monochrome. The temperatures, though, are extreme, as Stephen

leaves the hot mill for the cold and wet outdoors. There is no comfort to be had in Coketown, as the weather mirrors the dismal **atmosphere** of the factories. (p. 23)

Lewis, D. (2014). Melancholia and machinery: The dystopian landscape and mindscape in *Hard Times. Dickens Quarterly, 31*(1), 17–31.

Note: Emphasized words function as signal words or phrases to reinforce the descriptive scene.

2. Narration: A Sequential Development of Ideas

Purpose: We use narration when we want to reveal the significance of a sequence of events to our readers.

Context: Researchers regularly use narration to discuss the plot of a piece of literature; to overview a person's biography; to share the story of a particular community or location; or to discuss the historical chronology of an event.

Example: *Outlining the sequence of a historical event*

The actual revolt **began** on 10 June 1928. In the early morning hours, hundreds of villagers assembled in Kizburun II with the aim of freeing the prisoners from jail. **Before** making their way to Baksan, they plucked up their courage by dancing and were cheered on by the assembled women (Bystrova et al., 1928). According to the secret police report, the approximately 1500-strong mob, armed with 'pitchforks, poles, and hoes', was led by Urusov (Nal'chik, 2009). **Upon** their **arrival** in Baksan, the crowd marched to the district government building to demand the prisoners' release. **After** negotiations with the authorities failed, the militia opened fire on the crowd with a machine gun. However, the crowd managed to subdue and disarm the police officers. They beat up the head of the district administration as well as the police officers, severely injuring a policeman as well as the local state official. **Then** the crowd stormed the prison, released the inmates, and entered the arms depot. There, they seized two more machine guns, 13 rifles, and 2500 rounds of ammunition (Bystrova et al., 1928). **Then** the assembly dispersed, with many returning home. (p. 239)

Perovic, J. (2016). Highland rebels: The North Caucasus during the Stalinist collectivization campaign. *Journal of Contemporary History, 51*(2), 234–260. https://doi.org/10.1177/002200941456281

Note: Emphasized words function as signal words or phrases to reinforce the historical sequence.

3. Example: An Illustrative Development of Ideas

Purpose: We use examples to explain a complicated or abstract idea to our readers by using a concrete case or incident that they can understand.

Context: Researchers use examples in nearly every academic context to show how a theory works in practice or how an abstract idea plays out in concrete settings.

Example: *Exemplifying a set of behaviours common to a condition*

> Abnormal use of nonverbal communication, which is a diagnostic criterion for Autism Spectrum Disorder, may explain unusual or limited facial expressions. In addition, the observable behaviors reflecting self-regulation may differ. **For example**, adults with ASD have commented that self-stimulatory behaviors (**e.g.**, rocking) or intense focus on routines/rituals/circumscribed interests can be used for self-soothing (Lipsky & Richards, 2009). (p. 680)

Mazefsky, C.A., Herrington, J., Siegel, M., Scarpa, A., Maddox, B.B., Scahill, L., & White, S.W. (2013). The role of emotion regulation in Autism Spectrum Disorder. *Journal of American Academy of Child & Adolescent Psychiatry, 52*(7), 679–688. https://doi.org/10.1016/j.jaac.2013.05.006

Note: Emphasized words function as signal words or phrases to reinforce the pattern of example.

4. Definition: A Designative Development of Ideas

Purpose: We use definition when we want to set limits on or boundaries around a subject, or when we want to clarify one or more meanings of a term to our readers.

Context: Researchers use definition in nearly every academic context to establish the meaning of a word, term, phrase, concept, or idea, especially when it could have multiple meanings or could be understood differently in different contexts.

Example: *Defining a particular term to clarify its aspects*

> The palimpsest is a term commonly used in archaeology, and one widely used to **describe** large-scale rock art sites in Europe. The palimpsest originally **referred to** the act of writing, erasing, and rewriting a tablet or plaque (McDonagh, 1987). While often **referring to** the destruction of earlier activity by later work, a palimpsest may also **refer to** the superimposition or accumulation of activities, which may only partially destroy previous acts (Bailey, 2007, p. 203). Bailey (1987) **describes** the palimpsest as having

a dual understanding; both as a process of erasure and reworking, and as a process of accumulation and transformation. (p. 357)

Sapwell, M. (2017). Understanding palimpsest rock art with the art as agency approach: Gell, Morphy, and Laxön, Nämforsen. *Journal of Archeological Method and Theory, 24*(2), 352–376. https://doi.org/10.1007/s10816-015-9270-y

Note: Emphasized words function as signal words or phrases to reinforce the definition of terms.

5. Process Analysis: A Procedural Development of Ideas

Purpose: We use process analysis when we want to communicate to our readers a series of steps that leads to a particular outcome.

Context: Researchers often use process analysis to demonstrate the steps in a certain biological, physical, social, or chemical sequence; to outline a mathematical equation; or to show any step-by-step process necessary for explaining a result or outcome.

Example: *Analysing the process of stressors that result in certain outcomes*

Early life adversities thus serve as primary stressors that **set the stage for** and **interact with** secondary stressors in the form of **further** adversities. These proliferative **processes** flow through multiple life domains (education, work, relationships), **linking** chains of risk and **creating** interrelated hardships that **connect** ACEs and later life **outcomes** (Ferraro & Shippee, 2009; Pearlin et al., 2005). For example, early life adversity undermines learning and academic achievement, compromising success in adulthood across educational, workforce, and socioeconomic domains (Evans & Kim, 2010; Sansone et al., 2012; Zielinski, 2009). **In turn**, this undermined achievement **creates** contexts biased toward exposure to additional social stressors, a paucity of social and personal resources, and adult mental disorders (Turner, 2013; Wickrama et al., 2010). Increased exposure to later adverse life events may take a range of forms such as relationship problems, residential instability, disability, and involvement with the criminal justice system (Larkin & Park, 2012; Lu et al., 2008; Nurius et al., 2012; Schussler-Fiorenza et al., 2014). (p. 144)

Nurius, P.S., Green, S., Logan-Greene, P., & Borja, S. (2015). Life course pathways of adverse childhood experiences toward adult psychological well-being: A stress process analysis. *Child Abuse & Neglect, 45*, 143–153. https://doi.org/10.1016/j.chiabu.2015.03.008

Note: Emphasized words function as signal words or phrases to reinforce the pattern of process analysis.

6. Comparison and Contrast: A Correlative Development of Ideas

Purpose: We use comparisons and contrasts to explain the similarities and differences between two or more things, ideas, or experiences to our readers.

Context: Researchers use comparisons and contrasts to highlight the similarities and differences between people or things, between locations or locales; between activities; between processes; between ideas; or between experiences.

Example: *Comparing and contrasting two education models*

> The two epistemic modes are almost **inverses** of each other..., although they have the **same** end goal of conceptual understanding of core ideas. **In the first** epistemic approach, the core concepts, principles, and theory for a topic are explicitly presented, defined, and explained to learners, illustrated by demonstrations and example cases. This "theory" component of the topic is generally followed by a "practical" or "lab" component comprised of experimental activities where students aim to test and verify the theory, often working in groups. In this approach, the core ideas are treated as *ready-made science*, and students work with these ideas in tasks, activities, and problems. **In the alternative** epistemic approach a science topic or phenomenon is approached via focus questions and exploration, and the relevant concepts or laws are developed to account for observations and evidence. In this way, the core ideas and laws are "invented" or "discovered" by students and teacher together, in a concept-formation process stemming from a perceived need. Concept names are ideally introduced only *after* the concepts themselves have been grasped. This approach casts learning as *science-in-the-making*, and aims to reflect not only what we know but how we come to know it. (pp. 391–92)

Schuster, D., Cobern, W.W., Adams, B.A., Undreiu, A., & Pleasants, B. (2018). Learning of core disciplinary ideas: Efficacy comparison of two contrasting modes of science instruction. *Research in Science Education, 48*(2), 389–435. https://doi.org/10.1007/s11165-016-9573-3

Note: Emphasized words function as signal words or phrases to reinforce the comparison and contrast pattern.

7. Classification and Division: Categorical Development of Ideas

Purpose: We use classification and division to categorize multiple items for our readers, breaking ideas into parts or grouping them together as a whole.

Context: Researchers regularly use classification and division to categorize people, places, or things; to create taxonomies for plants and animals; to catalogue topics or books; to develop records; or to classify information and ideas.

Example: *Classifying species*

> In perennial *Glycine*, there are three **cases** where a **species** has diploid and polyploid cytotypes: two allopolyploids (*G. tomentella, G. tabacina*) and the putative autopolyploid (*G. hirticaulis*). In all three **cases**, the **name** belongs to the polyploid, not the diploid...but Barker *et al.* assumed that the **name** belonged to the diploid in each **case**. This may be reasonable as an evolutionary expectation, because polyploids at least initially will be a minority cytotype (Levin, 1975). However, **taxonomy** is a product of where, when, and by whom a **species** happens to be **collected** and **named** first, and may have little connection with evolutionary pattern or process. Indeed, the greater colonizing ability of polyploids (e.g. Pandit et al., 2011, 2014; te Beest et al., 2012) may make it more likely that taxonomists will encounter and **name** polyploid cytotypes first. (p. 489)
>
> Doyle, J.J., & Sherman-Broyles, S. (2017). Double trouble: Taxonomy and definitions of polyploidy. *New Phytologist, 213*(2), 487–493. https://doi.org/10.1111/nph.14276
>
> Note: Emphasized words function as signal words or phrases to reinforce the pattern of classification.

8. Cause and Effect: Causal or Consequential Development of Ideas

Purpose: We use cause and effect patterns to explain the reasons for or consequences of an action, or to show the relationships between various actions to our readers.

Context: Researchers often use cause and effect patterns to explain human behaviour and its outcomes; to show the results of certain interactions (biological, chemical, physical, etc.); and to highlight the reasons for or consequences of a historical, social, political, religious, economic, or ecological event.

Example: *Explaining the effects of family history on a behaviour*

> The **effects** of family history on hangover, however they manifest, appear to vary across the lifespan. Piasecki et al. (2005) noted that the **effects** of family history diminish after the college years, and frequency of hangovers during young adulthood may partially mediate the relationship between family history and the development of an AUD. These findings suggest that hangover frequency may be a developmentally limited risk marker

for later alcohol problems and highlight the need for greater hangover-related prospective research on younger samples. (p. 210)

Courtney, K.E., Worley, M., Castro, N., & Tapert, S.F. (2018). The effects of alcohol hangover on future drinking behavior and the development of alcohol problems. *Addictive Behaviors, 78*, 209–215. https://doi.org/10.1016/j.addbeh.2017.11.040

Note: Emphasized words function as signal words or phrases to reinforce the cause and effect pattern.

As we work to develop our ideas and demonstrate our logical train of thought, we choose the pattern of arrangement that makes the most sense for our purpose and our context. Are we describing something? Comparing something? Classifying something? Defining something? Our pattern of development should reflect the mental activity we are doing, showing our readers how we're reasoning through our research and ideas in a logical way.

Sometimes we engage in one category of mental activity in our reasoning process, but most of the time we are engaged in more than one at the same time. As a result, our body paragraphs rely on multiple patterns of development, some of them overlapping one another. For example, we may use one overarching pattern—like *comparison and contrast*—for the body as a whole, but use other patterns like *definition* and *description* to develop key areas within that larger framework.

It is also important to realize that a single paragraph may use more than one pattern of arrangement. For example, one paragraph may offer a historical overview (narration) with clear descriptive elements. Another paragraph may use a cause and effect organization with examples interspersed. We regularly combine patterns of arrangement to reflect our reasoning processes. Once we recognize these patterns and know how to use them, we can develop our ideas clearly, revealing a logical and organized train of thought to our readers.

EXERCISE 2
PATTERNS OF DEVELOPMENT

Consider the following passages and determine their main pattern of development. Do any of the excerpts include a secondary or tertiary pattern of development? See if you can locate all of them.

Excerpt 1

When Kant does talk about emotional cultivation, it seems to have at least three different meanings. First, he often equates it with strengthening. When Kant discusses cultivation of moral feeling, for example, he claims that our obligation is not to acquire it, but to "*cultivate* it and strengthen it through wonder at its inscrutable source" (*MM*, 6: 400, emphasis in original).... Elsewhere, Kant seems to suggest that cultivation requires paying careful attention (Papish, 2007). He claims for example that cultivating one's conscience requires one to "sharpen one's attentiveness to the voice of the inner judge" (*MM*, 6: 401).... Finally, cultivation sometimes seems to mean refining (*CPJ*, 5: 266). Kant claims that we have a duty of self-perfection, which consists in part in "*cultivating* one's *faculties* (or natural predispositions)," which involves raising ourselves from "the crude state" of our nature "more and more toward humanity" (*MM*, 6: 387, emphasis in original). (pp. 443–44)

Thomason, K.K. (2017). A good enough heart: Kant and the cultivation of emotions. *Kantian Review, 22*(3), 441–462. https://doi.org/10.1017/S1369415417000164

Excerpt 2

Given that caffeine modulates emotion, it is of interest whether caffeine may also modulate emotion regulation. Emotion regulation refers to processes that enable individuals to increase or decrease negative or positive emotions (Gross, 1999). According to the "modal model" of emotion, emotions begin with a situation, to which an individual then attends, then appraises, then responds (Gross & Thompson, 2007). Emotion regulation strategies may target any stage of the emotion generative process. Individuals who utilize emotion regulation strategies earlier in the emotion generative process, such as distraction and cognitive reappraisal, tend to experience more positive and less negative emotion, compared with individuals who utilize strategies after emotion generation (Gross & John, 2003). Thus, it is imperative to understand factors that influence both the extent to which individuals choose to employ emotion regulation strategies, and success with which they employ them, as both influence an individual's ultimate emotional experience. Distraction involves redirecting attention by focusing on non-emotional elements of a situation, whereas cognitive reappraisal involves re-evaluating the situation or emotional response to the situation to alter its emotional impact (Gross, 2002). (p. 192)

Giles, G.E., Spring, A.M., Urry, H.L., Moran, J.M., Mahoney, C.R., & Kanarek, R.B. (2018). Caffeine alters emotion and emotional responses in low habitual caffeine consumers. *Canadian Journal of Physiology and Pharmacology, 96*(2), 191–199. http://doi.org/10.1139/cjpp-2017-0224

Excerpt 3

In the village of St. Jacobs, public discourse (i.e., government policy) clearly favours growth over the preservation of historic structures. Our streetscape assessment finds that this position has impacted the built form of the commercial streetscape. Historic maps produced in 1857 and 1968 shed light on the removal of buildings in the core (Smith, 1968). The earlier map shows a total of 40 buildings in the village, with 14 found in the downtown. The latter diagram, produced in 1968, reveals that only 18 of the original structures remain, with seven still standing in the core district that we are focusing on here. We realize that the original streetscape began to change before the onset of heritage commodification, and before implementation of the first Interim Plan (Thompson, 2004).

This trend continued, however, after the plan was introduced in 1972. Although records are incomplete, we know that two of the original (residential) structures were replaced by two commercial buildings in 1976 (Smith, 1983), with three additional retail venues constructed in 1988 (CTW, 2012b). Removal continued even after the 1994 OP amendment, when in 1998 a large modern retail complex drastically changed the historic streetscape (CTW, 2012b, Figure 3). No other structures have been removed since this time (CTW, 2012b), as the development focus has shifted to the outlying market district (Mitchell & de Waal, 2009). These changes have given rise to a mix of historic and modern structures in the commercial core. Like other transforming spaces (e.g., Sennerville, Quebec), this duality has created a landscape lacking in "aesthetic harmonization" (Freidman, 2007, 360). (p. 437)

Mitchell, C.J.A., & Randle, K. (2014). Heritage preservation and the "differentiated countryside": Evidence from southern Ontario. *The Canadian Geographer, 58*(4), 429–444. https://doi.org/10.1111/cag.12131

D. CONNECTING IDEAS IN OUR TRAIN OF THOUGHT

Finally, we need to consider how to transition between ideas and connect our points as we write our body paragraphs. Transitions are like signposts that direct our readers from one thought to the next. We want them to follow our train of thought and not become lost or confused as they are reading; otherwise we'll have a difficult time convincing them of the value and validity of our ideas and our contribution to the current research dialogue.

Think for a moment about the importance of road signs in directing our travel. Imagine, for instance, that you are visiting a friend who has moved across the country. You fly to see her, rent a car at the airport, and ask for directions to her house. She responds by giving you a list of road names:

- Seventeenth Street
- Vine Road
- Pipeline Road
- Sycamore Street
- Archibald Terrace

It would be very difficult to get to her place with only a list of road names, especially if you are unfamiliar with the city and have no electronic means to direct yourself. It would be much easier if she provided direction markers, like *straight*, *right*, or *left*, so you knew which way to go on those streets, as well as landmarks to help situate you as you travel. For instance:

- Turn **right** out of the car rental agency onto *Seventeenth Street*.
- Take *Seventeenth Street* for ten minutes until you get to *Vine Road*.
- Turn **left** on *Vine Road* and go **straight** for three blocks until you hit *Pipeline Road*.
- Stay on *Pipeline Road* until you see a huge shopping centre on the **right**.
- The first street after the shopping centre is *Sycamore Street*. Turn **right** on *Sycamore Street*.
- In two blocks you'll see *Archibald Terrace*. Turn **left**.
- My house is the fourth one on the **left-hand** side: 27 *Archibald Terrace*.

The same goes for directing readers through our research and reasoning in our body paragraphs. We don't want to simply give readers a list of our points or findings and hope they can figure out how our ideas connect. Our readers take their directions from us, so we give them guiding words to help them follow our train of thought.

- Are our ideas sequential—illustrating a process, a chronology, or a narration?
  We use transition words and phrases like *first, second, third, then, next, it follows that, before, after, later, afterwards, subsequently, finally....*

- Is one idea building on another one?
  We use transition words and phrases like *in addition to, also, as well as, building on this idea, furthermore, in fact, moreover....*

- Is one idea set in comparison with another one?
  We use transition words and phrases like *similarly, likewise, also, analogous to, akin to, related to, in the same way, by the same token, in relation to, comparably, correspondingly....*

- Is one idea set in contrast to another one?
  We use transition words and phrases like *in contrast to, alternatively, inversely, conversely, unlike, on the other hand, however, distinct from, opposed to, different from....*

- Is one idea illustrating or exemplifying another one?
  We use transition words and phrases like *for example, for instance, to illustrate, to clarify, to demonstrate, as a case in point, to show what I mean....*

- Is one idea showing the effect or significance of another one?
  We use transition words and phrases like *consequently, so, thus, hence, therefore, as a result, the upshot is, the effect is, it follows that, in light of this....*

- Is one idea summarizing another one?
  We use transition words and phrases like *in sum, that is to say, to overview, in other words, to reiterate, to recap, in review, to sum up....*

Transitions are vital for readers to be able to see how our ideas fit together and to navigate through the research and reasoning in our body paragraphs. The most effective transitions occur at the beginning of a new paragraph and between each new sub-point. It only takes a few words or a short phrase to keep readers on track as we share our research material and ideas.

EXERCISE 3
TRANSITIONS

Circle the transition words in the following excerpts. Determine what the research writers' purpose is in each one—sequencing, building on, comparing, contrasting, illustrating, showing significance, or summarizing—and how the transition words help you, as a reader, to follow the writers' train of thought.

Excerpt 1

It was not until World War II that a major public exhibition of modern French art was held again in Ireland (Kennedy & Henry, 2003). By that time, the connection with avant-garde European art formed by Ellen Duncan's exhibitions had been lost. The interventions of younger female artists and activists, such as Mainie Jellett (1897–1944), Evie Hone (1894–1955), and Mary Swanzy (1882–1978), maintained connections with the wider cosmopolitan art world in the 1920s and 1930s. For these artists, especially Jellett, the art press continued to offer valuable avenues to ideas on art beyond Ireland (Kennedy, 2006). In a similar vein to Ellen Duncan, Jellett sought to promote the autonomy of art in the face of the increasing dominance of nationalist politics. Unlike Duncan, however, Jellett and Hone, choosing to remain in Ireland, used their knowledge of international artists and theories to connect modernist art to Celticism. (p. 70)

Kennedy, R. (2015). Transmitting avant-garde art: Post-impressionism in a Dublin context. *Visual Resources, 31*(1–2), 61–73. https://doi.org/10.1080/01973762.2015.1004780

Excerpt 2

Business ethics as a social movement and as a corporate practice has been associated with the corporate social responsibility (CSR) movement, especially in Europe and Asia.... The CSR discourse has been embraced by corporate circles, social movements and even international institutions (like the EU and the OECD). The CSR discourse is certainly a rich one and we cannot review its diversity here. However, the discourse and practice of CSR builds on three fundamental and interconnected assumptions which turned out to be false. The first is that of *voluntary compliance*: companies would be willing and able to become responsible. The second assumption is about the *potential role of the market*, while the third is about *the potential role of stakeholders* in promoting ethical business practices. (p. 98)

Boda, Z., & Zsolnai, L. (2016). The failure of business ethics. *Society and Business Review, 11*(1), 93–104. https://doi.org/10.1080/21681392.2017.1317457

Excerpt 3

The construction of North Arm Jetty in 1917 has resulted in the deflection of flow and sediment away from the north end of Sturgeon Bank (Levings, 1980). The North Arm was also dredged for navigation, whereas Middle Arm was not, and thus sand-sized sediment is now transported within North Arm and deposited north of Sturgeon Bank (Isfeld et al., 1996). Furthermore, the north end of Sturgeon Bank was closed off in 1961 at McDonald Slough as part of a sewage treatment plant project and this helped to further isolate North arm flows and sediment from Sturgeon Bank (Levings, 1980). (p. 792)

Atkins, R.J., Tidd, M., & Ruffo, G. (2016). Sturgeon Bank, Fraser River Delta, BC, Canada: 150 years of human influences on salt marsh sedimentation. *Journal of Coastal Research, 75*(2), 790–794. https://doi.org/10.2112/S175-159.1

CONCLUSIONS

Body paragraphs are meant to advance knowledge and deepen a community's understanding of a particular subject. The more insight and perspectives brought to the subject, the better we can understand its complex reality and its multifaceted nature. With this in mind, we write body paragraphs dialogically. In fact, we are engaged in two conversations at once! One conversation is with other research scholars: we interact attentively with a range of findings and ideas, discussing them in relation to our own ideas and structuring our body paragraphs accordingly. The other conversation is with interested and knowledgeable readers: we communicate our ideas and the research dialogue to our readers and invite their response. We put ourselves in their shoes in order to recognize what they need from us in order to make sense of our research and reasoning. In this chapter, we have learned some key ways to construct our body paragraphs and have come to recognize the main differences between the bodies of research essays typical of humanities disciplines and the bodies of research essays typical of the social sciences and sciences. We have also learned how to organize our body paragraphs with a logical train of thought and how to incorporate clear transitions between our ideas. As we have discovered, our body paragraphs combine complex ideas with clarity of thought in order to offer insights into the subject and contribute beneficially to our conversations and community.

QUESTIONS FOR REFLECTION

1. What are some specific ways we can respect and acknowledge other research scholars' ideas and findings in our body paragraphs?

2. How do we keep our readers in mind when we write? How can we anticipate their level of knowledge, questions, and responses as we attend to them in our writing?

3. How would you structure your body paragraphs to present your research and ideas in dialogue with other research scholars? As you think through this question, consider which field of study you are in and if your goal is to hypothesize a proposition or persuade others of an argument. Also, consider whether you are engaged in textual or visual interpretation (in the humanities), or whether you are doing qualitative or quantitative research (in social sciences or sciences).

4. What pattern(s) of development would you suggest to someone who needs help organizing their thoughts in each of the following contexts?

- In this section of my paper, I want to show how the War of 1812 had a powerful influence on Canada's formation.

- In this part of my paper, I want to define what *transcendentalism* means so that readers know what I'm talking about.

- In this section of my paper, I want to outline the production process for rayon fabric, from its raw material state to its final, sellable product.

- In this section of my paper, I want to illustrate the horrors of life in concentration camps in order to show the extent of Nazi atrocity during World War II.

- In this part of my paper, I want to show the advantages and disadvantages of a paleo diet versus a ketogenic diet for diabetic patients.

5. What transition words or phrases are needed to connect each set of ideas into a logical train of thought? Rewrite each example with transitions that make sense of the material.

    - Dexterity and fine motor coordination are important developmental skills in young children. Maria learned to tie her shoes at four years of age. Dylan used Velcro straps on his shoes until he was seven.

    - Pods of orcas have been found in the Strait of St. Peters. The death rate of orcas has risen in the last twenty years.

    - Landscape architects insist the roses should be planted this way. Horticulturalists argue that the roses should be planted that way. I have another way of planting roses.

    - Cognitive Behavioural Therapy and other forms of cognitive therapy are important treatments. Psychological disorders and thought distortions are prevalent.

CHAPTER THIRTEEN

CONCLUSIONS

Inviting Response and Responsibility

Endings are difficult matters. When we say goodbye to a good friend who we won't see for a while, or even when we close a meaningful conversation with someone who we don't know very well, we often experience a sense of awkwardness. We can easily imagine the following goodbye scenario at an airport:

Amari: "Okay then, I guess I'd better let you go."
Cameron: "Yeah. I don't want to miss that flight."
Amari: "No; that would be bad."
Cameron: "I can't believe I'm really actually going. It feels unreal."
Amari: "I know, right? For a whole year. How will I live without you? Ha ha."
Cameron: "Ha ha. Yeah."
Amari: "It will be a good experience, though."
Cameron: "For sure. I've always wanted to live in France."
Amari: "I know. And this is your chance."
Cameron: "Yeah. It will be good."
Amari: "And I'll see you next July!"
Cameron: "Right!"
Amari: "Alrighty then, get outta here."
Cameron: "Okay. I'll text you when I get there and keep you posted on all the happenings."
Amari: "For sure. And post some pictures of the Eiffel Tower."
Cameron: "Totally."

This can go on for quite a while, as many of us can attest to. We lob our words back and forth to avoid saying goodbye and facing the finality of leaving. Others of us don't linger, but mumble a quick goodbye and get out of there as fast as possible. This also feels awkward, but it avoids the endless stammering of repeated farewells. Our struggle with farewells becomes even more difficult when we are faced with a definitive departure, like leaving a job, a relationship, a community, or a country for good. We are left with the big question: "How do I end well?"

The same question applies to concluding an idea or set of ideas in a research essay. We have invested a lot of time and energy into our project, connecting with other researchers and communicating our ideas and findings to our readers. When we come to the end, we often don't know what to say. So we resort to one or both of the communication styles above: we repeat ourselves a few times and then breathe a sigh of relief as we flee. Deep down we know that this kind of ending is not quite satisfying, but we have a deadline to meet and most of us aren't sure how to wrap up our work.

If we return to our road trip analogy from Chapter 11, the conclusion to a research essay is like arriving at our destination. When we arrive we usually reflect on the trip and evaluate it. For example, when you reach your family home in Calgary after a long day of travel from Vancouver, your parents will probably ask, "How was your trip?" Answering that question requires you to reflect on and evaluate the journey. After a little thought, you might respond, "It was pretty good except for the traffic jam I hit in Kamloops. I think I'll go through Kelowna on the way back to avoid it." Reflection and evaluation are also common when it comes to discussing the trip with any friends who may have travelled with you. Together, you reflect on the highlights (or lowlights) of the trip and evaluate it according to certain criteria—like traffic congestion, outdoor scenery, car conversation, roadside rest stops, etc.

We can think of the readers of our research essay like the friends who have travelled with us on a road trip. Our readers have followed our train of thought from the beginning of our essay until now. They have been there for each of our points, our interactions with other researchers, our explanations and analyses, and our discussion of findings throughout the paper. By the time we reach our conclusion, they know our journey inside and out. Despite this fact, some of us have been told to recap our introduction or retrace the mental route we just took with our readers by summarizing our essay in our conclusion.

While a short summary of our stance can be a valuable reminder for readers at the end of an essay, a conclusion should not be a simple recapitulation of our work. What readers really want to know by the time they reach our conclusion is, What now? Where do we go from here? What should we do in response? Why does this research matter? The point of a conclusion in a research essay, then, is to discuss the *implications*, *applications*, and *future directions* of our ideas and findings for the research community. It also may raise *concerns*, *cautions*, or *obligations* in light of the research shown. In short, a conclusion is a guide that shows readers how they can respond to the information and ideas we've given them throughout our essay.

In this chapter, we will learn how to "end well" when it comes to writing research conclusions. We will hone our reflection and evaluation skills, addressing the questions our readers have for us by the end of our work and inviting their response. Specifically, we will consider three key features of conclusion writing: (a) the ability to step back and look at the big picture of our work in the research discussion; (b) the ability to look forward to the future of research and discussion on this topic; and (c) the ability to recognize the moral imperatives that our work raises in and for the community. We will consider conclusion exemplars from various fields of academic study and learn how to move away from repetition and towards significance as we close our work.

A. THE BIG PICTURE: CONTRIBUTING TO THE RESEARCH CONVERSATION AND COMMUNITY

The first characteristic of an academic conclusion is its "big-picture" focus. Conclusions require that we, as research writers, step back and consider the ***big picture*** of our work and its overall contribution to the research conversation on our topic. For example, if we imagine the body of our paper as a leaf we've been examining in detail under a microscope, then our conclusion zooms out from the leaf to consider the branch and tree that it came from: What is the significance of the leaf in regard to the branch on which it belongs? How do we understand the leaf in the context of the tree? When we focus on the big picture, we examine the significance of our work for a particular context and community. We communicate to readers why they should care about our stance, and show how our research contributes to our knowledge and actions as a community.

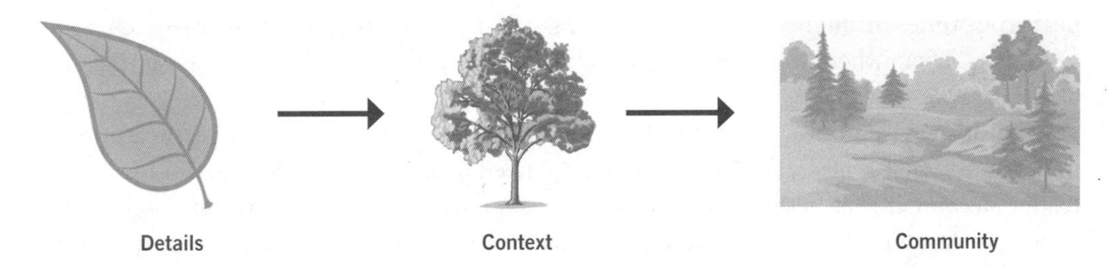

In order to highlight the big picture in our conclusion, we begin by reminding our readers of our claim and/or key ideas. We do this in a succinct summary, recognizing that our readers are already well familiar with our stance since they've just read our essay. Two ways we can acknowledge our readers' familiarity with our work in our summary is by using inclusive, plural pronouns like "we" and "us," and using phrases that evoke recall. For example, consider the following "reminder" templates:

- The issues that I have outlined in this study, namely ________, help **us** recognize that ________.
- Given the results of my hypothesis, specifically ________, **we** are now better situated to understand ________.
- As **we** can see, my claim that ________ is critical for ________.
- Without grasping that ________, as I have argued in this paper, **we** are less likely to ________.

As we can see in the templates above, we gently nudge our readers to recall our claim and key ideas with our intentional choice of words and sentence structure. We choose inclusive pronouns and embed our summary in the larger context and conversation of our research. As we focus on short summation, we are selective about the aspects of our research that we reiterate in our conclusion. Rather than try to sum up our whole essay, we focus on the key areas that have the most significance for the research discussion, and the greatest takeaway for the research community.

We may be wondering what sort of things count as significant or constitute a takeaway for the community. For researchers, ***significance*** involves two things: *thought* and *action.* A stance or set of ideas may be significant because it offers a new way of thinking about a subject. Significant ideas are those that provide new knowledge, contribute meaningful insights, or deepen our understanding of a topic in a research conversation. As we saw in Chapter 9, we know we are addressing the significance of our ideas when we ask ourselves, "So what?" and "Who Cares?" Answering these questions takes serious reflection and assessment. We do this numerous times throughout our body paragraphs, discussing the significance of each point or finding. Then, when we come to the conclusion, we provide readers with the significance of our essay *as a whole.*

Significance is not only a matter of intellectual gain—like new knowledge, meaning, or understanding; it is also a matter of action. We need to ask ourselves, "What do I want my readers to *do* with the research material I have shared with them?" "How do I want them to act as a result of the ideas I've communicated in this paper?" Answering these questions gives our readers a ***takeaway***, a practical way to respond to our work.

These two areas of significance—thought and action—are communicated in our conclusion by means of implications and applications. ***Implications*** refer to the *consequences* or *effects* of our ideas in the research conversation and community. For example, let's return to the sugar-versus-fat debate touched on in Chapter 8 and imagine that the research claim that we've attempted to prove in our research essay is, "human obesity is largely due to excess sugar consumption rather than fat consumption." We can point to one or more implications (consequences or effects) of this claim in our conclusion. Perhaps this claim has health and nutritional implications, consequences for food advertising, effects for digestive microbiology, ramifications for understanding food addiction, etc. Our conclusion will focus on the implication most fitting for the context and content of the rest of our essay.

If we combine one of the summary templates above with an implication-focused conclusion, it may begin something like this:

> **As we can see, my argument that** human obesity is largely due to excess sugar consumption rather than fat consumption **has critical implications for** understanding digestive health and dieting. If the body requires a balance of fat, sugar, and protein to function optimally, then excess consumption of any of these, especially over an extended period of time, causes alterations of the microbiome in the gut (Costos, 2012). Excess sugar,

> in particular, negatively affects gut bacteria, releasing compounds that can disturb digestive functioning and contribute to obesity (Fernandez, 2015; Abadi, 2018). As we approach the issue of weight loss through digestive health, our focus should be on developing a balanced diet that avoids excess sugar.
>
> Please note that the names and material used in this example are invented and any correspondence to actual research or researchers is purely coincidental.

This example illustrates the implications of a particular stance on the sugar-versus-fat debate in regard to obesity. Taking the view that excess sugar has a negative effect on digestive health naturally has consequences for how one diets. Here readers are guided from the specifics of the sugar-versus-fat debate to the broader context of digestive health and diet.

Like implications, ***applications*** focus on the significance of our research and ideas. Applications refer to the *use* or *purpose* of our ideas in the research community and beyond. They often focus on who will benefit most from our work and what will stimulate change in the community's actions and attitudes. If we return to the claim that "human obesity is largely due to excess sugar consumption rather than fat consumption," an application-focused conclusion would consider such questions as: What is the purpose or use of this stance? Who does it apply to? Who will most benefit from this standpoint? For example, the application of this claim may be geared towards those struggling with obesity or towards nutritional scientists. Or perhaps we wish to educate the public, offering general applications for food choices and eating habits.

If we combine one of the summary templates above with an application-focused conclusion, it may begin something like this:

> **Given that the results of my hypothesis suggest that** human obesity is largely due to excess sugar consumption rather than fat consumption, **we are now better situated to** educate children about healthy food choices, promoting snacks like nuts and seeds rather than sugar-laden foods in the school system. With children suffering from obesity at unprecedented rates in the United States (Foreman, 2014; Inglesburg, 2015), the role of food education at a young age is key to addressing this epidemic.
>
> Please note that the names and material used in this example are invented and any correspondence to actual research or researchers is purely coincidental.

As we can see, an application focuses on the specific ways our claim can be *applied* within a particular community. In this case the application focuses on educating children and recommending certain foods for snacks. Whether we tackle the applications or implications of our claim in our conclusion, we take a step back to look at the "big picture" of our work, showing the research community and our readers the significance of our ideas and providing a takeaway—something that can be reconsidered or something that can be done in response.

EXERCISE 1
THE BIG PICTURE, IMPLICATIONS AND APPLICATIONS

Examine the following excerpts taken from academic essay conclusions. In each example, what specific implications (consequences, effects) and/or applications (uses, purposes) do the researchers foreground to communicate the significance of their work?

Excerpt 1

Many, though not all, of our enthusiasts consider the Potter books a major contributor to both their self-identification as readers and their wider literacy development. Perhaps the most striking change they reported was the confidence and motivation to try more challenging books or more books in general. Thus, the Potter books—particularly the thicker ones—acted as a "Portkey" or "gateway," transporting readers into the world of more mature fiction. Pupils who persevered with the series considered it a positive achievement, which potentially heightened their LSC. As Marsh and Shavelson (1985) suggest, we observe that Literacy Self-Concepts have both cognitive and affective components. Readers thus know that reading Harry Potter has benefitted their reading; and moreover, they gain emotional payoffs such as pride and confidence in their abilities. These can motivate them towards further reading and trying more complex texts, which may subsequently result in higher attainments in school literacy activities (Archambault et al., 2010). (pp. 278–79)

Dempster, S., Oliver, A., Sunderland, J., & Thistlethwaite, J. (2016). What has Harry Potter done for me? Children's reflections on their 'Potter experience.' *Children's Literature in Education, 47*(3), 267–282. https://doi.org/10.1007/s10583-015-9267-x

Excerpt 2

This study encourages managers to examine the spiritual benefits of their CSR [corporate social responsibility] efforts and emphasize these benefits in marketing communications. Managers can incorporate spiritual benefits in their marketing messages by emphasizing the moral obligation associated with the purchase, the spiritual growth it can provide consumers and its symbolic spiritual meaning. For example, companies like Starbucks that emphasize their mission "to inspire and nurture the human spirit" benefit from being able to position their CSR effort as communicating spiritual benefits. (p. 284)

Alhouti, S., & D'Souza, G. (2018). Benefits of corporate social responsibility. *Journal of Consumer Marketing, 35*(5), 277–286. https://doi.org/10.1108/JCM-08-2016-1895

Excerpt 3

Through this transformative experience of art and art-making, ARTE (Art and Resistance through Education) views this as an opportunity to invite students to share their own stories about human rights. Through the work that ARTE engages in, we hope to create a culture where students do not feel that they need an invitation to speak, but realize it is their own space to share their stories as frequently as they wish. In this space, students and teachers are partners, utilizing the arts for reflection and growth to foster authentic expression. At this intersection of critical pedagogy and the arts ARTE believes a democratic space can and will exist. (p. 61)

Gutiérrez-Vicario, M. (2016). More than a mural: The intersection of public art, immigrant youth, and human rights. *Radical Teacher, 104*, 55–61. http://doi.org/10.5195/rt.2016.229

B. A FUTURE ORIENTATION: INVITING RESEARCHERS AND READERS TO RESPOND

Another important aspect of academic conclusions is their forward focus. In a conclusion, we have the opportunity to consider the future directions that our research and ideas can take in the research community. When we focus on the ***future directions*** of our work, we point to new areas for research development, areas we didn't touch on in our study that are relevant for developing further knowledge and understanding of the topic. We look forward by addressing questions like, "Now what?" "What next?" or "Where do we go from here?" Recognizing that there is always more research to do, we take the opportunity in our conclusion to invite our scholarly readers to build on our work. In this way, conclusions show the social objectives of a research community: readers from within that community share the desire to investigate the topic further and cooperate in developing new knowledge about it (Giltrow, 2005, p. 182).

To see how this works, let's return to the claim example in the previous section—"human obesity is largely due to excess sugar consumption rather than fat consumption." We could address the future directions of this claim by proposing *more* studies to support its stance. We could suggest research on *other* factors that contribute to obesity besides excess sugar consumption. We could propose research on the benefits of healthy fat consumption for *other* physical disorders or diseases. Alternatively, we might point to a specific limitation in our research: perhaps we only had a small pool of participants or a study of short duration. Maybe we think other factors have skewed the results of our study. If that is the case, we openly address it in our conclusion, asking pointed questions and suggesting ways to create a stronger and more effective study for future research.

If we combine one of the summary templates from Section A with a future orientation in our conclusion, it may begin something like this:

> **The issue that I have outlined in this study, namely,** that human obesity is largely due to excess sugar rather than fat consumption, **shows us that we need to** seriously consider the importance of healthy fat in the human diet and its benefits for human health (Stussi & Bengle, 2017). In our study, reducing processed sugar and adding healthy fats resulted in various benefits for obese participants, including weight loss, improved cognitive functioning, and higher levels of energy. With this in mind, further research should examine how boosting healthy fats may prove beneficial for other physical disorders or diseases, particularly those that involve low cognitive function and reduced energy levels.
>
> Please note that the names and material used in this example are invented and any correspondence to actual research or researchers is purely coincidental.

As we consider the questions, "Now what?" or "What next?" and look to the future of our work, we invite readers and scholars to respond to us by means of further research. In fact, we encourage them to respond to our research when we point to our unresolved questions or remaining knowledge gaps that they could address, answer, or fill with their work. In this way, we not only show how our work contributes to the ongoing conversation about the topic, but also invite others to continue the dialogue *beyond* our work, to take up our ideas and contribute to the conversation in their own way.

EXERCISE 2
FUTURE DIRECTIONS

Examine the excerpts of academic essay conclusions below and answer the following questions.

- How do each of the research writers present the future directions of their work—as *suggestions* for new areas of study or as *limitations* to address?
- How does each excerpt implicitly invite readers to respond?

Excerpt 1

> [This] is the first study to assess the manner in which spirituality might affect QOL [quality of life] among veterans with PTSD. Relying on multidimensional approaches for assessing these constructs, we found that spiritual functioning generated a significant overall effect on QOL in the presence of demographic risk factors, combat exposure, and severity of PTSD symptomatology. In addition, we

found that this association between spirituality and QOL was fully mediated by veterans' levels of forgiveness at the time of the study. Looking ahead, we hope that this study will promote further research on forgiveness in military populations and be a step to more fully illumining how veterans with PTSD may effectively draw upon their spirituality to cultivate QOL in their recovery process. (p. 176)

Currier, J.M., Dresher, K.D., Holland, J.M., Lisman, R., & Foy, D.W. (2016). Spirituality, forgiveness, and quality of life: Testing a mediational model with military veterans with PTSD. *The International Journal for the Psychology of Religion, 26*(2), 167–179. https://doi.org/10.1080/10508619.2015.1019793

Excerpt 2

Although our research provides important information about the risk factors for cyberbullying, there are limitations to the study. More sophisticated measures of cyberbullying are needed, in which the relationship to traditional bullying, the amount of time an adolescent spends using information and communication technologies, and personal characteristics, such as predisposition to violent acts, are considered. Also, we relied on self-reporting measures to assess cyberbullying, which means that the data could reflect the subjective perceptions of the adolescents and, thus, could be inaccurate, especially when the participants had no prior information about cyberbullying.... There is a need to further investigate cyberbullying to gain a better understanding of its dynamics. Researchers interested in this line of inquiry should examine the effects of using social network sites and the amount of time spent on the Internet. The influence of the interpersonal social context of peer groups and individual risk factors related to the personality of the adolescents are other possible risk factors that may be associated with their use of the Internet and communication technologies and their potential to become involved with cyberbullying. (pp. 1518–19)

Beyazit, U., Şimşek, S., & Ayhan, A.B. (2017). An examination of the predictive factors of cyberbullying in adolescents. *Social Behavior and Personality, 45*(9), 1511–1522. https://doi.org/10.2224/sbp.6267

Excerpt 3

The growing list of hemp's potential uses suggests that the crop has much promise for agronomic production systems in the United States. However, many of the claims surrounding hemp's productivity and utility must be taken with caution because in many cases, the production systems and markets for these products must be developed. Agronomic research will be needed to match cultivars to different soils and climates and determine resource input requirements (as fertilizer, herbicides, and pesticides) that optimize the volume and value of outputs. In addition, new harvest and processing systems are likely to be needed to capture these products. (p. 420)

Fike, J. (2016). Industrial hemp: Renewed opportunities for an ancient crop. *Critical Reviews in Plant Sciences, 35*(5–6), 406–424. https://doi.org/10.1080/07352689.2016.1257842

C. A MORAL ORIENTATION: ENCOURAGING ETHICAL ACTION AND RESPONSIBILITY

In addition to stepping back and looking forward, academic writers sometimes take a ***moral turn*** in their conclusions, highlighting obligations or responsibilities that arise from their work, as well as concerns or cautions resulting from their ideas. Similar to a forward focus, a moral orientation considers the questions, "Now what?" or "What next?" However, instead of concentrating on future intellectual contribution or direction, a moral orientation concentrates on ethical activity: What should we do in light of this research? What should we not do? What lessons can be learned? What changes or improvements should we make as a result of these findings? As Janet Giltrow (2005) puts it, "The call for action in the world flows from research-attested knowledge" and invites readers to respond accordingly (p. 183).

Returning once more to our example claim—"human obesity is due to excess sugar consumption rather than fat consumption"—we can offer a moral orientation and encourage ethical action by evaluating what needs to be done as a result of our research knowledge. Perhaps this takes the form of an imperative: We *must* change how we approach dieting in light of this information. Perhaps it takes the form of a caution or concern: We *should not* be reducing healthy fats to gain an optimal weight, but should cut out excess sugar instead. Or perhaps it takes the form of an obligation or responsibility: We *ought to* change how we think about fat in connection with health. We *should* educate patients with helpful guidelines to monitor fat and sugar intake.

If we combine one of the summary templates from Section A with a moral orientation in our conclusion, it may begin something like this:

> **Without grasping that** human obesity is due to excess sugar rather than fat consumption, **as I have argued in this paper, we are less likely to** offer effective dietary measures to obese patients under our care. We *should* be cautioning our patients against excess sugar intake and monitoring their fat intake, encouraging a moderate consumption of healthy fats rather than advising a low-fat diet (Smith, 2010; Jabula & Hahn, 2017).
>
> Please note that the names and material used in this example are invented and any correspondence to actual research or researchers is purely coincidental.

Notice how moral responsibility—whether in the form of imperatives, cautions, or obligations—is signalled by modal verbs. We have already seen how modality is used in academic research writing when we set up our claim (Chapter 9). In conclusions we see modality again, most often as verbs of necessity or obligation, which communicate a need for response. For instance:

- We *must* change our thinking.
- We *should* act differently
- We *ought* to care more about this issue.
- We *need* to support this cause.

Other forms of modality may also be present in conclusions. When we want to temper our imperatives or nuance our obligations in some way, we may choose to include other qualifiers. For instance:

- We *may* benefit from changing our thinking.
- We *might* begin by supporting this cause.
- We *could* consider alternatives to such-and-such.

When academic researchers focus on moral orientation at the end of their papers, they do so inclusively. The obligations they set forth are meant for *all of us*; hence, they use the plural pronoun *we*. In effect, researchers are saying, "Given the knowledge we now have, we have a responsibility to do something with it as a community." This community may be the academic one in which the research writer is situated, or it may be a wider community beyond this specific context. With a moral orientation, research writers offer suggestions to their readers about how best to respond to the research they've provided and how to be involved in responsible action.

EXERCISE 3
MORAL ORIENTATION

Review the list of modal qualifiers in Chapter 9, and then examine each of the following excerpts from academic essay conclusions.

- Find and highlight all the modal verbs that are used.

- What ethical actions are being promoted and/or what activities are being cautioned against?

Excerpt 1

This study is significant in identifying different patterns of change in mental health among older women. Many women will age with high levels of mental health-related quality of life. However, we identify a significant group of women with persistently poor levels of mental health throughout their later life, who are at risk of further decline in mental health as they age and in the period prior to death. This group of women may need additional support and specific mental health care in their last years. This mental health care should complement the care of their physical and medical needs, particularly as chronic diseases increase the risk of poor mental health among older women. Enhancement of mental health-related quality of life is an important component of the management of chronic disease in this older population. (p. 1052)

Leigh, L., Byles, J.E., Chojenta, C., & Pachana, N.A. (2016). Late life changes in mental health: A longitudinal study of 9683 women. *Aging and Mental Health, 20*(10), 1044–1054. https://doi.org/10.1080/13607863.2015.1060943

Excerpt 2

Now a final thought. Over the past two decades many historians of the USSR have privileged archival sources above others and in ways that may not always be justified. Naturally, the long absence of access to these sources gave them luster and appeal, especially to younger historians trying to develop new interpretations. But it may be time for the pendulum to swing and researchers to pay renewed attention to other kinds of sources. For many topics historians are most likely to reach balanced conclusions and ask good questions when they interact with the broadest range of sources. This is so, if only because multiple sources provide alternative prisms through which to view a given story. While we should continue to pay close attention to archival materials, we should remember that publications of all kinds and the insights supplied by live informants (oral history) matter no less for understanding and interpreting Soviet history. (pp. 417–18)

Solomon, P.H. (2015). Understanding the history of Soviet criminal justice: The contribution of archives and other sources. *The Russian Review, 74*, 401–418. https://doi.org/10.1111/russ.12022

D. CONCLUSIONS ACROSS THE DISCIPLINES

As we can see, there is a lot more to writing conclusions than reiterating our introduction or even providing a summary of our work. Conclusions are meant to show readers the big picture of our research and ideas—their implications and/or their applications. Conclusions also propose future directions for research and often take a moral perspective, offering suggestions about what responsible actions should be taken in light of our work in order to benefit a particular community. While conclusions are used wrap up a specific study and provide closure to an essay, they are not meant to shut down dialogue. Instead, conclusions are meant to provide new openings, inviting readers and researchers to respond and continue the conversation.

Now that we are familiar with the general aims and elements of a conclusion, let's consider how different disciplines in the sciences, social sciences, and humanities conclude their research. As you read the following examples, note how each one draws readers to look at the big picture. Also, notice the similar language—like plural pronouns and modality—used across the disciplines. Beyond providing a big-picture perspective, consider whether these scholarly writers have made any suggestions for future research or highlighted any responsibilities for the community to take up in response.

1. The Sciences: An Example from Agricultural Farming

> Growing demand for agricultural products has the potential to continue to shift landscapes and have negative environmental impacts at a global scale. ICLS have shown promise to create synergies between crop and animal systems with demonstrated environmental, yield, and economic benefits. Here, we examine this issue in the first paper globally to look at how farmers perceive the costs and benefits of integrating sheep into vineyard systems. Our results show that sheep integration in New Zealand is largely occurring on a seasonal basis, typically through exchanges between specialized systems, but this type of integration has the potential to provide both ecological and economic benefits to farmers of varying farm sizes and characteristics, in particular by reducing herbicide and mowing needs. In contrast to other forms of crop and livestock integration, using sheep in vineyards can reduce labor needs, resulting in higher profits. Our results also demonstrate that the full potential to integrate sheep into vineyard systems is not yet common, but among those utilizing sheep beyond the winter, additional economic and labor benefits are reported. Importantly, existing research, as well as our own, demonstrate the need for coordination and additional skill sets that would be necessary if farmers seek greater integration on-farm rather than across specialized systems.
>
> Finally, our results demonstrate a clear need for additional research in both the social and biophysical sciences related to sheep and viticulture integration. Further agronomic

research is needed on the effect of sheep integration on grape yield (perceived as a harm by two farmers), soil structure and diversity, animal health and well-being, input use, and potential conservation benefits. Expansion of farmer surveys into other regions in New Zealand and other countries can better assess whether these perceived benefits and costs are similar, and whether farmers who have not adopted the practice have different perspectives. This paper aims to be a first step in driving this future research agenda to more completely understand the potential benefits and costs of sheep integration in vineyards. (p. 8)

Niles, M.T., Garrett, R.D., & Walsh, D. (2018). Ecological and economic benefits of integrating sheep into viticulture production. *Agronomy for Sustainable Development, 38*(1), 1–10. https://doi.org/10.1007/s13593-017-0478-y

2. The Social Sciences: An Example from Psychotherapy

The present study investigated whether sleep disturbance serves as a predictor and/or a moderator of psychotherapy response in depressed individuals with bipolar disorder. Sleep neither predicted the likelihood of recovery nor the time to recovery in our analyses. Contrary to our hypothesis, receiving intensive psychotherapy as opposed to collaborative care did not offer a major advantage in terms of recovery rates. This is somewhat surprising, as individuals with bipolar disorder who are poor sleepers may experience more stressors in their lives or have less ability to manage the stressors, which would be addressed in intensive psychotherapy, but not collaborative care. This hypothesis is consistent with previous studies indicating that stressful life events can have a negative impact on sleep quality (Bernert et al., 2007; Frank et al., 2000; Haynes et al., 2006). Noteworthy shortcomings of the present study included that sleep duration was assessed by self-report, which is vulnerable to recall bias, and the study did not include objective measures of sleep quantity or quality such as polysomnography or actigraphy (Fernandez-Mendoza et al., 2011; Mercer et al., 2002). Therefore, it is not possible to formally diagnose individuals with insomnia or hypersomnia. Future research should utilize objective measures or daily sleep diaries to provide more data on weekly sleep patterns. Randomization to treatment group was not stratified according to sleep type, possibly confounding our finding of sleep on recovery. Of note, this study also does not examine the role of sleep on mania or hypomania on treatment response as participants were only enrolled if depressed at baseline. Further, due to sample size restrictions, we did not investigate the differential effects of the type of psychotherapy, which consisted of three treatments. Therefore, it is possible that the extent to which sleep was emphasized differed depending on the treatment modality received. Future research should more closely examine whether sleep patterns influence response to psycho-therapy differentially depending on type of services. Lastly, the measure of sleep only covered the previous past week, and it would be useful to know if habitual long-term sleep patterns had a similar relationship. Furthermore, it is possible that sleep variability rather than sleep duration alone may have a greater impact on treatment response. With these caveats in mind, in summary, our findings indicate that sleep during the past week does not seem to play a major role in predicting or moderating response to psychotherapy in bipolar disorder, suggesting that examining current sleep may not be a necessary factor that clinicians need to consider when determining the most appropriate type of psychosocial intervention for their patients. (p. 2001)

Sylvia, L.G., Salcedo, S., Peters, A.T., Magalhaes, P., Frank, E., Miklowitz, D.J., Otto, M.W., Berk, M., Nierenberg, A.A., & Deckersbach, T. (2017). Do sleep disturbances predict or moderate the response to psychotherapy in bipolar disorder? *The Journal of Nervous and Mental Disease, 205*(3), 196–202. https://doi.org/10.1097/NMD.0000000000000579

3. The Humanities: An Example from English and Literary Studies

In this paper, I have attempted to bring into focus Dorothy L. Sayers's knowledge and proficiency with a genre in which she is not generally acknowledged to be adroit or interested, that of writing original poetry, using allegories of classical myth and legend. My intent was twofold: first, to direct attention toward the poetry written by Sayers based upon her experiences and observations during her Oxford years, particularly to that of Sayers's first book of poetry, *OP. I.*, as it is a valuable portion of her literary heritage, and secondly, to direct attention toward a seldom recognized interest of hers in the worlds of classical mythology, legend, and fantasy, as well as in the allegorical devices inherent to those worlds which she explored within the sphere of poetry, particularly in her early published work, *OP. I.*...

I believe it is time to expand our consideration of the imaginative world of Dorothy L. Sayers, to include analyses of those themes of myth and legend as well as those allegorical devices that Sayers embraced in her early writing life, and to which she returned in her later, more seasoned, professional career, particularly with respect to her translation of *La Divina Commedia* by Dante Alighieri, a quintessential example of medieval allegorical verse dealing with supernatural other-worlds. By choosing to focus upon Dante in her later years, Sayers returned to her first loves of poetry and translation, completing full circle her interest in writing poems of mythic allegory, medieval romance, and Christian symbolism which she began as a young poet and in which she delved with enthusiasm during her Oxford University years. (pp. 67, 69)

Prescott, B. (2018). Allegorical reference to Oxford University through classical myth in the early poetry of Dorothy L. Sayers: A reading of "Alma Mater" from *OP. I. Mythlore, 36*(2), 43–71.

As we begin to craft our own conclusions, we can reflect on the kinds of conclusions that research scholars in our field of study write. What elements do they foreground—applications, implications, future directions, or moral actions? How do they organize these elements? What kind of language do they use? We draw on their frameworks as models for our own conclusion writing.

E. WRITING CONCLUSIONS: GENERAL PATTERNS

Now that we know the aims and elements of research conclusions and have seen examples from various disciplines, we are ready to tackle writing our own. As we start writing, it is helpful to remember that there is no "one size fits all" conclusion. However, research conclusions do often use the following format:

- **Summarize with a Purpose**
  We begin a conclusion by communicating to our readers the significance of our claim and our key research ideas. In the process, we summarize them very briefly, remembering that our summary always has a direction or purpose. It answers the question, "Why is this claim and research significant?" As we have seen, there are two main ways our research is significant in academic studies: our research is either *intellectually* important, adding to knowledge on the topic and understanding of the subject in the field of study, or our research is *practically* important, showing us what to do differently and what to change in order to benefit the community. In fact, it may well be both. We can use the templates in Section A to compose the beginning of our conclusion, summarizing our work briefly to highlight its importance.

- **Contextualize the Research**
  We spend the next few sentences of our conclusion on the applications or implications of our research. Applications and implications reinforce the significance of our work by showing how exactly our research affects or applies to a larger context and community: What are the consequences or potential effects of our research and ideas? How can they be used and applied? Who benefits most from our research and why?

- **Visualize the Future**
  We end our conclusion with an eye to the future. How do we want readers and researchers to respond to our work? What do we want them to do with our research and ideas? Perhaps we want to encourage scholars to continue the research conversation by suggesting areas for further study and future research. This may involve pointing out some gaps in our own study that still need to be filled. Or perhaps we want to encourage readers to make a change by proposing moral imperatives, highlighting what they could or should do in response to our research findings. Either way, we want to end our essay by opening up the conversation and inviting readers and researchers to respond to our work in order to continue the dialogue and benefit the future of the community.

Alongside this format, another area to take into account when writing a conclusion is the language typically used at the end of a research essay. Here are a few of the most common types of diction found in academic conclusions.

1. Concluding Phrases

Unsurprisingly, conclusions often use terms and phrases that signal that the current study is coming to a close. The most familiar examples of this are *in conclusion*, *to conclude*, *to close*, *finally*, *in the end*, *therefore*, *thus*, and *hence*. While these terms are important signals for our reader, we try not to overuse or repeat them as we conclude our ideas. One or two phrases of this kind will suffice.

2. Questions

Academic writers realize that no matter how much research they've done on a subject or how clearly they have developed their points and findings, there is always more knowledge to be gleaned; there are always more ways to look at the topic; and there are always other facets to address. Instead of hiding this fact, they draw attention to it by posing questions in their conclusions to highlight the limitations of their research and to suggest areas for future study.

3. Personal Pronouns

Academic writers are careful with the use of personal pronouns. The first-person singular, *I*, and first-person plural, *we*, are used sparingly and strategically in research writing. However, when it comes to conclusions, scholars often use *we* more liberally. They do so for three reasons: to include readers in their consideration of the big picture, to shift readers from the specificity of the research (in the body paragraphs) to the community in conversation, and to invite readers to respond to the research. By the end of their work, research scholars remind readers that they are all in this together—the research being done has applications, implications, obligations, and future directions for the community as a whole, and everyone can become involved.

4. Verb Tenses

When we sum up our claim or key research ideas at the beginning of a conclusion, we often use the past tense. For instance, if we return to the above example written by Prescott (Section D), we notice her use of the past tense as she begins her conclusion:

> In this paper, I **have attempted** to bring into focus Dorothy L. Sayers's knowledge and proficiency with a genre in which she is not generally acknowledged to be adroit or interested....

Sylvia et al. also begin with the past tense as they reiterate the basis for their study at the outset of their conclusion:

> The present study **investigated** whether sleep disturbance serves as a predictor and/or a moderator of psychotherapy response in depressed individuals with bipolar disorder.

In both these cases, only the first verb of the sentence appears in the past tense. It indicates that an activity—like a study—is now completed. However, the rest of the verbs in these examples are in the present tense. In fact, beyond recalling a study, most conclusions use the present tense throughout. Some conclusions even recall their study in the present tense. For instance, Niles, Garrett, and Walsh (Section D) sum up their study in the present tense:

> Here, we **examine** this issue in the first paper globally to look at how farmers perceive the costs and benefits of integrating sheep into vineyard systems. Our results **show** that sheep integration in New Zealand is largely occurring on a seasonal basis, typically through exchanges between specialized systems....

While verbs used for summarizing our study may be either in the past or present tense, verbs throughout the rest of a conclusion—those used to discuss applications, implications, obligations, and future directions—are consistently in the present tense. These areas are discussed in the present tense because they are recommendations being asserted *right now*, in the present moment of writing. They are also meant to direct readers from the present to the future: what we could study next or what we should do in response. This shift involves combining the present tense with modal verbs.

5. Modal Verbs

Modal verbs can be used in academic conclusions to indicate future directions, recommendations, or obligations. Conclusions open researchers and readers to new areas of exploration or action that can be taken up in the academic community and beyond. These areas are communicated with modal verbs—like *could*, *can*, *might*, and *may*—to suggest future potential or possible next steps. For example, Sylvia et al. (Section D) suggest the following:

> [E]xamining current sleep **may** not be a necessary factor that clinicians need to consider when determining the most appropriate type of psychosocial intervention for their patients.

Conclusions also implore readers to change their views or actions by using modal verbs, such as *should*, *must*, *need*, and *ought*. If the research shows that something needs to be improved or amended, readers are invited to respond accordingly. Returning to Sylvia et al., notice how they add a modal verb to communicate an obligation in regard to future research:

Future research **should** utilize objective measures....

As we can see, modal verbs help to qualify the future explorations and actions that readers are invited to take in response to the research provided.

When it comes to crafting a conclusion, our words count. There are certain words we use to communicate *closure* and others we use to communicate *opening*. There are particular verb tenses we use to convey the research we have undertaken and activities we would like to see in the future. There are also pronouns we use to express inclusion and cooperation at the heart of academic research, like "we." As we conclude a paper, we use our language strategically to foster community and to encourage the research dialogue to continue.

With a general pattern in place and particular words to incorporate, we can begin writing our conclusions with confidence. Try one of the following conclusion templates below to get started, and adapt it accordingly to make it your own:

In this paper, I have argued __________, with the intension of showing ____________. In the process, one key issue that has surfaced is __________. This issue has seldom been recognized as important because __________. I draw it to our attention here because it not only has implications for ____________ but also for ___________. As we explore this area further, we should ______________.

The findings that I have outlined in this study, namely _________, demonstrate that _________. These findings not only have benefits for ______________, but can also be applied to ___________. With this in mind, we must ___________. As we look to the future, it is also imperative that we _________ because ________. In particular, we recommend ______________.

In this study, I investigated ___________. Given the results of my hypothesis that _______, we are now better situated to understand _______. However, I was surprised to find _________, which highlights two limitations of this study, namely ________ and ________. Future research should more closely examine ________ as well as ________ in order to address these gaps. What we need to see as we move forward is _________.

CONCLUSIONS

In our road-trip analogy, we thought of a conclusion as a reflection we share with others once we reach our destination. To some extent this is an apt comparison. But really, when we come to the end of a research paper we are in the unique place of having completed a study while recognizing that there is always more exploration to come. The journey of knowledge is continuous. Perhaps a better image for a conclusion, then, is to imagine standing at a crossroads on a much longer journey, in which we are one of many travellers. Here we take stock of what we have accomplished in our study—how we've contributed to the research conversation on our topic and how we've shared the implications or applications of our ideas. But we also consider where to go from here. In fact, we suggest to other travellers on the knowledge journey which way we could or should go next. As we contemplate where we've been and where we're going, we invite our readers to respond and continue the research dialogue where we've left off.

Feeling anxious about writing conclusions is common for new research writers. It can be difficult to figure out the significance of our research and ideas in relation to the larger conversation about our topic. The most helpful way to overcome this anxiety is to look at how other researchers write their conclusions. We can adopt their format and methods of stating significance—like discussing the implications and applications of our work—to convey the intellectual or practical contribution of our ideas to the community. We can also apply their forward focus, suggesting future directions for studies in the field or pointing to the moral responsibilities emerging from our research. Finally, we can become aware of the common terms and language practices used in writing conclusions and apply them to our work. Once we become aware of the general purpose and patterns of a conclusion, we can become confident writers ourselves.

QUESTIONS FOR REFLECTION

1. Why do you think conclusions tend to be approached as either a recap of an introduction or a summary of the work done in the body paragraphs? Why do both approaches feel unsatisfying when we encounter them in other people's writing? What can be done differently that would result in a satisfying and substantial conclusion?

2. A key element in our conclusion writing is a big-picture approach to our research. We step back from our body paragraphs and show readers the significance of our findings and ideas. Determining the significance—the "So what?" and "Who cares?" of our research—is intellectually demanding and takes practice. It's hard work to ascertain why our findings and ideas are important and who they are important for. As you work on this dimension in your own writing, try practising your significance-finding skills on other statements. Take, for example, the following statement from NASA:

   Statement: NASA researchers recently created a model that analyzes various weather factors that lead to the formation and spread of fires. The Global Fire Weather Database (GFWED) accounts for local winds, temperatures, and humidity, while also being the first fire prediction model to include satellite-based precipitation measurements.

Significance (for what and for whom): Predicting the intensity of fires is important because smoke can affect air quality and increase the amount of greenhouse gases in the atmosphere.... The model has been especially helpful in Indonesia, which tends to have an intense fire season during El Niño years.

Patel, K. (2018, July 10). Can NASA help predict fires? New database includes fire danger forecasts. *Global Climate Change*. Retrieved from https://climate.nasa.gov/news/2762/

See what significance you can create from the following five statements. Use your imagination to indicate why a statement might be important and who it might most benefit or affect:

Statement 1

Fashion is one area in which consumerism has rapidly grown in recent years. Fast fashion has become more prevalent; clothing is produced on shorter timeframes with new designs appearing every few weeks to satisfy demand for the latest trends.... It has been estimated that there are 20 new garments manufactured per person each year and we are buying 60% more than we were in 2000.

The price of fast fashion. (2018). *Nature Climate Change*. Retrieved from https://www.nature.com/articles/s41558-017-0058-9

Statement 2

Canada's obesity epidemic is impacting children more than researchers previously thought. According to a new study, one in four 18-month-olds are already overweight, obese or at risk of becoming overweight.

Dubé, D. (2016, September 29). *1 in 4 Canadian toddlers overweight or obese, study says.* Global News. Retrieved from https://globalnews.ca/news/2972827/1-in-4-canadian-toddlers-overweight-or-obese-study-says/>

Statement 3

Oil is...the major transportation fuel and probably one of the most critical and indispensable raw materials of the contemporary industrial civilization. It is now the largest single component of international trade, the world's primary source of commercial energy, the mainstay of industry, the lifeblood of transport and often the cause of war.

Kubursi, A. (2018). What fuels oil prices? *Macleans*. Retrieved from https:www.macleans.ca/economy/business/what-fuels-oil-prices/

Statement 4

In advertising, there's a big difference between pushing the truth and making false claims. Many companies have been caught out for peddling mediocre products, using wild claims like "scientifically proven" with "guaranteed results."

Heilpern, W. (2016). 18 false advertising scandals that cost some brands millions. *Business Insider.* Retrieved from https://www.businessinsider.com/false-advertising-scandals-2016-3

3. In our academic conclusion, we invite readers to respond to the ideas and information we've given in our essay. Interestingly, the words *respond* and *responsibility* are closely linked in English. A *response* is an "answer" or a "reply to" and being *responsible* means "to be answerable to another for something" (*Oxford Dictionary of English Etymology*).

    - What kinds of responsibilities do you think research writers have in regard to their findings? Who are they answerable to? What are they responsible for?
    - What kinds of responsibilities do you think readers have in regards to their new knowledge? Who are they answerable to? What are they responsible for?
    - Why are response and responsibility so closely connected in a research conclusion?

4. It may be surprising to discover that academic conclusions are as much about opening as they are about closure. While our current project may be ending, our research is part of a much larger conversation on the subject that is continuing. Why is it important that openings and future directions make their way into our academic conclusions?

CHAPTER FOURTEEN

DRAFTS AND REVISIONS

Conversing Clearly

Crafting our prose is, for many of us, the hardest part about writing an essay. Like any skill, it takes practice to write well. Far from turning on a "word tap" that pours out perfect prose, the actual writing process consists of cutting, rewording, and reworking words and ideas over and over again. Our first draft is one of many, like the preliminary wash on a canvas or the raw footage for a film. It is only through the process of writing and the work of editing, rewriting, and revising that our ideas become clear to ourselves and to our readers.

Clarity is key for our communication to function and for our academic dialogue to flourish. If we are not clear in our own minds about what we think, we will not be able to communicate our research and ideas to others clearly. To develop clarity in our academic prose we need to engage in two practices: *detachment* and *immersion*. We need to be able to ***detach*** from our work—step back from it and cast a critical eye over it—in order to judge with honesty what we've written and how we've written it. At the same time, we need to be able to ***immerse*** ourselves in the world of our readers, putting ourselves in their shoes and anticipating what they need in order to understand our research and ideas. Developing clarity in our prose is thus an act of respect, both towards our own thoughts and towards our readers who want to understand what we have to say.

In this chapter we will learn how to craft our prose and develop editing and revising techniques. In particular, we will focus on clarifying our thoughts and choosing our words to communicate our ideas and research clearly. We will become familiar with two of the most common forms of editing—substantive editing and copy-editing—in order to evaluate our writing. We will also learn how to use our visual and auditory senses to catch problems in our prose.

A. LANGUAGE IS THOUGHT

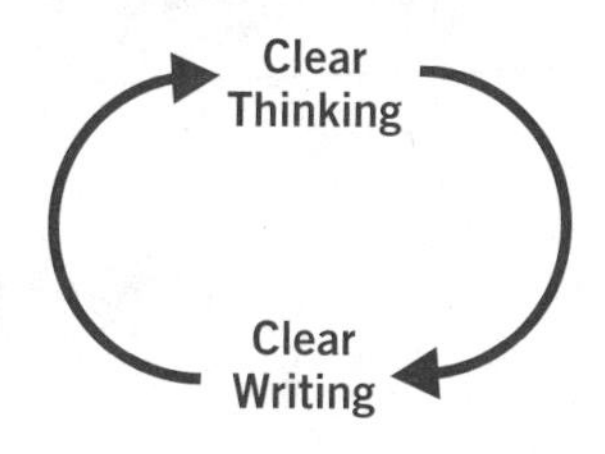

Learning how to write clearly is crucial for making our ideas known to our readers. Our writing is an expression of our thought. As we write our words we are engaged in the active process of thinking. Through the writing process, our thoughts become clearer. And the more we think through an issue or idea, the more clearly we can write about it. As William Zinsser aptly puts it in his well-known book *On Writing Well* (2006), "clear thinking becomes clear writing; one can't exist without the other" (p. 8).

That makes sense in ordinary experience, we may think, but isn't academic writing a different beast altogether? Isn't it notoriously opaque and full of jargon? Shouldn't we be using the longest, most abstract words we can find in order to sound intelligent? If our sentences are too simple, we may worry that we won't sound smart enough to belong to this community or participate in its conversations. Shouldn't we elevate our prose when it comes to writing for an academic audience?

These questions are legitimate. When we read scholarly research writing, we recognize that academics use specialized language to convey their research and ideas to others in their field of study. In a dialogue among experts, this specialized language fits the conversation's context and community. When this language is new to us, however, it seems pretentious and unapproachable. We may try to mimic it by burying ourselves in our thesaurus, digging for loftier words than the ones we normally use. But when we cobble our prose together with words from a thesaurus, our communication ends up sounding stilted or verbose and our research ideas are often lost in the process.

As it turns out, there is a big difference between the specialized language used and understood by academic experts and the obscure words we choose from a thesaurus to sound smart. The former reveals precise and expert thinking on a difficult subject; the latter suggests confused thought or a lack of knowledge hidden under a stream of big words. In time we may come to know the specialized language of an academic community well enough to use it convincingly in our own writing. In the meantime we strive for clarity using words we know well to communicate our research and ideas.

In fact, the most intelligent academics are those who understand their subject so thoroughly that they can communicate it to anyone and have that audience understand them. Think of the professors who make dense and difficult material accessible to everyone in the class. When we know what we think, we can be clear about it. Perhaps Friedrich Nietzsche (1882) says it best when he writes, "Whoever knows he is deep, strives for clarity; whoever would like to appear deep to the crowd strives for obscurity. For the crowd considers anything deep if only it cannot see the bottom" (p. 172). Our goal, then, is to think deeply and to communicate our ideas clearly to others. It is *clarity* combined with *substance* that makes for good academic writing.

B. SIMPLICITY: CHOOSING OUR WORDS WISELY

One of the key ways to make our research and ideas clear to readers is to simplify our prose by choosing our language carefully and strategically. When we simplify our prose, we streamline our words to make our research and ideas understandable and impactful. This keeps our readers interested in our work and lets our good ideas shine.

According to the famous British author and journalist George Orwell, simplifying our prose means eliminating the needless words, pompous phrases, and long-winded ramblings that often make their way into our professional and academic writing. In his famous essay, "Politics and the English Language" (1946), he pinpoints four problems that he sees plaguing the political and academic prose of his day: *dead metaphors*, *verbal clutter*, *pretentious diction*, and *meaningless words*.

Far from being resolved in the last 75 years, these problems still trouble our prose today. Interestingly, Orwell does not call these "writing problems," as if a few quick editorial changes will fix them. He calls them "mental vices," or problems with our *thinking*. To fix these problems and work towards simplifying our prose, we need to address the thinking behind our language, as well as the language itself. Let's look at each of these mental vices more closely.

1. Dead Metaphors

A metaphor is a figure of speech that connects or compares two things without using the connecting words *like* or *as*. For example:

- "She's weighed down by responsibility."
  Connects her responsibility to a heavy object

- "He fought tooth and nail."
  Connects his fighting to that of an animal

- "We're drifting apart."
  Connects a relationship to boats on the water

- "His speech is getting off track."
  Connects his speech to a wayward train

Metaphors help us think differently about a familiar subject by means of a new or surprising image. When we see something familiar in a new way we often have an "Aha!" moment. Our understanding has deepened; our view has changed. This means that a metaphor is not just a figure of speech; it is also a cognitive practice, revealing the depth or vitality of our thinking. If a metaphor makes a fresh connection, we come to new insights that we haven't had before.

The problem is, most metaphors we use have become so overused that they lull us to sleep rather than stimulate new thought. Take the above examples as cases in point. These metaphors are so overused that they don't cause us to think differently about responsibility, conflict, relational distance, or speech. But what if we were to infuse those metaphors with new life and surprising comparisons?

- "She's tangled in responsibility."
- "He fought brick and mortar until a wall was raised."
- "We're a meandering stream."
- "His speech is growing leaves."

Unlike the dead metaphors used above, these fresher metaphors help us to see responsibility, conflict, relationship, and speech in a new ways by using alternative images—a web, a wall, a stream, a tree. We create living metaphors by choosing alternative comparisons that generate new images and meanings for our readers. If we rely on clichés or dead metaphors, our language shows that we're not thinking in new ways. We are simply regurgitating well-worn paths and habits of thought. Academic conversation is meant to do the opposite: we are invited to contribute something new or different to the dialogue in order to inspire innovative thought. So we make comparisons that stimulate thinking rather than shut it down.

2. Verbal Clutter

Verbal clutter does to an essay what a mess does to a room. A messy room is unpleasant to be in. We can't get a good sense of the space or find what we are looking for. In the same way, verbal clutter disorganizes our ideas, muddles our research findings, and confuses our readers. In our academic writing, we aim to purge our work of verbal clutter in order to make our research accessible and our ideas impactful.

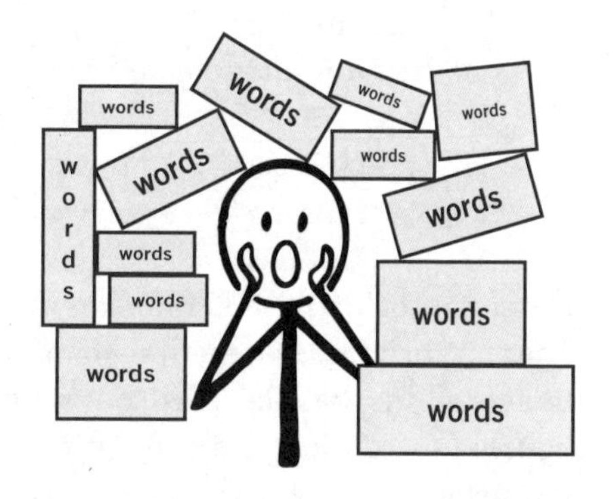

Eliminating verbal clutter begins with having enough research material and intelligent ideas to fill the parameters of our essay. When we don't have enough material or substance in our essay, we become anxious and start filling the space with extra words. As we try to hide our research shortcomings or insubstantial ideas, our writing becomes wordier and more convoluted. Unfortunately, most readers can see through this verbal disguise. We can too, once we recognize our verbal clutter by becoming aware of some of its most common culprits: *compound verbs*; *verbs constructed into nouns*; *passive voice*; *superfluous adverbs and adjectives*; and *padded phrases*.

Let's take a brief look at each of these so we can recognize which ones we habitually slide into when we lack content or feel apprehensive about our writing.

COMPOUND VERBS

Compound verbs are verbs strung together in a list. Rather than using one precise verb in its "simple" form, anxious writers often use the verb's "progressive" form and then compound it. Consider the differences between these forms:

- ***Simple form***: Marceau *argues* that....
- ***Progressive form***: Marceau *is arguing* that....
- ***Compound form***: Marceau *is trying to argue* that....

The progressive form combines the verb *to be* with *to argue* and makes the action continuous with the suffix *-ing*: *is arguing*. Compounding the progressive form means adding more verbs to the original, building verb upon verb. Verbs are action words, but using more verbs in a row doesn't make our prose more active. In fact, each extra verb makes us sound more hesitant and makes our prose more cumbersome. In academic writing we want to be assertive and confident in our prose in order to convince readers of the value and validity of our research and ideas. So we aim to use verbs in the simple form. Notably, using simple verbs does not make our writing simple; it simply cuts out the extra verbiage to make our prose more dynamic and our voice more confident.

VERBS CONSTRUCTED INTO NOUNS

Verbs constructed into nouns are action words that we have turned into abstract concepts. For example:

- Frose *examines* (verb) → Frose provides *an examination of* (abstract noun)
- Speer *observes* (verb) → Speer makes *the observation that* (abstract noun)

Turning verbs into abstract nouns deadens our prose and makes it tiring to read. We may think that heavy prose makes our ideas sound more substantial, but actually, abstract nouns have a dulling effect on our writing, making actions sound vague and insubstantial where they could be concrete and distinct. Wherever possible, we keep our academic prose direct and active with carefully chosen verbs instead of abstract nouns. It is verbs that give our writing power and impact.

PASSIVE VOICE

Another way to keep our prose direct and active is to use active voice rather than passive voice in our sentence construction. When we use the active voice, we focus on the person or thing (the "agent") performing the action by locating it up front in our sentence structure (e.g., ***The boy*** *threw the ball*). When we use the passive voice, we focus on the person or thing receiving the action by putting it up front (e.g., ***The ball*** *was thrown by the boy*). In the process, we relegate the agent to a later position in the sentence and have to add the verb *to be* and the preposition *by* to make the sentence grammatical (*was thrown by*). Using the passive voice not only clutters our prose with extra words, it also distances agents from their actions. Compare the following sentences that present the same material in active and passive voice:

- ***Active Voice***: **Researchers** regard obesity as a health concern.
  (agent) (action) (recipient)

- ***Passive Voice***: Obesity is regarded by **researchers** as a health concern.
  (recipient) (action) (agent)

- ***More Passive***: *It* is regarded by **researchers** that obesity is a health concern.
  (action) (agent) (recipient)

As the examples above show, using the passive voice emphasizes the recipient of the action (*obesity*) rather than the agents doing the action (*researchers*). While this sentence construction is appropriate to use in certain contexts, it does have the negative effect of making our prose more convoluted and cumbersome to read. Sticking the word *it* at the beginning of a passive sentence complicates our prose even further: readers now have to guess what *it* refers to in the sentence. This construction also produces extra verbiage since the verb *to be* must be used twice. While using passive prose can make us sound more detached and neutral in our writing, it can also make us sound less invested and engaged in our research. For this reason we are often asked to use the active rather than the passive voice in certain academic disciplines.

ADVERBS AND ADJECTIVES

Adverbs and adjectives are words that describe nouns and verbs. They are the most negligible parts of speech, and overusing them clutters our prose. Notice the difference between the following two sentences, where the first overuses descriptive words and the second minimizes them:

- ***More Description***: Sparken persuasively writes about the fascinating subject of shark-baiting practices off the Alaskan coast.

- ***Less Description***: Sparken persuades readers to consider shark-baiting practices off the Alaskan coast.

Writers who rely too heavily on adverbs and adjectives are often covering for poorly chosen nouns and verbs. Consider how in the first example the adverb *persuasively* is used to spice up the boring verb *writes*, while the adjective *fascinating* is used to elicit interest about the mundane noun *subject*. In the second example, the focus is on the nouns and verbs in the sentence. While descriptive words are excellent for creating emotion and narrative depiction (and are regularly used in genres like fiction and poetry), they don't suit the reason-driven genre of academic research writing. The point of academic writing is to inform and persuade readers of new research and ideas through logic and reasoning. Using descriptive words undermines that goal by making the tone of our prose emotional or effusive.

PADDED PHRASES

Padded phrases are unnecessary, bulky phrases used in the place of simple conjunctions (*and*, *or*, *but*, *so*, etc.) and prepositions (*at*, *by*, *from*, *with*, *in*, *on*, etc.). Notice the difference between the following two sentences:

- ***Padded Phrases***: In light of the fact that this year's flu vaccine can only be expected to become available in the springtime, it is critical to protect yourself from viruses with the constant cleansing of hands during the winter months.

- ***Clear Prose***: Because this year's flu vaccine will not be available until spring, protect yourself against viruses with extra hand-washing this winter.

Padded phrases give the appearance of substance, but weigh down our prose with needless bulk. Writers who use a lot of padding give the impression that they're trying to make up for their insubstantial ideas by using more words. In academic writing, we cut out all words that are not doing the work of communication. That way we can highlight our research material and emphasize our points, not hide them behind excess verbal clutter.

3. Pretentious Diction

If verbal clutter is a way to hide our insecurities or insubstantial ideas behind *more* words, then pretentious diction is a way to hide these issues behind *bigger* words. Writers often use pretentious diction to dress up simple ideas. When readers get to the bottom of the language, no substance can be found. We may be inclined to use pretentious diction to sound more educated only to end up using the words incorrectly or losing the clarity of our points.

One way we can cut back our pretentious diction is by drawing on Anglo-Saxon words in our academic writing. The English language is rooted in French (and Latin) and in German (Anglo-Saxon). In medieval and early modern England, the language of the church, legal court, and royal court was French and/or Latin. As a result, these languages became associated with aristocracy, power, and education. In contrast, Anglo-Saxon was the language of the common people. Consider the following words from Anglo-Saxon and their equivalents in French/Latinate English. Note the different effects they each create in your own mind as you read them.

Anglo-Saxon English	French/Latinate English
• House • To come • Car • To find • Goods • To see • Show	• Mansion • To arrive • Automobile • To retrieve • Merchandise • To regard • Spectacle
I came to her house by car. Did you find the lost goods? I saw the show.	I arrived at her mansion by automobile. Did you retrieve the missing merchandise? I regarded the spectacle.

Embedded in the English language is a hierarchy of class and power. It is not surprising, then, that we still choose words of Latinate or French origin when we want to sound more prestigious or educated in our prose. We tend to use nouns and verbs with Latinate suffixes like *-ion*, *-ate*, *-ize*, and *-ous* to sound especially brilliant: *conformation*, *exhortation*, *ameliorate*, *renegotiate*, *fraternize*, *contemporize*, *extemporaneous*, *instantaneous*. While words like these sometimes reflect the terminology used in a particular research context or conversation, we shouldn't choose them simply to sound smarter. Our academic readers can see through our big words and can recognize when we know what we're talking about and when we're using pretentious diction to fake it.

4. Meaningless Words

Finally, meaningless words refer to overused terms that have lost their meaning, or abstract terms that are too vague to be meaningful. Consider some of the words we use in ordinary conversation that have lost their significance: words like *nice*, *interesting*, *awesome*, *fun*, or *cool*. We might say, "That show is awesome," or "She seems cool." But what do these words actually mean? We know they signify something positive, based on their cultural context and typical use, but the words themselves are ambiguous expressions that have come to hold little meaning.

When we write, it is important to clarify what we mean by our terms. As C.S. Lewis, a well-known twentieth-century British author, observes, "The reader, we must remember, does not start by knowing what we mean. If our words are ambiguous our meaning will escape [him or her]" (2002, p. 263). Many of the words used in academia have become so ambigu-

ous that they have lost their significance: words like *society*, *culture*, *people*, *environment*, *advancement*, etc. Fortunately, we can give these words significance by using them in a particular context: Which society? Which culture? What people? What environment? Which advancement? It is critical to specify our ambiguous terms. If we are not sure what we are talking about, our readers won't know either.

Lewis gives us some good advice in this regard. He suggests that the way out of ambiguity is to know exactly what we want to say and to say exactly that (p. 263). This sounds simple, but any writer—academic or otherwise—will confirm just how difficult that is. It's hard to know exactly what we want to say and it's equally hard to say it. Sometimes we find ourselves writing on a deadline with few thoughts and little to say. We may try to hide this fact with verbal clutter or meaningless words, hoping that our lack of substance goes unnoticed. Unfortunately, the opposite tends to be true. Academic readers are usually quick to pick out our undeveloped ideas *because* of all the verbiage. If we have writer's block and find ourselves churning out words to compensate, we may need to step back and start over.

As we can see, the first order of writing well is to know what we think. Once our ideas and research are in place, we can ensure they are clear to our readers by choosing the best possible words to communicate them. We can cut verbal clutter down to its clearest components by focusing on nouns and verbs and by using the active voice. We can strive for clarity by using words of Anglo-Saxon origin and by defining our abstract terms; and we can communicate new and surprising ideas with a well-turned metaphor. This kind of crafting takes time. Given the process, it is wise to give ourselves at least as much time to edit and revise a research essay as we have given ourselves to write it. That way we can work towards communicating our good ideas in the clearest way possible, which will establish our credibility and make our work impactful in the research community.

EXERCISE 1
CONSIDERING WORDS

Imagine you are an editor who has been given the following passage of research writing. Locate all the problematic diction you can, looking specifically for dead metaphors, verbal clutter, pretentious diction, and meaningless words. Next, try your hand at revising the passage, addressing all the problems you found.

> Cybercrime is an insidious and devious crime committed online through the internet. Advancements in computer programming efficiency and hardware functionality have all accelerated the rate at which cyber criminals and private organizations have found ways to infiltrate national databases and personal computers

to access information at the press of a button. At the current time when technology is so readily accessible and available, any person has the potential of becoming an elaborate hacker. In this day and age, some members of the public seem completely oblivious to any threats of online credit card fraud, identity theft, or scams and, as a result, the hacking community is wholly and entirely at ease to take advantage of the fact. People these days may not realize that the rights they have guarded for centuries are slowly becoming eroded and washing away with the tide. The indispensable right to ownership and the essential right to privacy are two of the important rights that cyber criminals and private organizations are making obsolete with their hacking activities.

Please note that the material used in this excerpt is invented and any correspondence to actual research is purely coincidental.

C. EDITING AND REVISING PRACTICES

When we edit and revise a research essay, we need to be able to step back from our writing and view it with a detached or critical eye. We aim to judge our work fairly, deciding what material should stay and what should go. One helpful way to do this is to put ourselves in our readers' shoes and imagine how they will experience and respond to our work. Our writing is, after all, meant for our readers. The better we can step back and imagine our readers and their perspectives, the better we will be at predicting what they need in order to understand our research and ideas.

As readers, we have certain communication needs that must be met in order for us to track with a writer. Most of the time we are not aware of those needs, but they become clear when they are not met. If we're stumbling over sentences, tripping over careless mistakes, and struggling to follow a writer's train of thought, we are quickly put off by the effort. We also can't help but judge the quality of a writer's research and ideas by the quality of his or her writing. Because writing and thinking go hand in hand, we conclude that if the writing is unclear, disorganized, or littered with errors, then the writer's thinking is problematic too. Communication begins to break down and the possibility of a fruitful dialogue is sidelined. Keeping our experience as readers in mind, we can see how easy it is to lose our audience as writers. We need to develop our editing skills in order to help readers make sense of our research and track with our ideas.

There are a number of ways to edit our work. The two most common are substantive editing and copy-editing. Most editors use the term ***substantive editing*** to refer to the practice of revising a document's content, organization, and coherence. When we edit research writing substantively, we inspect each idea for its reasons and reasoning, and evaluate the arrangement of ideas within our paper as a whole. This includes revisiting our dialogic interactions with other researchers and reflecting on how we have engaged with their work. Most editors use the term ***copy-editing*** to refer to the practices of revising a document's diction, style, grammar, mechanics, sentence structure, format, and references. We use copy-editing to promote the clarity, precision, and flow of our research writing. Let's look more closely at how to use these two practices in order to develop our editing skills.

Substantive Editing	Copy-Editing
• Content • Organization and Relevance • Social and Cognitive Coherence	• Format and References • Style and Diction • Grammar, Sentence Structure, Mechanics

1. Substantive Editing

CONTENT

The ***content*** of our essay refers to the research material and ideas we develop in our paper. As we know, in an academic research paper our content is primarily composed of a claim, reasons, and reasoning, alongside explanations of their significance within a research context. When we edit for content, then, we examine these areas in our paper with a set of questions:

Claim

- Can the claim be easily located in the introduction?
- Is the claim debatable, clear, and precise?
- Is the claim presented in response to the work of other researchers?
- Does the claim fill a gap or offer a meaningful contribution to the current research dialogue?
- Is a trajectory for testing or proving this claim outlined up front?

Reasons (Research Evidence)

- Does the paper offer enough research material to make its case?
- Does all the research material work to test, support, or prove the claim?
- Is the research material scholarly, credible, and persuasive?
- Is the research explained and discussed in a way that demonstrates its purpose and value?
- Is the research expressed in a clear and meaningful way, contributing to the scholarly dialogue on the topic?
- Are the research sources acknowledged and cited?

Reasoning

- Does the reasoning work to support the claim and illuminate the research findings?
- Are all points of analysis clearly developed?
- Are there points that need further development, detail, or examples?

- Are there points that are overdeveloped at the expense of other points?
- Are there points that are confusing, dropped unexpectedly, or unrelated to the claim or research evidence?

Significance

- Is the significance or the "so what?" of the claim, research, and reasoning clear?
- Who will find this claim, research data, and analysis most compelling?
- In what context and community will this research have the most impact?

Most of us struggle with at least one of these aspects in communicating our content. It's useful to ask ourselves each of these questions when we edit our work to ensure that our research material and the development of our ideas make sense and fit the context of the academic dialogue in which we are participating.

ORGANIZATION AND RELEVANCE

Alongside content, editing for organization and relevance are also part of substantive editing. ***Organization*** refers to the *order* and *arrangement* of the material in a paper, and ***relevance*** refers to how closely ideas are *related* or *connected* to one another within that organization. As we saw in Chapter 12, organization and relevance require us to figure out how best to arrange our thoughts and ideas so that others can follow them and be convinced by our reasoning.

When we edit for organization and relevance, we first consider the order or *sequence* of our points and our research material. Sequence can be clearly shown with language markers, such as *first*, *second*, *third*, and *fourth*; *initially* and *subsequently*; *to begin with*, *then*, *next*, *later*, and *finally*. Sequence can also be emphasized with headings, as we have seen in examples from some research disciplines. To edit for sequence, we ask ourselves the following questions:

- Is the order of my points and research material clearly articulated with sequential language or carefully arranged with headings?
- Does this order make sense, or would a different sequence be clearer?
- Does each research point clearly follow or build on the previous point(s)?
- Are my abstract concepts and ideas developed with explanations and examples?
- Do I use transitions to lead my readers from one thought to the next?
- Do I offer my readers a clear line of reasoning from the beginning of the essay to the end?

Organizing a research essay is difficult because we don't necessarily think in a sequential way; we are, however, expected to write that way so others can make sense of our ideas. This disconnect between our natural flow of thought and the orderly construction of our research writing can cause us to struggle with organizing our research material and ideas. The good news is that many problems in a paper can be resolved by reorganizing our content—like putting our second idea first or moving our fourth sentence to the beginning of our paragraph.

As we edit for organization and relevance, our goal is to clearly communicate our line of reasoning by showing how each of our statements connects to the others. In the field of cognitive linguistics, Dan Sperber and Deirdre Wilson developed "relevance theory" (1996) to explain the conditions of connection that make statements easily understandable to an audience. A statement is "relevant" when it takes little effort to see how it is meaningful in relation to the statements around it (Giltrow et al., 2009, p. 161). The better we are at connecting our statements, then, the more understandable and relevant our train of thought will be to our readers. For example, consider how closely the following two statements are connected:

> Each of these passages has faults of its own, but, quite apart from the avoidable ugliness, two qualities are common to all of them. The first is staleness of imagery; the other is lack of precision. (Orwell, 1946, p. 331)

Orwell's second statement would be considered very relevant to the first one because its content directly relates. The first statement indicates that there are two qualities common to all the passages; the second indicates that those two qualities are staleness of imagery and lack of precision.

In contrast, consider this example where the statements lack a clear connection:

> Many students have been discouraged from using first-person pronouns in their research writing. Smith indicates that opinions aren't facts.

The second statement does not seem very relevant to the first statement. We cannot be sure how Smith's point that "opinions aren't facts" relates to students being discouraged from using first-person pronouns. Because the connection isn't clear, we have to work hard to decipher how the statements relate. We assume there must be a connection; if there were not, we think, the writer would not have placed the statements side by side. Still, we are hard-pressed to know what the connection is. After much deliberation, we may hazard a guess:

> Perhaps using first-person pronouns (*I* or *we*) suggests opinion, while using other pronouns (like *one*) suggests objectivity, which is more suitable for presenting facts. Perhaps this is why students have been discouraged from using first-person pronouns in their research writing: research writing is meant to be objective and factual rather than based on opinions.

We have now made the two statements connect in our minds, but making that connection took great effort and conjecture. The statements aren't meaningfully related in and of themselves. Significant work on our part as readers was required to guess at the statements' relationship and their relevance.

Finally, consider these two statements where no relationship can be found:

> By the time we reached Winnipeg, there were many people on the bus. Certain fish feed on shrimp, prawns, and blood worms.

We may do all sorts of mental gymnastics to ascertain the relationship between these two statements, but they still appear to be entirely disconnected. Each statement on its own would have to be placed in another context—like travel (for the first one) or the feeding habits of fish (for the second)—in order to be relevant.

As we can see, statements function on a "relevance continuum" (Giltrow et al., 2009, p. 161); that is, they are more or less relevant depending on how well they relate to other statements in their particular context. Their context can be *semantic* (between sentences) as the above examples show, but it can also be *social*. Since communication occurs *between people* in a social context, our statements become more or less relevant depending on our audience.

For example, a good friend might find something we say very relevant, whereas an acquaintance or stranger might not make any sense of it at all. Consider an inside joke, in which a statement is relevant to one person but lacks the social context to be meaningful or understandable to other people. In an academic context, our readers are most often part of our scholarly community. They are intelligent and interested in our topic. However, they cannot read our minds or guess at our meaning in the way a close friend or partner might. For this reason, we need to ensure that our statements clearly connect both semantically and socially as we edit and revise our research writing.

EXERCISE 2
THE RELEVANCE CONTINUUM

Semantic Relevance

How relevant (or closely related) are the two sentences in each example: very relevant, somewhat relevant, or not relevant?

1. Maria asked for my email address. I responded, "sandraiscool7@hotmail.com."
2. Body-builders inject steroids that get absorbed into the bloodstream. Steroid abuse leads to lower life expectancy.

3. "Honey," Mother asked, "Did you want to go to the party at the Thomsons' tonight?" Father replied, "I am tired from playing golf in the blazing sun all morning."

4. A Western education does not guarantee a good job. International students studying abroad receive limited job experience compared to immigrants and citizens.

5. Rodents are one of the most frequently used animals in experimentation. To maintain good health, athletes must eat the appropriate amount of calories to fuel their bodies for exercise.

Social Relevance
Would any of the less relevant examples become more relevant in a particular social context (e.g., between close friends or relatives, or within a particular community)? Why?

Moving towards Relevance
Change the three least-relevant examples by adding material or by rearranging the statements to make them more relevant to each other.

COHERENCE

Substantive editing also involves editing for coherence. Sometimes a person's ideas are ***incoherent*** to others, which means they are confusing, contradictory, illogical, or unintelligible. Either the ideas don't make sense *cognitively*—we can't reason through what the person is trying to say—or they don't make sense *socially*—they are inconsistent with our shared reality, or lack a genuine understanding of people in the past or present. We can all point to times when we've struggled to follow someone's reasoning or experienced a social disconnect with someone in conversation. What they are saying doesn't make sense to us, given our experience of the world, of other people, or of ourselves. We come to a standstill in our dialogue because our cognitive or social frameworks are at odds. In an academic context, the problems of social and cognitive incoherence need to be edited and revised so that our ideas make sense to our readers. Let's look at these two forms of incoherence more closely so that we can recognize and tackle them in our work.

Social incoherence occurs when statements are not socially or historically accurate in light of current research on a subject. Socially incoherent statements are often generalizations about a current event or a historical time period, or unqualified claims about a person or group of people. For example, the following claim would be considered socially incoherent by academic readers:

For centuries all women were dominated by men and had no chance of equality.

This claim is socially incoherent because it is an overgeneralization of human experience in history. It simplifies gender relationships in a one-size-fits-all statement, and does not reflect careful research on the subject.

Statements about people or events using extreme language like *always*, *never*, *everyone*, *no one*, *all*, or *nothing* tend to be socially incoherent because they are not true to reality or history as we know it. It is not true that *all* women were dominated by men across time and place. It is also not true that women have had *no* chance of equality anywhere in the world. Yet that is precisely what the generalization above implies with the language it uses. Rather than overgeneralized or unqualified claims, academic readers expect to see specificity and complexity in scholarly research.

In academic writing, we can correct social incoherence quite easily by adding a ***qualifier***—a word or phrase that limits, modifies, or specifies a statement so that it accurately reflects human experience within our social and historical reality. Some common qualifiers are *often*, *sometimes*, *somewhat*, *usually*, *few*, *many*, *more*, *most*, *less*, and *some*. With these or other modifiers, we can sometimes clear up social incoherence simply by changing a word. For example:

> In previous centuries women were ***often*** dominated by men and had ***little*** chance of equality.

Using the word *little* to describe the chance of equality for women is more socially and historically accurate than using the word *no*. Adding the word *often* qualifies male domination; it is not everywhere all the time. The statement above could be made even more socially coherent by adding other, more specific qualifiers and modifications. For instance:

> In ***eighteenth-century France***, ***many*** women experienced male domination and struggled for ***social*** equality.

As we can see, the more specific we can be about the complexity of social and historical realities, the more socially coherent our research writing will be.

It is worth noting that in popular online writing genres—blogs, posts, tweets, etc.—readers do not expect the same kind of social or historical precision that they do in scholarly research. Extreme claims, simplifications, and polarized language in these other genres may not give readers pause. However, in research writing, readers expect complex and critical thought. As a result, we edit our work for social incoherence by eliminating extreme or polarized language, overgeneralizations, and categorical statements. We revise by adding qualifiers and other modifiers to make our statements precise, accurate, and convincing.

Cognitive incoherence is the result of blurry or muddled thinking (cognition). It refers to a lack of clear connection between thoughts or ideas. Disconnected ideas lack relevance and leave readers struggling to make sense of the material before them. For example, consider the following two statements:

> Organic legumes can possess advantageous characteristics with regard to health. In the United States over 50 per cent of women suffer from iron deficiency during pregnancy.

Readers know that there must be a link in the writer's mind between organic legumes, health, and pregnant women suffering from iron deficiency. But it is not clear how they relate. An academic reader would likely respond with questions:

> I'm not sure what organic legumes have to do with pregnant women suffering from iron deficiency. Are there certain health advantages that organic legumes have for pregnant women? Do organic legumes contain more iron than conventionally grown legumes?

Our goal is to anticipate our readers' questions and possible confusion as we edit and revise our work. Most readers will grapple with our ideas and try to make their own cognitive connections where they are missing in our writing, but there is only so much work they will do. It is our responsibility as writers to connect our ideas and provide a coherent train of thought. If our work is littered with incoherence, we will lose our audience.

In academic writing, we edit for cognitive incoherence by identifying where our ideas are disconnected, disorganized, directionless, or nonsensical. We resolve cognitive incoherence by showing how one idea is relevant to another through *connecting words or phrases*. For example, we can connect the two ideas above as follows:

> Organic legumes possess advantageous characteristics with regard to health, ***particularly in their production of iron***. In the United States, over 50 per cent of women suffer from iron deficiency in pregnancy and would ***thus*** benefit from consuming organic legumes.

Alternatively, they could be connected like this:

> Organically grown legumes have ***a higher iron content*** than their conventionally grown counterparts. ***Consequently***, pregnant women suffering from iron deficiency in the United States can ***boost their iron levels naturally*** by increasing their consumption of organic legumes.

As we can see, there is usually more than one way to make our thoughts coherent. With the help of qualifiers and connecting phrases, we can turn disconnected ideas into relevant ones. This takes a careful eye and critical judgement; we need to step back and anticipate what our readers may need in order to make sense of our research and ideas.

EXERCISE 3
SOCIAL AND COGNITIVE COHERENCE

As a reader and editor, what problems of social and cognitive incoherence do you see in the following passage? What words, phrases, or sentences could be added, subtracted, or changed to make the text more accessible? In a separate document, rewrite the passage with the necessary changes.

> Since the beginning of time, food has played a significant role in all human life. People these days scrutinize their food to the very last calorie. Genetically modified foods are highly controversial across the globe. Something drastic like genetically modified foods is significant cause for concern. Genetically modified foods can take a leap forward in the direction of medical treatment, like vaccines. Allergic reactions to crops are a pressing matter. Americans have debated about whether genetically modified crops should be developed as a lot of precautions and prohibitions have been taken by Europeans. Genetically modified crops have the potential to resist herbicides at a faster pace, producing superweeds. Cross-pollination occurs when the wind carries the pollen from a genetically modified plant to an organic one. Genetically modified foods are crops that are altered genetically by splicing desirable traits from one organism and introducing them to a particular crop (Argan, p. 123). They give farmers everywhere increased yields and profits.
>
> Please note that the names and material used in this excerpt are invented and any correspondence to actual research or researchers is purely coincidental.

2. Copy-Editing

Alongside substantive editing, copy-editing plays an important role in the revision of our work. Copy-editing involves editing the format, references, diction, style, grammar, sentence structure, and mechanics of our document. Despite our familiarity with the concept, the practice of copy-editing can be daunting if we don't know what we are looking for or if our English-language skills are not strong. This section pinpoints what to look for as we copy-edit our work. Think of it as a copy-editing guideline.

FORMATTING AND REFERENCES

Formatting a paper and using appropriate referencing methods depend on our ability to use conventional academic structures, styles, and systems of arrangement in our writing, as well as on our ability to follow instructions. Regardless of how strong or poor we feel our writing is, we can format and reference our work impeccably.

- **Formatting**
  The format of a paper is usually stipulated by the professor or the publisher we are writing for. Formatting includes the word count and/or page count, the page numbering system, the font size and style, the margin setting, the line spacing, the indentation, the citation format, the inclusion of a title page and/or abstract, and the inclusion of a reference page or bibliography. Usually these are outlined in an assignment's instructions or in the rules of publication (when a research paper is submitted to be published) and can thus be followed easily.

- **References**
  The reference system we are asked to use in a research paper is dictated by the documentation style used in our field of study, like APA, MLA, Chicago, CSE, etc. There are multiple writers' handbooks and resources online that show us exactly how to reference research in our academic prose. We just need to make sure we are consulting an up-to-date reference guide (documentation styles change over time) and are following its instructions. There are also many free programs that we can use to format our bibliography. If we choose to use such a program, we need to be aware of the following shortcomings:

    - They do not guarantee correct bibliographic citation.
    - They are not helpful for properly formatting in-text citations.
    - They often falter in their spacing and punctuation.
    - They inevitably need to be reformatted to be consistent with the font size and style, spacing, and margin settings that we've used in the rest of our document.

  In short, our citations always need to be checked against an up-to-date writers' handbook or reference guide to ensure accuracy. For this reason, writing instructors recommend that we take the time to learn the referencing system most often used in our discipline or field of study, like APA in Sociology or MLA in English Literature. If we aren't familiar with how to reference our resources ourselves, we won't know whether the citation program we are using is documenting those sources correctly or not.

EDITING FOR DICTION AND STYLE

Editing for diction and style is the practice of examining our choice of words, tone, and voice in a document. As we edit our research writing, we ask ourselves, "Do the words I've chosen, the tone I've used, and the voice I've adopted fit the academic context I'm writing for and the conversation I'm participating in?"

- **Diction**
  Since words are the basis of all writing, we need to choose them carefully in order to communicate clearly. This is especially true in a research context where detail and precision count. As we learned in Section B of this chapter, it is important to focus on strong

nouns and active verbs in our writing, cutting away all our dead metaphors, verbal padding, pretentious diction, and meaningless words (including those we don't know the meaning of!). The less cluttered and muddled our diction, the better our careful research and good ideas can shine.

- **Tone**
  The tone of our writing also needs to fit our academic context and audience. Our context is a community of research experts and our audience is made up of academics and professionals. As apprentice researchers, we adopt a tone that is professional, instructive, confident, and compelling to share our research findings and ideas, showcasing our own expertise and intelligence.

- **Voice**
  Voice is connected to tone, but is not the same thing. Voice refers to the activity or passivity of our sentence construction. Active voice communicates actions directly. It sounds candid, credible, and confident. Passive voice communicates actions indirectly. It sounds detached, impartial, and deferential. We may automatically assume that passive voice sounds more academic; however, we can be both precise and professional using the active voice. Like tone and diction, the voice we use needs to fit our context and audience. While passive voice is used in certain academic disciplines, many others prefer the active voice.

EDITING FOR GRAMMAR, SENTENCE STRUCTURE, AND MECHANICS

If we want to communicate clearly in a particular language, especially at a high intellectual level, we need to know that language well. Many of us are familiar with the English language and may even have used it all our lives to communicate, but are less familiar with its inner workings—its grammar, sentence construction, and mechanics (spelling, punctuation, numbering, etc.). If we are not clear on how English works as a language, we may need to brush up on our language skills to be able to pinpoint problematic issues in our prose and fix them. As we develop our skills, here are some language fundamentals to look for in editing and revising our essay:

- **Basic Grammar**
  - ***Subjects and verbs must agree***. They must agree in number (singular/plural) and in person (first, second, third).
    - I sign the paper. (*first-person singular*)
    - You sign the paper. (*second-person singular*)
    - George signs the paper. (*third-person singular*)

- We sign the paper. (*first-person plural*)
- The company signs the paper. (*collective singular*)
- The class members sign the paper. (*collective plural*)
- Everyone signs the paper. (*indefinite singular*)

◦ ***Nouns and pronouns must agree***. Singular nouns agree with singular pronouns; plural nouns agree with plural pronouns.

- I am happy with my marks. (*singular*)
- The students are unhappy with their marks. (*plural*)
- One can be satisfied with one's marks. (*singular*)
- Maxwell and I are pleased with our marks. (*plural*)

◦ ***Plural nouns are different than possessive nouns***. Plural nouns often have an "s" at the end. Possessive nouns have an apostrophe before the "s".

- There are two tables in the house. (*plural*)
- This is the table's leg. (*possessive*)

◦ ***An exception to this rule***: The possessive form of the pronoun "it" takes an "s" with no apostrophe. The contraction of "it is" takes an apostrophe before the "s".

- The doll's shoe is untied. Its shoe is untied. (*possessive*)
- It is cold outside. It's cold outside. (*contraction*)

- **Basic Sentence Structure**

◦ ***Sentences always begin with a capital letter and end with a period.***

- **T**he research collected by Rohan and Schubert proves that climate change is a growing concern**.**

- ***Sentences must include a subject or agent (noun) and an action (verb).*** They may also have an object or recipient (noun).

  - The **cat** (*subject/agent*) hissed (*action*).

  - The **cat** (*subject/agent*) hissed (*action*) at me (*object/recipient*).

- ***A subordinate clause is not a sentence; it is only part of a sentence.*** A subordinate clause cannot stand alone as a sentence. It hooks into and modifies a grammatically complete sentence, or independent clause.

  - Although the train is late (*subordinate clause*), **we will still miss it by five minutes** (*full sentence*).

  - **John cannot seem to change his behaviour** (*full sentence*) regardless of what he tells himself (*subordinate clause*).

- **Basic Mechanics**

  - ***Commas (,) are most often used in lists or to separate a subordinate clause from the rest of the sentence.***

    - Everest ate two bananas**,** a handful of chocolate chips**,** and a bag of peanuts before dinner. (*commas used in a list*)

    - Despite snacking ahead of time**,** Everest was able to eat a full dinner. (*comma separating a subordinate clause from the rest of the sentence*)

  - ***Colons (:) and semicolons (;) cannot be used interchangeably.*** A semicolon is most often used to attach two related independent clauses, or two complete sentences. A colon is used to introduce a list, an example, or a long quotation.

    - I had to go home from work early**;** I was feeling sick. (*semicolon connecting two related independent clauses*)

    - The routine should include the following**:** twenty knee bends, fifty sit-ups, ten leg lifts, and five minutes of jogging on the spot. (*colon introducing a list*)

- ***Hyphens (-) and dashes (—) are not the same thing***. A hyphen creates a compound word. This compound word may take the form of a noun or an adjective. In contrast, a dash is used to set apart parenthetical material for emphasis.

  ➢ I need to take my mother-in-law to the doctor for a check-up. (*hyphens for compound nouns*)

  ➢ Blaire is a well-known candidate. (*hyphen for compound adjective*)

  ➢ In Vancouver, the cost of essentials—housing, food, and clothing—are more expensive than in Winnipeg. (*dashes to set apart parenthetical material*)

As we can see, copy-editing focuses on how we construct our writing to communicate our research and ideas. Some aspects of copy-editing (like formatting and references) are quite easy to address by consulting guides and following instructions. Other aspects of copy-editing (like diction and style) require us to think carefully about our context and audience so that our communication is fitting. Still other aspects of copy-editing (like grammar, sentences, and mechanics) depend on a strong grasp of the English language in order to pinpoint and correct problematic prose. We combine copy-editing with substantive editing in order to create a precise, professional, and compelling research essay that joins the scholarly dialogue on our topic.

D. MULTI-SENSORY PRACTICES OF EDITING

Once we have reviewed a paper with our substantive and copy-editing skills, we benefit from reading through our work one or two more times, using as many senses as possible to catch the niggling issues that remain. When we edit, we normally depend on our eyes to find the problems to revise in our prose. ***Visual editing*** focuses on the writing problems that can be *seen*. It develops our critical observation skills and often picks up problems in structure, formatting, referencing, and mechanics. We can easily see if we have forgotten a citation or missed a set of quotation marks. We can also see when the margins or fonts are inconsistent. Visual editing can also pick out other key problems. For example:

- *This sentence is missing a verb.*
- *The punctuation is incorrect in this sentence.*
- *These in-text citations aren't formatted consistently.*
- *I see some spelling mistakes here.*
- *There are extra spaces between these paragraphs.*
- *I don't see a claim in the introduction.*
- *I can't find a discussion of the research evidence presented here.*

While our computer programs might underline some of these issues for us, we often benefit from printing out our work to edit it. On paper, we tend to read more carefully and comprehensively than we do on a screen. Screen-based editing is also more physically and mentally taxing than reading and revising our work on paper.

While visual editing is familiar and commonly used, our work benefits from incorporating other senses into our editing practice as well by reading our work aloud. This practice not only involves our eyes, but also our mouth and our ears. ***Oral editing*** forces us to read slowly—word for word—and more carefully than when we read silently to ourselves. In silent reading, our eyes slide over a page relatively quickly and our mind automatically corrects many of our mistakes. It reads what we meant to write and not what we have actually written. This is why sentences seem smoother and why cluttered prose is often overlooked when we edit visually. It is only when we slow down and read our work aloud that we pick up on awkward sentences and convoluted prose.

Oral editing helps us catch writing problems that can be *heard*. In particular, we can apprehend shortcomings in our flow, style, coherence, and clarity of thought and expression. For example:

- ***I've repeated this word five times in two sentences.***
- ***This sentence is so convoluted that I have no idea what I'm trying to say.***
- ***My voice is getting lost in all the research jargon and quotations. What am I adding to the discussion?***
- ***I'm struggling to follow my own train of thought!***
- ***My claim sounds like an observation. It needs to be reworked.***
- ***This point sounds really abstract. I need to include some examples to help clarify it.***

Both written and oral editing skills are indispensable. The eye misses things that the ear can hear. The ear misses things that the eye can see. The more senses we involve in our editing process, the better. This is why reading our work aloud and making corrections on a physical document can be highly beneficial; not much can get past all these senses working together, and we end up with a well-rounded evaluation our work.

EXERCISE 4
VISUAL AND ORAL EDITING

Consider the following paragraph. Read it *with your eyes*, scanning the paragraph for problems in structure, formatting, mechanics, and citation. Make a list of revisions in these areas that you would suggest to the writer. Then read the paragraph *out loud*, listening for problems in flow, style, coherence, and clarity of thought and expression. Add these to your list of suggested revisions.

> Andrew Bing interviews undergraduates at some American university, indentifies binge drinking (defined as consuming 5 or more alcoholic drinks in a row for men and four or more for women) as an activity in which "approximately 63% of college students have drunk at least once in their lifetime. (123) Andrew also demonstrates that various consumptative patterns among college students that are fuelled by two different drives, those that drink for "social inhancement" or "sensation seeking" and those who drink do to underlying psychological problems stemming from depression. But the problem then is in distinguishing which of the two. Scientific evidence by numerous researchers proves that adolescence is a period of rapid grow and physical change. During this time alcohol consumption affect physiological systems and biological processes a lot. Through drinking among adolescents may not cause "chronic disorders such as liver cirrhosis, hepatitis, gastritis and pancreatitis its affects growth in a way that scope for future danger is increased (Smythers, 2013, p. 456).
>
> Please note that the names and material used in this excerpt are invented and any correspondence to actual research or researchers is purely coincidental.

CONCLUSIONS

Language and thought are intimately connected. The more we know what we think about our research material, the better we can write about it. The clearer we write, the clearer our thinking comes across to our readers. When we edit and revise our work, we take our written drafts and craft them into a coherent and professional document for our academic readers. There are two main things to consider in this process: the quality of our research and ideas, and our ability to communicate them. In *substantive editing*, we examine our ideas, research, and thought processes. We edit our claim, research evidence, reasoning, and the significance of our ideas; the organization and relevance of our thoughts; and the social and cognitive coherence of our reasoning. In *copy-editing*, we examine the writing itself. We edit our formatting and references; our diction, tone, and voice; and our grammar, sentence structure, and mechanics. We then catch any remaining issues by reading our work aloud, using as many senses as possible to detect what we've missed. As we develop our editing and revising skills, we become more adept at communicating our research and ideas clearly to others. In this way, we contribute to the scholarly dialogue on our topic with strong and compelling prose.

QUESTIONS FOR REFLECTION

1. Expressing our thoughts in words is no easy matter. Many of us can identify with the feeling expressed by the speaker in T.S. Eliot's famous poem, "The Love Song of J. Alfred Prufrock": "It is impossible to say just what I mean!" If language is thought, why is it so difficult for us to articulate to others what we are thinking?

2. When it comes to academic writing, we often assume that our readers—our professors or other scholars—expect lofty ideas wrapped in pretentious jargon. The more opaque our writing is, we reason, the smarter we sound. In fact, the opposite is true: the smartest thinkers can make their complex ideas accessible to any audience. What are some ways that you can make your good ideas clearer and more comprehensible to your audience in your academic writing?

3. One of the basic skills required for editing and revising our writing is that of fair judgement. We need to be able to step back from our work and view it with a detached and critical eye so that we can determine what material should stay and what needs to be cut. What are some ways you can develop your critical eye?

4. Another skill we need when editing and revising our work is the ability to put ourselves in our reader's shoes and consider what they, as our audience, need from us in order to understand our ideas and track with our train of thought. When you read the work of other writers, what communication needs do you expect them to fulfill? What happens when those needs aren't met? With your experience as a reader in mind, what are some ways you can meet the needs of your readers as you write for them?

5. Each of us has editing strengths and weaknesses. Some of us are detail-oriented and can pick out niggling mistakes in our prose with ease. We like to focus on the craft of writing and gravitate towards copy-editing, but we often miss the big-picture problems with content, organization, and coherence in our work. Others of us can see the big picture with no trouble and notice when ideas are weak, jumbled together, or missing entirely. We like to focus on research and concepts in our work

and gravitate towards substantive editing, but we often miss the details of craft that can obscure our good ideas with writing problems. What are your editing strengths? How can you hone them so that they become even stronger? What are your editing weaknesses? What are some ways you can develop them so that they do not hamper your work?

6. We often think about editing as a visual practice of scanning our work for mistakes. How does incorporating more senses into our process broaden and benefit our editing capabilities? What kinds of mistakes can we catch on printed paper that we might miss on a computer document? What might our ears catch that our eyes miss?

REFERENCES

Abrams, M.H., & Harpham, G.G. (2009). Rhetoric. In *A glossary of literary terms* (9th ed.) (pp. 311–312). Wadsworth.

Apel, K. (1996). The rationality of human communication. In E. Mendiata (Ed.), *Karl-Otto Apel: Selected essays* (Vol. 2). Humanities Press.

Aristotle. (1976). *Ethics* (J.A.K. Thomson, Trans.). Penguin Books.

Aristotle. (1991). *On rhetoric: A theory of civic discourse* (G. Kennedy, Trans.). Oxford University Press.

Arnett, R.C., Fritz, J.M.H., & Bell, L.M. (2009). *Communication ethics literacy: Dialogue and difference*. Sage.

Arnett, R.C., Fritz, J.M.H., & Bell, L.M. (2010). Dialogic learning as first principle in communications ethics. *Atlantic Journal of Communication, 18*(3), 111–126. doi:10.1080/15456871003742021

Austin, J.L. (1962). *How to do things with words: The William James lectures delivered at Harvard University in 1955*. Oxford University Press.

Bakhtin, M.M. (1984). *Problems of Dostoevsky's poetics* (C. Emerson, Trans.). University of Minnesota Press.

Bakhtin, M.M. (1986). *Speech genres and other late essays* (V.W. McGee, Trans.). University of Texas Press.

Bakhtin, M.M. (1993). *Toward a philosophy of the act* (V. Liapunov, Trans.). University of Texas Press.

Barber, K. (Ed.). (1998). *The Canadian Oxford dictionary*. Oxford University Press.

Baxter, L.A. (2004). Dialogues of relating. In R. Anderson, L.A. Baxter, & K.N. Cissna (Eds.), *Dialogue: Theorizing difference in communication studies* (pp. 107–124). Sage.

Birks, R., Eng, T., & Walchli, J. (2004). *Landmarks: A Process Reader* (2nd ed.). Pearson Canada.

Buber, M. (1958). *I and thou* (2nd ed.) (R.G. Smith, Trans.). Charles Scribner's Sons.

Buber, M. (1965). *The knowledge of man: A philosophy of the interhuman* (M. Friedman, Trans.). Harper.

Cissna, K.N., & Anderson R. (1994). The 1957 Martin Buber-Carl Rogers dialogue, as dialogue. *Journal of Humanistic Psychology, 34*(1), 11–45. doi:10.1177/00221678940341003

De Bono, E. (1967). *The use of lateral thinking*. Penguin.

Fisher, A. (1989). Suppositions in argumentation. *Argumentation, 3*(4), 401–413.
Frye, N. (1990). *Words with power*. Penguin Books.
Giltrow, J. (2005). Modern conscience: Modalities of obligation in research genres. *Text, 25*(2), 171–199.
Giltrow, J., Gooding, R., Burgoyne, D., & Sawatsky, M. (2009). *Academic writing: An introduction* (2nd ed.). Broadview Press.
Graff, G., & Birkenstein, C. (2014). *They say, I say: The moves that matter in academic writing* (3rd ed.). W.W. Norton & Co.
Henderson, E. (2011). *Writing by choice* (2nd ed.). Oxford University Press.
Holquist, M. (1990). *Dialogism: Bakhtin and his world*. Routledge.
Hyde, M.J. (2011). Ethics, rhetoric, and discourse. In G. Cheney, S. May, & D. Munschi (Eds.), *The handbook of communication ethics* (pp. 31–44). Routledge.
Jaksa, J.A., & Pritchard, M.S. (1994). *Communication ethics: Methods of analysis* (2nd ed.). Wadsworth.
Kahneman, D. (2011). *Thinking, fast and slow*. Anchor Canada.
Lewis, C.S. (2002). Cross-examination. In W. Hooper (Ed.), *God in the dock: Essays on theology and ethics* (pp. 258–267). William B. Eerdmans Publishing Company. (Original work published 1970)
Nevo, I. (2013). The ethics of human scholarship: On knowledge and acknowledgement. *Journal of the Philosophy of History, 7*, 266–298. doi:10.1163/18722636-12341254
Nietzsche, F. (2000). The gay science (P. Gay, Trans.). In W. Kaufmann (Ed.), *Basic writings of Nietzsche* (pp. 171–178). The Modern Library. (Original work published 1882)
Oliver, K. (2001). *Witnessing: Beyond recognition*. University of Minnesota Press.
Onions, C.T. (Ed.). (1996). *The Oxford dictionary of English etymology*. Oxford University Press.
Orwell, G. (2004). Politics and the English language. In R. Birks, T. Eng, & J. Walchli (Eds.), *Landmarks: A process reader* (pp. 329–339). Pearson/Prentice Hall. (Original work published 1946)
Ricoeur, P. (1992). *Oneself as another* (K. Blamey, Trans.). University of Chicago Press.
Scarafile, G. (2014). Introductory essay: «Sob o mesmo céu». Listening and dialogue as ethics of communication. In D. Riesenfeld & G. Scarafile (Eds.), *Perspectives on theory of controversies and the ethics of communication* (pp. 1–17). Springer.
Searle, J. (1979). *Expression and meaning*. Cambridge University Press.
Sperber, D., & Wilson, D. (1996). *Relevance: Communication and cognition* (2nd ed.). Wiley-Blackwell.
Tannen, D. (1998). *The argument culture: Moving from debate to dialogue*. Random House.
Taylor, C. (1994). The politics of recognition. In A. Gutmann (Ed.), *Multiculturalism: Examining the politics of recognition* (pp. 28–73). Princeton University Press.
Voloshinov, V.N. (1986). *Marxism and the philosophy of language* (L. Matejka & I.R. Titunik, Trans.). Harvard University Press. (Original work published 1929)
Zinsser, W.K. (2006). *On writing well: The classic guide to writing nonfiction* (30th anniversary ed.). HarperCollins.

PERMISSIONS ACKNOWLEDGEMENTS

Bennett, Roger. "Factors Contributing to the Early Failure of Small New Charity Start-ups." *Journal of Small Business and Enterprise Development* 23.2 (2016): 333–48. Copyright © 2016 Emerald Group Publishing Limited. Reprinted by permission of Emerald Publishing Limited conveyed by Copyright Clearance Center, Inc.

Brown, M. "Children's Literature Matters (?)." *English Academy Review* 34.1 (2017): 8–22. Reprinted by permission of Taylor & Francis Group, www.tandfonline.com, conveyed by Copyright Clearance Center, Inc.

DeCamp, Whitney, and C.J. Ferguson. "The Impact of Degree of Exposure to Violent Video Games, Family Background, and Other Factors on Youth Violence." *Journal of Youth and Adolescence* 46.2 (2017): 388–400. Copyright © 2016 Springer Science Business Media New York. Reprinted by permission of Springer Nature Customer Service Centre GmbH conveyed by Copyright Clearance Center, Inc.

Gilardi, S., and E. Lozza. "Inquiry-Based Learning and Undergraduates' Professional Identity Development: Assessment of a Field Research-Based Course." *Innovative Higher Education* 34.4 (2009): 245–56. Copyright © 2009 Springer Science Business Media, LLC. Reprinted by permission of Springer Nature Customer Service Centre GmbH conveyed by Copyright Clearance Center, Inc.

Hawkes, J. "A Quick Reference Guide to Mental Health on University Campus: A Brief Rhetorical Analysis of Fear." *Disability & Society* 34.1 (2019): 1–7. Reprinted by permission of Taylor & Francis Group, www.tandfonline.com, conveyed by Copyright Clearance Center, Inc.

Kaufmann, Robert K., Heikki Kauppi, Michael L. Mann, and James H. Stock. "Reconciling Anthropogenic Climate Change with Observed Temperature 1998–2008." *Proceedings of the National Academy of Sciences of the United States of America* 108.29 (2011): 11790–93. Reprinted by permission of the author.

Lunt, D., L. Chonko, and L.A. Burke-Smalley. "Creating a Culture of Engagement in Business Schools." *Organization Management Journal* 15.3 (2018): 95–109. Reprinted by permission of Taylor & Francis Ltd, http://www.tandfonline.com, and Eastern Academy of Management, www.eaom.org, conveyed by Copyright Clearance Center, Inc.

Minteer, B.A., and J.P. Collins. "Move It or Lose It? The Ecological Ethics of Relocating Species under Climate Change." *Ecological Applications* 20.7 (2010): 1801–04. Reprinted by permission of John Wiley & Sons, Inc. conveyed by Copyright Clearance Center, Inc.

Morrow, O., R. Hawkins, and L. Kern. "Feminist Research in Online Spaces." *Gender, Place, and Culture* 22.4 (2015): 526–43. Reprinted by permission of Taylor & Francis Group, www.tandfonline.com, conveyed by Copyright Clearance Center, Inc.

Pundik, Amit. "Against Racial Profiling." *University of Toronto Law Journal* 67.2 (2017): 175–205. Copyright © 2017 University of Toronto Press. Reprinted with permission from University of Toronto Press (https://utpjournals.press). https://doi.org/10.3138/UTLJ.3883

Sinker, R., M. Phillips, and V. de Rijke. "Playing in the Dark with Online Games for Girls." *Contemporary Issues in Early Childhood* 18.2 (2017): 162–78. Reprinted by permission of SAGE Publications, Ltd. conveyed by Copyright Clearance Center, Inc.

Sylvia, Louisa G., et al. "Do Sleep Disturbances Predict or Moderate the Response to Psychotherapy in Bipolar Disorder?" *The Journal of Nervous and Mental Disease* 205.3 (2017): 196–202. Reprinted by permission of Wolters Kluwer Health, Inc. doi: 10.1097/NMD.0000000000000579

Watterson, B. Cartoon. CALVIN AND HOBBES © 1993 Watterson. Reprinted with permission of ANDREWS MCMEEL SYNDICATION. All rights reserved.

Zivkovik, T., M. Warin, M. Davies, and V. Moore. "In the Name of the Child: The Gendered Politics of Childhood Obesity." *Journal of Sociology* 46.4 (2010): 375–92. Reprinted by permission of SAGE Publications, Ltd. conveyed by Copyright Clearance Center, Inc.

INDEX

From the Publisher

A name never says it all, but the word "Broadview" expresses a good deal of the philosophy behind our company. We are open to a broad range of academic approaches and political viewpoints. We pay attention to the broad impact book publishing and book printing has in the wider world; for some years now we have used 100% recycled paper for most titles. Our publishing program is internationally oriented and broad-ranging. Our individual titles often appeal to a broad readership too; many are of interest as much to general readers as to academics and students.

Founded in 1985, Broadview remains a fully independent company owned by its shareholders—not an imprint or subsidiary of a larger multinational.

For the most accurate information on our books (including information on pricing, editions, and formats) please visit our website at www.broadviewpress.com. Our print books and ebooks are also available for sale on our site.

broadview press
www.broadviewpress.com

This book is made of paper from well-managed FSC®-certified forests, recycled materials, and other controlled sources.